Negotiating Patriarchy and Gender in Africa

Negotiating Patriarchy and Gender in Africa

Discourses, Practices, and Policies

Edited by
Egodi Uchendu and Ngozi Edeagu

LEXINGTON BOOKS
Lanham • Boulder • New York • London

Published by Lexington Books
An imprint of The Rowman & Littlefield Publishing Group, Inc.
4501 Forbes Boulevard, Suite 200, Lanham, Maryland 20706
www.rowman.com

6 Tinworth Street, London SE11 5AL, United Kingdom

British Library Cataloguing in Publication Information Available

Library of Congress Cataloging-in-Publication Data

Names: Uchendu, Egodi, editor. | Edeagu, Ngozi, editor.
Title: Negotiating patriarchy and gender in Africa : discourses, practices, and policies / edited by Egodi Uchendu and Ngozi Edeagu.
Description: Lanham : Lexington Books, 2021. | Includes bibliographical references and index. | Summary: "This book examines the entrenchment of patriarchy in Africa and its attendant socioeconomic and political consequences on gender relations"— Provided by publisher.
Identifiers: LCCN 2021021712 (print) | LCCN 2021021713 (ebook) | ISBN 9781793642066 (cloth) | ISBN 9781793642059 (epub)
Subjects: LCSH: Male domination (Social structure)—Africa. | Sex discrimination against women—Africa. | Patriarchy—Africa. | Women's rights—Africa. | Women—Africa—Social conditions.
Classification: LCC HQ1090.7.A35 N44 2021 (print) | LCC HQ1090.7.A35 (ebook) | DDC 305.31096—dc23
LC record available at https://lccn.loc.gov/2021021712
LC ebook record available at https://lccn.loc.gov/2021021713

Dedication
To our mothers and daughters
... and especially to Chika Edeagu for being a
driving force in our academic pursuits.
She makes it all worth it.

Contents

Foreword

Samuel Zalanga

Director of Research and Publications
African Studies and Research Forum

The phenomenon of patriarchy and gender inequality is a global problem, but its manifestation in Africa is far more serious than in other regions of the world. Of course, even within Africa, it varies by countries, region within a country, ethnic groups, and religious communities. No country in the world has made serious progress in the area of inclusive development without seriously addressing the issue of patriarchy and gender inequality as formidable as they are. They are formidable challenges because often, by the time when one becomes conscious of such inequality, they have already been socialized to internalize the structures and processes of inequality as normal and natural. Challenging such structures and processes of inequality are made extravagantly difficult for numerous reasons, but in many cases, this is because the majority of people are so preoccupied by the urgent struggle for daily survival which leaves little time to think more deeply and critically about structures and processes that normalize domination. It is in this respect that I find the initiative and determination of Professor Egodi Uchendu to edit this book as very inspiring and pushing the needle in the long struggle for gender equality and fairness in Africa.

My first encounter with Professor Uchendu was at the 2007 annual meeting of the Association of Third World Studies in Lima, Peru. Subsequently, it was opportune for me to get to better know the scope of her scholarship and intellectual contribution to higher education in Nigeria and Africa when I was serving as a US Fulbright Scholar at Nnamdi Azikiwe University, in Anambra State, Southeastern Nigeria, during the 2017–2018 academic year. She organized a scholarly forum for me to present in her department at the University of Nigeria, Nsukka, Enugu State, Southeastern Nigeria. That occasion gave me the opportunity to appreciate the depth and scope of her scholarship and the role she is playing in mentoring younger scholars from diverse backgrounds. Compared to many professors in African universities, she is unique because she is intellectually restless and inquisitive about knowledge. She does not restrict herself to teaching alone but commits herself to empirical research with the primary goal of bringing greater cross-cultural hermeneutic understanding as a step towards the struggle for a more just and fair society for all. It is in this respect that she needs to be highly commended for this book on patriarchy and gender inequality that she has edited together with another brilliant Nigerian female historian, Ngozi Edeagu, who teaches at Alex Ekwueme Federal University, Ndufu-Alike, Ebonyi State, Nigeria. Ms. Edeagu previously studied for her B.A. at the University of Nigeria, Nsukka, where Professor Uchendu recognized her potential. She subsequently received an M.A. from Oxford University in England, and is currently pursuing a Ph.D. in Germany.

After working for six years as the Associate Editor for Africa in charge of peer review process for the then *Journal of Third World Studies*, I quickly arrived at the conclusion that, broadly speaking, one of the scholarly areas that received the least attention in terms of journal articles submitted to the journal from Africa was gender inequality and patriarchy. It appeared that many concerns crowd out the focus on patriarchy and gender inequality. But a subliminal factor and explanation for such a situation is that most of the scholars in Africa are males and many male scholars in Africa for numerous reasons find it less interesting to engage deeply with scholarship in the area of patriarchy and gender inequality. I was therefore highly excited in my capacity as the Director of Research and Publications for the African Studies and Research Forum when she offered to pursue this book project as part of the African Studies and Research Forum Book Series.

There are several reasons why this book is a phenomenal contribution to the study of patriarchy and gender inequality as part of the broader struggle for a more just and egalitarian African society. Any society that ignores the need to seriously and honestly address the issue of gender inequality and patriarchy will do so at its own peril. This is so because social science research has extensively documented the enduring role of mothers in shaping children, the effect of which remains with them sometimes throughout their lives. The book in terms of methodological approach emphasizes interdisciplinary and triangulated method of interrogating a question using different sources of data and methods of analysis. It also examines the issue of gender inequality and patriarchy as a multifaceted issue while acknowledging how diversity across Africa mediates how gender and patriarchy are manifested. The social science literature has documented as part of the broader study of inequality and stratification that gender inequality and patriarchy can be traced back to ancient times and it exists universally in diverse forms. In addition to that, it is dynamic and consequential as it affects the life chances of women in decisive ways. One major highlight of the book is the logic that informed its structure.

The first part of the book deals with the implicit and explicit gender categories of mediation by interrogating discourses in the normal functioning of society to see how gender inequality and patriarchy are legitimated and reproduced. With that issue addressed, the next section leads one to documentation of women's experiences in the trenches of the gender lifeworld. It helps the reader appreciate the concrete spheres in which women are struggling as it documents the concrete manifestations of gender inequality in the regular rhythm of life that often passes without being formally acknowledged. It is sad to say "women struggle" because women are part of the human race and, ideally, we should all see this as a collective human struggle. The third section of the book is focused on the sphere of politics and how power in Africa is reproduced in the public sphere in a manner that marginalizes women. It is amazing to see the diverse tactics that have been used in different countries and times to keep women in the social margins and periphery of political institutions. Yet, the struggle for a more just and fair society is continuing notwithstanding ambivalent results. The last section of the book focuses on public policy implementation to seriously address gender inequality and patriarchy even if it cannot be totally eradicated. It is at this juncture that the reader encounters the problem of state failure or quasi-state failure in many African countries. The gravity of the problem of gender inequality and patriarchy is worsened by the fact that many Africans have been culturally socialized and have internalized the legitimacy of such inequality in very intricate ways. This means the first struggle for gender equality and the diminishing of patriarchy is the need to effectively problematize the part of the people's psyche, which sees it as normal and legitimate and therefore produces categories of mediation that reinforces such understanding of social reality in the private and public spheres of life. We need to reorient the African mindset in this respect to a point where we can see and appreciate the beauty in creating social spaces and environment that enable women to thrive and flourish.

Professor Uchendu is a solid scholarly African woman. I know from experience that this can be challenging to deal with because in a patriarchal society, she would experience a high degree of emotional labor in terms of how she manages social relations across gender. But her work and scholarly commitment always remind me of coming to know as I grew older that my mother had a voice in the family and church, and even though she just attended Bible school, she was highly engaged with scripture through reading and interpretation. She was puritan but compassionate. It was that experience that made me to develop special and keen interest in the struggle for gender equality and fairness. At a personal level, the struggle for gender equality and the diminishing of patriarchy is for me a way to honor my mother. It is the equivalent of affirming her desire and aspiration to have a voice as a woman and human being, which some must have found threatening, but at the same time all those who know her acknowledge without hesitation that she was a compassionate person. It is in this same spirit that I want to appeal for all readers of this book to see it as part of our collective struggle to create a new Africa that does not devalue men's contribution but is vehemently committed to diminishing gender inequality and patriarchy in order to give women optimum social space and environment to thrive and flourish as a step towards producing a new generation of young Africans, males and females, that will see themselves as brothers and sisters in the struggle for meaningful existence that affirms our shared humanity irrespective of gender.

Acknowledgments

Scholarly endeavors come with a price and the investment of several stakeholders. We appreciate the leadership of African Studies Research Forum that envisioned this project. We also acknowledge the commitment and cooperation of all chapter contributors. In addition, we would like to thank our colleague and friend, Professor Dr Dmitri van den Bersselaar, for his professional advice and support in this book process. They and several others who worked behind the scenes, made this project a reality. To all, we say, "Thanks."

Introduction

Egodi Uchendu and Ngozi Edeagu

Globally, males disproportionately predominate leadership roles and exert power in diverse forms of social systems and institutions. Patriarchy, the supremacy of fatherhood whereby women and children rely totally on the male line, is entrenched in many societies around the world. Differential enjoyment of rights and dignity predetermined for women and men, based on their social, cultural, and legal disposition, typify gender inequality. Thus, patriarchy and gender inequality are two important but complex and debatable issues facing the African continent today. Argued to be the main cause of gender inequality, patriarchy plagues Africa in spite of immense progress made in the last two decades to address the prolonged impacts of gender injustice and male dominance. On the occasion of the fifteenth anniversary of the protocol to the African Charter on Human and Peoples' Rights on the Rights of Women in Africa, the editors announced a call for chapter proposals to critically analyze the situation of girls and women in Africa. Thus, under the broad themes of gender and patriarchy, the outcome of this call aims to assess the state, role, and impact of gender inequality and patriarchy on African girls and women. This work therefore juxtaposes work on discourse and policy, as well as material oppression and discourse in a similar way to the work of Daniel Goldstein, political and legal anthropologist, who brings literature, policy, and academe together in his work, *Outlawed: Between Security and Rights in a Bolivian City*.[1] Thus, this text, for instance, explores how policy and literature are used to approach issues of gender, domination, and equality from different angles, providing different perspectives that illuminate each other. Consequently, Onwuegbuchi's critical reading of the literature in this volume helps readers understand why gender policies are not implemented.

The contributions to this book are organized around four major themes: gender discourse and domination; women, work and exploitation; women in power and male dominance; and policy implementation. The authors come from a range of institutional and disciplinary backgrounds and deploy different methodologies to discuss the themes of this edited volume from multiple regional African scopes. The editors are pleased to include the work of early career researchers and researchers with noninstitutional affiliations.

GENDER DISCOURSE AND DOMINATION

Chapters under this category examine how people talk about women and men in literature, film, newspapers but also in official sources. At the same time, they explore what this discussion does to entrenching expectations of gendered (violent) behavior. These chapters are less concerned with changing and more with describing and understanding processes.

So, Berger's "Black Peril, White Peril? Challenging Racialized Gender Hierarchies in Early Twentieth-Century South Africa," highlights the intriguing "Commission on the So-Called Black Peril Case" in South Africa to explain the functionality of the powerful Black Peril narrative for the South African experience, particularly shortly after the unification of South Africa. On the other hand, through a critical review of film, Ezepue's "Isoken: An Exploration of Differential Enjoyment of Rights and Dignity" takes readers on a journey of how women's lives, careers, and futures are changed by choices they were forced to make and how these sociocultural demands highlight differences in the privileges males and females enjoy in two different cultural settings. Furthermore, Fourshey and Jaksch challenge the notion of patriarchy as "eternal and natural" through their examination of the Uyango, a women's knowledge system in East Africa, in their "Challenging Patriarchy: East African Women's Knowledge Systems."

As sexual and intimate partner violence is part of the landscape that women and children live with in today's society,[2] chapters 4 and 5 in this section are important additions to this discussion. Thus, in "'I Paid Lobola!' The Interface between Bride Price and Domestic Violence: A Case Study of Epworth, 2007–2017," Muguti and Mlambo investigate how the cultural practice of legalizing a marriage union exacerbates gender-based violence in one of the poorest high-density suburbs in Zimbabwe. On the other hand, Ndhlovu and Tanga's "The Interconnection between Youth Gangs, Toxic Masculinity, and Gender-Based Violence in South Africa" explores how black African youth gangs from marginalized communities use high levels of violence to prove their masculinity, and how this toxic masculinity translates into gender-based violence. Finally, Okafor's "Structuration

Theory and Patriarchy System in Africa: The Silent and the Salient in a Lifeless Structure," on the principles of Gidden's Structuration theory, captures the indices of self-victimization, ignorance, and unseen reinforcement of the patriarchy system.

WOMEN, WORK AND EXPLOITATION

The chapters under this theme give more attention to female agency. However, they are still focused on challenges that women face. While some chapters are more hopeful in content, like those of Agofure, and Smyrilli, others such as Adjoh-Davoh, Hannah and Endeley, and Slyvanus are more despondent. The section thus begins with a historical study by Adjoh-Davoh who examines archival documents to account for male domination against women and girls through the institution of pawning in her work, "Patriarchy and Cultural Values in Nineteenth- and Twentieth-Century Ghana." In continuation of the theme of female labor, Agofure uses Marxist feminism to determine the extent to which women are circumscribed and made socially and economically unequal to men through unpaid labor. Specifically, in "Patriarchy, Inequality, and Housework: An Assessment of Sefi Atta's Everything Good Will Come," Agofure explores the concept of women's unpaid housework through fiction to illuminate the struggles women face in a patriarchal conservative Nigerian society. Similarly, Slyvanus in "Women as Composers in Nollywood: Evidence of Absence or Absence of Evidence?" goes beyond the descriptive and/or representative forms ascribed to women in the film music industry to examine how questions of gender and gendered politics have shaped film music and its practice in Nigeria's Nollywood industry. Finally, Smyrilli's evidence-based study, "An Analysis of Gender Roles around Water and Sanitation in Rural Uganda," investigates gender roles in water and sanitation infrastructure and practices, in rural Uganda to determine how this infrastructure can challenge existing gender roles.

WOMEN IN POWER AND MALE DOMINANCE

In the third category, contributions discuss how women in Africa are not as visible in politics as they should be—in sharp contrast to women in America like Nackey Scripps Loeb who used her political influence to shape presidential politics in America.[3] So, Hannah and Endeley in "Patriarchy, Gender, and Deliberative Democracy: How Does it Play Out in the Ugandan Parliament?" explore patriarchal manifestations in the Ugandan parliament during deliberative sessions and how women parliamentarians have sought to attain visibility and voice during deliberations. In particular, they argue that "countering barriers associated with patriarchy and gender schemes is central to women's voice" and this "voice adds value to the theories of critical mass and deliberative democracy." The discrimination and marginalization against women in politics is also the central theme of Iwuoha's "New Dimensions to Discrimination against Party Women and Women in Power" which seeks to establish the extent to which democratic consolidation in Nigeria has impacted on women's political inclusion.

Through the lens of poststructuralism, Onwuegbuchi in "Silence and Power in Yejide Kilanko's *Daughters Who Walk This Path*" interrogates the myth of sexual violence and the various shades of silence foisted on women through the eyes of Kilanko's central fictional protagonist. Her work aptly articulates the primary symbol of male power. Similarly, through fiction, Zamanpour explores new forms of masculinity as presented through the sacred and exclusive-male kola nut ceremony which is deeply rooted in Igbo patriarchy and its initiation ceremony, as depicted in *GraceLand*. His work thus "addresses complex problematics of the relationship between masculinity, marginality, and liminality." Through "Becoming Man, Becoming Kola Nut: Rite of Passage in Abani's *GraceLand*," the author takes readers on the journey through the first stepping stone of becoming a man in Igbo society.

POLICY IMPLEMENTATION

The last theme covers policy implementation in particular reference to gendered violence and gender equality. Thus, these papers analyze how policies, that in principle are uncontroversial, are often not or inadequately implemented. For example, Oluwafunminiyi's "UN Women and the Pitfalls of Gender Equality and Representation in Nigeria" interrogates one of the United Nations Women's priority areas—the achievement of equality between men and women in political life—by focusing on post-1999 Nigeria. On the other hand, du Toit and Boshoff in "Transitional Justice, Sexual Violence, and Women's Status in Africa" argue for the use of transitional justice processes in Africa to address women's citizenship status in post-colonial and post-conflict states. They simultaneously argue that "continued systemic sexual violence" against women across the three stages of conflict must be acknowledged. Similarly, Petillo and Eggers in "Rendered as Political Pawns: Chibok Girls, Ebola, and the Exercise of Political Will" employ a feminist sociolegal comparative analysis of the Nigerian response to both the Ebola pandemic and the 2014 abduction of Chibok school girls. The authors suggest that the state's failure to effectively respond to the school abduction was "neither simple nor about competence."

Still focusing on the girl child, Isaac's "Gender Imbalance and Girl Child Education in Niger State, North-Central Nigeria" discusses the imbalance affecting girl child education in north central Nigeria from multiple levels using a social-historical approach. However, in "To be Introduced by my Daughter is a Blessing," Tavrow, Otieno, and Muindi approached this theme differently. The trio focused on the commodification of daughters through early marriage which deprives girls of getting an education and improved socioeconomic lives in the future as adults. Nonetheless, the success of a community project, launched in 2017, has shown that social norms that border on strict patriarchal domination of women and girl children can be reformed to squeeze the gender gap and improve the lot of girls and women in their societies.

Despite the multiple themes established in this volume, the authors are united on one point: that the struggle to achieve gender equality is far from over and they have identified a range of solutions ranging from "disruption" to community participation to challenging and redefining reconstructions of masculinity. Although there is an urgent need for increased advocacy to narrow the gender gap in many African societies, government will and internal solutions are paramount. Thus, the realization of the significant gender reform will involve the key actors in the gender equation working together to create a new and beneficial future for both groups.

NOTES

1. Daniel Goldstein, *Outlawed: Between Security and Rights in a Bolivian City* (Durham, NC: Duke University Press, 2012).

2. Angela J. Hattery and Earl Smith, *Gender, Power, and Violence: Responding to Sexual and Intimate Partner Violence in Society Today* (Lanham, MD: Rowman & Littlefield, 2019).

3. Meg Heckman, *Political Godmother: Nackey Scripps Loeb and the Newspaper That Shook the Republican Party* (Lincoln, NE: University of Nebraska Press, Potomac Books, 2020).

Part I

GENDER DISCOURSE
AND DOMINATION

Chapter 1

Black Peril, White Peril? Challenging Racialized Gender Hierarchies in Early Twentieth-Century South Africa

Claudia Berger

The Black Peril was arguably the most infamous racialist fear narrative in the British Empire during the nineteenth and twentieth century.[1] It led to extreme cases where White women's rights activists condoned extreme racial terror, as the lynchings in the southern states of the United States, a former British settler colony, in the late nineteenth century.[2] This short example, although not located in South Africa, illustrates the uneasy relationship between the women's rights movement and emancipation movements by people of color in regard to the Black Peril narrative. Yet in the following, a document authored (among others) by activists of both movements will be the focus of the analysis, the report of the "Commission on the So-called Black Peril," which was written for the General Missionary Conference in Cape Town in 1912. How did it challenge or maintain racialized notions of sexual violence? Also, the use of the commission as an administrative instrument by activists will be of particular interest.

THE BLACK PERIL NARRATIVE IN SOUTH AFRICA

Black Peril narratives were, in short, instrumental in racializing male violence against White girls and women in colonial South Africa (and later during the Apartheid era). In the formalized urban settler societies in South Africa at the beginning of the twentieth century, as in other (former) British colonies at the time, the hegemonic masculinity was White and British. This was by far not the only masculinity available, as there were others which survived in their specific spheres during the conquest; others evolved during the changes of South African society after the Mineral Revolution.[3] But, in the hegemonic discourse of colonial press and politics, only White men with British backgrounds were conceptualized as embodying the possibility of perfection—they were conceptualized as civilized and controlled, while their binary opposite Black[4] masculinity was thought of as violent and uncontrolled, remaining vulnerable to an intrinsically predatory sexual nature. This predatory nature was in turn conceptualized as being directed specifically toward White women, and this kind of endangerment, personified in Black masculinity, was coined the Black Peril (or by similar vague terms: social evil, social pest, outrage, and so on). At the heart of the construction, White womanhood was the embodiment of the vulnerability of the Empire, in need of protection by White men.[5]

As even contemporaries were aware, the term "Black Peril" was used as an umbrella term to cover all kinds of minor and major allegations and was also applied to consensual interracial relationships.[6] The inner logic conceptually connecting the cases was the ability of the Black Peril narrative to naturalize and essentialize the racist and sexist hierarchies of colonial societies at a time, when emancipatory movements by people of color and the suffragists' movement fought for participation and democratization of society.[7] To avoid the destabilization of the colonial society and a shift of power to the disadvantage of the dominant White masculinity, any alliance between the movements had to be penalized and deemed as unrespectable.

But, White women were not innocent of these constructions. They were rewarded for their complicity with an elevated status within the racialized hierarchy of the colonial society which placed them above people of color—and most notably above women of color. White affluent women were able to realize their limited freedoms despite their domestic duties due to the services, and consequently the oppression, of people of color.[8] At the same time, they were urged to be careful in terms of their exposure to men of color, which led to particular tensions in the domestic sphere. White housewives were advised not to order their Black male servants to assist them with more intimate tasks, like dressing and bathing. Jeremy Creighton Martens coins the terms of "besieged settler homes" in this context.[9] He also stresses that at least in Natal, South Africa, Black men preferred domestic employment over work in mines or on plantations because it offered a variety of tasks instead of monotonous work. Also, they had been employed with domestic duties from the very beginning of the British settlement in Natal. The obsession of White settlers with the male Black domestic servant was rather a projection of their own insecurities concerning the standards of "real" masculinity and a sense of endangerment, which sprang from the presence of Black men in the heart of the home.[10]

Lynchings as in the southern states of the US and in the British South African Colony Natal in the late nineteenth century were legitimized and framed as spontaneous acts of vengeance connected to Black Peril cases, and resulted in or from "rape scares," which seemed to errupt spontaneously in White colonial populations with devastating consequences for people of color. Instead, at least in the US, lynchings were not spontaneous at all, but planned and calculated as a spectacle to entice fear and maintain control over the African-American population.[11]

Already contemporary experts in Natal were hinting that these "rape scares" were not fueled by a real increase in cases of sexual violence.[12] Rather, they occurred in strange synchrony with broader feelings of economic or political insecurity. Retrospectively, the rape scares have been linked by historians to the fear of White men to lose their political or economic advantage over Black men. Consequently, they resulted quite effectively in repressive legislation, aimed especially at people of color.[13]

By purporting the dangerous nature of Black men, Black Peril narratives stressed the dependency of White women on their White male "defenders" and were instrumental in confining both Black men and White women to their places.[14] In short, the Black Peril narratives were instrumental in keeping the racialized colonial order intact. They also constructed and perpetuated a reality where interracial love became increasingly unimaginable and left a void to be filled with narratives of violent encounters.[15]

EARLY TWENTIETH-CENTURY COMMISSIONS AND THE BLACK PERIL

The early twentieth century was a period characterized by a growing economic concern in South Africa and a global climate in which various emancipation initiatives and their struggles were unfavorably portrayed in the daily press from the South African emancipation movements by people of color to the independence movement in India and the suffragette movement in the United Kingdom. These, combined with White anxieties, caused by the victory of Japan in the war with Russia in 1905 and the vital example of Black rule in Haiti seemed to indicate a global climate opposing White supremacy in the long term and was echoed by academic scholars of the time.[16] This sense of endangerment, as Marilyn Lake and Henry Reynolds observed, resulted in a worldwide attempt by British settler colonies to consolidate White supremacy by implementing new segregative policies.[17] As Martin Legassick has analyzed for South Africa, the reach and the totality of the "native policies" aspired for implementation was unprecedented in South African history at that time.[18]

This was also partly the result of the defeat of the two Boer republics in 1902 by the British Empire, which motivated policymakers to standardize "native policy" in all four British South African colonies, which would eventually form the South African Union in 1910. Also, the economic well-being of the mining industry depended on affordable, exploitable Black labor. While importation of workers from India and China was unpopular with the rising xenophobic sentiments in the colonies, Black men were often reluctant to enter into the highly exploitative mining work environments, where wages had also reached a new low since the South African War. The industry hoped with good reasons that legislators would act in its favor and pressure Black men to return to work in the mines.[19]

The discoursive needed for this concerted effort was channeled through the strategic use of the commission as an administrative instrument to "create" truth. At the same time, it recreated the authority of the state by the formulation of a certain "problem" and by regulating the terms in which this perceived problem could be acceptably addressed.[20] The South African Native Affairs Commission (SANAC, 1903–1905) was the most impressive example of the power, the administrative instrument of the commission could exercise in the period in question. It was highly successful insofar that its outcomes were not only vital to the tightening of settler control. Its report also unified the White South African political establishment, incorporating most of the political spectrum.[21]

Notably, the commission itself consisted only of White male administrators with an overwhelmingly British South African background. While there were Black male witnesses, no woman of color was heard. Although gender relations were frequently discussed, male participants generally assumed their ability to speak for women of color. SANAC, therefore, constitutes an example not only of opposing agencies of White and Black men but also the attempt to enforce and secure patriarchal control especially over Black girls and women.[22] Interestingly enough, the Black Peril narrative was of no importance to SANAC.

This situation had already changed in 1907 when the report of the Natal Native Affairs Commission was published, which decidedly mentioned and problematized interracial sexual relationships.[23] The mentioning of the Black Peril in the Natal commission report can be attributed to a Black Peril scare rocking the colony in the aftermath of the Bambatha rebellion, a Zulu uprising which had profoundly terrified the settler community in 1906.[24]

CRITICISM AND ALTERNATIVES

There are some White people who always color us with the opprobrium paint of disloyalty. They will always distort our humble and harmless appeals into a

"Black Menace," "Black Peril" or some other stygma. We would inform them that these ideas only exist in their brain

—"Koranta ea Becoana," December 31, 1902

This complaint was most likely written by Sol Plaatje, one of the founding fathers of the African National Congress (ANC) and the editor of the widely circulated English and Tswana-speaking *Koranta ea Becoana* in Mafikeng. As shown by the quotation above, he was also an outspoken critic of the Black Peril narrative. In 1921, he even discussed his views on the subject in a novel.[25]

In 1902, ten years prior of the founding of the ANC, Plaatje was already an outstanding political figure championing emancipatory causes like the position of Black South Africans and women's rights, most actively in the Cape Colony and the Bechuanaland Protectorate. The industrious Black Press, which tried to argue against the Black Peril narrative and stressed the endangerment of women of color by White men in South Africa, was another indicator of society's change since the end of the nineteenth century. In this sense, the newspapers, edited by Black South Africans and often bilingual, were most notably even perceived as a further endangerment of White supremacy.[26]

Already in advance of the South African unification in 1910, activists of all kinds widened their scope and sought cooperation in the other South African British colonies. This was true for the Black emancipation movement as it was for the women's rights movement. The women's rights movement in South Africa meant mostly White middle- and upper-class female activists since Black people were confronted with such massive suppression that an inclusive women's vote was simply not a prioritized issue for people of color.[27] But even among White people, at the beginning of the twentieth century, the women's suffrage movement in South Africa was still very young and not as influential as the corresponding movements in Britain.[28]

However, as embodied by Sol Plaatje himself, both emancipatory movements shared a similar inner logic, which prompted some rare activists of both movements to align their struggles. Sol Plaatje being an exception, most Black male activists did not demand a women's suffrage. At the same time, many White women's rights activists were adamant in fighting for the right to vote mainly for White women to overcome their perceived weak position almost under Black men who were, unlike women, theoretically able to vote under the Cape Colonial qualified franchise. Olive Schreiner was a world-famous author and women's rights activist and like Plaatje an exception of sorts. She left The Cape Women's Enfranchisement League in 1909 after it officially abandoned its goal to achieve the franchise for *all* women and instead focused on White women's franchise only.[29]

Olive Schreiner herself was aware that most of the women's rights activists did not share her concern for an inclusive suffrage for all women. She dedicated a lot of time trying to persuade Julia Solly, a very influential fellow suffragist, to abandon racist categories and fight for a franchise for all women.[30] But, while she did disagree with Solly's narrow political agenda, she simultaneously knew that there were White women possibly believing and spreading the Black Peril narrative to achieve their goals. In a letter to her brother, she writes, mentioning a fellow women's rights activist: "I'm sorry Mrs Macfadyen is going to air the wickedness & debasedness of our natives, & the sweet innocence of our white women who the men won't defend them!"[31] And in another letter to Julia Solly, she mentions the same women with an even more drastic condemnation: "She is the bitterest enemy the natives have. [. . .] But if I write on the matter at all it will be quite an impersonal letter showing how small & cowardly the action of all of us is, who raise the Black Peril cry."[32]

Plaatje also became more pronounced in his condemnation of the Black Peril theme and its injustices, which he with the reality of violence and intimidation by White men against women of color. Describing in *Koranta ea Becoana* a case of a White man, who managed to get his Black female victim sent to prison for alleged perjury against him, he stated in 1911:

> This man deserves a decoration from the White Peril "fraternity." His action has created such a sheepish submission among victims of the White Peril and given the fraternity the satisfaction of knowing that no matter how deeply injured Black girls will keep their mouths shut.[33]

The term "White Peril" as used by Sol Plaatje hints at a modernization of the Black Peril narrative, which came to life in the early twentieth century. It argued that not only were White men endangering women of color. Some White proponents of the "White Peril" narrative also suggested that White men's disregard or seduction of and sexual violence against Black women motivated Black men to avenge this behavior by laying an eye on White women. The subnarrative shifted the majority of the blame from Black to White masculinity. At the same time, it retained women of either race, but in particular women of color, as a bargaining tool for male power.[34]

DISSECTING THE BLACK PERIL

In January 1912, the South African Native National Congress, later ANC, elected John Langibele Dube as first President, and Sol Plaatje as General

Secretary. Incidentally, both Dube and Plaatje were also involved with the "Commission of the So-called Black Peril" at the General Missionary Conference held in Cape Town from 3 to 9 July that same year. The appointment of this commission was directly influenced by a widespread Black Peril scare, which had already started in 1911.[35] Plaatje was only a witness to the commission, while John Dube, John Tengo Jabavu, another Black activist and publicist, and Olive Schreiner were members of the commission. Instrumental in bringing these people together was James Henderson, Convener of the commission and Principal of the Lovedale Missionary Institution.[36]

The extent of the cooperation of Black Peril opponents was at least partially veiled. The commission argued in its report not to disclose the full identities of the witnesses due to the sensitive subjects discussed. Instead, witnesses were only identified in the final report by a racial descriptor and their occupation, as in "6 Salvation Army officers, 8 ladies [. . .] a Native newspaper editor" listing a total of 68 persons, of whom eight were supposedly White females ("ladies") and sixteen men of color.[37]

In a relatively closed environment like the South African media and political establishment, some of the descriptions might have indeed already been quite telling. Indeed, of all the existing people in South Africa who would have merited the description "a Native newspaper editor," already two major figures were employed in the commission itself, namely John Dube and John Tengo Jabavu.

Given the importance of commissions in shaping and defining South African policies in the early twentieth century, it is adequate to assume that the "Commission of the So-called Black Peril" was an attempt to shape the discourse in a similar conclusive way. Although the impact of the commission was most likely imagined as being limited from the beginning (after all it was no official government commission, but born from a missionary context), most prominently the name of the commission was a giveaway in this respect and also subject to some criticism by the organizers of the conference: "'The So-called Black Peril' may be misleading and give a wrong impression as if we did not believe in the reality of that peril. The Executive would suggest that the title should be simply 'The Black Peril'."[38] Evidence indicates that James Henderson, after receiving this letter, followed up on the claim and asked the organizer of the conference whether the name of the commission would be approved. It was suggested that the name commission on the "'Black Peril' Question" would be fine.[39] However, in the final report of the conference, the commission was simply called "Commission IV on the Black Peril." Preceded by Commission VI "The Problem of Native Young Men in Large Cities" and V "Native Girls in Towns," it is initially obvious that the General Missionary Conference was no attempt to challenge racialized colonial hierarchies.[40]

To be fair, the still existing recruiting letter, written on October 30, 1911, and addressing a woman, does not indicate that Henderson wanted to question the Black Peril narrative in particular, but was merely aiming for a balanced approach concerning "the serious problem of the so-called 'Black Peril'," which should be discussed by "not only missionaries, but public men and women in various capacities."[41]

Henderson was not only successful in recruiting the outspoken Black Peril opponent Olive Schreiner who immediately informed him how she planned to approach the subject.[42] In the end, there were five (White) women and two men of color among a total seventeen members of the commission; in this respect, the commission was outstanding. While Commission V "Native Girls in Towns" was a women-only commission, no other commission at the conference had people of color among their members. The attempts of Henderson to include White women and men of color can still be seen as only a very modest achievement since both groups were by far outnumbered by the White male members of the commission. Nonetheless, the argumentation of the resulting report is quite remarkable and worth a closer look.

The report starts its argument by using a statistical approach. Therefore, the number of rape cases in Great Britain (using statistics from the late nineteenth century) were compared to the number of rape cases in South Africa (separated numbers for White/Black ("native") perpetrators, using statistics of the year 1904) *relative to the population.*[43] While the number of rape cases in Great Britain was not as low as the number for White perpetrators in South Africa, it was not as high as the number for Black perpetrators.[44] While this seems not the least surprising and indeed even seems to fit the Black Peril narrative, the commission points out explicitly that "[t]hese figures [the South African figures] include offenses against women and children of all races. But the great majority were against Native women."[45]

In the report now follows a rather compelling argument, which in opposition to the Black Peril narrative, did not naturalize or essentialize the racist and sexist hierarchy of the colony, but instead problematized it. Of course, Great Britain was not comparable to South Africa since there were fewer people of color there; which meant that, according to the report, there was no "easy outlet for the vicious tendencies of potential European offenders in the Native and Coloured population." This easy outlet was ascribed to differences in access to money and authorities, which made the Black population especially vulnerable and possibly helped European offenders to circumvent prosecution in South Africa.[46] The realization that the injustices of the colonial society placed a specific burden especially on Black women sets the different figures for Great Britain and South Africa in perspective, concluding that South Africa was, in fact, *safer* for *White* women than Great Britain. On the other hand, women of color were specifically imperiled by the colonial power structure.[47]

Afterwards, the report takes a closer look at the rape statistics for South Africa. While it assigns an upward trend to cases of sexual violence, these cases were also in the vast majority directed at women of color. Also, the report argues that the most significant growth did not occur in rape cases, but in minor allegations.[48]

After having successfully desensationalized the topic, the argumentation follows two implicit questions. First, the commission explains under which circumstances a Black Peril allegation would probably be issued; second, the circumstances which lead to a "real" Black Peril offense are examined. In answer to the first question, the commission concludes that there is no real distinction made between rape and "illicit intercourse" in the reporting of Black Peril cases. Once again the specific constitution of the colonial society creates a problem for the examination of the phenomenon. As the commission notes:

> It is natural that modest women should shrink from the ignominy of having their name before the public in such a connection, and undoubtedly there do occur from time to time genuine cases of assault which are not reported. The consensus of information and opinion, however, is that there are not many, and that concealment is rather less to be expected in native assaults than in those by Europeans.[49]

The report also mentions unfortunate misunderstandings, in which housewives feel threatened by the "undue familiarity" of a servant, which is ascribed to the shared space of the home, where a wrong move could be interpreted as a threat, even if not intended as such.[50] This aspect reminds the reader instantly of Frantz Fanon's interpretation of Octave Mannoni's famous analysis of the dreams of individuals in the colonies, who were haunted by symbols of their racialized paranoia and burdened by the perception of a permanent and imminent threat.[51] Also, the commission cites cases where Black men were merely accused of an offense out of spite or revenge.[52]

Implicitly arguing only a fraction of Black Peril cases could legitimately be classified as cases of violent assault, the commission's tone becomes significantly more patronizing. In the report, the situation of Black laborers who were forced to live in poverty apart from their families is cited,[53] including their exposition to liquor[54] and temptations as prostitution and pornography. Even movie theaters were considered a harmful influence.[55] The commission also cites possible mental health issues of the laborers[56] as well as spheres of intimacy, which were deemed to be especially difficult to navigate as a Black domestic servant.[57] Facing the evidence, the report concludes that the number of violent cases was, contrary to popular belief, strikingly small, compared to the hostile environment of Black men in South Africa.[58]

While describing the situation of Black South African men in detail, the question of how White South African men would behave themselves under these exact same circumstances is never asked directly, but implicated. And despite the often patronizing tone and the constant reproduction of the structurally racist cliches of Black masculinity (naivety and general unfitness for the Western lifestyle in general), a small revolution is almost hinted at when the report mentions the possibility of sexual violence just being, well, sexual violence: "'The evil is much more sexual than racial,' says another witness, 'if it is at all racial'."[59]

CONCLUSION

The report of the commission does not end with this sentence, but with rather conventional recommendations, which are at the same time advising the exertion of more control on White women as on Black women and the reaffirmation of the patriarchal structures of the colonial society.[60] Similarly, the commission still did not recognize women of color as equal interlocutors in their own right. Also, the recommendations for better living conditions for Black workers are tainted with racist assumptions and can also easily be read as a demand for better-segregated infrastructure.[61]

Nevertheless, the report tries to take into account the responsibility of society, even accusing the media and extreme jurisdiction of stirring up "the spirit of a bravado."[62] It states that small towns which felt overwhelmed by the influx of Black workers should not "build iron school churches, and preach to the people, and teach the children more or less to read. What has also to be done is to assist the dwellers in the location."[63] Being well-meaning and flawed at the same time, the deracialization of rape appears surreptitiously included in the report rather than being the climax of the argumentation.

Nonetheless, it can be recorded that, using an instrument of official discourse, the commission, a diverse group of activists tried to dissect the Black Peril narrative and relate it to the fabric of the South African colonial settler society. This detailed and compassionate perspective does not only inspire sympathy with the plight of people of color in the colonies, but it also desensationalizes the issue and enables a rational discussion of the issue at hand.

The fabric of society though is never openly challenged and it is rather suggested that a governmental commission should take up the work and arrive at its own conclusions.[64] Although intermarriages between Black men and White women are quickly mentioned and rehabilitated from being threatening to the respectability of White women,[65] the tone clearly implies that interracial relationships are not desirable in general: the familiarity between a housewife and her servant is "undesirable" and interracial intercourse "illicit."[66]

This lack of appreciation and imagination leads us back to the Lucy Valerie Graham's observation that although the White Peril narrative was able to question the hegemonic settler masculinity and voice a counter perspective, it still shared some basic assumptions with the Black Peril narrative: it rendered interracial love as impossible and interracial relationships therefore undesirable, demanding segregation. Graham attributes this lack of imagination to a "cultural-instituted melancholia," and refers thereby to Judith Butler who condensed in this term the inability to love someone who is deemed an unlovable object by discourse—and the resulting inability to mourn this loss since any affection toward the "other" is deemed unthinkable by society.[67]

NOTES

1. The research leading to this paper was conducted in the context of my PhD project on political activism in the early twentieth century Cape Colony at the University of Duisburg-Essen. I am grateful to Jan-Hendryk de Boer, Eva Lehner and Rita Schäfer for their kind and generous support while writing this article.

2. Vron Ware, *Beyond the Pale. White Women, Racism and History* (London: Verso, 2015), 206.

3. Belinda Bozzoli coined the term "Patchwork of masculinities" in: Belinda Bozzoli, "Marxism, Feminism and South African Studies," *Journal of Southern African Studies* 9, no. 2 (1983): 149. 'Mineral Revolution' is the term commonly used for the diamond (1867, Kimberley) and gold discoveries (1880s, Witwatersrand) in South Africa and the immediate social change and industrialisation prompted by them.

4. The capitalized term "Black" is used as in South African historiography as an emancipatory term which embraces different racial identities formerly suppressed by the Apartheid system. When used in the context of the Black Peril narratives and its mechanisms, however, it is used in a Fanonian sense as the conceptualized opposite of 'White' in colonial thought, e.g. Frantz Fanon, *Black Skin, White Masks* (London: Pluto Press, 2008), 3.

5. On *Hegemonic Masculinity* in White settler societies in South Africa see Robert Morell, "Of Boys and Men: Masculinity and Gender in Southern African Studies," *Journal of Southern African Studies* 24, no. 4 (1998): 618.

6. Gareth Cornwell, "George Webb Hardy's The Black Peril and the Social Meaning of 'Black Peril' in Early Twentieth-Century South Africa," *Journal of Southern African Studies* 22, no. 3 (1996): 442; Ware, *Beyond the Pale*, 38, 41.

7. A possible hint on this interpretation is that Black Peril scares in South Africa reached their peak during the late nineteenth century when emancipation movements were on the rise and turning towards a more aggressive struggle.

8. Cherryl Walker, "The Women's Suffrage Movement: The Politics of Gender, Race and Class," in *Woman and Gender in Southern Africa to 1945*, ed. Cherryl Walker (Cape Town/London: David Philip Publishers, 1990), 320–321.

9. Jeremy C. Martens, "Settler Homes, Manhood and 'Houseboys': An Analysis of Natal's Rape Scare of 1886," *Journal of Southern African Studies* 28, no. 2 (2002): 394.

10. Ibid., 392–394.

11. Ibid., 171.

12. Martens, "Settler Homes, Manhood and 'Houseboys,'" 381.

13. Ibid., 386.

14. Ibid., 388. Ann Laura Stoler, *Carnal Knowledge and Imperial Power: Race and the Intimate in Colonial Rule* (Berkeley, CA: University of California Press, 2010), 60.

15. Graham, *State of Peril*, 11.

16. Marilyn Lake and Henry Reynolds, *Drawing the Global Colour Line: White Men's Countries and the International Challenge of Racial Equality* (New York, NY/Cambridge: Cambridge University Press, 2008), 2, 10–11, 259.

17. Ibid., 8–9; This network also included the United States of America.

18. Martin Legassick, "British Hegemony and the Origins of Segregation in South Africa, 1901–14," in *Segregation and Apartheid in Twentieth-Century South Africa*, ed. William Beinart and Saul Dubow (New York, NY: Routledge, 1995), 44–45.

19. Adam Ashforth, "On the 'Native Question': A Reading of the Grand Traditions of Commissions of Inquiry Into the 'Native Question' in Twentieth-Century South Africa" (PhD dissertation, Oxford, 1987), 88.

20. Adam Ashforth, *The Politics of Official Discourse in Twentieth-Century South Africa* (Oxford: Clarendon Press, 1990), 6–7.

21. Legassick, "British Hegemony and the Origins of Segregation in South Africa," 47–48.

22. South African Native Affairs Commission, *Report of the South African Native Affairs Commission 1903-1905. Presented to both Houses of Parliament by demand of His Majesty, April 1905* (Cape Town: Cape Time Printers, 1905), 52, 58–59, 83. The often underexplored role of gender relations to the SANAC hearings will be thoroughly discussed in my upcoming thesis.

23. Cornwell, "George Webb Hardy's The Black Peril," 443.

24. Ibid.

25. Sol T. Plaatje, *The Mote and the Beam: An epic on Sex-Relationship 'Twixt White and Black in British South Africa* (New York, NY: Young's Book Exchange, 1921).

26. Graham, *State of Peril*, 45.

27. Walker, "The Women's Suffrage Movement," 315.

28. Lou Haysom, "Olive Schreiner and the Women's Vote," *Searchlight South Africa* 3, no. 3 (1993): 30.

29. Ibid., 32.

30. The Olive Schreiner Letters Online, "Julia Solly," http://www.oliveschreiner.org/vre?view=personae&entry=222 (accessed January 30, 2019).

31. Olive Schreiner to William Philip ('Will') Schreiner, July 1911, UCT Manuscripts & Archives, Olive Schreiner Letters Project transcription, lines 14–16.

32. Olive Schreiner to Julia Solly nee Muspratt, May 24, 1911, UCT Manuscripts & Archives, Olive Schreiner Letters Project transcription, lines 13–16.

33. Sol T. Plaatje, "sub-rosa," Tsala ea Becoana, February 11, 1911.

34. As Lucy Valery Graham points out, Olive Schreiner's novel "Trooper Peter Halket of Mashonaland" (1897) was one of the first to focus on the rape of Black women by White imperialists (Graham, *State of Peril*, 26). In 1907, Francis Bancroft's "Of like Passions" gave the Black/White Peril narrative a more typical novel depicting the pain inflicted on Black and White women by the mechanisms of Black and White Peril. Bancroft was a white female author and women's rights activist writing under a male pseudonym. Her book demanded self-restraint from men and a better standing for (White) women. The depicted Black women, in contrast to her White heroine, stay muted during the novel and remain victims, Gareth Cornwell, "Francis Bancroft's of Like Passions and the Politics of Sex in Early Twentieth-Century South Africa," *English in Africa* 25, no. 2 (1998); Graham, *State of Peril*, 69–100.

35. Cornwell, "George Webb Hardy's The Black Peril", 443–444.

36. "Report of Commission VI, 'The Black Peril'," *Report of the Proceedings of the Fourth General Missionary Conference of South Africa held at Cape Town, 3rd to 9th July, 1912* (Cape Town: Townshend, Taylor and Snashall, 1912), 80.

37. Ibid.

38. Samuel Bovet to Rev. J. Henderson, May 24, 1912, Cory Library, MS 14 847, 19.

39. Rev. J. du Plessis to Rev. J. Henderson, June 5, 1912, Cory Library, MS 14 847, 19.

40. "Report of Commission VI, 'The Black Peril'," 4.

41. Rev. J. Henderson to N.N., October 30, 1911, Cory Library, MS 14 847, 22.

42. "The subject of the so called Black-Peril is one that interests me deeply. My feeling, of course, is that peril which has long over shadowed this country, is one which exists for all dark skinned women at the hands of white men."—Olive Schreiner to James Henderson, 26th December 1911, Cory Library, Olive Schreiner Letters Project transcription, lines 13–16.

43. This approach acknowledges therefore the relative proportions of the White and Black population. While White South Africans were and are significantly outnumbered by Black South Africans, absolute figures would have severely distorted the results.

44. "Report of Commission VI, 'The Black Peril'," 81.

45. Ibid.

46. Ibid.

47. Ibid.

48. Ibid., 82–83.

49. Ibid., 85.

50. Ibid.

51. Fanon, *Black Skins, White Masks*, 75–81. A similar point is made in Graham, *State of Peril*, 71.

52. "Report of Commission VI, 'The Black Peril'," 85.
53. Ibid., 84.
54. Ibid., 84–85.
55. Ibid., 86–87.
56. Ibid., 85.
57. Ibid., 88–89.
58. Ibid., 90.
59. Ibid., 91.
60. Ibid., 94. The control of Black women is achieved via the suggestion to replace the male domestic servants with Black maids, who had, in turn, to be 'protected' and controlled by their White mistresses.
61. Ibid., 93–94.
62. Ibid., 94.
63. Ibid., 95.
64. Ibid.
65. Ibid., 89.
66. Ibid., 84, 88.
67. Graham, *State of Peril*, 11, 35.

BIBLIOGRAPHY

Ashforth, Adam. "On the 'Native Question': A Reading of the Grand Traditions of Commissions of Inquiry Into the 'Native Question' in Twentieth-Century South Africa." PhD diss., University of Oxford, 1987.

Ashforth, Adam. *The Politics of Official Discourse in Twentieth-Century South Africa.* Oxford: Clarendon Press, 1990.

Bozzoli, Belinda. "Marxism, Feminism and South African Studies." *Journal of Southern African Studies* 9, no. 2 (1983): 139–171.

Cornwell, Gareth. "George Webb Hardy's The Black Peril and the Social Meaning of 'Black Peril' in Early Twentieth-Century South Africa." *Journal of Southern African Studies* 22, no. 3 (1996): 441–453.

Fanon, Frantz. *Black Skin, White Masks.* London: Pluto Press, 2008.

Graham, Lucy Valerie. *State of Peril: Race and Rape in South African Literature.* Oxford/New York, NY: Oxford University Press, 2012.

Haysom, Lou. "Olive Schreiner and the Women's Vote." *Searchlight South Africa* 3, no. 3 (1993): 30.

Lake, Marilyn and Henry Reynolds. *Drawing the Global Colour Line: White Men's Countries and the International Challenge of Racial Equality.* New York, NY/Cambridge: Cambridge University Press, 2008.

Legassick, Martin. "British Hegemony and the Origins of Segregation in South Africa, 1901–14." In *Segregation and Apartheid in Twentieth-Century South Africa*, edited by William Beinart and Saul Dubow, 43–59. New York, NY: Routledge, 1995.

Martens, Jeremy C. "Settler Homes, Manhood and 'Houseboys': An Analysis of Natal's Rape Scare of 1886." *Journal of Southern African Studies* 28, no. 2 (2002): 379–400.

Morell, Robert. "Of Boys and Men: Masculinity and Gender in Southern African Studies." *Journal of Southern African Studies* 24, no. 4 (1998): 605–630.

Plaatje, Sol T.. *The Mote and the Beam: An epic on Sex-Relationship 'Twixt White and Black in British South Africa.* New York, NY: Young's Book Exchange, 1921.

Stoler, Ann Laura. *Carnal Knowledge and Imperial Power: Race and the Intimate in Colonial Rule.* Berkeley, CA: University of California Press, 2010.

Walker, Cherryl. "The Women's Suffrage Movement: The Politics of Gender, Race and Class." In *Woman and Gender in Southern Africa to 1945*, edited by Cherryl Walker, 313–345. Cape Town/London: David Philip Publishers, 1990.

Ware, Vron. *Beyond the Pale. White Women, Racism and History.* London: Verso, 2015.

Willan, Brian. *Sol Plaatje: A Life of Solomon Tshekisho Plaatje, 1876–1932.* Auckland Park: Jacana Media, 2018.

Chapter 2

Isoken

A Cultural Exploration of Differential Enjoyment of Rights and Dignity

Ezinne Ezepue

In this study, patriarchy is defined as systematic and institutionalized gender inequality in favor of men. As I reflect on the extent to which patriarchy, gender inequality, and gender roles have continued to impact family and personal choices, two stories readily come to mind: one involves my mother and the other my cousins. I am compelled to tell these stories in this study to make a contribution to how women's lives, careers, and futures are altered by choices they were compelled to make—choices that were made and forced on them because they are girls. Their situations are quite interesting because circumstances prove that these decisions could have been different had they been male rather than female. My mother is the first daughter and the third child of ten children born to my grandfather. Having just obtained her West African Examination Council (WAEC), a high school diploma, by the time the Nigeria–Biafra war broke out in 1967, she halted school to keep safe with other members of the family. But by the time the war was over in 1970, poverty and hardship spread across all south-eastern families and they struggled to feed. While her brothers resumed school because they were boys who required careers to lead successful lives, my mother assisted her mother in her small business. The family engaged in subsistence farming to augment whatever her father's salary and mother's income could afford them. My grandfather was a teacher and his salary was meager.

My father's family was more fortunate than my mother's as they had plenty of farmlands. Both his parents were merchants and at the start of the war, he was already a qualified teacher with a job. They had more food than they needed for a family of four children and two parents. When my father's family proposed marriage, my maternal grandmother disliked the idea, arguing that her daughter needed some form of a career. However, because my mother had been pulled out of school so that her brothers could continue their education, her remaining unmarried made little sense. My grandfather presented a clearer picture of what the family stood to benefit from the union: one mouth less to feed, an extended family (in-laws) that had ample food supply, and possibilities of grandchildren. No one gave a thought to what my mother felt or wanted. Marriage arrangements were made and she was duly given away. She was unhappy and wanted to return home at every opportunity she had, but she knew better than to cross her father. So, she endured. She tried various small trades as she struggled to make a contribution to her new family. In the process, she was involved in an accident that dislocated her hip and deformed one of her feet. Yet, my mother painfully carried on with her duties including childbearing, having as many as ten children to fill up a home where my dad was an only son. The accident prompted her return to school and she trained to be a teacher, the number one career for women and mothers in her time. Whenever my mother reflects on these events, she feels like a sacrificial lamb, believing her life, story, and contribution to the society could have been different were decisions not made for her based on her gender.

Until 2014, my uncle was both affluent and influential. He had eight children not because he wanted that many, but he was hoping the next one would be a male child. When he mentioned that he was taking a second wife, everyone was astounded. My uncle did not have a university education, but he obtained his secondary school certificate and was well traveled. Not minding what anyone said or how his wife and daughters felt, he married a second wife. Then, he lost a few business investments and began to experience some hardship. Subsequently, his resentment toward the children from his first wife for being all girls turned into hostility. Instead of love, he lorded over them, controlling their decisions and dictating their choices. He made all decisions for them including choosing courses for them to study at the university. It had to be nursing, pharmacy, or medicine as he was unwilling to invest in any woman who declined to study a medical science course. In keeping with his word, he refused to pay fees for one of his daughters who opted to study political science.

The purpose of this study is neither to establish nor measure society's fixation with patriarchy as, according to Solati, no society has any quantifiable measure for patriarchy.[1] Therefore, the aim of this study is to explore the sociocultural demands on the woman and how these demands differ from expectations on the man, especially within similar circumstances. Through this exploration, this study highlights differences in the privileges males and females enjoy within the society as well as the level of dignity each commands within the same cultural setup.

METHODOLOGY

The intended methodology for this research was purely qualitative, but due to the industrial strike action by the Academic Staff Union of Universities which terminated academic activities within university campuses across Nigeria, final year students of the select departments could not be reached en masse for data collection. I thus adopted a method I term qualitative narrative methodology. This methodology combines an aspect of qualitative method together with critical narrative analysis (CNA). In other words, it combines CNA's interplay of critical discourse and narrative analysis with qualitative methodology's case study. Each element of the qualitative narrative methodology is important because together they offer a flexibility and diversity in approach which a single method is incapable of providing especially to the study of an intangible phenomenon such as patriarchy. Although patriarchy is established within Nigerian society, how firmly rooted it remains in the modern-day Nigerian society is debatable. For this reason, critical narrative discourse becomes essential as it is employed to:

> Explore often opaque relationships of causality and determination between (a) discursive practices, events, and texts, and (b) wider social and cultural structures, relations and processes; to investigate how such practices, events, and texts arise out of and are ideologically shaped by relations of power and struggles over power.[2]

From Fairclough's submission, CNA can be further interpreted as an approach that examines a text's form, structure, and content, from the grammar employed to audience reception and interpretation. When this text is a film, every tool employed in its making becomes as relevant as the spoken words, its content and tone. Sriwimon and Zilli's demonstration indicates that CNA constitutes a suitable conceptual framework for investigating gender stereotypes.[3] They however note the method's major criticism—"selecting and using only a small number of texts, leading to concerns of representativeness of the texts selected, and thus susceptibility to the researcher's bias in text selection for an intended analysis."[4] To overcome this challenge, I have opted for text from a film that entered for the 2018 Africa Magic Viewers' Choice Award (AMVCA)—*Isoken*. It was nominated for the Best Movie West Africa category alongside five others and emerged the winner. Besides its emergence as a winner, among the other films that also enjoyed public screening, *Isoken* best addresses the issue of societal demands on the woman as well as the role her parents play in it. In essence, to make my text selection, I banked on the impeccable standard AMVCA has set with its last five editions of the award, its truthful submission of viewers' choices, the film's useful content as well as its contemporary nature. My supporting text, *Hope Dances*, however, was randomly selected. This random selection does not counter Sriwimon and Zilli's criticism of CNA. However, the focus and emphasis of this study lie with the Nigerian society and its demands on the woman in terms of choices and expectations. *Hope Dances* paints a perfect picture of the pressure women are put through as they struggle to meet these family and sociocultural expectations. It serves to further illustrate and reinforce this phenomenon, and highlight the role parents play in influencing the decisions their female children take in life. Most importantly, *Hope Dances* serves to distinguish between the sociocultural support for and demand on the Nigerian and Western woman.

CNA is important to this methodology because it facilitates an assessment that is based on the functionality of the text under discourse—in terms of its production, dissemination, and consumption. Its meticulous attention to details balances narrative analysis' tendency to produce generalizations in thinking, actions, and meanings related to given phenomenon. Hence, Souto-Manning's submission that CNA unites critical discourse analysis and narrative analysis in a mutually beneficial union in order to address the theoretical and methodological predicaments inherent in discourse analysis.[5] Rather than measure and deduce value from interviews, this method ensures an appraisal of value in cultural narrative tools such as films and texts. Films not only affect the society, but equally reflect them as well as influence the social, moral, and cultural lives of the people. This method will be applied to the critical interpretation of the select movies to understand the extent to which differential enjoyment of rights and dignity, predetermined by the society, impact on women's choices.

ART AND THE SOCIETY

Films have been understood as technological arts that are crucially defined by their ability to automatically register sight and sound. They inevitably contain elements of the culture they represent visually. For this reason, to fully retrieve and comprehend a film's discourse, Dudley prescribes that a film analyst should be both a historian and an interpreter of art.[6] In essence, he/she should retain the ability to objectively examine the context of a film text as well as subjectively engage with the experience contained therein. Films promote the self-image of a culture, and beyond recording experiences and history, it informs change in daily cultural experiences. Films influence the culture of their consumers, form an integral part of the culture, are products of such culture and reflect the peoples' belief system, outlook in life, ideologies, concerns and cares, among other elements. These elements are constantly changing just as the people contained within these cultures change. Hence, ideologies, concerns, attitudes, belief systems, and so on, prevalent in one era or period, may not be the same in another. For instance, in the Nigerian film industry, films produced in the 1990s explored themes of ill-gotten wealth (via prostitution, money rituals, or dubious means), family brouhaha, love, deception, among others. Classic examples include *Living in Bondage* (1991), *Glamour Girls* (1994), *Rattle Snake* (1995), and *Forever* (1997). In the early 2000s, Nollywood movie themes became more daring, exploring sensitive themes such as rape, domestic violence, and love, for instance, *Slave to Lust* (2007), *Last Girl Standing* (2004), among others. The industry embraced digital technology, capturing the entrepreneurial spirit of Nigerians who exploited the technology's accessibility, affordability, and user-friendliness. As themes expanded, so did genres and approaches since the industry became an all-comer's affair. By the end of 2009, Nollywood film themes became more serious and diverse as filmmakers began to make higher quality films that demanded larger budgets; films that became known as the New Nollywood[7], New Nigerian cinema, or New Wave.[8] Some examples include *The Figurine* (2009), *Ijé* (2010), *Black Gold* (2011), and *Tango with Me* (2011).

New Nollywood, according to Adejunmobi, has a differing ideology (in terms of production, distribution, and consumption) from the Old Nollywood (referring to pre-2009 Nollywood videos). Unlike the New Nollywood films made with a large budget, entered in film festivals and screened in local and international cinemas, Old Nollywood films have only begun to tighten storylines, produce better picture quality, and engage formally trained filmmakers. Like industry players have argued, the New Nollywood is a creation of the state. Its uneven investment into the industry warranted that huge film capital circulated in the hands of only a few lucky filmmakers. Nonetheless, this has prompted an influx of film professionals, willing private and corporate investors, access to improved digital technology, and most importantly, an exploration of controversial issues such as gender-based themes that have remained sensitive subjects in Nigerian society. While most of the storylines for these films are often fictional, I have established above that movies and the society as well as its cultures are in constant communication with each other.

CRITICAL DISCOURSE ANALYSIS OF *ISOKEN*

While the story of *Isoken* is not based on a true life story, it is based on the familiar realities that young females face within the Nigerian society. It tells the story of a lady who has come of age to get married, yet remains not only unmarried but without a known suitor. Being a familiar situation in the society, the filmmaker goes straight into the storyline, introducing Isoken, the unmarried thirty-four-year-old who is not only beautiful, but successful, smart, independent, and intelligent. The story opens as Isoken's cousin's wife goads her over her single status at her younger sister's wedding ceremony. Establishing how exasperated she had become with the situation of being constantly reminded, she moans to her friends:

> So, I expected a few "ahh . . ., God will do your own oo" or "don't worry, your own will soon come," but my family is not playing. Even that my deadbeat cousin's wife, who has three children under five at twenty-five, even that one has something to say to me. I wanted to slap that her nonsense mouth. Yes, I am thirty-four and two of my younger sisters are married. No, I don't have a boyfriend. And no, I am not going to kill myself. I am freaking fine.

Notwithstanding Isoken's contentment at this point in her life, her mother desperately carries on with her match-making attempts to find her a befitting husband. This time, Isoken is in luck as she fancies her mother's newest pick, Osaze, who lived in America and hails from a good Edo Christian family. She confides in her friends: "If there ever was a checklist of what a great guy would be, Osaze would tick every box. Ah..ah, one person. Handsome, check. Successful, check. Ambitious, check. Great kisser, check, check, check." And through her friends, the society questions her reluctance to commit to Osaze. While Isoken is attracted to Osaze, she finds herself living a life of artificiality and pretense in order to appeal both to him and his overbearing matriarch of a mother. Meanwhile, she meets a Caucasian, Kevin, with whom she can be herself and live a life devoid of "forming" or "packaging" However, the society again judges her. Her marriage to Osaze would be ideal, the perfect union of two Edo persons, rather than with an individual who knows nothing about a Nigerian and more specifically, an Edo woman.

Isoken confides in her father who describes her as the typical Nigerian woman who from an early age always ensures that everyone else around her is happy and comfortable at the detriment to her own comfort. While her father is supportive and proud of his daughter and hopes she makes the right decision for her happiness rather than please him or her mother, Isoken's mother objects vehemently. Like the typical Nigerian mother, she wants nothing less than see her daughter become a great, but typical Nigerian mother like herself. Hence, it beats her imagination when Isoken calls off her engagement to Osaze on the grounds that she could not continue to live a life of pretense. Isoken's mother believes it is better to live such life with one's own kind rather than be committed or married to an "oyinbo" (white man). Thus, when Isoken eventually opens up on her feelings for Kevin, her mother wails, "This girl has disgraced me ooo. I knew it, I knew it. Isoken, why can't you be normal like your sisters? Why can't you be normal? Na only you go school? Na only you go London?" This indicates that, however well-schooled or widely traveled a woman is, she is expected to return and realign with traditional expectations from a typical Nigerian woman. She is not expected to value career, choice of lifestyle, or personal preferences on/about marriage over what the society demands or expects of her. It was alright for Osaze to make life-altering decisions such as deciding when to settle down and with whom, but Isoken, as a woman, brings disgrace to her family and herself by choosing to follow her heart.

While enlightening Kevin on the dignity predetermined for Nigerian female by the society, Isoken observes, "It doesn't matter what a woman accomplishes in her life. She can find a cure for AIDS, she could find a cure for world hunger, even cancer and it still wouldn't matter, unless she was able to buy herself a husband and pop out some babies." According to Ntoimo and Isiugo-Abanihe, "[R]emaining unmarried by constraint or choice, beyond the age considered conventional in the Nigerian society (late teens and twenties) [*sic*] places women on the fringe of life. Their reasons for non-marriage and lifestyle are often misinterpreted,"[9] leaving the women feeling like failures, their accomplishments notwithstanding.

Unable to comprehend this advocacy for the difference in the rights enjoyed by males and females, Isoken snaps at her mother to the utter disbelief of her family and relatives:

> I nearly married Osaze who would have made me miserable, just because I wanted to please you. So that maybe just for once, for once in my life, I can say I finally did something to make mummy happy, to make you proud of me. But I know now that that would never happen, unless I do exactly what you want me to do. And that's not going to happen, because you know what? I am not normal. I never was, and I never will be. So the earlier you start to accept that, mummy, the better.

Isoken's mother represents a culture that upholds a tradition which limits the rights, choices, and dignity of the woman. She symbolizes a culture that upholds gender inequality, and distinguishes between roles played by the man and woman within the family and society. Most importantly, Isoken's mother is portrayed as the typical Nigerian mother who inadvertently bears the burden and shame of a failed or childless marriage, unruly or unsuccessful children as well as unmarried, mature daughters. Saddled with such responsibility, Isoken's mother's joy is boundless at the prospect of a perfect in-law—Osaze, a handsome Edo man, successful, driven, religious who hails from a reputable family.

Isoken's father is not characterized as the typical Nigerian patriarch, but a modern, if not, westernized man, who is proud of the woman his daughter has become despite the flaws society finds in her. He encourages her to dare to be different and happy, even if that meant displeasing everyone else including her parents. He infers that society has no moral standing to subject her to a life of misery. While studies are yet to establish what percentage of the modern Nigerian fathers are this liberal minded with their female children and the choices they make, it is worth noting that filmmakers deliberately switch roles for dramatic purposes as well as to differ from the norm. For instance, in the film, Isoken's mother enjoys privileged matriarchal authority despite her husband's active presence in the lives of their children. Osaze's mother enjoys the same privilege, but her husband's existence is never established. His absence is further reinforced with Isoken's mother's submission to her husband's decision. The director, Jadesola Osiberu, allows Isoken's father his moment to be the typical, protective dad by openly questioning Osaze's intentions toward his daughter. Ntoimo and Abanihe argue that patriarchy and existent patriarchal structures remain major limiting factors to women's opportunity to marry on their own terms.[10] While the authors contend that patriarchy not only creates this limitation, but equally stigmatizes the unmarried women, the film *Isoken* and other films in such categories like *From Lagos with Love* (2018) establish that much of the stigmatization and judgment arise from fellow women. Gender roles, gender relations, and patriarchal or matriarchal authority are social and cultural constructs, which according to Makama[11] differ from place to place and equally changes with time.

Isoken highlights other issues Nigerian women struggle with within the society like abuse, childlessness, and societal pressures. Although the director, Jadesola Osiberu, does not engage with these issues, it is important to note her portrayal of women's disposition toward addressing these issues—they confide in one another and take consolation from the fact that they are unable to change or affect their situation. In essence, Osiberu neither empowers nor sensitizes the women to stand up to gender and sociocultural inequality, but simply motivates them to be resilient rather than docile in such situations. Hence, she presents a rational and distinctive protagonist as a model to other female characters who would rather conform and adapt to the status quo. One conformist, Isoken's immediate younger sister, Rene, struggles with self-neglect due to an early marriage contracted to please her mother. She is only able to speak to Isoken whose courage she admires. Isoken's determination not to enter into an unhappy marriage in spite of societal and cultural pressures and expectations motivated Rene's self-reflection. Despite being an "ideal" woman by fulfilling her sociocultural responsibility as a mother and wife, Rene yearns for self-discovery, personal fulfillment, and purpose; a venture for which Isoken is paying by being judged and misunderstood. As she confides in Isoken, she states:

[S]ometimes I wish I had just told them that I was not ready [*for marriage*], you know? Or I told them that I needed a little bit more time. I don't know what I am doing, Isoken. And between school runs and taking care of Tega [*her husband*], there is no time for me. I don't know who I am anymore. . . . I just wish I could press the reset button.

Another conformist, Kukua, Isoken's Ghanaian friend, is characterized as a fun-loving, determined, doting, and loyal person. Yet, overwhelmed by the realities of societal demands on the woman, she is willing and ready to date more than one man at once in order to increase her chances of finding a husband within the year. Besides societal demands, the film equally indicates that women deal with biological issues. Unlike the men, women are encouraged to bear children early as their fertility begins to drop by the age of thirty. In relation, the film *Biological Clock* illustrates the emotional, financial, and mental distress Nigerian women go through in order to find husbands in time for childbearing.

CRITICAL DISCOURSE ANALYSIS OF *HOPE DANCES*

The gender-based discrimination which Nigerian women and girls contend with and the choices they make or are able to make differ from that in the western society. The differential enjoyment of rights and predetermined privileges existent between men and women in the Nigerian society warrants that women sacrifice dreams and aspirations essentially for family life, while men are allowed little or no limitations on their ambitions. Unlike in *Isoken* where preconceived social privileges, family pressure, and the social allocation of responsibilities have been established as major influencers of decisions made by young Nigerian women, the young girl, Hope Douglas, in *Hope Dances*, faces differing challenges and circumstance around making career choice. While her parents are divided on what career path they deem fit for their talented daughter, they are more concerned about Hope pursuing a career in a field where she has talent rather than a field socially acceptable and befitting for a woman.

Hope Douglas is the first of two children born to former ballerina Tina Douglas, and sports loving Jay Douglas. Hope is a talented ballet dancer as well as a star athlete. Her success in both worlds leaves her parents in disagreement on what the right choice is for Hope. While her mother aspires that Hope becomes a prima ballerina, her father desires her to become a professional softball player. Hope feels the pressure of not wanting to disappoint either of her parents, but remains completely uninfluenced by and indifferent to the society. Her introduction of herself differs remarkably from

Isoken's. While Isoken portrays herself an individual tortured by the society, Hope depicts a person unwilling to become a disappointment. Isoken's introduction of herself ends in exasperation; Hope's concludes with a hint of uncertainty.

> Hi, I am Hope. Welcome to my world. Ballerina and ball. Half the time, I don't know which one I am. My dad makes sure it's all about softball, softball, softball. And whenever dad is not looking, mum swoops in and suddenly its adagio, allegro, plié, plié. Sometimes I think my parents are getting more out of it than I am.

Like Isoken, Hope wishes to please her parents. However, their desires for her, especially her mother's is not prompted by societal demands, cultural expectations, or gender orientation. Instead, her mother perceives Hope as a realization of dreams she could not actualize. In essence, Tina Douglas' ambition for Hope is personally, rather than socioculturally, motivated. While both parents are consistent in their persuasion, Hope is equally being groomed to take charge of her life and life decisions. However, as Hope is only eleven years old, her parents understand that it is their time to make the most of influencing her career decisions. Nonetheless, rather than be forceful like Isoken's mother, each of Hope's parents employ persuasive tactics, taking their time to convince Hope of her capabilities in their own chosen fields.

Jay Douglas: I spend hundreds of hours pitching to you and hitting to you.
Tina Douglas: Honey, this isn't about what we've done. This is an opportunity for Hope to be able to express herself. And dance does that.

It is important to note the differences in social and cultural expectations and obligations for Isoken and Hope in these films. Isoken's mother attempts to forestall being perceived as a failure; a mother whose daughter could not fulfil cultural expectations by remaining unmarried despite being beautiful and successful. Hope's parents on the other hand worry about other forms of fulfillment quite unrelated to social expectations—success, personal expression, and satisfaction. Although subtle rather than aggressive in their persuasions, Hope's parents mount nonverbal pressure on her. The director, Dillion, highlights Hope's state of mind as he introduces her to the viewers. Tender music plays, creating an atmosphere for the audiences to sympathize, if not empathize with Hope. Her bed rests on a wall decorated with images of her soft ball and ballet idols. It also contains other images from the field and stage. Among the writings on the wall, positioned close to her awards and trophies are two rather contrasting pieces of encouragement. One, located closer to images that represent the two careers her parents desire for her, reads, "DO WHAT YOU LOVE." The other, however, placed closest to her trophies prompts, "Be Reasonable! DO IT MY WAY." These are significant to understanding Hope's state of mind. While undecided on what path to choose, she has dotting, loving parents who support her but have differing dreams for her. Each encourages her, giving time to bringing out the best in her. Although they would want her to do whatever she loves, each prefers she pursued the dream each believes she has great talent in. They unknowingly appear to force her on two paths that she cannot commit to simultaneously but loves, because she is great at both of them. Desiring to please her ever supportive parents, Hope reflects, "Sometimes I wonder, can I do both?"

Hope eventually commits fully to ballet in spite of numerous challenges. Her father relents in his push for her to become an athlete, trusting that dance will afford Hope the opportunity to accomplish her dreams and offers her both moral and material support. This action indicates a prioritization of Hope's dreams, personal goals and ambition, career, and personal satisfaction as well as happiness and contentment. On the other hand, Isoken does not enjoy such a privilege. This is not because her parents are unaware, unexposed, uneducated, or nonchalant. For while her father remains proud of Isoken, her mother is deliberately oblivious to Isoken's personal achievements and desire for a perfect and happy marriage. Isoken's mother is anxious to fulfill her social expectations by Isoken and anticipates that Isoken does exactly the same. To Isoken's mother, it is crucial that all her daughters are married when expected so that "her enemies," encapsulated in the society, do not mock her. Her disappointment in and objection to Isoken's desired union with a Caucasian, Kevin, further affirms her rootedness and belief in the sacredness of culture and tradition.

The difference in the rights enjoyed by women in these two distinct societies is brought to the fore when Kevin struggles to comprehend the demands and pressure which society places on the Nigerian woman and what dignifies her before her peers. While Hope's society makes positive and consistent impacts on her career dreams and promotes her personal ambitions, Isoken's society serves as a consistent reminder of gender inequality and limitation, differential enjoyment of rights and dignity predetermined for men and women based on their sociocultural and legal disposition.

CONCLUSION

Although these films, *Isoken* and *Hope Dances* are completely fictional, I established earlier that films as art, reflect as well as impact on a people's culture. So, both films are perceived as a reflection on the society as well as an advocacy. Hope attains personal satisfaction as she builds a budding and promising career in dance, while Isoken finds peace of mind and love with

Kevin who is receptive to her passionate and feisty personality, stubbornness, and quirkiness. On the other hand, Isoken's sister, Rene, recovers from the exaction of early marriage, rediscovers, prizes and loves herself as much as she loves her family. Like Adeniyi and Akinrefon observe of early marriage, Rene's early marriage posed some limiting impact on her personal growth.[12] Her self-rediscovery is the only point of social liberation which *Isoken* offers the woman. In other aspects, it yields to the social and cultural demands on the woman. This is observable in the resolution of the conflict in Isoken's life as well as those of her friends—Joke, Agnes, and Kukua. Joke delivers a baby after numerous miscarriages, Kukua gets married, Isoken finds love, and there is an admirer for Agnes who equally desires to be married. Isoken's brother, however, remains clueless and unpressured on what career to pursue.

The film *Isoken*, symbolizes a sociocultural reality—only a thin line separates the modern Nigerian woman struggling with internalized misogyny from the traditional, pseudo-progressive one who advances gender inequality and patriarchal ideals. While the film *Isoken* explores this troubling sociocultural reality, it makes no attempt to fully advocate for the abolition of cultural expectations that burden specific gender groups. The director of *Isoken*, Osiberu, sacrifices the seriousness and relevance of the matter under discourse for a contrived happy ending. She represents the mentality of the typical woman formed within the Nigerian society who believes in a needfulness to meet societal demands on the woman, but at the woman's own time. Hence, she characterizes the ladies in *Isoken* to be almost desperately desirous of marital union. Their discussions are focused on social expectations—how and when to meet these demands rather than how and when to challenge them. She does not proffer any objective criticism on or solution to the pressure only women face in certain circumstances like marriage. Nonetheless, it makes a clear point of encouraging self-discovery before succumbing to societal demands and pressures. Osiberu's role reversal for Isoken's mother and father is purely dramatic. Her interpretation and portrayal of roles are in agreement with and deference to society's conception of gender roles, privileges, and superiority.

This study thus concludes that by simply portraying and reiterating the sociocultural conceptions of gender, gender roles, and privileges, art and artistes are re-enforcing them. Art needs to become controversial by depicting dimensions that contradict predetermined expectations. It must correct established conceptions in order to educate and sensitize the audiences whose social, moral, and cultural lives can be potentially influenced. Art needs to explore and represent the impact of these social pressures, demands and inequalities, and predetermined privileges on career choices, attitude to work, and work ethics of women in the society. By doing this, art can empower women to protest against gender-specific pressure and preconceived privileges. Like Oyewumi observes, gender and gendering are not static conceptions, but continuous processes that are made and remade via everyday personal experiences.[13]

NOTES

1. Fariba Solati, *Women, Work, and Patriarchy in the Middle East and North Africa* (Cham: Palgrave Macmillan, 2017), 5.
2. Norman Fairclough, *Critical Discourse Analysis* (London: Longman, 1995), 132.
3. Lanchukorn Sriwimon and Pattamawan Zilli, "Applying Critical Discourse Analysis as a Conceptual Framework for Investigating Gender Stereotypes in Political Media Discourse," *Kasetsart Journal of Social Sciences* 38 (2017): 136–142.
4. Ibid., 136.
5. Mariana Souto-Manning, "Critical Narrative Analysis: The Interplay of Critical Discourse and Narrative Analysis," *International Journal of Qualitative Studies in Education* 27, no. 2 (2014): 160.
6. Andrew Dudley, *The Major Film Theories* (Oxford: Oxford University Press, 1976).
7. Alessandro Jedlowski, "From Nollywood to Nollyworld: Processes of Transnationalization in the Nigerian Video Film Industry," in *Global Nollywood: The Transnational Dimensions of an African Video Film Industry*, eds. Matthias Kring and Onookome Okome (Bloomington, IN: Indiana University Press, 2013).
8. Moradewun Adejunmobi, "Neoliberal Rationalities in Old and New Nollywood," *African Studies Review* 58, no. 3 (2015): 31–53.
9. Lorretta Ntoimo and Uche Isiugo-Abanihe, "Patriarchy and Singlehood among Women in Lagos, Nigeria," *Journal of Family* 20, no. 10 (2013): 2.
10. Ibid., 7
11. Allanana Makama, "Patriarchy and Gender Inequality in Nigeria: The Way Forward," *European Scientific Journal* 9, no. 17 (2013): 115–144.
12. Olakiitan Adeniyi and Adesupo Akinrefon, "Variation in age at first marriage among women in Nigeria: A Multilevel Logistic Analysis," *Mathematical Theory and Modelling* 4, no. 13 (2014): 122.
13. Oyeronke Oyewumi, "Introduction," in *Gender Epistemologies in Africa: Gendering Traditions, Spaces, Social Institutions, and Identities*, ed. Oyeronke Oyewumi (New York, NY: Palgrave Macmillan, 2011), 2.

BIBLIOGRAPHY

Adejunmobi, Moradewun. "Neoliberal Rationalities in Old and New Nollywood." *African Studies Review* 58, no. 3 (2015).

Adeniyi, Olakiitan and Adesupo Akinrefon, "Variation in age at first marriage among women in Nigeria: A Multilevel Logistic Analysis." *Mathematical Theory and Modelling* 4, no. 13 (2014).

Biological Clock. Directed by Reginald Ebere. Divine Touch Productions, 2017. Film.

Black Gold. Directed by Jeta Amata. Jeta Amata Concepts, et al., 2011. Film.

Dudley, Andrew. *The Major Film Theories.* Oxford: Oxford University Press, 1976.

Fairclough, Norman. *Critical Discourse Analysis.* London: Longman, 1995.

Figurine, The. Directed by Kunle Afolayan. Golden Effects, 2009. DVD.

From Lagos with Love. Directed by Tola Odunsi. FilmOne Productions, 2018. Film.

Glamour Girls. Director by Kenneth Nnebue. NEK Video Links Production, 1994. Videocassette.

Hope Dances. Directed by Andrew Dillon. Bright River Productions, 2017. Film.

Ijè. Directed by Chineze Anyaene. Nollywood: Xandria Productions, 2010. Film.

Isoken. Directed by Jadesola Osiberu. Tribe 85 Production, 2018. Film.

Jedlowski, Alessandro. "From Nollywood to Nollyworld: Processes of Transnationalization in the Nigerian Video Film Industry." In *Global Nollywood: The Transnational Dimensions of an African Video Film Industry*, edited by Matthias Kring and Onookome Okome. Bloomington, IN: Indiana University Press, 2013.

Living in Bondage. Directed by Chris Obi Rapu. NEK Enterprise, 1992. Videocassette.

Makama, Allanana. "Patriarchy and Gender Inequality in Nigeria: The Way Forward." *European Scientific Journal* 9, no. 17 (2013).

Ntoimo, Lorretta and Uche Isiugo-Abanihe. "Patriarchy and Singlehood Among Women in Lagos, Nigeria." *Journal of Family* 20, no. 10 (2013).

Oyewumi, Oyeronke, "Introduction." In *Gender Epistemologies in Africa: Gendering Traditions, Spaces, Social Institutions, and Identities*, edited by Oyeronke Oyewumi. New York, NY: Palgrave Macmillan, 2011.

Solati, Fariba. *Women, Work, and Patriarchy in the Middle East and North Africa.* Cham: Palgrave Macmillan, 2017.

Souto-Manning, Mariana. "Critical Narrative Analysis: The Interplay of Critical Discourse and Narrative Analysis." *International Journal of Qualitative Studies in Education* 27, no. 2 (2014).

Sriwimon, Lanchukorn, and Pattamawan Zilli. "Applying Critical Discourse Analysis as a Conceptual Framework for Investigating Gender Stereotypes in Political Media Discourse." *Kasetsart Journal of Social Sciences* 38, 2017.

Tango with Me. Directed by Mahmood Ali-Balogun. Brickwall Communications, 2011. Film.

Chapter 3

Challenging Patriarchy

East African Women's Knowledge Systems

Catherine Cymone Fourshey and Marla L. Jaksch

Patriarchy, a system of hegemony that systematically privileges men while systematically disadvantaging and oppressing women, is all around us everywhere in the world in the twenty-first century.[1] In hegemonic systems, violence is a paramount tool to maintain domination; global statistics reveal this is true of patriarchy too.[2] Deeply unequal power relations and women's under-representation in the twenty-first century in almost every sphere of everyday life and centers of power—state institutions, decision-making processes, and economic systems—are emblematic of this pervasive problematic. We contend that in present-day East Africa, where men dominate national politics, university posts, and nearly all sectors of the formal business arena, the trappings of patriarchal power structures exist primarily as a legacy of colonialism and nationalist movements. While women face multiple oppressions because position in life, age/life-stage, wealth, and sexuality often intersect with patriarchy's oppression, some women do garner and hold positions of prestige and control even in a patriarchal world. Due to history, intersectionality, and exceptions to the rule, pinpointing meanings of gender as a category of authority, power, and oppression is knotty and misunderstood; thus, historicizing patriarchy is important. Centering women's knowledge and authority is critical to rethinking patriarchy's usefulness.

Since the vast majority of the world today exists under patriarchy, much of the scholarship presumes patriarchy is eternal and natural. African feminists challenge these assumptions about patriarchy's universality across time and space. Evidence reveals that many communities in Africa historically not only afforded women authority in central social, political, and economic institutions and decision-making processes, but also created configurations other than patriarchy. What does a system other than patriarchy look like? Some scholars have pointed to the idea of matriarchy. Matriarchies may have existed somewhere historically, yet there is greater evidence to suggest communities historically drew on more multifaceted systems than a simple hegemony of patriarchal or matriarchal power.[3] A critical examination of women's knowledge systems related to education, health and wellbeing practices, and decision-making processes challenges patriarchy as 'natural'.

We argue that historical context and African feminist theories reveal that power relations pivoting on false dichotomies of gender do not bear out in the evidence. The dynamics of sex and gender relations and expressions have historically been less influential in determining leadership roles than current patriarchal assumptions and displays allow us to imagine. Starting with an analysis of African feminist scholarship, we suggest a framework that decenters patriarchy to understand power and authority dynamics outside these hegemonic constructs. We provide examples drawn from our work with East African women regarding their knowledge production—specifically their intellectual, social, political, and artistic uses of *khanga* cloth. *Khanga* is a *Kiswahili* (language) term denoting a cloth form *Waswahili* (people) value, and it holds cultural currency throughout eastern Africa. The importance of centering the legitimate influence eastern African women's knowledge has— rather than privileging neocolonial, patriarchal, nationalist understandings of what constitutes legitimate knowledge forms in discourse and analysis—to disrupt patriarchy. Local communities and nations are more likely to achieve their stated visions for social action and to arrive at solutions to women's oppression if women's knowledge systems are valued in the national policy.[4] The following section discusses African feminism to frame the importance and meaning of *khanga* cloth as sites of authority that women have carved out for themselves in East Africa's patriarchal systems.

AFRICAN FEMINIST SCHOLARSHIP
AND PATRIARCHY

As scholars based in the United States, we acknowledge the essential work and thinking of feminist scholars from the African continent who have shaped our thinking on patriarchy—highlighting the value of excavating the history of African feminisms and womanist work and the importance of the continental scholarship. Scholars must draw on knowledge generated and framed on the continent to effectively pose questions and to reach more meaningful understandings about women, men, and gender as categories both in people's thinking and lived daily experiences in East Africa. By the 1980s and more fully in the 1990s, a number of African-descended women and feminists were recognized for their contributions as they posed entirely new questions rooted in their lived experiences. Their analyses challenged what Western feminist scholarship dictated about patriarchies, gender, and oppression.[5] African women had long understood other examples and possibilities existed and used that knowledge to deconstruct gender and its universal significance in people's self-identity and its role in determining societal authority.

Some scholars pointed to the ways colonial and postcolonial male-dominated politics (patriarchy) negatively impacted women's aspirations for the futures of their own communities. The work of Amina Mama, Patricia McFadden, Gwendolyn Mikell, Obioma Nnameka, Oyèrónkẹ́ Oyěwùmí, Sylvia Tamale, to name a few, marked a shift in thinking about social categories of identity, power, and privilege. Knowledge of African languages, which are rarely gendered, combined with African institutions and categories one must recognize that positions and titles are seldom gendered in Africa. Many African feminists challenged biosocial essentialism and discuss such determinism as a colonial product. Oyěwùmí contends, physical bodies were not a logical means of deciding who could be an authority and make decisions. Physical, biological, and socially constructed differences of male and female were not the basis of doling out responsibilities and influence; instead familial and social relationships, knowledge, ability, and privilege of time on earth (age) determined one's status and authority.[6] African feminists have consistently insisted that identities like mother, aunt, sister, daughter, wife, in-law, grandmother, or ancestor (the same would hold for individuals labeled relationally as father, uncle, brother, son, husband, in-law, or grandfather) are what mattered. African feminists provide important models for postcolonial African women to turn to reassert a rightful place in societal decision making.[7]

Historian Onaiwu Ogbomo demonstrates "contemporary gender relations in Africa are not a true reflection of women's exercise of power and influence on the continent in the past."[8] The challenge in much of Africa is that identity is determined by categories deemed more salient than gender; categories like sibling, cousin, parent, child, and grandparent; generation, age, and stage of life; and knowledge or skill attainment like medical practitioner, educator, or cloth producer, to name a few. There is a critical need for deeper engagement with research from Africa on gender history, to understand the significance of the erosion of rights—particularly rights of people gendered female—during the twentieth century.

Mikell's work and Nwando Achebe's recent publication on female leaders make a compelling case, that women across Africa—from the Tswana in southern Africa to the Dogon and Soninke in northwestern Africa to rural women in Ethiopia—have long pursued and acquired various forms of authority and engaged in activism for centuries.[9] Women employ networks, mobilize resources, produce knowledge, and spread information widely, a fact that challenges patriarchy as natural and infinite. What is clear in African feminist scholarship is that power, influence, and authority were complex and most often transcended or operated outside the confines of gender. Scholars of Africa have repeatedly pointed to precolonial and contemporary indigenous practice rooted less in gender parameters and far more in the importance of kith and kin relationships and culturally linked forms of public participation. In the twenty-first century, women have less authority over wider society economically, politically, and socially, because of the erosion of local cultural models that historically afforded women meaningful participation and central roles in processes of decision making. We must seriously consider if and where patriarchy was historically the norm in Africa and attend to categories that mattered to those at the center of the narrative.[10] Rethinking categories opens up new possibilities for thinking about social status historically and the assumptions one ought to question regarding authority.[11]

Maxwell Shamase points to the failure of Western feminist paradigms that do not account for the intersections of race, social class, health and wellbeing, sexuality, ability, nationality, and other constraints that intersect with gender.[12] Shamase turns to early African feminist scholar activists to highlight precolonial strategies for correcting imbalances in the distribution of authority across gender—where women drew on local values to serve as political, social, and technical authorities even without patriarchy's consent.[13] In the next section, we share an example of women's knowledge systems that exemplify East African feminist praxis and women's clear understandings of patriarchy.

HISTORICAL SITES OF LEADERSHIP

Eastern Africa's history reveals that the rise and entrenchment of patriarchal forms are both recent and anathema to the multidimensional forms, processes, and choices regarding authority, position, and accountability that large groups of people in the region inherited, upheld, adhered to, modified, and passed on to descendants for many centuries. In precolonial eastern Africa, the territories between the Indian Ocean and Lake Tanganyika, the generational process carried great weight in determining one's authority. *Waswahili*, East African Muslims who speak a Bantu language, privilege elderhood and maintain elements of matrilineal organizing in decision making. These seemingly random factors are highly relevant in understanding the roots and importance of East African women's knowledge systems. In precolonial contexts, women and men held socially, politically, and economically influential roles.[14] People increasingly gained privilege and inhabited more authority and responsibility in critical decision-making roles within their social, familial, political, and economic networks as they gained knowledge and advanced in age and through stages of life. Like men, East African women ascended to powerful rank and standing such as *mganga/waganga* (medical healer/healers); teachers of *unyago* (education processes for youth); managers of *shamba/mashamba* (farms) and *ghala/maghala* (food barn/granaries); political leadership as chiefs; and producers of food, textiles, and jewelry to name some economic and political positions women held.[15]

Sites of power shifted increasingly during the later nineteenth and the entire twentieth century away from these systems and toward positions in the colonial/nation state, control over inedible cash crops, and production of factory goods for example—positions from which women were almost entirely excluded. The clamber of colonial capitalism and later neoliberalism in people's lives reinforced patriarchy and infringed on women's ability to have influence and positions in official national politics. Rhetoric of Islam and Christianity were also used to bolster patriarchy. After independence, African countries failed to remedy much of the erosion to women's social, political, and economic positions that colonial rule set in motion or accelerated. In their roles as public and private sphere brokers, women produced knowledge and perfected skills to assert their influence and power in their communities.[16] Next, we present *khanga* as an example of East African women producing new knowledge and maneuvering to challenge their disempowerment within the patriarchal system.

Khanga: East African Women's Knowledge Systems Personal to the Political

It is hard to imagine the power embodied in three-foot rectangles of cloth printed with decorative central motif (*mji*), ornate symmetrical borders along all four sides (*pindo*), and a few words (*jina*) along the bottom. Yet, it is their pithy, proverbial, and poetic messages that give them power. Elinami Swai likens *khanga* to popular written forms such as novels, graffiti, and cartoons. *Khanga* are multipurpose cloths used for head wraps, scarves, baby slings and diapers, menstrual absorption, postpartum blood measure, and to bundle loads. Tailors transform them into market bags or contemporary clothing styles. Its ubiquity and low-cost belie its power as a strategic tool. Outsiders dismiss *khanga* as unexceptional material, yet the intellectual and political significance of *khanga* must not be underestimated.

Its power lies in the multilayered visual, symbolic, and proverbial double messaging embedded in the cloth, that make them a "literary genre, where knowledge is produced, used, and disseminated" by women and girls.[17] We assert that *khanga* is a critical example of an East African women's knowledge system used to challenge patriarchal forms of power and control. Borrowing from Nnamaeka's Nego-feminism, we argue that contemporary

East African women employ the art and legacy of negotiation through *khanga* as political and antipatriarchy strategies. East African women's uses of *khanga*—a cultural norm of speech that is at once polite and subversive—is resistance to negotiate around patriarchal practices using a locally familiar form while also working to dismantle patriarchy.[18]

Khanga transcends class, ethnicity, and even race. Virtually all women in eastern Africa possess many *khanga* in a lifetime. A woman will walk through a market, see a *khanga* with the perfectly phrase or an ideal color combination; another day, she will be gifted *khanga* as a sign of respect and affection possibly even as recognition of her *unyago* instruction and bonding marking a transition away from childhood. Women give away and wear *khanga* to convey messages to their inner circle; they tighten bonds with family and friends. It is within the personal intimacies that women assert their authority, and subvert and violate norms with *khanga* messages for more political ends. In the face of patriarchal limits from colonial times to the present, *khanga* became a means for ordinary women across East Africa to assert position, persuasion, pressure, and prestige.[19]

Khanga are a creation of the nineteenth century, an era when patriarchal industrial capitalist demands were trying to pull women in eastern Africa more tightly into that orbit.[20] They first appeared as a small bandana-sized cloth that women of meager financial means used to display style and express their values. Over time individuals accumulated and sewed kerchief pieces together; they used them in increasingly complex ways to exhibit the semblance of luxury and affluence and to voice discontent. It began to carry political weight and became a commodity that British colonial representatives restricted to prevent anti-British and anticolonial protests. Over time this cloth came to hold clear political associations for people as resistant colonial subjects often deployed them like banners.[21] *Khanga* contain visual, verbal, and even kinesthetic messages when worn, literal messages on *khanga* are entangled with opaque and philosophical connotations whose meanings are manifold and poetic. For example, *Utu ni Kutendeana Mema* (see Figure 3.2), which might be read by some as "human-ness is treating each other well." Another *khanga* imprint reads *Kama Unaweza Basi Mtie Kamba Mumewe* (see Figure 3.3). This *khanga* phrase communicates in the literal translation "if you can, just tie your husband up." The social com-mentary might be read as women critiquing patriarchy itself. The proverbial sense of the phrase and perhaps the message an individual woman wants to send to her own family or neighbors might be a message about issues of (in)fidelity, other transgression, or annoyance.[22] *Khanga* wearers employ the cloth as "radi-cal aesthetics of double-coding," a useful strategy when direct speech is not pos-sible or desirable.[23] Double-coding subverts patriarchal norms and conventions of gendered speech and space use and serves as a powerful social commentary on people's actions.[24]

While *khanga* are ubiquitous, they are also an incredibly intimate and personal item of material culture. The meaning women make and how they engage the complex messages on *khanga* is critical. Women use them as public pedagogy—to praise, chastise, shame, glorify, or commemorate ideas and individuals. Individuals can and do utilize *khanga* subversively to express disdain while hiding disdain, to seduce while hiding seduction, expressing social taboos in coded ways. The cloth's wide circulation paired with its multilayered messaging has allowed East African women to exert power and authority with language, express their thoughts privately and publicly, and maintain plausible deniability when transgressing social norms in a system that became increasingly rigidly patriarchal during the nineteenth century. In East Africa, where oratory and incisive command of language is power, the depth of meaning in *khanga* sayings provide women opportunities to discuss meanings, teach lessons, and voice concerns through poetic proverbial expressions. Women strategically place this motif inscribed cloth on objects and bodies and "created, structured, and routinely provided learning experiences, as well as produced knowledge and articulated women's influence and authority in society."[25] Through extensive knowledge of proverbs combined with choices they make daily in fashioning *khanga*, women's actions construct and control an important form of public knowledge while transcending patriarchal control and often critiquing its norms.

Circulated among family members, *khanga* collections carry sentimental and archival value. Women collect *khanga* over a lifetime as they are gifted at puberty, weddings, engagements, births, funerals, and other important life events to signify social bonds. They can be used to express loyalties and to allay or stoke conflict. They are even often seen at political rallies and national events to signal allegiances.[26] For example, a father gifts *khanga* to a mother postpartum that states *Mama ni Mama aliaumtupa haiana maana* (Figure 3.3). The words express respect for motherhood and her experience of childbirth. *Khanga* reflect loyalties between parents for the labor they will collectively do in raising a child. A mother might redeploy this very *khanga* to contest treatment she interprets as disrespect. A *khanga* that states *penzi la mama haliishi* (A mother's love is endless) might be given by a mother to her daughter to express a bond as a daughter transitions leaving home to go off to school or build her own family. The message might assert her power and position of influence over her children and their decisions.

People carefully consider *khanga* messages and decide what is appropriate to impact the intended audience. *Khanga* designs and sayings are activated as creative and symbolic power when women consciously deploy them to demonstrate their authoritative knowledge of proverbs, communication, and relationships. It is unclear who authors and approves *khanga* phrases, yet it is women who use them to speak back, open space for dialogue, and transmit knowledge.[27] This is illustrated by a long-popular *khanga* with the subtle, concise *Alaa Kumbe* (Figure 3.1) meaning "indeed I see" or "alas I see."

This popular saying and bright *khanga* convey far more than what is at the surface. It can also make a statement about exposing another person's deceptive actions or convey innuendo of either positive or negative commentary, depending on the context.

Khanga employ well understood modes of communication that contain verbal, symbolic, and visual messages tied to deeper historical elements in motifs, color combinations, and proverbs. Closer examination of what women do in conversation with family members and friends as they choose, purchase, fashion, and strategically brandish *khanga* reveals ways that individuals subvert while seemingly affirming rules and norms of modesty and politeness.[28]

These catalogs of women's social and political thought and creative public pedagogy constitute education women use to produce "epistemic contradictions and transformations" that fall outside formal patriarchal curriculums and learning spaces.[29] Women's knowledge systems include systematic ways of assessing health of individuals with *khanga* (see Figures 3.1–3.4), which have a myriad of important uses for knowledge production, transmission, and preservation around health issues to compliment biomedicine.[30] In the context of maternal health, *khanga* are used to educate new mothers, for example, on how to protect newborns and to monitor postpartum blood loss. Given the ubiquity and the standardization of *khanga*, birth attendants have used the uniform size to soak up and measure blood loss to determine if a woman experiences postpartum hemorrhage. Regardless of the access women have

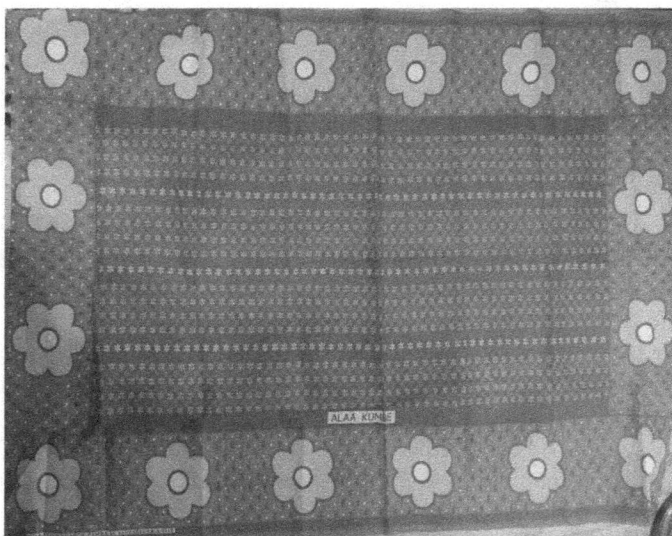

Figure 3.1 **"Alaa Kumbe."** Photo credit: Catherine Cymone Fourshey

Figure 3.2 "Utu ni Kutendeana Mema." Photo credit: Catherine Cymone Fourshey

to biomedical training or university style education in patriarchal systems, women have continued to forge their own forms of knowledge as a means of circumventing patriarchal landmines.[31]

Figure 3.3 "Mama Ni Mama Anaemtupa hana Maana." Photo credit: Catherine Cymone Fourshey

Because women wear *khanga* daily, it is not always known by observers whether the wearer consciously chose a particular *khanga* to send a message or if the wearer grabbed it from the top of a neatly organized stack in the wardrobe. It is precisely the control women have over meanings given to *khanga* and the power to reveal or conceal when the cloth is intentionally deployed to register a complaint that make them a powerful form of resistance.[32] Women's uses of *khanga* as an additional strategy allows them to make strong statements about their concerns, while at the same time avoiding direct conflict, which might arise from more less socially sanctioned actions. In line with African feminist praxis, *khanga* functions as a clear example of one feminist approach in action. *Khanga* represent cultural expectations of indirectness in language as a politeness strategy, and symbolize strategies of resistance that work around patriarchy. *Khanga* provide avenues to express thoughts both to specific individuals and/or the community at large. With this form of knowledge, women cleverly and at the right time display cloth and words—working within and against the constraints placed upon them.[33]

The familiar and politically charged words, images, and colors conjure up histories of regional liberation struggles and revolutions as well. Zanzibari feminist scholar Amina A. Issa situates *khanga* as a political intervention, through which women were central figures in the liberation struggle. Using them to display slogans and complaints, Zanzibari women instituted using *khanga* as a "weapon of political struggles." Much like the anti-British anti-colonial protesters of the 1890s and 1910s, Zanzibar revolutionaries used *khanga* as a foundational vehicle to raise women's consciousness about the struggle for independence in the 1960s.[34]

A *khanga* developed for the women's wing of the party—*Umoja wa Wanawake wa Tanzania* (UWT)—reflects women asserting their place in the political arena (see Figure 3.4). Printed in the colors of the nationalist ruling party *Chama cha Mapanduzi*, the cloth proclaims *Tunaweza* and centers a woman with a child presumably unhindered, capable of political action while mothering. The statement reinforces that collectively with unity women can author and achieve political goals and agendas. UWT wisely utilized *khanga* cloth in ways that were functional and emotively impactful in mobilizing political support. As Bibi Titi Mohamed expressed it, *khanga* was an important "nationalist tool of empowerment and self-expression."[35] Two decades later in the 1980s and the 1990s, women in UWT deployed *khanga* to question government leadership's unfulfilled promises regarding rights and opportunities for women made during the liberation struggle and documented in the constitution. UWT members exposed the assurances as empty rhetorical political slogans that needed to be fulfilled. Believing the anticolonial liberation movement demanded and the constitution enshrined their rights, women began to make more demands with their own rhetorical

Figure 3.4 **"Umoja wa Wanawake wa Tanzania—Tunaweza (Women's Union/Party of Tanzania—We Can!)."** Photo credit: Marla L. Jaksch

proclamations printed on *khanga*. UWT *khanga* serve as historical records archiving political thought.[36]

When women's contributions and their historic demands and the legitimate positions they hold are excluded or go unaccounted for in the official national record in favor of a uniform representation, everyone is left with a distorted and incomplete nation and history. Erasures of women's agency allow patriarchy to persist.

CONCLUSION

At first glance *khanga* appears to be mundane cloth; however, through an African feminist lens it becomes clear that these practices and art forms have power as political, social, and personal commentary. In particular, *khanga* serve as the very loci of decisions being made in society, and as such, they are reproducing culture and teaching new generations about multiple sites of authority. Although *khanga* is a more recent historical invention, women deploy the cloth to assert authority and voice against patriarchy. Throughout this chapter we assert that by over privileging neocolonial and patriarchal understandings of what constitutes legitimate knowledge forms, failing to attend to the complexity of influences, and ignoring diverse sites of knowledge production and power in communities, our understanding and vision for challenging patriarchy and solutions to inequality will continue to be incomplete and problematic. In particular, we have argued that women's knowledge systems captured in practices and uses of *khanga* cloth are one of the important sites of authority that can allow us to access women's visions for the nation and the ways they have challenged patriarchal institutions.

Centering questions on African women's knowledge systems, we contend that there are effective, indigenous feminist approaches to and negotiations with patriarchy that demand greater attention. We believe that these examples hold significant power for women advocating legal change and policy makers looking to implement effective disruption to patriarchy in localized contexts. We believe this work demonstrates that *khanga* are potent sites and spaces where women's power and knowledge are articulated text and subtext. We see women employ *khanga* to co-construct knowledge and maneuver through the world in savvy ways. Women have made this hybrid foreign–local product wholly indigenous in form and function to assert African feminist values as they contest patriarchy without overtly ruining anyone's *sifa*, reputation or *heshima*, honor. *Khanga* cloth is a space through which women bring their knowledge to the table to shed light on a host of injustices and aspirations they are pursing. More significantly, a range of historical examples provide important insights for women legal advocates and policy makers working to expand human-centered public policy agendas that do not exclude or discount "women" as a category. Gender equity, education, community-based health practices, and people's rights could all benefit by engaging women's knowledge systems while challenging patriarchy in all its forms. *Khanga* is an important site for understanding how East African women challenge patriarchy and all the limitations it engenders.

NOTES

1. The authors would like to acknowledge the work of African feminists who provide critical theoretical frameworks necessary in challenging patriarchal forms of oppression and violence. We also acknowledge our own daughters Winnie Nunungha and Wangui Kilima for lessons they learn and teach about navigating patriarchy across multiple culture.

2. Some examples of statistics include: https://www.who.int/news-room/fact-sheets/detail/violence-against-women; http://www.unwomen.org/en/what-we-do/ending-violence-against-women/facts-and-figures; http://www.endvawnow.org/en/articles/299-fast-facts-statistics-on-violence-against-women-and-girls-.html.

3. James Lorand Matory, *Black Atlantic Religion: Tradition, Transnationalism, and Matriarchy in the Afro-Brazilian Candomble* (Princeton, NJ: Princeton University Press, 2005), 36–37, 189–191; Ifi Amadiume, *Re-Inventing Africa: Matriarchy, Religion, and Culture* (London: Zed Books, 1997).

4. Sylvia Tamale, *Decolonization and Afro-Feminism* (Ottawa: Daraja Press, 2020).

5. Damlègue Lare, "Debunking Patriarchal Legacy in African Traditional Setting: A Reading of Efo Kodjo Mawugbe's in the Chest of a Woman," *Littera Aperta* 2 (2014): 103–123; Maxwell Z. Shamase, "A Theoretical Exposition of Feminism and Womanism in African Context," *Gender and Behaviour* 15, no. 2 (2017): 9210–9222; See also Molara Ongundipe-Leslie, *Recreating Ourselves: African Women and Critical Transformations* (Trenton, NJ: Africa World Press, 1994), 222; Ifi Amadiume, *Male Daughters, Female Husbands: Gender and Sex in an African Society* (London: Zed Press, 1987).

6. Abosede George, "*AHR* Conversation: Each Generation Writes its Own History of Generations," *The American Historical Review* 123, no. 5 (2018): 1514–1515.

7. Josephine A. Beoku-Betts and Wairimu Ngaruiya Njambi, "Be African Feminist Scholars in Women's Studies: Negotiating Spaces of Dislocation and Transformation in the Study of Women" *Meridians: Feminism, Race, Transnationalism* 6, no. 1 (2005): 113–132; Gwendolyn Mikell, *African Feminism: The Politics of Survival in Sub-Saharan Africa* (Philadelphia, PA: University of Pennsylvania Press, 1997), 3–7; Oyèrónké Oyěwùmí, *The Invention of Women: Making an African Sense of Western Gender Discourses* (Minneapolis, MN: University of Minnesota Press, 1997), 3–7; Patricia McFadden, "Becoming Postcolonial: African Women Changing the Meaning of Citizenship," *Meridians: Feminism, Race, Transnationalism* 6, no. 1 (2005): 1–22.

8. Onaiwu W. Ogbomo, "Women, Power and Society in Pre-Colonial Africa," *Lagos Historical Review* 5 (2005): 49–74.

9. Mikell, *African Feminism*; Nwando Achebe, *Female Monarchs and Merchant Queens in Africa* (Athens, OH: Ohio University Press, 2020).

10. Oyěwùmí, *Invention of Women*, 1997; Oyěwùmí Oyèrónké, *African Women and Feminism: Reflecting on the Politics of Sisterhood* (Trenton, NJ: Africa World Press, 2003).

11. Onaiwu W. Ogbomo, *When Men and Women Mattered: A History of Gender Relations Among the Owan of Nigeria* (Rochester, NJ: University of Rochester Press, 1997).

12. Shamase, "A Theoretical Exposition," 9181–9193; See original Ongundipe-Leslie, *Recreating Ourselves*, 222.

13. Lare, "Debunking Patriarchal," 103–123.

14. Catherine Cymone Fourshey, Rhonda M. Gonzales, and Christine Saidi, *Bantu Africa: 3500 Bce to Present* (New York, NY: Oxford University Press, 2018), ch 2.

15. Derek Nurse and Thomas T. Spear, *The Swahili: Reconstructing the History and Language of an African Society, 800-1500* (Philadelphia, PA: University of Pennsylvania Press, 1985), 22–25, 83, 87.

16. Sarah M. Mirza and Margaret Strobel, eds., *Three Swahili Women: Life Histories from Mombasa, Kenya* (Bloomington, IN: Indiana University Press, 1989), 13–14, 105–108.

17. Elinami Veraeli Swai, *Beyond Women's Empowerment in Africa: Exploring Dislocation and Agency* (New York, NY: Palgrave MacMillan, 2010), 82.

18. Sinmi Akin-Aina, "Beyond an Epistemology of Bread, Butter, Culture and Power: Mapping the African Feminist Movement," *Nokoko*, no. 2 (2011): 65–89; Nkiru Nzegwu, "O Africa: Gender Imperialism in Africa," in *African Women and Feminism*, Oyěwùmí, vii–viii, 102–103.

19. For varied uses of *khangas* see, Cheryl McCurdy, "Fashioning Sexuality: Desire, Manyema Ethnicity, and the Creation of the Kanga, ca. 1880-1900," *International Journal of African Historical Studies* 39, no. 3 (2006): 441–469; Jeanette Hanby and David Bygott, *Kangas: 101 Uses* (Nairobi: Ines May-Publicity, 1984).

20. Mahfoudha Alley Hamid, "Kanga: It is More Than What Meets the Eye—A Medium of Communication," *African Journal of Political Science* 1, no. 1 (1996): 103–109.

21. Elisabeth Linnebuhr, "Kanga: Popular Cloths with Messages," *Sokomoko: Popular Culture in East Africa* 3, no. 9 (1992): 138–141.

22. MacKenzie Moon Ryan, "A Decade of Design: The Global Invention of the Kanga, 1876–1886," *Textile History* 48, no. 1 (May 2017): 101–132; Maria Suriano, "Clothing and the Changing Identities of Tanganyikan Urban Youths, 1920s-1950s,"*Journal of African Cultural Studies* 20, no. 1 (2008): 95–115; Rose Marie Beck, "Texts on Textiles: Proverbiality as Characteristic of Equivocal Communication at the East African Coast (Swahili)," *Journal of African Cultural Studies* 17, no. 2 (2005): 131–160; David Parkin, "Textile as Commodity, Dress as Text: Swahili Kanga and Women's Statements," in *Textiles in Indian Ocean Societies*, ed. Ruth Barnes (New York, NY: Routledge, 2004), 44–61; Mahfoudha Alley Hamid, "Kanga: It is More Than What Meets the Eye—A Medium of Communication," *African Journal of Political Science* 1, no. 1 (1996): 103–109.

23. Swai, *Beyond,* 87.

24. Saida Yahya-Othman, "If the Cap Fits: Kanga Names and Women's Voice in Swahili Society," *Afrikanistische Arbeitspapiere: Schriftenreihe Des Kölner Instituts Für Afrikanistik* 51 (1997): 135–149.

25. Swai, *Beyond,* 82.

26. Katalin Medvedev and Lioba Moshi, "Female Tradition in a New Context: The Case of the Khanga," in *The Meanings of Dress*, eds. Kimberly Miller-Spillman and Andrew Reilly (New York, NY: Fairchild Books, 2019); Rose Marie Beck, "The Creation of a Visual Discourse 'From Below': Exploring the History of the East African Leso," (unpublished manuscript, 1997); Mahfoudha Hamid, "Nini Historia Na Matumizi Ya Kanga," *Jukwaa*, no. 13–17 (1995).

27. Amina A. Issa, "Wedding Ceremonies and Cultural Exchange in an Indian Ocean Port City: The Case of Zanzibar Town," *Social Dynamics: A Journal of African Studies* 38, no. 3 (2012): 467–478.

28. Rose Marie Beck, "Gender, Innovation and Ambiguity: Speech Prohibitions as a Resource for 'Space to Move'," *Discourse and Society* 20, no. 5 (2009): 531–553; Katrina Daly Thompson, "Zanzibari women's Discursive and Sexual Agency: Violating Gendered Speech Prohibitions through Talk about Supernatural Sex," *Discourse and Society* 22, no. 1 (2011): 3–20; Joanne B. Eicher and Sandra Lee Evenson, *The Visible Self: Perspectives of Dress, Culture and Society* (New York, NY: Fairchild Publications, 2008).

29. Swai, *Beyond*, 81–82.

30. N. Prataa, T. G. Mbarukub and M. Campbel, "Using the Kanga to Measure Postpartum Blood Loss," *International Journal of Gynecology and Obstetrics* 89 (2005): 49–50.

31. Obioma Nnaemeka, "Nego Feminism: Theorizing, Practicing, and Pruning Africa's Way," *Signs* 29, no. 2 (2004): 375–385.

32. Hildi Hendrickson, ed., *Clothing and Difference: Embodied Identities in Colonial and Post-Colonial Africa* (Durham, NC: Duke University Press, 1996).

33. Nnaemeka, "Nego Feminism," 375–385.

34. Amina A. Issa, "Women, Kanga, and Political Movements in Zanzibar, 1958-1964," *JENdA: A Journal of Culture and African Women Studies* 28 (2016): 24.

35. Susan Geiger, *TANU Women: Gender and Culture in the Making of Tanganyikan Nationalism, 1955-1965* (Portsmouth, NH: Heinemann, 1997), 180.

36. Marla Jaksch, "Mapping Differential Geographies: Women's Contributions to the Liberation Struggle in Tanzania," in *Global Perspectives on Gender and Space: Engaging Feminism and Development*, eds. Ann Oberhauser and Ibipo Johnston-Anumonwo (New York, NY: Routledge, 2014), 138–160.

BIBLIOGRAPHY

Achebe, Nwando. *Female Monarchs and Merchant Queens in Africa*. Athens, OH: Ohio University Press, 2020.

Akin-Aina, Sinmi. "Beyond an Epistemology of Bread, Butter, Culture and Power: Mapping the African Feminist Movement." *Nokoko*, no. 2 (2011): 65–89.

Amadiume, Ifi. *Re-Inventing Africa: Matriarchy, Religion, and Culture*. London: Zed Books, 1997.

Amadiume, Ifi. *Male Daughters, Female Husbands: Gender and Sex in an African Society*, London: Zed Press, 1987.

Beck, Rose Marie. "Gender, Innovation and Ambiguity: Speech Prohibitions as a Resource for 'Space to Move'." *Discourse and Society* 20, no. 5 (2009): 531–553.

Beck, Rose Marie. "Texts on Textiles: Proverbiality as Characteristic of Equivocal Communication at the East African Coast (Swahili)." *Journal of African Cultural Studies* 17 (2005): 131–160.

Beck, Rose Marie. "The Creation of a Visual Discourse 'From Below': Exploring the History of the East African Leso." Unpublished manuscript, 1997.

Beoku-Betts, Josephine A. and Wairimu Ngaruiya Njambi. "Be African Feminist Scholars in Women's Studies: Negotiating Spaces of Dislocation and Transformation in the Study of Women." *Meridians: Feminism, Race, Transnationalism* 6, no. 1 (2005): 113–132.

Eicher, Joanne B. and Sandra Lee Evenson. *The Visible Self: Perspectives o Dress, Culture and Society*. New York, NY: Fairchild Publications, 2008.

Fourshey, Catherine Cymone, Rhonda M. Gonzales and Christine Saidi. *Bantu Africa: 3500 Bce to Present*. New York, NY: Oxford University Press, 2018.

Geiger, Susan. *TANU Women: Gender and Culture in the Making of Tanganyikan Nationalism, 1955-1965*. Portsmouth, NH: Heinemann, 1997.

George, Abosede. "*AHR* Conversation: Each Generation Writes its Own History of Generations." *The American Historical Review* 123, no. 5 (2018): 1514–1515.

Hamid, Mahfoudha Alley. "Kanga: It is More Than What Meets the Eye—A Medium of Communication." *African Journal of Political Science* 1, no. 1 (1996): 103–109.

Hamid, Mahfoudha Alley. "Nini Historia Na Matumizi Ya Kanga." *Jukwaa*, July 3–30, 1995.

Hanby, Jeanette and David Bygott. *Kangas: 101 Uses*. Nairobi: Ines May-Publicity, 1994.

Issa, Amina A. "Wedding Ceremonies and Cultural Exchange in an Indian Ocean Port City: The Case of Zanzibar Town." *Social Dynamics: A Journal of African Studies* 38, no. 3 (2012): 467–478.

Issa, Amina A. "Women, Kanga, and Political Movements in Zanzibar, 1958-1964." *JENdA: A Journal of Culture and African Women Studies* 28 (2016): 23–37.

Jaksch, Marla. "Mapping Differential Geographies: Women's Contributions to the Liberation Struggle in Tanzania." In *Global Perspectives on Gender and Space: Engaging Feminism and Development*, edited by Ann Oberhauser and Ibipo Johnston-Anumonwo, 138–160. New York, NY: Routledge, 2014.

Lare, Damlègue. "Debunking Patriarchal Legacy in African Traditional Setting: A Reading of Efo Kodjo Mawugbe's in the Chest of a Woman." *Littera Aperta* 2 (2014): 103–123.

Linnebuhr, Elisabeth. "Kanga: Popular Cloths with Messages." *Sokomoko: Popular Culture in East Africa* 3, no. 9 (1992): 138–141.

Matory, James Lorand. *Black Atlantic Religion: Tradition, Transnationalism, and Matriarchy in the Afro-Brazilian Candomble*. Princeton, NJ: Princeton University Press, 2004.

McCurdy, Cheryl. "Fashioning Sexuality: Desire, Manyema Ethnicity, and the Creation of the Kanga, ca. 1880-1900." *International Journal of African Historical Studies* 39, no. 3 (2006): 441–469.

McFadden, Patricia. "Becoming Postcolonial: African Women Changing the Meaning of Citizenship." *Meridians: Feminism, Race, Transnationalism* 6, no. 1 (2005): 1–22.

Medvedev, Katalin and Lioba Moshi. "Female Tradition in a New Context: The Case of the Khanga." In *The Meanings of Dress*, edited by Kimberly Miller-Spillman and Andrew Reilly. New York, NY: Fairchild Books, 2019.

Mikell, Gwendolyn. *African Feminism: The Politics of Survival in Sub-Saharan Africa*. Philadelphia, PA: University of Pennsylvania Press, 1997.

Mirza, Sarah M. and Margaret Strobel. *Three Swahili Women: Life Histories from Mombasa, Kenya*. Bloomington, IN: Indiana University Press, 1997.

Nnaemeka, Obioma. "Nego Feminism: Theorizing, Practicing, and Pruning Africa's Way." *Signs* 29, no. 2 (2004): 375–385.

Nurse, Derek and Thomas T. Spear. *The Swahili: Reconstructing the History and Language of an African Society, 800-1500*. Philadelphia, PA: University of Pennsylvania Press, 1985.

Nzegwu, Nkiru. "O Africa: Gender Imperialism in Africa." In *African Women and Feminism: Reflecting on the Politics of Sisterhood*, edited by Oyèrónkẹ́ Oyěwùmí. Trenton, NJ: Africa World Press, 2003.

Ogbomo, Onaiwu W. *When Men and Women Mattered: A History of Gender Relations Among the Owan of Nigeria.* Rochester, NJ: University of Rochester Press, 1997.

Ogbomo, Onaiwu W. "Women, Power and Society in Pre-Colonial Africa." *Lagos Historical Review* 5 (2005): 49–74.

Ongundipe-Leslie, M. *Recreating Ourselves: African Women and Critical Transformations.* Trenton, NJ: Africa World Press, 1994.

Oyěwùmí, Oyèrónkẹ́. *The Invention of Women: Making an African Sense of Western Gender Discourses.* Minneapolis, MN: University of Minnesota Press, 1997.

Parkin, David. "Textile as Commodity, Dress as Text: Swahili Kanga and Women's Statements." In *Textiles in Indian Ocean Societies*, edited by Ruth Barnes. New York, NY: Routledge, 2004.

Prataa, N., Campbel M. and Mbarukub T. G. "Using the Kanga to Measure Postpartum Blood Loss." *International Journal of Gynecology and Obstetrics* 89 (2005): 49–50.

Ryan, MacKenzie Moon. "A Decade of Design: The Global Invention of the Kanga, 1876-1886." *Textile History* 48, no. 1 (2017): 101–132.

Shamase, Maxwell Z. "A Theoretical Exposition of Feminism and Womanism in African Context." *Gender and Behaviour* 15, no. 2 (2017): 9210–9222.

Suriano, Maria. "Clothing and the Changing Identities of Tanganyikan Urban Youths, 1920s-1950s." *Journal of African Cultural Studies* 20, no. 1 (2008): 95–115.

Swai, Elinami Veraeli. *Beyond Women's Empowerment in Africa: Exploring Dislocation and Agency.* New York, NY: Palgrave MacMillan, 2010.

Tamale, Sylvia. *Decolonization and Afro-feminism.* Ottawa: Daraja Press, 2020.

Thompson, Katrina Daly. "Zanzibari Women's Discursive and Sexual Agency: Violating Gendered Speech Prohibitions through Talk about Supernatural Sex." *Discourse and Society* 22, no. 2 (2011): 3–20.

Yahya-Othman, Saida. "If the Cap Fits: Kanga Names and Women's Voice in Swahili Society." *Afrikanistische Arbeitspapiere: Schriftenreihe Des Kölner Instituts Für Afrikanistik* 51 (1997): 135–149.

Chapter 4

"I Paid Lobola!" The Interface between Bride Price and Domestic Violence

A Case Study of Epworth in Zimbabwe, 2007–2017

Tasara Muguti and Nyasha Mlambo

This chapter endeavors to explore the correlation between bride price payment (lobola) and gender-based violence (GBV) in Zimbabwe using Epworth high-density suburb in Harare as a case study. Lobola payment is a practice among Africans that serves as an exchange between two families to legalize a marriage union. Lobola is usually paid in form of cattle or cash and every woman's dream is to have bride price paid for her as it gives her and her family greater status in the society. The study seeks to evaluate the extent to which this age-old cultural practice has been used by men to abuse their female partners under customary law in Zimbabwe's highly patriarchal society. More precisely, the study seeks to determine participants' knowledge, experiences, and views on domestic violence against women (VAW), identify factors that sustain abusive marriages, identify the most pervasive forms of violence women face, and determine perceptions of participants regarding bride price payment and domestic violence.

The study concludes by examining how GBV impacts on the victims. On the whole, the study reveals that the majority of women in Epworth believed there are certain acts that deserve a beating from a husband and that women receive pressure from various actors such as the church and family to endure in abusive marriages. While generally there are multiplicities of socioeconomic and cultural factors that drive VAW, the researchers believe that the payment of lobola strongly influence male partners to become abusive to their female partners in marriages.

Despite national governments, local and international nongovernmental organizations' intervention to protect women against domestic violence,

women are still vulnerable to abuse across the world as they still live in predominantly patriarchal societies. Although Zimbabwe enacted its Domestic
Violence Act way back in 2007 in an attempt to outlaw domestic violence,
since the issue needed to be addressed proactively using legal instruments,
the practice is still prevalent across the country. Perhaps, it is important to
highlight from the outset that domestic violence is not necessarily perpetrated
against women by their male counterparts but it can also be perpetrated by
women against men. Nonetheless, for the purposes of this study, GBV will
be confined to violence directed at women which affects them disproportion-
ally. GBV is a type of violence girls and women are subjected to by virtue of
their gender identity.

The United Nations Declaration on the Elimination of VAW defines
domestic violence as "the use of force or threats by a husband or boyfriend
for the purposes of coercing and intimidating a woman into submission."[1]
GBV is intended to cause subordination based on assumed men's superiority.[2] In general terms, the term "violence" is conceptualized as any attack by
one person on another carried out with the intention of causing physical pain
and injury to the other person. Wife beating or VAW in the context of this
study is defined as any act of aggression directed by a husband against his
wife. It is used specifically to cover incidents of physical attacks and sexual
violations such as punching, beating, choking, slapping, stabbing, throwing
harmful objects like household items, and forced sex, which all cause physical injury and or death. It also includes psychological violence which consists
of repeated verbal abuse, harassment, belittling one in public, cursing via the
use of vulgar language, and deprivation of physical, financial, and personal
resources.

Bride price payment is a contextual factor perceived and associated with
domestic violence and having serious sexual and reproductive health implications for women. While it is generally acknowledged that there is no single
factor that is associated with instigating VAW, it is the contention of this
study that there is a direct link between bride price payment and the occurrence of domestic violence within marriages. Bride price payment is a common practice used to cement relations between two families within African
societies. The practice is fundamental to marriage rites and is deeply embedded as a prized cultural norm as it legitimizes marriages and as demonstrated
by Dery, there is burgeoning evidence to show that bride price payment has
far reaching negative influences on domestic violence.[3]

The system of bride price payment is not peculiar to sub-Saharan African
countries alone; it is a global practice which dates back to 3000 BC.[4] Most
women see the payment of *lobola* (bride price) as a sign of honor while families need it for social security, increased status in the community; hence, its
commercialization, which has exacerbated the occurrence of domestic violence

in marriages. In precolonial Zimbabwe, lobola generally took the form of a hoe or cattle. Although being a concept rooted in patriarchy, it has been corrupted by modernity through avarice that seems to consign women to the level of purchased household furniture. Domestic VAW and violation of women's reproductive rights have also been reported to have a direct or indirect link with bride payment.[5] This study seeks to explore the connection between the cultural practice of bride wealth payment and domestic violence in Epworth suburb in Harare, Zimbabwe. Epworth, one of the poorest high-density suburbs in Harare, is located about 15 kilometers south-west of the capital city.

The increasing statistics on domestic violence among married people with a bride price tag have prompted the need for this research as domestic violence appears to be expanding in Zimbabwe. The study augments the already existing literature on bride payment, related domestic violence and builds an understanding of abused women's perceptions of what perpetuates domestic violence in marriage settings.

METHODOLOGY AND THEORETICAL FRAMEWORK

The study was largely qualitative in nature drawing heavily on appropriate data from Musasa Project Centre, Harare.[6] It was principally based on the "lived realities" of fifty married and divorced women clients (aged between eighteen and fifty) of Musasa Project from the Epworth Community who have suffered from one form of intimate partner violence (IPV) or another and have come for help at one point at Musasa Project Centre in Harare. The study was further augmented by interviews with a sample of men and women from Epworth, focus group discussions, and ten key informants. Pseudo names were used to guarantee privacy and confidentiality. The study was influenced by feminist theories such as radical feminism and liberal feminism. These were useful in understanding how women's weak economic status in the society leaves them vulnerable when faced with domestic violence. The study is influenced by these theories especially when establishing the extent to which culture and the notion of "preserving marriages" has impacted on the victims' choice to pursue legal options. The ecological theoretical framework was also used in order to understand the interaction between personal, situational, and sociocultural factors in accomplishing women abuse.[7]

AN OVERVIEW OF VAW

Domestic violence is a cause of concern all over the world and has emerged as a serious global health, human rights, and development issue. The practice of bride price payment is increasing the frequency of domestic violence globally, and Zimbabwe is no exception. The fact that VAW and the need to reduce it has progressively been receiving international attention is reflected through the adoption of several international and regional instruments.[8] These legal benchmarks have assisted in changing people's attitudes toward domestic violence resulting in its treatment as a public issue in most countries across the world today. Cases of domestic violence have been on the rise and no continent has been spared. Feminist movements have also been very proactive in pushing governments to take action through enacting laws and legislations protecting women against abuse.

Since the adoption of the Convention on the Elimination of all Forms of Discrimination against Women, there has been significant progress in eradicating VAW. Zimbabwe has enacted various pieces of legislation including the Domestic Violence Act (2007) to protect women from various forms of abuse.[9] It has established national frameworks such as the Ministry of Women Affairs Gender and Community Development to ensure women protection against abuse. It also observes the sixteen days of activism against GBV annually from November 25 which helps in creating awareness on issues related to violence and rights.

Various factors have been presented as causes of VAW. In China, risk factors for violence include patriarchal beliefs, sexual jealousy, low male socioeconomic status, low female contribution to household income, and alcohol consumption. A 2011 study in Shenzhen revealed that 94 percent of violence that occurred in marriage had been perpetrated by husbands.[10] According to Moxley, 66 percent of the rural populace in China have been victims of domestic violence due to the traditional belief that boys are more precious than girls and the subordinate position of women in the country side.[11] Moxley further argues that about 157,000 women in China kill themselves annually as they are no longer able to endure the abuse.[12] In countries like India where dowry is the form of bride wealth paid by the woman, domestic violence still occurs within marriages.[13] Interestingly, in Europe where the practice of bride wealth payment is alien, cases of domestic violence are also reportedly widespread largely due to alcohol and drug abuse.[14] It is alleged that one in every four European women have experienced domestic violence in their lives and that between 6 to 10 percent have suffered domestic violence annually.[15] This shows that the causes of domestic violence in marriages are widespread and multifaceted.

In the African context, bride wealth payment has emerged as one of the factors connected with men's authority and VAW as it not only gives men authority to dominate and abuse women but also rationalizes the use of VAW.[16] In recent years, the practice of bride wealth payment has been spotlighted. A number of objections have been raised in the media and in political and academic discourses. These stem from the view that the transactional nature of the bride price practice results in the commoditization of women with adverse effects on marriages. For example, husbands may feel they can mistreat their wives because they paid for them, leaving women in marriages prone to physical violence.

Bride price payment demands have become excessive nowadays as they are paid in form of cash, cars, groceries, and so on. Consequently, women are "purchased" thus implying that men have a license to do whatever they deem fit. African culture expects wives to be quiet, submissive, and accepting of abuse within marriage and the family.[17] The scourge of domestic violence is a daily occurrence in Africa where an unhealthy mix of tradition, inequality, and even ignorance conspire. It is estimated that one in three women have directly experienced either or both forms of VAW: IPV or sexual violence from a nonpartner.[18] The regional prevalence rates of VAW are high approaching 50 percent which is a symptom of underlying gender inequalities and power imbalances between men and women which may be closely linked to patriarchy.[19] Historically, gift exchange has been an important integral part of marriage rites and ceremonies in African culture. It involves the exchange of materials or money from the man's to the woman's household. Consequently, Levinson argues that bride payment perpetuates the culture of male dominance in prestige, power, and decision making, and also perpetuates economic inequality.[20]

The history of VAW is tied to the history of women being viewed as property and the gender role assigned to them to be subservient to men. Makahamadze *et al.*, argue that bride price payment is a custom which reduces and undermines women's role in marriage, turning women into a man's property.[21] It has practical implications for women's choices in marriage, making them more vulnerable to physical, intimate, and economic violence, thereby breeding submissiveness and silencing their voice at the family level. The payment of lobola renders women weak as they have no say in family decisions and even their own sexuality. Thus, men have a sense of entitlement to sex after paying lobola. The conviction that men have the right to sex even without consent stems from sexual violence related to social norms of being a man. In addition to encouraging men to behave violently, social norms can cultivate tolerance and silence about sexual and other forms of violence within communities. Flood and Pease are of the view that such norms can contribute to stigma against survivors and prevent people from speaking out or taking action against violence.[22] Bride price payment has left women in compromising positions and susceptible to all forms of violence within the marriage institution. Before the economic meltdown and dollarization process in Zimbabwe in 2008, it can be argued that the practice of bride price payment had value as its main purpose was to strengthen relations between two families (*kusunga hukama*) among the Shona. Scholars like Tawanda Chabata[23] argue that the commercialization of lobola is the problem with the practice not the practice itself. The exorbitant lobola prices that parents call for these days can be excessive where the bride is well-educated, for instance a graduate. In this regard, one can note that amassing wealth has become more important than lobola's traditional purpose of establishing ties among families. Factors such as the woman's level of education, virginity, and financial status of the groom are all considered during lobola negotiations. It is against this background that one notes the different meanings attached to bride wealth payment in different societies.

FACTS ABOUT VAW IN EPWORTH

In table 4.1 below, from the targeted fifty female respondents all were interviewed, twenty were clients from Epworth who came to Musasa Project seeking assistance and the other twenty were interviewed individually from their homes in Epworth. Two focus group discussions with female participants of five members each were held at Musasa Project. Only one key informant failed to attend the interviews as planned. The response rate was 99 percent.

ATTITUDES TOWARD DOMESTIC VIOLENCE

Responses from the participants in Epworth indicated that the high tolerance of domestic violence by society makes its eradication extremely difficult. One of the recurrent reasons given in the study as to why many cases of VAW were not reported was that society has accepted domestic violence as natural and that the men, as heads of households, have the right to do anything they want to their female counterparts. Both male and female respondents were asked what actions were justified for a woman to be beaten, and the responses included: going out without telling the husband, refusing the husband sex, and arguing with him. The researchers noted that generally, the acceptance

Table 4.1: Individual and group interviews

Respondents	Interview target	Number of people interviewed	Response rate (%)
Males	10	10	100%
Females	50	50	100%
Key informants	10	9	90%
TOTAL	**70**	**69**	**99%**

Source: Individually generated

attitudes for wife beating were higher among women (80 percent) than men in most cases. Indeed, this clearly indicates that wife beating is an expression of male dominance and the institution of marriage reflects patriarchal norms of male supremacy which society generally tolerates.

The pattern of responses also clearly indicated that it is difficult for behaviors to change and that both women and men still view violence as acceptable. This conviction renders all efforts by the government, local nongovernmental organizations, and other interested parties in eradicating VAW futile. For instance, 50 percent of male respondents argued that a woman deserved a beating if she was to insist on the use of condoms during sex. In particular, one male respondent affirmed: "If she insists on using protection it means that there are other men she is sleeping with, if not I do not see the need because we are married."

PARTICIPANTS' KNOWLEDGE, EXPERIENCES, AND VIEWS ON DOMESTIC VIOLENCE

The researchers were able to probe for issues like family relations, level of education, and life history. The women gave various responses as to what they thought domestic violence meant. An overwhelming 90 percent of these women referred to battering (wife beating) as domestic violence and they justified these beatings where a woman neglected her children or disrespected the husband. The other 10 percent cited verbal insults, forced sex, and denial of finance as acts of domestic violence. When asked during the discussions if they regarded forced sex in marriage (marital rape) as an act of domestic violence, the majority gave "NO" as their response on the basis that they were taught that it was their duty as wives to be sexually active whenever the husband requested it. The researchers got the impression that women had little knowledge of their rights in marriage especially sexual rights and their rights in general. The ten male participants concurred that there was nothing called domestic violence in a marriage. The researchers interpreted this response to be a result of men's socialization whereby men are raised to think that women should be corrected by beating. All female participants in the study had experienced one form of violence or another in their marriage.

Table 4.2 summarizes key marriage-related experiences of ten respondents in Epworth. An indication of age, number of children, types of violence exposed to, current years spent in the marriage, family size, and occupation is provided. Forced sex, physical abuse, psychological abuse, verbal (cursing, insulting in private or public), and economic abuse were mentioned by women as experienced. These results summarize classical perverse forms of violence that include emotional, verbal, sexual, physical, and economic violence.

Table 4.2:   Participants' profiles and their experiences in domestic violence

Pseudonym	Age in years	Number of children	Form of violence exposed to	Years in marriage	Occupation
Mrs. Mango	48	3	denied financial resources; forced unprotected sex when husband drunk; threatened with knife	23	Housewife
Mrs. Musasa	27	1	locked in house without food; belittled in front of neighbors; kicked and slapped	4	hair dresser
Mrs. Kusawgu	33	4	restricted from visiting friends and relatives; brings girlfriends home and forced to watch them being intimate; choking; forced sex without protection	11	self-employed (vendor)
Mrs. Muwonde	23	0	forcibly kept awake when husband drunk; pushed; shouted at in public using vulgar language, name calling; forced sex denied financial resources	6 months	Housewife
Mrs. Mutohwe	40	2	punched in the face; forced daily unprotected sex; pulled by the hair; name calling in presence of children	20	Teacher
Mrs. Mahogany	29	5	flushed away birth control pills; denied money to buy food and other basics; clothes burnt; mother insulted using vulgar language; forced sex when drunk	8	Housewife
Mrs. Mupfuti	25	2	beaten using a stick; forcibly kept awake at night when husband drunk; extra-marital affairs; called a prostitute	5	police woman

(Continued)

Table 4.2   Participants' profiles and their experiences in domestic violence (Continued)

Pseudonym	Age in years	Number of children	Form of violence exposed to	Years in marriage	Occupation
Mrs. Mupfura	35	1	forced sex; damaged property; threat of physical assault; denied visits relatives, to go to work	10	Teacher
Mrs. Mutondo	47	3	beaten with electric cables; extra-marital affairs; husband's willful transmission of HIV to her; forced unprotected sex; kicked, punched; stalking; denied permission to go to work, locked in house	22	Soldier
Mrs. Mukute	30	1	beaten while pregnant; swearing; forced sex; stalking; cell phone taken and all communication cut off with relatives; slapped, forced to skip work; extra-marital affairs; no financial support for family; name-calling-referred to by her private parts in presence of child	6	crèche teacher

Source: Individually generated

WOMEN'S UNDERSTANDING OF DOMESTIC VIOLENCE

While opinions may differ as to what domestic violence is or what its causes and effects may be, the reality is that the problem simply will not go away and is getting progressively worse. Women were asked what actions they would classify as violence between a husband and a wife. In summary, they said domestic violence include

1. threats of physical violence;
2. physical aggression, for example, kicking, squeezing, punching, and pushing;
3. physical assaults that damage the body, for example, bruising, broken teeth or bones, swollen body, and forced sexual intercourse; and

4. verbal abuse, for example, belittling in front of children or one's family, insulting or cursing.

Women who had been subjected to domestic violence reported during the interviews that, at the time, they found it difficult to define their experiences as "violence." For example, women felt that they had caused it, and this confused them; they did not see their husbands' actions as violence. Thus, for some wife beating was first regarded as a family problem to be settled in the privacy of the home. Also, many of the women believed that a wife is subordinate to her husband. Some emphasized that wife beating was part of the social norm. For these reasons, their families tended not to interfere in domestic violence issues. At the time of the interviews, several women whose life stories are captured in table 5 had bad bruises on their faces, necks, and hands. Despite this, the women had the tendency to forgive as they often thought that their partners would not hit them again. The women hoped their men would change, and chose to transform themselves to meet these gendered social expectations. Braithwaite and Heather state that domestic violence includes a range of behaviors and coercive tactics; it is often repetitive, meaningful, and strategic, reflecting deeply held attitudes and beliefs rather than an isolated incident, and there are social and cultural dimensions that give meaning to this violence.[24] Women suffer violence at the hands of husbands who are family heads because these males have been raised to feel superior to their female counterparts.

Although both men and women in intimate relationships have been shown to be victims of their partners' violence, this research has been limited to female victims since women usually bear the brunt of immense suffering. Men relative to women have the potential to cause more physical damage and to escape an abusive attack more easily because of their size and strength (biological buildup) advantages. Women's greater social and economic dependence often prevents them from escaping abusive relationships. This is evident in this study since most women took a long time before seeking intervention.

Women may be required to engage in unwanted sexual practices more frequently than desired. Married women who request the use of condoms are often subjected to violence as it is suspected that they are committing adultery. Regrettably, cultural norms have pronounced silence and submissiveness and conformity for women in sexual relations. The study also noted from given responses that decisions on how and when to have sex remain exclusively with men. The payment of lobola, as a customary practice, gives ultimate power to the husband in the home and it causes untold suffering to women who have no negotiating power on sexual issues as they are often habitually subjected to unprotected sex and marital rape thereby exposing them to HIV and AIDS. The forms of violence and abuse undermine every aspect of women's lives, making it difficult for them to live functional lives and contribute to development as the effects of domestic violence affect them.

FACTORS THAT SUSTAIN ABUSIVE MARRIAGES

Women in Epworth revealed why they stayed in marriages even though they were abused and risked endangering their health and lives. It was observed that 80 percent of the female respondents had not attained ordinary level in their secondary school education and could not further their studies. As a result, they were either unemployed or self-employed as vendors earning very little income. Due to their economic dependence on their male partners, they had to endure in otherwise "dysfunctional" marriages. Some of the responses given were influenced by the women's children, and influential sociocultural forces like the church and close family relations which encouraged women to be strong despite the impact of the abuse just to preserve their marriages. The few educated degree holders and formally employed women revealed how relatives, the community, and the hope that their partners would change influenced them to remain in their marriages. The women revealed that when abused, they sought assistance and advice from their immediate family members especially aunties, the church, and friends to try and save their marriages. The abused women rarely sought legal redress because society deems domestic violence a "private" rather than a public issue.

Although organizations like Musasa Project may provide counseling services as well as education for its female clientele, all their intervention programs come to naught when the customary laws and practices take precedence over general law. Another reason stated by the women as to why they stay in abusive marriages was because of their children since they had no source of income to cater for them alone. One interviewee retorted:

> I have to stay in the marriage because of my children, if I leave I have no means of getting money and there is no hope of me getting a job. I attended school up to Grade 7 and besides there are no jobs. I have to be strong for the children no matter what.

Another female weighed in by stating: "I am afraid of leaving him because he threatened to hunt me down and kill me if I were to run away."

The above statements characterized some of the general feelings on why abused women could not leave their abusive husbands in Epworth.

THE MOST PERVASIVE FORM OF VIOLENCE WOMEN ARE EXPOSED TO IN MARRIAGES

Married women in Epworth are susceptible to all forms of violence but sexual abuse stood out as the major form of abuse particularly marital rape which they experience but is grossly under reported. Economic abuse, comprising the denial of permission to go to work, and the denial of financial resources to buy food, is one example. Fifty percent of women reported that the psychological effects attributed to the "small-house" phenomenon whereby the husband spends all his money and neglects his family's welfare were some of the worst forms of violence they experienced. Excessive drinking of alcohol among male spouses was also a significant factor. Psychological abuse, physical and verbal abuses were the other forms of abuse identified by the women.

PERCEPTIONS REGARDING BRIDE WEALTH PAYMENT AND DOMESTIC VIOLENCE

The respondents had both positive and negative perceptions regarding bride wealth payment. Most female participants believed that the payment of lobola was proof that a man values his wife and their union. Eighty-five percent of the respondents agreed with the view that lobola payment gave status to a marriage. This is in agreement with Bourdillon's study among the Shona people which identified that the payment of a high bride price conferred a higher status on the bride and reflected the value the husband places on the marriage.[25] The respondents provided mixed thoughts on the amounts charged as bride price with some saying it is a sign of love and others saying the effects of lobola in its commercialized form is violence as men liken it to purchasing property and so if their needs are not met they resort to violence to "discipline" women. The respondents unanimously revealed that gender constructions of masculinity condone violence in their marriages. Kambarami maintains that lobola gives men all rights while women are stripped of their freedom and rights. Thus, the woman is reduced to the level of property.[26] It is important to note that gender roles and expectations are not exclusively created by men but by both women and men. Men are often seen as fueling the paying of lobola as well as gender violence yet both women and men engage in these practices. Prevailing norms of masculinity cover a man's discipline of his wife occasionally whether in the physical, emotional, economic, or psychological form. Not surprisingly, a male respondent referred to the wife as a little less than his property and in his own words retorted:

> I paid six cows, US$4000 dollars cash when I married my wife in 2011. My wife is unemployed and I do everything for her so I discipline her every now and then to remind her of her place. She needs to know I am the head of the family.

The male participants used gender socialization to explain the violence perpetrated against their partners. The man is afforded a right to sanction what is regarded as undesirable behavior in the African culture. Some of the women interviewed suggested that their husbands saw wife beating as their "cultural right." Cultural and societal expectations and norms create an environment where marital violence is acceptable and justified by the payment of lobola as the participants in the study indicated. The cultural practice of paying lobola widens the gap between women and men and subordinate women. According to SAFAIDS, the Zimbabwean society is a patriarchal one which teaches girls and women that there is nothing wrong with being beaten by a husband. The ability of the man to pay lobola from his own earnings and savings reduces the power and influence of his extended family in regulating the relationship especially in conflict resolution and the women have no power to make decisions.[27] Despite the respondents' conflicting views on the impact of lobola on domestic violence, the participants wanted the practice of lobola to continue and the bride prices charged to grooms' strictly monitored so as to maintain a rational balance between the cultural value of lobola and the need to avoid unwanted cases of domestic violence in the home.

Notwithstanding the direct link between domestic violence and lobola payment, there are other causal factors of domestic violence. These include drug abuse, jealousy, infidelity, and norms of masculinity as identified by respondents in the study. Male respondents cited disrespect on the part of women as an action deserving some sort of "correcting" through beating and to remind women about "who the head of the family is." Some women in this study revealed that their husbands became more violent after the consumption of alcohol or drugs forcing them to stay awake at night. Through acts of domestic violence, perpetrators (primarily men) seek to maintain privileges, power, and control over women. During the in-depth interviews with the men, the researchers noted that nine out of ten interviewees were of the view that women should be constantly reminded of their place in the home and that a little beating was the only way for them to understand who the head of the family is.

REFLECTIONS ON THE STUDY FINDINGS

The study raised recurring themes including the perpetuation of the patriarchal system which further widens the gap between men and women. The participants made reference to the unequal relations of both sexes which are exacerbated by the payment of lobola. These have been a major source of conflict between partners within marriages. That the payment of bride price can be a major stimulant of VAW can be discerned from the sentiments of one female respondent who indicated that violence between partners who were just cohabiting was less frequent than between partners whose marriage was endorsed by lobola.

The effectiveness of measures to deal with domestic violence is however debatable as cases of domestic violence are still on the rise and many cases go unreported as people view it as a "private matter." Violence is considered integral to African culture and repletes sayings such as "stay, things will get better," all in the name of preserving the marriage union. However, VAW has serious physical, emotional, psychological, and health effects on the victims and their children. Health effects such as physical injuries, unwanted pregnancies, STIs (including HIV), miscarriages, and emotional challenges emanating from anxiety and depression are not uncommon among victims.[28] Violence erodes the self-esteem of the victims. It is a traumatic experience that results in untold trauma to the victim and is a violation of the victim's human rights. It also propagates the stereotyping of gender roles that denies the dignity of women as individuals and in the process stifles human development.

CONCLUSION

From the preceding discussion, it is evident that the cultural practice of lobola payment exacerbates domestic violence. The payment of lobola in its commercialized form widens the gap between men and women as women tend to become men's property. Nonetheless, the study, like others before it, demonstrates that there is no one single cause of domestic violence as other factors like alcohol abuse, norms of masculinity, infidelity, jealousy, among others, tend to fuel violence in the home. It can be further concluded that while Zimbabwe has made significant strides in complying with its human rights obligations that address the problem of VAW at national, regional, and international level, these cases are still prevalent within Zimbabwean communities particularly among the poor and the marginalized communities such as Epworth. Domestic violence continues to be a hideous, global social setback. Domestic violence should not be condoned in any way, traditionally, socially, or legally. Perhaps, a multisectoral approach by various players and employing strategies which influence norm change could provide a lasting solution in ending VAW in Zimbabwe where the payment of lobola is an exacerbating factor in violence.

NOTES

1. United Nations, Committee on the Elimination of All Forms of Discrimination against Women (CEDAW), Geneva, UN General Assembly, 1993, 1.

2. Fummilola B. Akokan, "Domestic Violence against Women: A Family Menace," (paper presented at the 1st Annual International Interdisciplinary Conference, AIIC, Azores, Portugal, April, 24–26, 2013), 100-107.

3. Isaac Dery, "Bride-price and Domestic Violence: Empirical Perspective from Nandom District in the North Western Region of Ghana," *International Journal of Development and Sustainability* 4, no. 3 (2015): 258–271.

4. Swan Anderson, "The Economics of Dowry and Bride Price," *Journal of Economic Perspectives* 21, no. 4 (2007): 151–174.

5. Tompson Makahamadze, Anthony Isacco and Excellent Chireshe, "Examining the Perceptions of Zimbabwean Women about Domestic Violence Act," *Journal of Interpersonal Violence* 27, no. 4 (2012):706–727.

6. Musasa Project is a nongovernmental organisation that deals with women rights issues in Zimbabwe including violence against women.

7. Mary Ellsberg and Lori Heisi, *Researching Violence against Women, A practical Guide for Researchers and Activists* (Geneva: WHO Press, 2005), 5.

8. These organizations include the United Nations CEDAW adopted in 1979, the United Nations DEVAW in 1993, The Beijing Declaration of 1995, The Protocol to the African Charter on Human and Peoples' Rights on the Rights of Women in Africa of 2003.

9. The year 1993 is significant as it was the first time that the United Nations organ, CEDAW established an official definition of the term violence against women.

10. Mitch Moxley, "RIGHTS-CHINA: For Too Many, Domestic Violence Part of Family Life,"http://www.ipsnews.net/2010/10/rights-china-for-too-many-domestic-violence-part-of-family-life (accessed December 14, 2018).

11. Ibid.

12. Ibid.

13. S. Strinivasan and S.A Bedi, "Domestic Violence and Dowry: Evidence from a South Indian Village" (Working Paper Series No. 429, The Hague, Institute of Social Sciences, 2006), 2.

14. "Domestic Violence against Women Report," (Special Eurobarometer 344, European Commission, Brussels, TNS Opinion and Social, 2010), 67.

15. Ibid., 5.

16. Makahamadze, Isacco and Chireshe, "Examining the Perceptions," 710.

17. Alima Katembo, "Reducing Cases of Gender Based Violence in Mashonaland Central Province: Zimbabwe" (MA Thesis, Durban University of Technology, 2015), 12.

18. World Health Organization, "Violence against Women," November 29, 2017, https://www.who.int/news-room/fact-sheets/detail/violence-against-women.

19. Ibid.

20. D. Levinson *Family Violence in Cross-Cultural Perspectives* (Newbury Park, CA: Sage, 1989), 439–455.

21. Makahamadze, Isacco and Chireshe, "Examining the Perceptions," 710.

22. Michael Flood and Bob Pease, "Factors Influencing Attitudes to Violence against Women," *Journal of Trauma and Violence* 10, no. 2 (2009): 128, 125–141.

23. Takunda Chabata, "The Commercialisation of Lobola in Contemporary Zimbabwe, A Double-Edged Sword," *A Journal on African Women's Experiences* 2, no. 1 (2012): 10–14.

24. John Braithwaite and Heather Strang, *Restorative and Family Violence* (Cambridge: Cambridge University Press, 2002), 1–288.

25. M.F.C. Bourdillon, *The Shona Peoples* (Gweru: Mambo Press, 1976), 50.

26. M. Kambarami, "Femininity, Sexuality and Culture: Patriarchy and Female Subordination in Zimbabwe" (ARSRC: University of Fort Hare, 2006).

27. SAFAIDS, *Best Practices on Challenging Gender Dynamics in Cultural Context* (Harare: SAFAIDS, 2009).

28. Ellsberg and Heisi, *Researching Violence*, 18.

BIBLIOGRAPHY

Anderson, S. "The Economics of Dowry and Bride Price." *Journal of Economic Perspectives* 21, no. 4 (2007): 151–174.

Bourdillon, M. F. C. *The Shona Peoples.* Gweru: Mambo Press, 1976.

Braithwaite, J. and Heather Strang. *Restorative and Family Violence.* Cambridge: Cambridge University Press, 2002.

Chabata, T. "The Commercialisation of Lobola in Contemporary Zimbabwe, A Double-Edged Sword." *A Journal on African Women's Experiences* 2, no. 1 (2012): 10–14.

"Domestic Violence against Women Report," (Special Eurobarometer 344, European Commission, Brussels, TNS Opinion and Social, 2010).

Ellsberg, M. and L. Heisi. *Researching Violence against Women: A Practical Guide for Researchers and Activists.* Geneva: WHO Press, 2005.

Flood, M. and B. Pease. "Factors Influencing Attitudes to Violence against Women." *Journal of Trauma and Violence* 10, no. 2 (2009): 125–141.

Fummilola, B. and A. B. Akokan. "Domestic Violence against Women: A Family Menace." Paper presented at the 1st Annual International Interdisciplinary Conference. AIIC, Azores, Portugal, April, 24–26, 2013, 100–107.

Isaac, D. "Bride-price and Domestic Violence: Empirical Perspective from Nandom District in the North Western Region of Ghana." *International Journal of Development and Sustainability* 4, no. 3 (2015): 258–271.

Kambarami, M. "Femininity, Sexuality and Culture: Patriarchy and Female Subordination in Zimbabwe." ARSRC: University of Fort Hare, 2006.

Katembo, A. "Reducing Cases of Gender Based Violence in Mashonaland Central Province: Zimbabwe." MA Thesis, Durban University of Technology, 2015.

Levinson, D. *Family Violence in Cross-Cultural Perspectives*, 439–455. Newbury Park, CA: Sage, 1989.

Makahamadze, T., A. Isacco and Excellent Chireshe. "Examining the Perceptions of Zimbabwean Women about Domestic Violence Act." *Journal of Interpersonal Violence* 27, no. 4 (2012): 706–727.

Moxley, M. "RIGHTS-CHINA: For Too Many, Domestic Violence Part of Family Life." http://www.ipsnews.net/2010/10/rights-china-for-too-many-domestic-viol ence-part-of-family-life (accessed December 14, 2018).

SAFAIDS. *Best Practices on Challenging Gender Dynamics in Cultural Context.* Harare: SAFAIDS, 2009.

Strinivasan, S. and S. A. Bedi. "Domestic Violence and Dowry: Evidence from a South Indian Village." Working Paper Series No. 429, The Hague, Institute of Social Sciences, 2006.

United Nations, Committee on the Elimination of All Forms of Discrimination against Women (CEDAW), Geneva, UN General Assembly, 1993.

World Health Organization. "Violence against Women," November 29, 2017. https ://www.who.int/news-room/fact-sheets/detail/violence-against-women (accessed January 10, 2019).

Chapter 5

The Interconnection between Youth Gangs, Toxic Masculinity, and Gender-Based Violence in South Africa

G. Nokukhanya Ndhlovu and Pius T. Tanga

The issue of youth and gang violence is still endemic and profound in the lives of many marginalized Black African and Colored South Africans. Not only does it have significant consequences on the youth involved, it also has adverse effects on communities.[1] In addition to contending with psychological violence, substance abuse and abnormal levels of crime including gun battles,[2] communities also have to contend with gender-based violence (GBV), which remains one of the country's greatest concerns.[3] GBV can be physical, sexual, or psychological[4] and is closely linked to toxic masculinities. In essence, it is about the exercise of power by men over women and other men who are considered weak.[5]

This chapter provides a synopsis of how Black African youth gangs from marginalized communities use high levels of violence to prove their masculinity; and also discusses how their construction of masculinity translates into GBV. It explores the intricate intersection between youth gangs, toxic masculinity, and GBV. The chapter builds on existing literature on toxic masculinities and GBV in South Africa. However, it notes that not much has been done on the intersection between youth gangs, toxic masculinities, and GBV in marginalized Black African communities; hence, the need for this chapter to contribute in filling this knowledge gap.

The chapter begins by defining GBV, including the different types of GBV as well as a brief introduction to its link with violence against women and toxic masculinity. It then presents a picture of GBV in South Africa, using statistical evidence, and the patriarchal attitudes within the country that legitimize violence against women. This will be followed by a discussion of toxic masculinity and the social constructs of what it is to be a man along with the negative impacts of these constructs. The chapter will then focus on gang violence, toxic masculinity, and rape in Bophelong, including the use of extreme levels of violence by gangs to prove their manhood resulting in communities going through various forms of violence. It will then discuss the methodology followed by the findings from the study. The chapter ends with a conclusion and recommendations.

LITERATURE REVIEW

Defining Gender-Based Violence

GBV is a destructive action committed against a person or people on the basis of their gender. This includes early or forced marriage, risky traditional or cultural practices, and trafficking.[6] However, women and girls are disproportionately affected because of the specific violence they suffer such as genital mutilation, domestic violence, rape, and sexual assault.[7] GBV is a "general term used to capture violence that occurs as a result of the normative role expectations associated with each gender, along with the unequal power relationships between the two genders, within the context of a specific society."[8] It is a human rights violation with major social and developmental impacts for survivors, their families, communities, and society; and is embedded in institutions, cultures, and traditions.[9]

GBV is used interchangeably with the term "violence against women," which is defined as injurious and damaging actions against women with the intention of causing psychological, physical, and sexual harm because of their gender.[10] It is profoundly embedded in the patriarchal doctrines of control and subordination of women and girls.[11] Behind GBV is an intricate trap of male privilege, toxic masculinity, and patriarchal dominance,[12] which is an infringement of human rights.

Gender-Based Violence in South Africa

South Africa has made numerous strides in addressing the issue of GBV. However, despite these strides, the magnitude of violence in the country is still widespread. As Mathews and Benvenut observed:

> Social acceptance or tolerance of various forms of violence…is a major factor in the continued perpetuation of violence. These social norms are carried forward from one generation to the next as men are viewed to have authority over women and children in the family and the community. The patriarchal (male-centred) South African society legitimises violence against women and children as a means of maintaining men in a position of power and control. In addition,

widespread violence in communities desensitises children and normalises the use of violence.[13]

While women and girls endure different kinds of violence in the hands of men, studies indicate that rape is the most common type of violence in the country. Statistics South Africa reports that while crime in general saw a decline between 2013 and 2014, violent crimes against women, especially sexual assault, radically increased between 2015 to 2016 and 2016 to 2017.[14] They further report on the situation in the country noting the seriousness of the rape of women and girls. The 2016/2017 Crime Statistics show that 250 out of every 100,000 women fell victim to sexual violence in comparison to 120 out of 100,000 men. Combining the 2016/2017, South African Police Service statistics and the Statistics South Africa's estimates, it was concluded that the number of women who were victims of rape per 100,000 was 138 and this figure is the highest in the world, consequently, securing South Africa the position of the rape capital of the world.[15]

However, these statistics underestimate the magnitude of GBV. The numbers of GBV could be higher but since most cases go unreported due to various barriers to reporting, a lot of women and girls suffer in silence. Some of these barriers include the patriarchal and condescending attitudes of some police officials.[16] Due to the multifaceted nature of GBV, one cannot identify a single cause of the high levels of violence in South Africa. However, some of the reasons are the rape culture, growing up in an abusive environment, and the discriminatory patriarchal practices against women.[17]

The Dynamics of Toxic Masculinity

While the term femininity might be almost universal, masculinity is not and this is dependent on geography, race, and culture[18] among others. These differences have seen the emergence of terms such as *indoda kuzwa* (real man), *indoda emadodeni* (a man among men), or *indojelana* (weak man). It is for this reason that the term masculinity is linked with power, dominance, and control.[19] This dominance is also displayed on other men considered weaker than others.[20] Patriarchy is the foundation from which the definition of gender is derived and it is the notion that men are superior to women. Masculinity therefore intersects with the male identity, manliness, and men's roles. This male identity linked to masculinity is interconnected with violence and men and boys are at the forefront of this violence.[21] To this end, it is noted that "violence is frequently used to resolve a crisis of male identity."[22]

Masculinity entails those social constructions that define what it is to be a man. These definitions are sometimes toxic because not only do they put men at risk, they also put women and other men at risk. Toxic masculinity is where the notions and ideals of what it means to be a man lead to negative consequences for the man himself and the people around him.[23] It is consequently linked to men's execution of violence against women as well as sexual aggression toward women in order to exert dominance[24] and it is reportedly the leading cause of rape.[25] "Perpetration of sexual violence can serve as a tool for men and boys to prove their manhood, achieve the social status of a "real man," and establish power over others."[26] Violence is linked with masculine gender identity, where some men perceive that they have no alternatives other than violent crime to prove that they are real men.[27] These men resort to rape and violence as tools for exerting power, control, and dominance.

Gang Violence, Toxic Masculinity, and Rape in Bophelong: Connecting the Dots

In the Black African township of Bophelong, gangs fight for territory, power, and recognition. Weapons of choice are pangas and knives and these have resulted in numerous deaths.[28] Gangs violently kill each other in public spaces to prove who is smarter, braver, and stronger.[29] They are fearless, cause destruction and want to be feared. They will stop at nothing to remain dominant in the communities, and consequently, violent crime is used to prove who the real man is.[30] These gangs are young drug addicts who torment communities and gang rape young girls. When one boy is interested in a girl, he can walk into her home armed, abduct and rape her.[31]

In marginalized communities like Bophelong, where young men have no access to socio-economic opportunities, joining gangs and committing violence becomes a platform for them to practice masculinity.[32] This masculinity is toxic as it allows them to engage in antisocial behavior where many die, get maimed, lose their loved ones or put them in danger while trying to prove that they are the better gang and the better man.[33] Being a real man is about power and hierarchy; accordingly in Bophelong, "masculinities are sustained by violence"[34] because no gang wants to be called weak. There are a number of characteristics that play a role in the understanding of the term masculinity, and they include the way men understand themselves as well as their sexual relationships. Consequently, sexual violence is used as a tool for boys and men to prove that they are real men.[35]

In Bophelong, youth are forced to find alternative means of survival and many have turned to gangs as they negotiate backgrounds of marginalization in search of masculinity.[36] In contexts facing socio-economic marginalization, gang membership becomes the platform where young boys and men, construct masculinity.[37] There is a link between social constructions of masculinity, gangs, violence, and offending. In some contexts, hyper-aggressive forms of masculinity are what define gangs.[38] The luxurious lifestyle and the qualities of gangs are linked with definitions of masculinity. These qualities are strength, respect, power, and multiple female sexual partners. Consequently, young men from marginalized communities who do not fit the masculine definition create their own pathways of respectable manhood.[39] Gangs empower them to become *indoda kuzwa* (real man). Gangs and violence are interconnected because one has to ensure that no traces of femininity or weakness are traceable in him and this entails exerting extreme levels of violence in order to assert one's masculinity.[40] Baird also had this to say:

> Many young men join gangs to emulate and reproduce successful local male identities. The accumulation by the gang of "masculine capital," the material and symbolic signifiers of manhood, and accompanying stylistic and timely displays, means that youths often perceive them to be spaces of male success, driving the social reproduction of the gang. Once in the gang, they become increasingly "bad" using violence to defend the gang's interests in exchange for masculine capital.[41]

Some of the characteristics that define youth gangs are high-risk sexual behaviors that include relationship violence and substance abuse.[42]

METHODOLOGY

This study was explorative in nature. An exploratory qualitative approach is adopted when exploring the perceptions of participants about a particular topic in which the researcher wants to develop initial ideas.[43] We therefore intended developing some initial ideas and an understanding of the perceptions of relevant participants on the interconnection between youth gangs, toxic masculinity, and GBV in Bophelong.

Thirty-four participants were purposefully sampled, as this is the best nonprobability sampling technique.[44] Permission from the relevant authorities was sought. The researchers were interested in locating a Black African township that is faced with the issue of youth and gang violence. In consultation with various forms of media, Bophelong was identified. The township is located in the Vaal area in Gauteng.

The first group of participants comprised of eight unemployed youths, followed by seven young-rehabilitated gang members. Additionally, nineteen informants were interviewed. The list of informants included seven government officials at both provincial and local level, one community leader, one nongovernmental organization representative, two participants from nonprofit organizations, two law enforcement officials, and six civil society actors working on and dealing with the issue of youth and gang violence. Thus, we had three subsamples that were interviewed, namely eight unemployed youths, seven rehabilitated gang members, and nineteen informants.

In-depth interviews were conducted with informants as well as with young-rehabilitated gang members. Focus group discussions were also used to collect information from unemployed youths. Both interviews and focus group discussions were used to obtain information on participants' insights and perspectives on the link between youth gangs, GBV, and toxic masculinities. A recording device was used to ensure accurate capturing of data.

The study adopted Tesch's method of analysis. The subsequent steps were used to guide the process of analysis: reading through each transcript for meaning; assigning labels to the meanings of the text in the margins of the transcripts; classification and grouping of labels into main themes and subthemes; developing a framework that depicted the revised themes and subthemes; and presentation and discussion of findings using the main themes as main headings and subthemes as subheadings.[45] The researchers used the actual quotes of participants for discussing the findings linking them to the literature review.

In order to ensure that findings were credible and trustworthy, we used triangulation to cross-check, validate, and verify information. This meant that participants did not only come from one institute but from different sources with different viewpoints. This helped curb bias and the provision of unreliable information.

Given the nature of the topic, anonymity was a vital aspect of the research process. In order to ensure the anonymity of the research participants, the researchers hid their identities through the use of pseudonyms. Confidential information was not disclosed to anyone. The researchers sought informed consent from the participants prior to the research process. All participants were informed about the research and this entailed information about the goals, methods, and objectives of the study. Participants were not forced to participate in the study and were adequately informed that they were under no obligation to participate and in the event that they did, they had the right to withdraw anytime they felt uncomfortable.

THE FINDINGS

This section extricates the themes and subthemes that emerged from the findings that came from the interviews. The themes include normative role expectations, masculine norms, and youth gang masculine identities.

Normative Role Expectations

The main theme bordered on "normative role expectations." The subtheme that was identified from this main theme was "community circumstances." This is presented and discussed below.

Community Circumstances

Research findings suggest that the levels of violence caused by gangs in Bophelong are staggering. This is in consonance with other findings which noted the levels of violence perpetrated by gangs in Bophelong and the dire consequences of this violence on community members.[46] Consequently, a majority of the participants shared that communities live in fear. One unemployed youth even refused to reveal the names of the most popular gangs in Bophelong, remarking, "*Ausi* (my sister), I am afraid to give you the names of the gangs in Bophelong, those people are very dangerous. They could kill me just for speaking their name." An informant also admitted that "our biggest challenge is that communities do not cooperate, we think that they are afraid of getting killed because these gangs can be ruthless." Commenting on the violence inflicted by these gangs on the communities, three local informants noted:

> These gangs are causing problems in the community. They are not giving our people a break. They rob them, at night and during the day. They do house breaking, they stab our people, and they kill them. With these young ones what is worse is that if they try to rob you and you have nothing valuable on you, you will pay with your life. They won't hesitate to kill you if you have nothing.[47]

> We are afraid of these children. If they are robbing you, and they don't find anything on you, they will kill you, just because you have nothing to give them. If they are not killing each other, they are burning our houses. They kidnap children to take them *entabeni* (mountains), if they kidnap you and find that you are already medically circumcised they can kill you. We are very afraid of these gangs.

> Whatever they are taught *entabeni* (in the mountains) is really making them behave like *izilwane* (lions)…There is a lot of violence here . . . they stab each other a lot.

The above narratives underscore the issue of gang violence in Bophelong. It was also revealed that in the absence of socio-economic opportunities, violence is a normative role expectation associated with gangs and a way of communicating their masculinity although very destructive. Many former gangs shared that among gangs one has to portray the desired levels of masculinity in order to be a gang member because gangs cannot be "sissies". These results concur with those of other studies which noted that violence is the tool used by gangs to eradicate all traces of femininity or weakness within them. Gangs enable men to assert their manhood hence they have to use high levels of violence to show that they are indeed men.[48]

Masculine Norms

The next theme was "masculine norms" and the subtheme that was identified from this theme was toxic masculinity. This is discussed as well.

Toxic Masculinity

There was a general consensus that the definition of what it means to be a real man among gangs is toxic and very detrimental to the gangs themselves as well as their communities. Many participants identified the masculine norms of power, control, being in command, disrespect, and aggression as some of the defining factors of *izinja ze game* (top dogs; powerful gangs). Also, there was an element of show off where they displayed this so-called prowess on the streets so that they could intimidate communities and cause destruction. Some of the former gangs as well as informants shared that gangs instil fear in the communities to show off their manhood. A former gang member admitted:

> We fought for power, we wanted to be the most powerful gang in our area. It belonged to us and no one else. You feel like you are a man if your gang is powerful but there is so much violence and there is so much revenge. My sister was raped by rival gangs as an act of revenge.

Commenting on gangs showing off their prowess in the streets and their need to be the top gang in control of the area, an unemployed youth revealed:

> Our challenges are that we are exposed to gangs, they don't care who is watching when they fight for territory. Our children grow up seeing this violence. They fight to be the top gang in the area, they want to be feared, and they want to be in control.

A local informant also gave his take on how these gangs show off their masculinity on the streets.

> They no longer respect us as elders, a young boy can say *voetsek* to you and there is nothing you can do to him. I think that they are taught that they are now

men and they don't have to listen to anyone, but what kind of man does the things that they do?

The above narratives highlight the link between gangs and toxic masculinity; this toxic display of masculinity is observed in how gangs present themselves in their respective communities. It seems that a lot of violence takes place within their communities, because it is where gangs either loose or gain the title of *indoda kuzwa* (real man). These findings corroborate those of other studies who reported that masculinity is strongly linked with power and a desire to control others; hence, some men use violence and aggression in order to maintain their dominance in communities.[49]

In many studies, young men have identified violence as an important way to display power and to prove their masculinity in their communities.[50] As a result, it also emerged that young gangs are exerting their violence on other men. To this end, some male participants shared their disdain for the way gangs disrespected them hence they questioned the way gangs define the term masculinity, for example, a number of them remarked "what kind of man does that?" or "what kind of man does the things they do?" It could be that, perhaps they do not believe that men should be violent to other men; or perhaps, it could be that they themselves feel emasculated by these young boys who disregard their manhood. Or it could be that these are progressive men who have different ideas about what it means to be *indoda kuzwa* (real man); alternative ideas that are neither patriarchal, toxic, nor harmful.

Youth Gang Masculine Identities

The next theme was "youth gang masculine identities." The subtheme that was identified from it was "rape as a weapon used by gangs."

Rape as a Weapon Used by Gangs

Narratives highlight the link between youth gangs, toxic masculinity, and GBV. Many participants said that rape was a "weapon" used by gangs to assert their manhood. It was found that, not only did gangs confine their violence to rival gangs; they also extended it to the women and girls around them. This rape took on many dimensions, with some wondering whether in order to test their "thing," it was prerequisite that they rape women in the community. One informant explained:

> They start raping girls around the area. I don't know, maybe they are told that they are now men they must test their thing.

Explaining how these rapes by gangs work, another informant also expounded:

The serial rapes is when you have a gang that goes out into a certain area, they mark their territory and they have one or two guys that go out and rape women.

Studies show the intricate link between gangs and sexual violence[51] and this was no different in Bophelong. One informant specifically indicated that the issue of gangs is about power which goes beyond physical violence and plays right into the GBV domain. It appears this power sees women's bodies used as "battlegrounds" in gang-related wars; and it is seen in men displaying their power over rival gangs by raping women as well as marking territory through raping women in the selected territory. The informant maintained:

You find that you are a gang member and you belong to a certain group. How do we hurt you? We hurt you by either touching your daughter, your wife, or your girlfriend. So now again you see gender-based violence. You will again see the issues about power playing out in gangs beyond just physical violence. It plays right into the sexual violence domain and it is normally very gruesome because it is a gang . . . they are doing it with intent. And you will find that the injury is more severe and the trauma is more severe...you have higher levels of fear because you know what they are capable of beyond of sexual violence, you know the members, you know that your family might be in real perceived danger.

Findings also show that one's manhood in a gang is tested through raping a woman or women. Other studies indicate that due to their financial and social status in marginalized communities, gangs can afford to get any woman they want; hence, they construct their masculinity through promiscuity and having many sexual partners.[52] Research findings, however, show that in Bophelong, rape is a weapon used by gangs to construct their masculinity. Other findings corroborate these findings. For instance, it is reported that sexual violence is used to prove one's manhood as well as to achieve the status of real man.[53] Consequently, many participants reported that women and girls experience high levels of sexual violence in the hands of gangs where violence against women is accepted and encouraged in order for one to maintain the status of a real man.

CONCLUSION

Studies have shown that in many marginalized communities, where young men seem to be "emasculated" by poverty, violence becomes an outlet to prove their manhood. This study has therefore shown how Black African gangs from the marginalized community of Bophelong construct and practice masculinity and how this has affected their community. It also focused on the GBV experienced by women at the hands of gangs; linking it to toxic masculinity which sees women being raped in gang-related wars. There is an urgent need for various government departments, civil society, and communities to work together to deny toxic masculinity its breeding ground. It is therefore recommended that focus should be on addressing the underlying interlinked root causes of GBV and this includes a change in attitudes, socialization, behaviors, and beliefs about masculinity and manhood. The way *indoda kuzwa* (real man) is defined in many Black African communities should be challenged and redefined to ensure that it is not detrimental to wellbeing. Families and communities need to teach young boys that manhood and masculinity do not entail behaving in ways that cause harm to others, their communities, or the women around them. Boys and men should be taught to love, respect, and protect women. Interventions that bring together government, civil society, communities, and boys/men to challenge toxic masculinities should also be prioritized.

NOTES

1. Richard Mamabolo, "Global Effects of Gangsterism and Policing – POPCRU," *Politics Web*, June 27, 2019, https://www.politicsweb.co.za/politics/global-effects-of -gangsterism-and-policing--popcru.

2. Christopher Morris, "The Violent Work of South African Gangs," *Alternative Information and Development Centre*, July 8, 2019, http://aidc.org.za/the-violent -work-of-south-african-gangs.

3. Amos Phago, "Gender-Based Violence Still a Major Concern," *SABC News,* August 9, 2018, http://www.sabcnews.com/sabcnews/gender-based-violence-still-a -major-concern/.

4. "Gender-Based Violence," United Nations Economic Commission for Europe, accessed August 1, 2020, https://www.unece.org/stats/video/violence.html#:~:text =Meetings%20%26%20Events-,Gender%20based%20violence,occurring%20in%2 0public%20or%20private.

5. UN Women Training Centre, *Self-Learning Booklet: Understanding Masculinities and Violence against Women and Girls* (Santo Domingo: UN Women Training Centre, 2016), 18, https://trainingcentre.unwomen.org/RESOURCES_ LIBRARY/Resources_Centre/masculinities%20booklet%20.pdf.

6. Office of the High Commissioner for Human Rights, Sexual and Gender-Based Violence in the Context of Transitional Justice (Geneva: Office of the High Commissioner for Human Rights, 2014), n.p, https://www.ohchr.org/Documents/Iss ues/Women/WRGS/OnePagers/Sexual_and_gender-based_violence.pdf.

7. "Council of Europe Convention on Preventing and Combating Violence against Women and Domestic Violence," Council of Europe, https://www.coe.int/fr/ web/conventions/full-list/-/conventions/rms/090000168008482e.

8. Shelah S. Bloom, *Violence against Women and Girls: A Compendium of Monitoring and Evaluation Indicators* (Chapel Hill, NC: Carolina Population Center MEASURE Evaluation, 2008), 14.

9. Elizabeth Dartnall and Ali Channon, "Gender Based Violence in South Africa," accessed May 30, 2017, https://www.saferspaces.co.za/understand/entry/gender-based-violence-in-south-africa.

10. Annemiek J. M. Richters, *Women, Culture and Violence: A Development, Health and Human Rights Issue* (Leiden: Women and Autonomy Centre, 1994), 205.

11. Nkiru Igbelina-Igbokwe, "Contextualizing Gender Based Violence within Patriarchy in Nigeria," *Pambazuka News*, May 30, 2013, https://www.pambazuka.org/gender-minorities/cintextualising-gender-based-violence-within-patriarchy-nigeria.

12. Christopher Kilmartin and Julie Allison, *Men's Violence against Women: Theory, Research, and Activism"* (Mahwah, NJ: Lawrence Erlbaum Associates Publishers, 2007), 5.

13. Shanaaz Mathews and Patrizia Benvenut, "Violence against Children in South Africa: Developing a Prevention Agenda," in *South African Child Gauge 2014*, ed. Shanaaz Mathews, Lucy Jamieson, Lori Lake and Charmaine Smith (Cape Town: Children's Institute, UCT, 2014), 29.

14. Statistics South Africa, *Crime against Women in South Africa: An In-Depth Analysis of the Victims of Crime Survey Data 2018* (Pretoria: Statistics South Africa, 2018), 6, http://www.statssa.gov.za/publications/Report-03-40-05/Report-03-40-05 June2018.pdf.

15. Statistics South Africa, *Crime against Women in South Africa*, 8.

16. Rachel Jewkes, and Naeema Abrahams, "The Epidemiology of Rape and Sexual Coercion in South Africa: An Overview," *Social Science & Medicine* 55, no. 7 (October 2002): 1231–44, https://doi.org/10.1016/S0277-9536(01)00242-8.

17. Centre for the Study of Violence and Reconciliation, *Gender-Based Violence (GBV) in South Africa: A Brief Review* (Johannesburg: Centre for the Study of Violence and Reconciliation, 2016), 8.

18. Jay C. Wade and Aaron B. Rochlen, "Introduction: Masculinity, Identity, and the Health and Well-Being of African American Men," *Psychology of Men and Masculinity* 14, no. 1 (January 2013): 2–3, https://doi.org/10.1037/a0029612.

19. Christian Groes-Green, "Hegemonic and Subordinated Masculinities: Class, Violence and Sexual Performance among Young Mozambican Men," *Nordic Journal of African Studies* 18, no. 4 (2009): 288.

20. Robert Morrell, Rachel Jewkes, and Graham Lindegger, "Hegemonic Masculinity/Masculinities in South Africa: Culture, Power and Gender Politics," *Men and Masculinities* 15, no. 1 (March 2012): 11, https://doi.org/10.1177/1097184X12438001.

21. Brian Heilman and Gary Barker, M*asculine Norms and Violence: Making the Connections* (Washington, DC: Promundo-US, 2018), 8.

22. Rachel Jewkes, "Intimate Partner Violence: Causes and Prevention," *The Lancet* 359, no. 9315 (April 2002): 1423, https://doi.org/10.1016/S0140-6736(02)08357-5.

23. Lauren October, "Toxic masculinity and violence in South Africa," accessed May 30, 2019, https://www.saferspaces.org.za/understand/entry/toxic-masculinity-and-violence-in-south-africa.

24. Rachel M. Smith et al., "Deconstructing Hegemonic Masculinity: The Roles of Antifemininity, Subordination to Women, and Sexual Dominance in Men's Perpetration of Sexual Aggression," *Psychology of Men and Masculinity* 16, no. 2 (April 2015): 160, https://doi.org/10.1037/a0035956.

25. Rachel Jewkes, *Rape Perpetration: A Review* (Pretoria: Sexual Violence Research Initiative, 2012), 1.

26. Heilman and Barker, *Masculine Norms*, 11.

27. Chris Crowther-Dowey, and Marisa Silvestri, "The Gendering of Violent Crime: Towards a Human Rights Approach," *British Journal of Community Justice* 14, no. 3 (2017).

28. Steven Tau, "Increasing Gang Violence Worries Bophelong," *The Citizen*, November 22, 2016, https://citizen.co.za/news/south-africa/1352829/increasing-gang-violence-concerns-bophelong-community/.

29. News24.com, "Gang Boss Chopped Up," *Daily Sun*, November 16, 2016, https://www.dailysun.co.za/News/National/gang-boss-chopped-up-20161116.

30. SAFM, "Gangs Rule Bophelong in the Vaal," *SAFM*, November 30, 2016, https://iono.fm/e/361427.

31. Vicky Abraham, "Gangs Using Initiation Schools to Recruit New Members, Commission Told," *The Citizen*, March 8, 2017, https://citizen.co.za/news/south-africa/1451611/initiation-schools-used-to-recruit-gangsters-commission-told/.

32. Ross Deuchar, "Policing Youth Violence: Transatlantic Connections," (London: Trentham Books/IOE Press, 2013), 19–20.

33. Pharie Sefali, "Young, High and Dangerous: Youth Gangs and Violence in Khayelitsha," *Ground Up,* May 27, 2014, https://www.groundup.org.za/article/young-high-and-dangerous-youth-gangs-and-violence-khayelitsha_1823/.

34. Diana Gibson and Godfrey Maringira, *Gang Relationships in a Black Township in South Africa* (New York, NY: Social Science Research Council, 2020), 6, https://s3.amazonaws.com/ssrc-cdn1/crmuploads/new_publication_3/gang-relationships-in-a-black-township-in-south-africa.pdf.

35. Heilman and Barker, *Masculine Norms,* 8, 11.

36. Adam Baird, "Negotiating Pathways to Manhood: Rejecting Gangs and Violence in Medellín's Periphery." *Journal of Conflictology* 3, no. 1 (May 2012): 32–33.

37. Adam Baird, "The Violent Gang and the Construction of Masculinity amongst Socially Excluded Young Men," *Safer Communities* 11, no. 4 (September 2012): 179.

38. Ross Deuchar, "Gang Members 'Doing Masculinity,'" in *Gangs and Spirituality: Global Perspectives*, ed. Ross Deuchar (Cham: Palgrave Macmillan, 2018), 19–20.

39. Adam Baird, *Breaking Bad: Recognizing the Role of Masculinities Can Help Prevent Gang Formation in Latin America and the Caribbean*, 2017. LSE Latin America and Caribbean Blog. https://blogs.lse.ac.uk/latamcaribbean/2017/07/18/

breaking-bad-recognising-the-role-of-masculinities-can-help-prevent-gang-formati
on-in-latin-america-and-the-caribbean/.

40. Baird, *Breaking Bad.*

41. Adam Baird, "Becoming the Baddest: Masculine Trajectories of Gang Violence in Medellín," *Journal of Latin American Studies* 50, no. 1 (June 2017): 183, https://doi.org/10.1017/S0022216X17000761.

42. Julia Dickson-Gomez et al., "Gang Masculinity and High-Risk Sexual Behaviours," *Culture, Health and Sexuality* 19, no. 2 (August 2016): 165, https://doi.org/10.1080/13691058.2016.1213422.

43. W. Lawrence Neuman, *Social Research Methods: Qualitative and Quantitative Approaches*, 7th ed. (Essex: Pearson, 2014), 38.

44. John. W Creswell, *A Concise Introduction to Mixed Methods Research* (London: SAGE Publications, 2014).

45. Renata Tesch, *Qualitative Research: Analysis Types and Software Tools* (New York, NY: Falmer, 1990), 117.

46. Sefali, "Young, High and Dangerous."

47. As already noted under the methodology section, in order to ensure the anonymity of the research participants, the researchers used pseudonyms.

48. Baird, *Breaking Bad.*

49. Smith et al., "Deconstructing," 160.

50. October, "Toxic Masculinity."

51. Morris, "The Violent Work."

52. Dickson-Gomez et al., "Gang Masculinity," 165.

53. Heilman and Barker, *Masculine Norms,* 11–12.

BIBLIOGRAPHY

Abraham, Vicky. "Gangs Using Initiation Schools to Recruit New Members, Commission Told." *The Citizen*, March 8, 2017. https://citizen.co.za/news/south-africa/1451611/initiation-schools-used-to-recruit-gangsters-commission-told/.

Baird, Adam. "Becoming the Baddest: Masculine Trajectories of Gang Violence in Medellín." *Journal of Latin American Studies* 50, no. 1 (June 2017): 183–210. https://doi.org/10.1017/S0022216X17000761.

Baird, Adam. *Breaking Bad: Recognizing the Role of Masculinities Can Help Prevent Gang Formation in Latin America and the Caribbean*, 2017. LSE Latin America and Caribbean Blog. https://blogs.lse.ac.uk/latamcaribbean/2017/07/18/breaking-bad-recognising-the-role-of-masculinities-can-help-prevent-gang-formation-in-latin-america-and-the-caribbean/.

Baird, Adam. "Negotiating Pathways to Manhood: Rejecting Gangs and Violence in Medellín's Periphery." *Journal of Conflictology* 3, no. 1 (May 2012): 30–41.

Baird, Adam. "The Violent Gang and the Construction of Masculinity amongst Socially Excluded Young Men." *Safer Communities* 11, no. 4 (September 2012): 179–190.

Bloom, Shelah. S. *Violence against Women and Girls: A Compendium of Monitoring and Evaluation Indicators.* Chapel Hill, NC: Carolina Population Center MEASURE Evaluation, 2008.

Centre for the Study of Violence and Reconciliation. *Gender-Based Violence (GBV) in South Africa: A Brief Review.* Johannesburg: Centre for the Study of Violence and Reconciliation, 2016. http://www.csvr.org.za/pdf/Gender%20Based%20V iolence%20in%20South%20Africa%20-%20A%20Brief%20Review.pdf.

Council of Europe. "Council of Europe Convention on Preventing and Combating Violenceagainst Women and Domestic Violence." https://www.coe.int/fr/web/con ventions/fulllist/-/conventions/rms/090000168008482e.

Creswell, J. W. *A Concise Introduction to Mixed Methods Research.* London: SAGE Publications, 2014.

Crowther-Dowey, Chris and Marisa Silvestri. "The Gendering of Violent Crime: Towards a Human Rights Approach." *British Journal of Community Justice* 14, no. 3 (2017).

Dartnall, Elizabeth and Ali Channon. "Gender-Based Violence in South Africa.". https://www.saferspaces.co.za/understand/entry/gender-based-violence-in-south -africa.

Deuchar, Ross. "Gang Members 'Doing Masculinity.'" In *Gangs and Spirituality: Global Perspectives*, edited by Ross Deuchar, 19–37. Cham: Palgrave Macmillan, 2018.

Deuchar, Ross. *Policing Youth Violence: Transatlantic Connections.* London: Trentham Books/IOE Press, 2013.

Dickson-Gomez, Julia, Katherine Quinn, Michelle Broaddus and Maria Pacella. "Gang Masculinity and High-Risk Sexual Behaviours." *Culture, Health and Sexuality* 19, no. 2 (August 2016): 165–178. https://doi.org/10.1080/13691058.20 16.1213422.

Gibson, Diana and Godfrey Maringira. *Gang Relationships in a Black Township in South Africa.* New York, NY: Social Science Research Council, 2020. https://s3 .amazonaws.com/ssrc-cdn1/crmuploads/new_publication_3/gang-relationships-in -a-black-township-in-south-africa.pdf.

Groes-Green, Christian. "Hegemonic and Subordinated Masculinities: Class, Violence and Sexual Performance among Young Mozambican Men." *Nordic Journal of African Studies* 18, no. 4 (2009): 286–304.

Heilman, Brian and Gary Barker. *Masculine Norms and Violence: Making the Connections.* Washington, DC: Promundo-US, 2018.

Igbelina-Igbokwe, Nkiru. "Contextualizing Gender Based Violence within Patriarchy in Nigeria." *Pambazuka News*, May 30, 2013. https://www.pambazuka .org/gender-minorities/cintextualising-gender-based-violence-within-patriarchy- nigeria.

Jewkes, Rachel. "Intimate Partner Violence: Causes and Prevention." *The Lancet* 359, no. 9315 (April 2002): 1423–1429. https://doi.org/10.1016/S0140 -6736(02)08357-5.

Jewkes, Rachel. *Rape Perpetration: A Review.* Pretoria: Sexual Violence Research Initiative, 2012.

Jewkes, Rachel and Naeema Abrahams. "The Epidemiology of Rape and Sexual Coercion in South Africa: An Overview." *Social Science and Medicine* 55, no. 7 (October 2002): 1231–1244. https://doi.org/10.1016/S0277-9536(01)00242-8.

Kilmartin, Christopher and Julie Allison. *Men's Violence against Women: Theory, Research, and Activism.* Mahwah, NJ: Lawrence Erlbaum Associates Publishers, 2007.

Mamabolo, Richard. "Global Effects of Gangsterism and Policing – POPCRU." *Politics Web,* June 27, 2019. https://www.politicsweb.co.za/politics/global-effects -of-gangsterism-and-policing--popcru.

Marlow, Christine. *Research Methods for Generalist Social Work.* Belmont, CA: Thomson Brooks/Cole, 2011.

Mathews, Shanaaz and Patrizia Benvenut. "Violence against Children in South Africa: Developing a Prevention Agenda." In *South African Child Gauge,* edited by Shanaaz Mathews, Lucy Jamieson, Lori Lake and Charmaine Smith, 26–34. Cape Town: Children's Institute, UCT, 2014.

Morrell, Robert, Rachel Jewkes, and Graham Lindegger. "Hegemonic Masculinity/ Masculinities in South Africa: Culture, Power and Gender Politics." *Men and Masculinities* 15, no. 1 (March 2012): 11–30. https://doi.org/10.1177 /1097184X12438001.

Morris, Christopher. "The Violent Work of South African Gangs." *Alternative Information and Development Centre,* July 8, 2019. http://aidc.org.za/the-violent -work-of-south-african-gangs.

Neuman, W. L. *Social Research Methods: Qualitative and Quantitative Approaches,* 7th ed. Essex: Pearson, 2014.

News24.com. "Gang Boss Chopped Up." *Daily Sun,* November 16, 2016, https://ww w.dailysun.co.za/News/National/gang-boss-chopped-up-20161116.

October, Lauren. "Toxic Masculinity and Violence in South Africa." Accessed May 30, 2019. https://www.saferspaces.org.za/understand/entry/toxic-masculinity-and-violence-in-south-africa.

Office of the High Commissioner for Human Rights. *Sexual and Gender-Based Violence in the Context of Transitional Justice.* Geneva: Office of the High Commissioner for Human Rights, 2014. https://www.ohchr.org/Documents/Issues /Women/WRGS/OnePagers/Sexual_and_gender-based_violence.pdf.

Phago, Amos. "Gender-Based Violence Still a Major Concern." *SABC News,* August 9, 2018. http://www.sabcnews.com/sabcnews/gender-based-violence-still-a-major -concern/.

Richters, Annemiek J. M. *Women, Culture and Violence: A Development, Health and Human Rights Issue.* Leiden: Women and Autonomy Centre, 1994.

SAFM. "Gangs Rule Bophelong in the Vaal." *SAFM,* November 30, 2016. https:// iono.fm/e/361427.

Sefali, Pharie. "Young, High and Dangerous: Youth Gangs and Violence in Khayelitsha." *Ground Up,* May 27, 2014. https://www.groundup.org.za/article/ young-high-and-dangerous-youth-gangs-and-violence-khayelitsha_1823/.

Smith, Rachel M., Dominic J. Parrott, Kevin M. Swartout and Andra T. Tharp. "Deconstructing Hegemonic Masculinity: The Roles of Antifemininity,

Subordination to Women, and Sexual Dominance in Men's Perpetration of Sexual Aggression." *Psychology of Men and Masculinity* 16, no. 2 (April 2015): 160–169. http://dx.doi.org/10.1037/a0035956.

Statistics South Africa. *Crime against Women in South Africa: An In-Depth Analysis of the Victims of Crime Survey Data 2018.* Pretoria: Statistics South Africa, 2018. http://www.statssa.gov.za/publications/Report-03-40-05/Report-03-40-05June2 018.pdf.

Tau, Steven. "Increasing Gang Violence Worries Bophelong." *The Citizen*, November 22, 2016. https://citizen.co.za/news/south-africa/1352829/increasing-gang-violen ce-concerns-bophelong-community/.

Tesch, Renata. *Qualitative Research: Analysis Types and Software Tools.* New York, NY: Falmer, 1990.

United Nations Economic Commission for Europe. "Gender-Based Violence." Accessed August 1, 2020. https://www.unece.org/stats/video/violence.html#:~:te xt=Meetings%20%26%20Events-Gender%20based%20violence,occurring%20in %20public%20or%20private.

UN Women Training Centre. *Self-Learning Booklet: Understanding Masculinities and Violence against Women and Girls.* Santo Domingo: UN Women Training Centre, 2016. https://trainingcentre.unwomen.org/RESOURCES_LIBRARY/Re sources_Centre/masculinities%20booklet%20.pdf.

Wade, Jay C. and Aaron B. Rochlen. "Introduction: Masculinity, Identity, and the Health and Well-Being of African American Men." *Psychology of Men and Masculinity* 14, no. 1 (January 2013): 1–6. https://doi.org/10.1037/a0029612.

Chapter 6

Structuration Theory and Patriarchy System in Africa

The Silent and the Salient in a Lifeless Structure

Samuel O. Okafor

Patriarchy as a social concept is embedded in the everyday activities of members of the society, making it a tool of control over especially uneducated women. Technically, patriarchy goes beyond the surface argument of whose responsibility it is to carry out certain activities in the family, church, and other public settings. It involves inherent feelings in men to see women as property and subordinate rather than equals.[1] Similarly, the patriarchal system to most women across Africa appears in the form of inherent self-deprecation. This is due to women's subordinate roles in societies where status hierarchy runs on the string of achievements and relevance in the social system. At worst, in some traditional settings, women, overwhelmed by the dominant influence of patriarchy, tend to surrender their achieved social status to the nearest male counterparts, thereby acquiescing to the patriarchal system and its attendant social consequences.

As a microsocial institution of its own, patriarchy has grown beyond other socially induced inequalities, causing more harm in the current twenty-first century epoch when the door for self-manifestation has been opened for all.[2] As a concept, patriarchy operates to reinforce masculine ego and desire for domination over others;[3] both of which are instinctive in every living thing including humans, and which can only be made possible by undue socially and environmentally stimulated advantages held by a family, group, or gender over the other. It also operates as the socially accepted strategy developed over periods of time to help men (even the economically and physically weak ones) enforce feminine obedience even to the women's own detriment provided it makes the man appear to be in charge of affairs and the situation.[4]

Although at the surface, the patriarchal system seems to be dominant in the gender relations of most human societies studied;[5] beneath the surface, according to available ethnographic data, the patriarchal institution is weak.[6] For instance, in most studied societies in Africa, there were indices of gender equality in both the family structure and in the society at large save for ritualized social functions and conditions that excluded women making them appear socially lower to men.[7] Responsibilities assigned to women in these small-scale societies—anthropologically defined unit of analysis for societies beyond the family and kinship—were akin to the position occupied by the Queen of England in today's sociopolitical outlook of modern England.[8] Almost all positions of authority allowed women, which gave the small-scale African societies a gender-balanced image, gradually fizzled away in the face of colonialism's gender-specific approach to the management of the affairs of the colonized.[9]

With the colonial authorities privileging men, the subsequent changes in Africa's small-scale societies resulted in the total domination of the society by men and relegation of women to the background.[10] Having been exposed to the colonial perception that men were more important to the colonial administration and women best as housewives, African men strengthened patriarchy and institutionalized it. From this point onwards, members of Africa's small-scale societies that were later merged into countries in the different regions of the continent became the instruments for reinforcing patriarchy.[11] While men by their postures bully women into accepting that they were in charge, women on their own became instruments of generational reinforcement of patriarchy by training their children along the same understanding. By doing so, women reinforced the very elements that subjugated them and unconsciously upheld male dominance.

This chapter, therefore, aims to bring to the fore factors that reinforced patriarchy in selected small-scale African societies through the framework of structuration theory. More importantly, it puts forward a model for a behavioral transformation of African women from the wave of self-deprecation to conscious understanding of gender equality and its place in everyday life.

STRUCTURATION AND HUMAN-INDUCED SLAVERY IN THE SOCIAL SYSTEM

Structuration theory has its conceptual basis on the concept and schema of structure. It is one of the social theories that see human behavior as the product of a man-built social system.[12] In the sociological theoretical parlance, structure is the supporting network that reinforces and upholds the status quo of any social system,[13] provided it serves the interest of the dominant group.[14]

According to Giddens, structuration theory advances the structuralisms' perspective embedded in the understanding that the social system operates on invisible structure that had been created, and at some point preceded the individuals living in such structure.[15] Meanwhile, those living in this structure can either in ignorance or fear continue to reify the structure over their affairs irrespective of the implication of such action to their survival.[16] Structuralisms' perspective also observes the tendency of every phenomenon in the social system such as language, family, religion, politics, and economy, upholding a structural setting, which in extension foretells the actions and attitudes required toward other phenomenon such as gender and power relations.[17]

Social structure and human actions are the two sides of the same coin,[18] with human actions appearing as the forerunners of the intents of the structure.[19] The structure of the social web, which appear first as rules of engagement over certain human activities, continue to be expanded upon and reinforced by the actions of the members of the society. In most circumstances, these actions are the unconscious moves and reactions of the members of the social system[20] that later become a reified order or superimposition on the same people in the social web who have created the situation.[21]

In a more distinct framework, which created a fluid departure for the Giddens' structuration theory from the dominant structuralism paradigm, Giddens maintained that the social structure has no existence independent of the knowledge that the agents have about what they do in their day-to-day activities.[22] In essence, what people believed and what people do and follow are all products of their past experience reproduced in the context of the prevailing order, norms, and expected attitude.[23] Using English language grammar as an instance, Giddens explained how the elements of the social system survived through the acknowledgment by human activities. In Giddens' structuration theoretical concepts are the concepts of rules and resources and their applications in daily human activities. Rules are appropriated with their interpretations in the daily lives of the members of the society. These rules are interpreted, applied, and extended by individuals and groups in the society to unfamiliar circumstances that were absent in the time of the rules. Again, the resources, whether material or nonmaterial, are put in use by the members of the society such that in the absence of human manipulation and application, these resources may be irrelevant and unnoticed as valuable.[24]

In the social system, according to Giddens, human beings are the agency of reproduction; something that manifests through the daily use of what the structure has offered the members of the society. There are some scholarly affirmations of Giddens propositional concepts regardless of the superficial and axiomatic appearance of his theoretical imagination.[25] In the works of Max Weber on interpretive sociology and social-cum-economic organization, which appeared more deductive when compared to a number of other classical theories, human actions were seen to be strongly attached to structural dictates from the social super structure.

The dictate by the social structure is not visible but operates through the same members of the society who at one point or the other feel uncomfortable with the system.[26] Human agency in the social structure concept as captured in Giddens' structuration theory has not only appeared in the axiomatic and superficial analysis of the society as some scholars against Giddens theoretical orientation claimed but has appeared in the everyday living of the members of the society via language,[27] kinship relationship,[28] gender relations,[29] family structure,[30] religion, politics,[31] and economy.[32] The structure and the agent, in Giddens' Structuration theory, cannot be separated as both work in tandem to reinforce each other. However, Giddens observed that human actions in the social structure are voluntary and subject to change in view of the prevailing circumstances in the hierarchy of human developmental needs.[33]

PRE- AND POST-COLONIAL AFRICAN WOMEN: POTENTIAL OPPORTUNITY FOR GENDER EQUALITY/PATRIARCHY

Historically, we may not have encompassing information of the nature of gender relation in all African small-scale societies compared to the other regions of the world. However, from the pages of ethnographic documentations, we can piece together what the situation looked like in the past in the selected small-scale precolonial African societies.

Among different small-scale African societies then, women were perceived and treated differently from what became the norm after the culture contact with European colonialists.[34] Evidence of consistency about social and cultural respect for women has survived in some small-scale societies showing that women's social status and positions were appreciated.[35] In some other societies, evidence of serious relegation of the women to the background has also survived.[36] In whichever way it is considered, the position of women before European colonial domination of Africa were not as bad as it was latter presented often by the same colonialists whose interests were served in using men for empire building and excluding women.

Among the people of Dahomey, women were active in political activities making them, more or less, the major stakeholders in the political and leadership affairs of the kingdom.[37] According to Bohannan, the political decision among the people as at the time of his study was not reached except with inputs from the women. Women activities according to him were extended to family affairs where, incidentally, they were not presented or viewed as men's property. In the military affairs of the kingdom, women were recruited into the indigenous army giving them equal stake with their male counterparts. However, as recent as the nineteenth century, Benin Republic, which rose on the ashes of the Kingdom of Dahomey, degenerated socially and women became marginalized in politics and other human affairs following the crushing of their original indigenous system by the French colonialists.

In pre-colonial Ghana, the Ashanti were a formidable force politically and otherwise with respect for gender equality. Among them, the political office of the king's mother was practically replicated withal of the attendant responsibilities at all levels of leadership.[38] The position of the king's mother at all levels of political and social affairs in Ashanti did not occur in passivity but with some level of robustness that saved women from being devalued by men.[39]

Furthermore, among the Lovedu or Balobedu, women were as sacred as men. For instance, women were made rain queens; a position that ascribed sacredness in some other small-scale African societies to men. The rain queen in Lovedu was an independent queen whose existence symbolized the powerful nature of women in public functions. Women's leadership functions did not create misrepresentation of their members in that society, but instead fostered gender equality among the sexes. However, the exportation of foreign socio-cultural orientations gradually misrepresented the activities that bestowed leadership position on women as article of religious taboo and made women vulnerable to subjugation by men.

In Mende, women were organized to be competent and ready for political activities prior to the domination of the westernization influence.[40] Mende women organized a secret society that assisted them in manipulating and obtaining political power in the society. Sexual abuse against women was controlled in all ramifications by the women. This led to a regime of fines and imposition of other levels of punishments on men found wanting in the rules of societal ethics on sexual relationship.[41]

Among the Yoruba and Nupe, women were economically influential in the social logic of family and communal economy. They commanded economic respect at both the family and communal levels. Yoruba and Nupe women were so influential that they could determine the direction of the public decisions by the male elders via their financial contributions to the communal purse.[42] Nupe women, especially, were revered by men who perceived them to possess strong witchcraft powers.[43]

In the ancient Zulu system, women were respected as sacred beings as long as their fertility lasted; thereafter, they were accorded great social status like men after the age of menopause.[44] While women's sacredness during the years of fertility enhanced their social value, the social status accorded them during the age of menopause offered them the leverage to live above abuse and domination by men.

Among the Igbo and Ijo (or Ijaw), women were more or less at liberty to influence their social status in terms of marriage and participation in the social and political affairs of the society.[45] For the Igbo before colonialism, the male traditional leadership, the Eze-in-council, reserved a seat in the cabinet for women who were represented by a symbolic leader known as *Ilumandinate*. This was case with the structure and arrangement of the last Eze Nri. It was shown that this had existed for centuries before the last Eze Nri. Similarly, among the Ijaw women, the forms of marriage they entered into determined their chances of self-determination.[46]

Among the Hausa subscribers to Islam, women became subjugated to men when married and under some other social circumstances. Purdah according to Smith and Onwuejeogwu was introduced by Mansa Musa of the Songhai Empire after his visit to Saudi Arabia in the fifteenth century. In the absence of purdah, Hausa women were as free as other women in the ethnic groups mentioned above before the culture contact with foreign cultures.[47]

The status of women in view of the social structures of the small-scale societies presented above showed the indices of gender neutrality making them, more or less, open societies for women. The nature of these societies as open, compared to closed societies, made it possible for the women to indirectly exercise their right through active engagement with the society. However, the passivity of women in some of these societies equally made them vulnerable to domination by men. The current status of these societies mentioned above, reconfigured in the colonially created new nations, make them appear as internationally designated systems for women abuse and men domination after the culture contact with the outside world. In Dahomey where women were recruited into the military like men and operated in every facet of the society, the report of the social watch as at 2012 showed that women participation in economic activities were as low as 0.14 percent, gender equality 0.41 percent, and empowerment 0.66 percent.[48]

Ghana, which once had a gender-equal Ashanti society, now ranks among the nations with the poorest score in gender equality, women empowerment, and women participation in economic and political activities. Same applies to Yoruba, Hausa and Igbo in Nigeria and Lovedu in South Africa. In present-day Benin Republic, a study carried out within the framework of the 2020 Empowerment project, reported that sexual harassment against women was the most common manifestation of sexual abuse; 37 percent of respondents declared being victims of sexual harassment, followed by rape 20 percent, and incest 10 percent.[49] Between 2003 and 2011, the percentage of elected women was consistently low, rising from 7.2 percent (or six out of eighty-three ministers) to 10 percent (or nine out of eighty-three ministers) between 2007 and 2011. The poor representation of women in the political sphere is explained in part according to CEDAW, by the fact that, as stated in the JICA country profile for Benin, "Women's involvement in any activity, whether social, economic, or cultural, was subject to men's decision."

WOMEN AS THE REJUVENATING FORCE TO PATRIARCHY SYSTEM IN AFRICA

Patriarchy's crude definition, as shown earlier in this chapter, is about men's domination of women in the society. Its indices include institutional domination by men, women subjugation by the social structure, and relegation of the dignity of women to the background. More than this crude definition of patriarchy are other perspectives that have come into play as far as the concept and phenomenon of patriarchy is concerned. More specifically, in the Hegelian–Marxian concept of thesis, antithesis, and synthesis,[50] patriarchy in Africa, going by the available historical and anthropological data, appears to be an ongoing process of the social relationship aptly defined and sustained by the weaknesses and strengths of one group over another. Nevertheless, the situation in the sociological parlance of social structure and the ongoing system can be defined as the accepted but not inherent status of women to serve as the opposite of the strong (weak), head (tail), leader (led), super ordinate (subordinate), and so on.

While the concept of patriarchy in its crude form focuses on the social institutions and their contribution to the survival of male domination in the society, the Hegelian–Marxian concept of socio-historical movement of the society singles out the problem of epoch-making decision of the members of the society to pursue, or not to pursue, the needed change in gender relations.

The institution of patriarchy in Africa has continued to survive through with the help of the social structure upheld and reenforced by the members of the society.[51] While the men have exploited the opportunity as resources lying potentially for use, women have ignorantly/fearfully maintained the same system without the understanding that they were supporting the survival of patriarchy.[52]

In the language structure, especially in the indigenous dialects and adages, women are depicted as lower in status to their male counterparts. This is observable in the attitude of some women when they want to psychologically submit to difficult tasks; they simply look for the terminology of women weaknesses in the local dialects to defray their mind from striving further. From the classical text of Ferdinand de Saussure, there is the inherent capacity of language to socialize man into his permanent status as a superior gender category in the society. Similarly, Levi Strauss indicated that language in the kinship system appear so powerful that the members of the society become classified in their relationship with one another in the microcomponents of the local dialects leading to the situation by which the members of the society become inherently weak or strong[53] toward each other on the basis of their gender.[54] Although the role played by the language structure in sustaining patriarchy appear to be general; in the specific, women unconsciously transfer this inherent antigender equality in the language to their wards knowing that they are the custodians of child upbringing in the family and society at large.[55] What the children learn become basically what they are thought and exposed to by their mothers and they grow to keep these in sustenance of the system in the direction of male dominance.[56] In certain circumstances where the female children try to be actively involved in social activities with their male counterparts, their mothers speak into their ears certain words that promote gender inequality and inherent submission such as: "are you aware that you are a woman who will be married to a man?" Such silent statements appear salient in understanding the social logic of gender relations in the mind of the female folk when they gradually start seeing themselves secluded and isolated from active participation in the social activities.[57]

There are countless instances in the local dialects across Africa that psychologically induce weakness and self-dehumanization among the female folk. Such words carrying gender-sensitive image ought to have fallen into disuse so that feminine courage could gradually grow through childhood until women of all classes recover their humanity with dignity and enjoy equal rights with men.[58] As it is, the ignorance of the women over these unconsciously acts merely reinforce indignity against their persons in the language and social system.[59]

In Giddens' theme of rules and resources, the rules guiding a particular social setting cannot be absolutely comprehensive as to involve all behaviors and rules guiding them at the same time; likewise, the resources such as the opportunity to act and control situation can lie potentially dormant until when human beings put them into use. The rules guiding human behavior in the family and public setting though in unwritten form in African societies did not specify the limit of women participation or how women should train their female wards. However, these rules have been given strength, and sometimes new dimensions, by the people applying them. For instance, among the people of Obowo in south eastern Nigeria, women are expected to respect their husbands but not to bow to the excesses of the husbands. In the case of abuse of a woman, the husband was to be reported to *umu nna, umu ada* and the community women association. Strictly speaking, women can only be divorced with the support of the family, *umu nna, umu ada* or the community women association on the grounds of marital infidelity and socially abominable acts. In view of the unwritten code of respect to the husbands, many women in the past and currently have given further interpretations to this unwritten code to the detriment of gender equality and the socio-cultural rights of women.

By extension, some women have included the habit of keeping quiet in the face of abuse, spousal maltreatment, and husband infidelity to be part of the way of showing respect to their husband. For example, some men can easily abuse their wives, abandon their wives and children, and even initiate extra-marital affair with another woman. Normally, it is the duty of the rightful wife to bring such to the knowledge of the family through the elderly person in the family or other avenues the entire community used to handle such mat-ters. But, instead, many victims of such abuse and maltreatment keep silent giving the impression that taking up cases against their husbands will earn them problems from the husband. Notwithstanding, cases abound of men sanctioned by the community cum kinship heads over their mistreatment of their wives, and instead of further troubles, brought peace to the family and protected the dignity of the women involved.

The unconscious rules guiding individual participation in the socio-eco-nomic and political affairs in most African societies have depended on who may likely interpret and give the rules life of its own. In Giddens' example, it is the daily interaction with the members of the community that give the rules life and expands their scope for continuity, while the interpretation goes in the favor of who understands and is willing to exploit the rules. From the pages of ethnographic documentations, the pseudo patriarchal rules governing small-scale societies in Africa had operated and continued to operate as a potential opportunity for who cares to activate them in their own favor.

Resources in Giddens' theoretical paradigm are both material and nonma-terial resources. In Durkheimian theoretical parlance, the society runs on the principles of social facts—i.e., values, cultural norms, and social structures that transcend the individual and can exercise social control over the individ-uals. Social facts according to Durkheim are divided into material and non-material social facts. In comparative as well as chronological arrangement, the Giddens nonmaterial resources stems from the Durkheim's concept of nonmaterial social facts. In Giddens' theoretical legacy, material resources, such as land and raw materials, cannot be operational without human beings putting them into use. The nonmaterial resources, which lie more invisible, cannot be put to use except by human beings who observe and understand them. There were resources at the disposal of women in Africa both before and after the colonial intervention. These resources included beauty, which had appealed to the hearts of most powerful kings and heads of authorities; wisdom, which had exposed many women to public leaders and personalities; talents, which have given the entire society a good image before the outside world; leadership opportunities, which have put the decision of women on records across generations, and so on. These resources in most cases were underutilized women in the pursuit of gender equality.

In the absence of international intervention for gender equality in Africa, most women in Africa even those with access to political and economic power still lack conviction and indigenous strategy to pursue gender equality and the elimination of patriarchy. Most of the efforts made so far for gender equality in Africa still have the taste of an external agenda, which appear alien to the indigenous social institutions and by implication were viewed as derogatory and an anti-indigenous culture.

CONCLUSION

As Giddens observed, the social structure and the human actions are two dual structures that reenforced each other. While the human beings in the society grow into the structure being nurtured by the structure, the structure itself depends on human beings in the society to continue in existence. Patriarchy as a social construction is dependent on human actions to survive. According to Giddens, even though the social structure affects the way the members of the society behave and operate, there is still the lacuna between the lifeless social structure and the human action, which offers opportunity for self-determination and self-liberation from the unfavorable rules of the social structure; what Giddens called determinism, voluntarism, and agency transformation. In the case of patriarchy in the selected small-scale African societies, the condition had existed unconsciously for years and has now metamorphosed into the new colonially created nations' outlook and posture. This continued legacy is based on women's passivity even after colonial rule that accelerated gender inequality in the system. From the structuration theory perspective, what appeared to be ceaseless patriarchy among African societies did not appear as definite rules compelling everybody to obey them; rather, they were the expansion of microconcepts by the members of the society especially the women through their actions and inactions.

NOTES

1. Kamla Bhasin, *What is Patriarchy* (New Delhi: Women Unlimited, 2006), 52.
2. Solomon O. Ademiluka, "Patriarchy and Women Abuse: Perspectives from Ancient Israel and Africa," *Old Testament Essay* 31, no. 2 (2018): 339–362.
3. Joey Sprague and Diane Kobrynowicz, "A Feminist Epistemology," in *Handbook of the Sociology of Gender*, ed. Janet S. Chafetz (New York, NY: Plenum Press, 1999), 25–43.

4. Nkiru I. Igbokwe, "Contextualizing Gender Based Violence within Patriarchy in Nigeria," *Old Testament Essays* 5, no. 30 (2013): 630–632.

5. Kevin Stainback, Sybil Kleiner and Shryl Skaggs, "Women in power: Undoing or Redoing the Gendered Organization?" *Gender and Society* 30, no. 1 (2016): 109–135.

6. Ibid., 87.

7. Laura Bohannan, "Dahomean Marriage: A Revaluation," *Africa* 19 (1949): 12–17.

8. Eileen J. Krige and Daniel Jacob, *The Realm of a Rain Queen* (London: Oxford University Press, 1943), 121–125.

9. Samuel O. Okafor, "Globalization and the Indigenous Concept of Sexuality in African Tradition: Charting a New Course for Sexual Right and Safe Society," *CPQ Women and Child Health* 1, no. 2 (2018), 1–9.

10. Olajumoke Jenyo, "Patriarchy and Gender Inequality in Nigeria: A Threat to National Development," *Journal of Business and Economic Management* 6, no. 7 (2018): 148–156.

11. Ibid., 150.

12. Anthony Giddens, *Studies in Social and Political Theory* (London: Hutchinson, 1977), 54–61.

13. Tocqueville S. Kalberg and Max Weber, "The Sociological Origins of Citizenship: The Political Culture of American Democracy," *Citizenship Studies* 1, no. 2 (1997): 199–222.

14. Lise Vogel, *Marxism and the Oppression of Women: Toward a Unitary Theory* (New Brunswick, NJ: Rutgers University Press, 1983), 154–157; and Jean Stockard, "Gender Socialization," in *Handbook of the Sociology of Gender*, 215–227.

15. Anthony Giddens, *The Constitution of Society* (Cambridge: Polity Press, 1984), 162–167.

16. Ruth Wallace, *Feminism and Sociological Theory* (Newbury Park, CA: Sage, 1989), 34–41.

17. Jack Sattel, "The Inexpressive Male: Tragedy or Sexual Politics?" *Social Problems* 23–24 (1976): 469–477.

18. Mike Haralambose and Martin Holborn, *Sociology, Themes and Perspectives* (Hammersmith: Harper Collins Publishers, 2008), 482–489.

19. Ibid., 103.

20. Ibid., 87.

21. Namok Choi and Dale Fuqua, "The Structure of the Bem Sex Role Inventory: A Summary Report of Validation Studies," *Educational and Psychological Measurement* 63 (2003): 872–887.

22. Ibid., 74.

23. Man, Y. Kan, Oriel Sullivan and Jonathan Gershuny, "Gender Convergence in Domestic Work: Discerning the Effects of Interactional and Institutional Barriers from Large Scale Data," *Sociology* 45, no. 2 (2011): 234–251.

24. Peter Burke, *History and Social Theory* (New York, NY: Cornell University Press, 1992), 215–219.

25. Margaret Archer, "Morphogenesis Versus Structure and Action," *British Journal of Sociology* 33, no. 4 (1982): 1–14.

26. Francis Fukuyama, *The Great Disruption: Human Nature and the Reconstruction of the Social Order* (New York, NY: Free Press, 1999), 251.

27. Ferdinand de Saussure, *Course in General Linguistic* (New York, NY: Mcgraw-Hill, 1966, first published in 1959), 52.

28. Claude Lèvi-Strauss, *Structural Anthropology* (Harmondsworth: Penguin, 1963), 27.

29. Nancy Bonvillain, *Women and Men: Cultural Constructs of Gender* (Englewood Cliffs, NJ: Prentice-Hall, 1995), 57.

30. Janet Chafetz and Jacqueline Hagan, "The Gender Division of Labor and Family Change in Industrial Societies: A Theoretical Accounting," *Journal of Comparative Family Studies* 27 (1996): 187–217.

31. Lawrence Scaff, *Fleeing the Iron Cage: Culture, Politics, and Modernity in the Thought of Max Weber* (Berkeley, CA: University of California Press, 1989), 38.

32. Zillah Eisenstein, "Developing a Theory of Capitalist Patriarchy and Socialist Feminism, and Some Notes on the Relations of Capitalist Patriarchy," in *Capitalist Patriarchy and the Case for Socialist Feminism,* ed. Z. Eisenstein (New York, NY: Monthly Review Press, 1979), 5–55.

33. Anthony Giddens, *Central Problem in Social Theory* (London: Macmillan, 1979), 148.

34. Angulu Onwuejeogwu, *The Social Anthropology of Africa: An Introduction* (London: Heinemann, 1975), 36.

35. William Bascom, "The Esusu: A Credit Institution of the Yoruba," *Journal of the Royal Anthropological Institute* 82 (1952): 66–73.

36. Michael Smith, *The Economy of Hausa Communities of Zaria* (London: HMSO, 1955), 59.

37. Melville Herskovits, *Dahomey: An Ancient West African Kingdom* (New York, NY: J. J. Augustine, 1938), 142.

38. Robert Rattray, *Ashanti* (Oxford: Clarendon Press, 1923), 109.

39. Phyllis Kaberry, *Women of the Grass Fields* (London: HMSO, 1952), 241.

40. Kenneth Little, "The Changing Position of Women in Sierra Leone Protectorate," *Africa* 18 (1948): 128–139.

41. Kenneth Little, *The Mende of Sierra Leone* (London: Routledge and Kegan Paul, 1951), 158.

42. Ibid., 25.

43. Ibid., 31.

44. Godwin Woodson, "Zulu Woman," *Journal of Negro History* 33, no. 1 (1948): 371–372.

45. Simon Ottenberg, "The Changing Economic Position of Women Among the Afikpo Ibo," in *Continuity and Change in African Cultures,* eds. W. R. Bascom and M. Herskovits (Chicago, IL: University of Chicago Press, 1959), 172.

46. Kay Williamson, "Changes in the Marriage System of the Okirika Ijo," *Africa* 32, no. 1 (1962): 109–118.

47. Ibid., 52.

48. Social watch, poverty eradication and gender justice (Social Watch-Benin Network, 2012), 4.

49. UN Committee on the Elimination of Discrimination Against Women (CEDAW), Consideration of reports submitted by States parties under article 19 of the Convention on the Elimination of All Forms of Discrimination against Women: 4th periodic reports of States parties/Benin, 21 March 2012, CEDAW/C/BEN/4.

50. George Ritzer, *Classical Sociological Theory* (New York, NY: McGraw Hill, 2011), 250.

51. Godiya Makama, "Patriarchy and Gender Inequality in Nigeria: The Way Forward," *European Scientific Journal* 9, no. 17 (2013): 115–144.

52. Preeti Rawat, "Patriarchal Beliefs, Women's Empowerment, and General Well-being," *Vikalpa* 39, no. 2 (2014): 43–55.

53. Lilian Atanga, Edith Ellece, Lia Litosseliti and Jane Sunderland, "Gender and Language in sub-Saharan African Contexts: Issues and Challenges," *Gender and Language* 6, no. 1 (2012): 1–20.

54. Ndimande-Hlongwa Nobuhle and Rushubirwa Leonce, "Gender Inequality and Language Reflections in African Indigenous Languages: Comparative Cases from IsiZulu and Kiswahili," *Alternation Special Edition* 13 (2014): 390–410.

55. Veronica Tichenor, "Maintaining Men's Dominance: Negotiating Identity and Power When She Earns More," *Sex Roles* 53 (2005): 191–205.

56. Roberto Cubelli, Daniela Paolieri, Lorella Lotto and Remo Job, "The Effect of Grammatical Gender on Object Categorization," *Journal of Experimental Psychology* 37, no. 2 (2011): 449–460.

57. Lera Boroditsky, "How Does Our Language Shape the Way We think?," in *What's Next? Dispatches on the Future of Sciences*, ed. M. Brockman (New York, NY: Vintage, 2009), 206–214.

58. Sheryl Feinstein, Rachel Feinstein and Sophia Sabrow, "Gender Inequality in the Division of Household Labour in Tanzania," *African Sociological Review* 14, no. 2 (2010): 98–109.

59. Sinfree Makoni and Ulrike Meinhof, "Western Perspectives in Applied Linguistics in Africa," *AILA Review* 17 (2004): 77–104.

BIBLIOGRAPHY

Ademiluka, Solomon O. "Patriarchy and Women Abuse: Perspectives from Ancient Israel and Africa." *Old Testament Essay* 31, no. 2 (2018): 339–362.

Archer, Margaret. "Morphogenesis versus Structure and Action," *British Journal of Sociology* 33 no. 4 (1982): 1–14.

Atanga, Lilian, Edith Ellece, Lia Litosseliti and Jane Sunderland. "Gender and Language in sub-Saharan African Contexts: Issues and Challenges," *Gender and Language* 6, no. 1 (2012): 1–20.

Bascom, William. "The Esusu: A Credit Institution of the Yoruba," *Journal of the Royal Anthropological Institute* 82 (1952): 66–73.

Bhasin, Kamla. *What is Patriarchy.* New Delhi: Women Unlimited, 2006.

Bohannan, Laura. "Dahomean Marriage: A Revaluation," *Africa* 19 (1949): 12–17.

Bonvillain, Nancy. *Women and Men: Cultural Constructs of Gender.* Englewood Cliffs, NJ: Prentice-Hall, 1995.

Boroditsky, Lera. How Does Our Language Shape the Way We think? In *What's Next? Dispatches on the Future of Sciences,* edited by M. Brockman, 206–214. New York, NY: Vintage, 2009.

Burke, Peter, *History and Social Theory.* New York, NY: Cornell University Press, 1992.

Chafetz, Janet and Jacqueline Hagan. "The Gender Division of Labor and Family Change in Industrial Societies: A Theoretical Accounting." *Journal of Comparative Family Studies* 27 (1996): 187–217.

Choi, Namok and Dale Fuqua. "The Structure of the Bem Sex Role Inventory: A Summary Report of Validation Studies." *Educational and Psychological Measurement* 63 (2003): 872–87.

Cubelli, Roberto, Daniela Paolieri, Lorella Lotto and Remo Job. "The Effect of Grammatical Gender on Object Categorization." *Journal of Experimental Psychology* 37, no. 2 (2011): 449–460.

de Saussure, Ferdinand. *Course in General Linguistic.* New York, NY: Mcgraw-Hill, 1966.

Eisenstein, Zillah. "Developing a Theory of Capitalist Patriarchy and Socialist Feminism, and Some Notes on the Relations of Capitalist Patriarchy." In *Capitalist Patriarchy and the Case for Socialist Feminism,* edited by Zillah Eisenstein, 5–55. New York, NY: Monthly Review Press, 1979.

Feinstein, Sheryl, Rachel Feinstein and Sophia Sabrow. "Gender Inequality in the Division of Household Labour in Tanzania." *African Sociological Review* 14, no. 2 (2010): 98–109.

Fukuyama, Francis. *The Great Disruption: Human Nature and the Reconstruction of the Social Order.* New York, NY: Free Press, 1999.

Giddens, Anthony. *Central Problem in Social Theory.* London: Macmillan, 1979.

Giddens, Anthony. *Studies in Social and Political Theory.* London: Hutchinson, 1977.

Giddens, Anthony. *The Constitution of Society.* Cambridge: Polity Press, 1984.

Haralambose, Mike and Martin Holborn. *Sociology, Themes and Perspectives.* Hammersmith: Harper Collins Publishers 2008.

Herskovits, Melville. *Dahomey: An Ancient West African Kingdom.* New York, NY: J. J. Augustine, 1938.

Igbokwe, Nkiru I. "Contextualizing Gender Based Violence within Patriarchy in Nigeria." *Old Testament Essays* 5, no. 30 (2013): 630–632.

Kaberry, Phyllis. *Women of the Grass Fields.* London: HMSO, 1952.

Kalberg, Tocqueville S. and Max Weber. "The Sociological Origins of Citizenship: The Political Culture of American Democracy." *Citizenship Studies* 1, no. 2 (1997): 199–222.

Kan Man, Y., Oriel Sullivan and Jonathan Gershuny. "Gender Convergence in Domestic Work: Discerning the Effects of Interactional and Institutional Barriers from Large Scale Data." *Sociology* 45, no. 2 (2011): 234–251.

Krige, Eileen J. and Daniel Jacob. *The Realm of a Rain Queen.* London: Oxford University Press, 1943.

Lèvi-Strauss, Claude. *Structural Anthropology.* Harmondsworth: Penguin Books, 1963.

Little, Kenneth. "The Changing Position of Women in Sierra Leone Protectorate." *Africa* 18 (1948): 128–139.

Little, Kenneth. *The Mende of Sierra Leone*. London: Routledge and Kegan Paul, 1951.

Makama, Godiya, "Patriarchy and Gender Inequality in Nigeria: The Way Forward." *European Scientific Journal* 9, no. 17 (2013): 115–144.

Makoni, Sinfree and Ulrike Meinhof. "Western Perspectives in Applied Linguistics in Africa." *AILA Review* 17 (2004): 77–104.

Nobuhle, Ndimande-Hlongwa and Rushubirwa Leonce. "Gender Inequality and Language Reflections in African Indigenous Languages: Comparative Cases from IsiZulu and Kiswahili." *Alternation Special Edition* 13 (2014): 390–410.

Okafor, Samuel O. "Globalization and the Indigenous Concept of Sexuality in African Tradition: Charting a New Course for Sexual Right and Safe Society." *CPQ Women and Child Health* 1, no. 2 (2018): 1–9.

Olajumoke, Jenyo. "Patriarchy and Gender Inequality in Nigeria: A Threat to National Development." *Journal of Business and Economic Management* 6, no. 7 (2018): 148–156.

Onwuejeogwu, Angulu. *The Social Anthropology of Africa: An Introduction*. London: Heinemann, 1975.

Ottenberg, Simon. "The Changing Economic Position of Women Among the Afikpo Ibo." In *Continuity and Change in African Cultures*, edited by W. R. Bascom and M. Herskovits, 172. Chicago, IL: University of Chicago Press, 1959.

Rattray, Robert, *Ashanti*. Oxford: Clarendon Press, 1923.

Rawat, Preeti. "Patriarchal Beliefs, Women's Empowerment, and General Well-Being." *Vikalpa* 39, no. 2 (2014): 43–55.

Ritzer, George. *Classical Sociological Theory*. New York, NY: McGraw Hill, 2011.

Sattel, Jack. "The Inexpressive Male: Tragedy or Sexual Politics?" *Social Problems* 23–24 (1976): 469–477.

Scaff, Lawrence, *Fleeing the Iron Cage: Culture, Politics, and Modernity in the Thought of Max Weber*. Berkeley, CA: University of California Press, 1989.

Smith, Michael. *The Economy of Hausa Communities of Zaria*. London: HMSO, 1955.

Social watch. *poverty eradication and gender justice*. Social Watch-Benin network, 2012.

Sprague, Joey and Diane Kobrynowicz. "A Feminist Epistemology." In *Handbook of the Sociology of Gender*, edited by Janet S. Chafetz, 25–43. New York, NY: Plenum Press, 1999.

Stainback, Kevin, Sybil Kleiner and Shryl Skaggs. "Women in power: Undoing or Redoing the Gendered Organization?" *Gender and Society*, 30, no. 1 (2016): 109–135.

Tichenor, Veronica. "Maintaining Men's Dominance: Negotiating Identity and Power When She Earns More." *Sex Roles* 53 (2005): 191–205.

UN Committee on the Elimination of Discrimination Against Women (CEDAW). *Consideration of reports submitted by States parties under article 19 of the Convention on the Elimination of All Forms of Discrimination against Women.*

4th periodic reports of States parties/Benin, 21 March 2012, CEDAW/C/ BEN/4.

Vogel, Lise. *Marxism and the Oppression of Women: Toward a Unitary Theory.* New Brunswick, NJ: Rutgers University Press, 1983.

Wallace, Ruth. *Feminism and Sociological Theory.* Newbury Park, CA: Sage, 1989.

Williamson, Kay. "Changes in the Marriage System of the Okirika Ijo." *Africa* 32, no. 1 (1962): 109–118.

Woodson, Godwin. "Zulu Woman." *Journal of Negro History* 33, no.1 (1948): 371–372.

Part II

WOMEN, WORK, AND EXPLOITATION

Chapter 7

Patriarchy and Cultural Values in Nineteenth- and Twentieth-Century Ghana

Valerie Delali Adjoh-Davoh

Earlier writers on gender have focused on the rights of men in allocating land to women in matrilineal and patrilineal societies.[1] Other writers have concentrated on the exploitation of unpaid female labor in both domestic settings and on cocoa farms for commercial purposes.[2] However, there are limited historical accounts on sexual abuse and the exploitation of women and girls by men by virtue of the patriarchal rights being enabled by cultural values in the former Gold Coast (now Ghana). Also, the discussion of issues on sexual abuse is often frowned upon in the twenty-first century Ghanaian society making it difficult to interview victims today. As a result, this chapter makes use of archival documents such as reported court cases, reports by colonial officials, and the Basel Mission to provide a historical account of how women and girls were treated by virtue of patriarchal and cultural norms through the institution of pawning, marriage and its complexities with Christianity in the nineteenth and twentieth century Ghana. This chapter begins by discussing the case of women with some examples in the Gold Coast followed by some examples on girls. Also, this chapter discusses some measures taken by the colonial government to end pawning in order to free these women and girls although it persisted for many years.

THE PRACTICE OF PAWNING IN GHANA AFTER 1874

Pawning in precolonial Africa was an act of offering a person as security for a debt.[3] In 1874, during the period of the abolition of domestic slavery in Ghana, slave holders demanded that their slaves should provide pawns as their replacement in order to be manumitted.[4] Besides being a means of manumission, the act of pawning became the main source by which Ghanaians in the nineteenth and twentieth century obtained loans and only a prominent person or elder of a community could guarantee a loan. However, pawning became the main source of guarantee for obtaining a loan since it was easier to pawn a family member than get an elder to guarantee a loan who in case a default, would be held responsible for repayment. The evidence for this research demonstrates that women and girls were mostly pawned.[5] The female pawn was obliged to stay with the creditor until the debt was paid, and was expected to work for the creditor.[6] The work which the pawn did for the creditor during that period was considered to be the interest on the loan taken by the debtor. As a result, a debtor was only expected to pay the principal amount of the money borrowed to redeem a pawn. Therefore, in cases where a pawn absconded, she was sent back to the creditor or replaced by the debtor.[7] In such cases, the process of replacing a pawn continued until the debt was fully paid. However, it was only in few cases that a pawned pawn absconded. Nonetheless, female pawns were hardly redeemed which led to a number of cases of unredeemed pawns being reported to the colonial courts in the Gold Coast after the abolition of domestic slavery in the nineteenth century.

Yet, the act of pawning intensified after abolition because there was short supply of labor often referred to as the "early colonial labor problem."[8] An example of the effects of the labor shortage could be given in an 1875 case when Noguah (wife of a debtor) and six of her children were pawned to Kuaco Amoah (chief of Berinoosoo), the creditor, by Sampson (Noguah's husband or debtor to the chief of Berinoosoo).[9] However, Noguah absconded after a period of service and had to be sent back to the chief but in the process was assaulted by the chief's messenger. Noguah complained to the court that she had absconded because she was sexually abused by the chief.[10] She thought that the forced sex she had with the creditor sufficed for the debt but the creditor refused to release her.[11] On the other hand, the creditor claimed she was at his pleasure until she was redeemed. Like the case of other female pawns, Noguah was assaulted by her master's messenger in her husband's home when she absconded from the creditor. Noguah's plight is an indication that women, often seen as a weaker sex, were sometimes maltreated by their holders who as men are considered to be the sex from which each family grows. This stance is sustained by traditional patriarchal values in Ghana. So although gender studies have focused on the sexual abuse of women, historical studies on the issue is lacking because the discussion of sex was frowned upon by most communities in Ghana in the past.[12]

Also, in the court, there were reported cases of women being kept by their creditors because they bore children for them.[13] The holders who had sexual interests in the women pawned to them, seduced them and bore children with them in order to keep them permanently. The documents consulted were, however, silent on the agency of women pawns in seducing their holders. In these circumstances, it is probable that beautiful women or a hard-working woman whose labor was needed on the holder's farm could be seduced and kept. For example, in 1874, Affuah Obiri was recorded by the court for having been seduced and kept by her holder. The court reports made it clear that Affuah Obiri was pawned at a young age.[14] The comments on Affuah Obiri's seduction by the Acting Chief Magistrate confirm that, "the sum of £12 amount advanced you [Otabil] with interest for and on account of Affuah Obiri whom you pawned to him [Kwabena Kotchie] but seduced and kept by you [Kwabena Kotchie] now."[15] As a woman was expected to live with the father of her children, any woman who did otherwise was not respected in the Ghanaian society. This cultural norm placed a burden on a female pawn who was obligated to stay with her holder, heed to her holder's instructions at home, and serve him as the father of her children.

The report of the attempt by Friedrich Ramseyer of the Basel Mission to redeem these pawned girls shows that very young children, even below age five, could be pawned. Unfortunately, the girls could hardly resist being pawned because of societal norms that expected them to obey the directives of their parents or elder. The plight of pawned girls was also reported by Ramseyer of the Basel Mission in 1882 as follows:

> In a recent special case he was glad to buy free from the fetish priest of Atie Yaw (Bowu) 2 small girls aged 3 and 5 from the family of their best convert in Mpraeso. They had been sold in his absence to cover debts. The price involved was £27 . . . Bowu wanted Ramseyer to pay £6 but R. talked about the crimes of the fetish priest which he [R.] knew about, and he lowered the price out of fear.[16]

Besides societal norms, no value was placed on educating girls as compared to boys in the nineteenth-century Ghana. As reported on the education of girls in Fankyeneko, it was made clear that "[g]irls they cannot get to come to school at all. They reason is the parents' use of the children-girls to mind the younger ones."[17] Thus, in the nineteenth century, it was a common practice in Fankyeneko to keep girls at home while boys went to school. Culturally, girls catered to the need of their younger siblings while the boys went to school. This reasoning was due to the belief that a girl would get married and her sole responsibility in her husband's home would be to cook and cater to the needs of her husband and children. Therefore, educating a girl was not as important as educating a boy.[18] The idea of not educating girls compared to boys is better understood by an Akan proverb which states: *se obia totua etswire berima danmu.* This proverb literally means when a woman buys a gun she keeps it in her husband's room. That means what a woman acquires or achieves was handed to her husband as the head of the home. This saying thus creates the impression that educating a girl is not as important as educating a boy since a girl's future role was to manage the home. Therefore, it was more important to educate the boys who would take up the fatherly role of providing for their immediate family.

Marriage, Patriarchy and the Christian Doctrine in Gold Coast (now Ghana)

The institution of marriage was one of the means by which men dominated women and girls. In nineteenth- and twentieth-century Gold Coast, marriage was contracted through the *adehye awadie* or *awowa awadie*. However, this traditional marriage custom which will be discussed later had generated a lot of controversy among missionaries in the Gold Coast. In 1890, the Basel Mission missionary Sitzler in his report of marriage among the Akyems, criticized it as follows:

> Troubled by the casualness with which Akyems approach marriage questions. The man wants a woman for his lust, and to look after the farms he makes. But, if a woman does not please him he can divorce her easily, and gets back from her relatives the head-money he had to pay at the time of the marriage. It often happens too that the relative let a girl go without head-money, saying that, then, if the man finds he does not like her he can send her back without them having to worry about head-money.[19]

In Akan, *adehye* in Akan refers to royals, while *awadie* means marriage. Therefore, *adehye awadie* refers to a royal marriage.[20] This form of marriage, *adehye awadie*, was also used for those contracted between free born people.[21] In matrilineal societies of the Gold Coast, the children from such a marriage inherited wealth from their mother's family, particularly from their maternal uncle known as *wofa*. Therefore, since these children inherited wealth from their maternal uncle, he had rights over the children. In the same vein, when someone from the mother's lineage needed a loan, the girls could be pawned by their maternal uncles who already had rights over them.

On the other hand, *awowa* in Akan refers to a pawn. Therefore, *awowa awadie* refers to pawn or pledge marriage. *Awowa awadie* may be contracted under two circumstances.[22] In the first example of this, the woman becomes the pawn of her husband by reason of her family taking a loan from her husband after the customary marriage rites have been performed.[23] In this case, the woman's lineage takes a loan from the husband after the *adehye awadie* has been contracted. If the loan was given to the woman's lineage after the *adehye awadie,* she could not divorce her husband until the loan was paid. In the second example of *awowa awadie*, marriage rites were not performed so a woman's lineage could take a loan from a man who was not yet her husband in the hope that she would cohabit with the man in order to serve him until the loan was settled. The loan was often taken by a lineage head upon agreement with the other members of the lineage to advance a particular course such as loans for funerals since funerals were revered among the Akan. In this case, the woman's family was hopeful that the man would marry her to offset their loan. This means, that the head-money which would have been paid in contracting the marriage was paid prior to the performance of the customary marriage.[24] If the man did not marry the woman in question, the woman's family was expected to repay the loan in order to redeem her.

From Sitzler's criticism of marriage above, it is clear that the relationship between a man and a woman, where head-money has been paid, refers to *adehye awadie*. The second description would refer to *awowa awadie* or cases where a girl was pawned for a loan and so cohabited with the man. In all these descriptions, one important fact to note was that the labor of the girl pawn was exploited. Usually, the labor provided became interest paid on the loan acquired. Therefore, the debtor was only expected to pay the principal. The number of unmarried females in a lineage became the commodity or wealth of the lineage that could be traded for a loan. Sitzler's second sentence also mentions lust and labor of pawned young girls on the farms of creditors. This raises the twin issues of sexual abuse and the exploitation of female labor on farms. Therefore, one can argue that marriages in the nineteenth century were in most cases conducted to secure a loan, to exploit the labor of girls, and for the lust of the men they married. This is because from Sitzler's report, one can conclude that the only reason some men married was to satisfy their lust and have the girls work on their farms. Similarly, these girls tended to be the labor force on cocoa farms in the peak season of cocoa production from November to March.

In 1908, the Chief Commissioner of Ashanti indicated that "a pawn remains with the creditor until the debt is paid in full and no provision for a period of labor, on the completion of which the former may be held to have discharged the debt exist."[25] This quotation demonstrates that there was no specific labor period or number of years by which a pawn could be discharged. As a result, the labor of a pawned woman could be exploited for many years without pay by her holder. Therefore, holding female pawns became a means by which their holders obtained free labor for their farms especially after the abolition of domestic slavery when labor was in short supply.[26]

It is important to note that, since women in matrilineal societies did not have direct control over their children, children's labor was exploited through pawning by their maternal uncles, thus, Grier posits that, especially in cocoa growing areas, men pawned their children or nieces for an advance to purchase land.[27] During the colonial period, the pawning of women and girls worsened with the unfavorable conditions faced by Gold Coast businessmen in obtaining a loan from the existing European banks.[28]

The circumstances under *awowa awadie* where a pawned girl cohabited with a creditor for temporary service, was further noted by J. C. de Graft Johnson in 1927. He maintains:

> Today there are very probably some pawns, but without questions they know they are only doing temporary service, that they are free persons and can leave at any time. Moreover the family giving and the family receiving the pawn are usually on very friendly terms, one temporary adopting the daughter or son of the other and no crime or wrong is ever intended by either by the transaction.[29]

This kind of cohabitation involving pawned girls was a great challenge to Christian missionaries because the Christian doctrine encouraged marriage by mutual consent of the parties involved. In other words, this act was against marriage which was contracted by convenience of the families of the pawned girl and their creditor. The Basel Mission also criticized this form of marriage for several reasons. First, the man involved could easily divorce the girl or request for the loan from the pawned girl's family when he desired. It was against the Christian doctrine that a man and woman or young girl cohabit throughout their life time at the pleasure of her holder without the security of marriage. Secondly, this kind of cohabitation encouraged promiscuity between both men and women. In a case where a pawned woman found a man who could pay the debt, she left the creditor that she had cohabited to live with the man who paid the debt in question. Furthermore, the creditor could easily divorce her for another girl or marry another woman in addition to his first wife.[30] These scenarios ensured a cycle of remarriage, adultery and promiscuity, especially among the mission's new converts, all in the name of customary marriage and credit. Thus, the challenges of marriage in Akyem Abuakwa were reported by the Basel Missionary as follows:

> Woman has been married before [*sic*] they simply see what it is like living together, and if it works, they persist. The woman knows she will not find it hard to marry again: often she has her eye on another man, and will create difficulties until her husband divorces her. Many women make their husbands' lives a misery . . . on the whole Akyem marriages lack true mutual love, though, praise be, there are exceptions to this rule among the heathen. And it takes a long time and much effort to [*sic*] put over to the Christians what the Bible's teachings about marriage are. And when you do talk to people about Christian marriage, they have so many ifs and buts that you are tempted to doubt if the old spirit and the old attitudes will be ever uprooted from their heads.[31]

To further illustrate the aforementioned challenge of marriage, the missionary Sitzler gave an example of the marriage of Kwateng in Akyem Abuakwa:

> A case in . . . Kwateng a young catechumen, without saying a word to anyone, married a girl under customary law, the relative asking no head-money, so that the two were- as far as they were concerned free to part if they found they did not lived in peace. All went well for a year then the man began to wish to marry a different girl, and started to pick quarrels with his wife. S. was involved in hearings in which it was explained clearly to him that being a Christian involves behaving by Christian standards, which in turn involves not playing with marriage. If he sent his existing wife away he would be excluded tout [*sic*] court: and indeed, his wife loved him and did not want to leave him.[32]

The case of Kwateng of Akyem Abuakwa is a clear case of cohabitation without the payment of head-money or *awowa awadie* which has been explained above. The report, however, does not mention the whereabouts of the first wife after Kwarteng left town. Sitzler's subsequent report indicated that Kwarteng married a second wife upon his return to Akyem Abuakwa albeit his first wife's desire to remain married to him because of her love for him.[33] Furthermore, since Kwarteng had not divorced his first wife at the time of his second marriage, he committed adultery which is abhorred by the Christian doctrine. However, his second marriage explains the freedom which men exploited by customary marriage where they could marry a woman to work on their farms but later request for the head-money to be returned once he sent the woman away and married another woman.

COLONIAL GOVERNMENT RESPONSE TO END PAWNING IN THE GOLD COAST

The colonial government put up a number of measures to curtail pawning in the Gold Coast colony when it still persisted after the abolition proclamation in 1874. The attempts included the enactment of laws, use of notes, fines, specified period of redemption, and the prohibition of hereditary pawning.

First, the colonial government enacted laws under Section 439 Subsection 3 of the criminal code.[34] Under this code, persons engaged in pawning could be sentenced to imprisonment. This included both the creditor and the debtor and thus explains the case of the chief of Berinosoo who was sentenced to some weeks of imprisonment after judgment had been passed in the case between him and Noguah.[35]

Also, the colonial government instituted the use of promissory notes to end pawning.[36] These promissory notes were supposed to be written by licensed letter writers in the colony who collected fees for their services.[37] The creditor had the right to present a promissory note to the court in case the debtor did not pay the debt by the agreement stated on the note. Once the note was presented, it was then the responsibility of the court to ensure that the debt was recovered.[38]

The introduction of fines or head-money in accordance with customary law was also enforced by the colonial government.[39] They requested that families of female pawns should induce creditors who had children with their pawns to pay head-money.[40] Furthermore, after the head-money had been paid, the families would need to consent to the marriage between the holder and the female pawn in accordance with customary and colonial government law.[41] Also, since the Akan practiced the maternal system of inheritance under customary law, the children would belong to the woman's family once the marriage was contracted.

Another measure the colonial government used to end pawning was the introduction of a maximum period of seven years' service of a pawn to a creditor.[42] The debt was supposed to be equally divided to match the service of a pawn in each year[43]. As a result, debts of all pawns were to be recorded with the appropriate division of a pawn's service per year to a holder to determine the number of years a pawn would work for a holder. The years of service of a pawn to pay a debt was not to exceed seven years. This time period was proposed as a means of redeeming pawns and eventually putting an end to pawning. However, this law was only supposed to redeem existing pawns, beginning from 1908, while subsequent loans were to be obtained by promissory notes. In addition, people who become pawns after January 1, 1908, would not be liable to pay any debt.[44] Thus, the court would not assist any creditor to recover his debt after entering into a pawning agreement from 1908. The pawn would be released with the sole responsibility of the debtor to pay the amount involved absolving the government.[45] If pawning persisted without the release of those in bondage, both the creditor and the debtor would receive equal punishment.[46]

Furthermore, pawning, by the colonial government's instruction, was to cease to be hereditary.[47] Prior to the executive order with regard to pawns, the practice of pawning was hereditary. This meant that the practice where children became pawns by virtue of the death of their pawned parents had to cease. Eventually, the act of passing on pawning from one generation to another would then cease.

In spite of the attempts by the colonial government to end pawning, it persisted throughout the Gold Coast colony until the late 1930s. This is made evident by the reports of the Committee of Experts on Slavery in 1939 that found people who were given as security for a loan as late as 1939.[48]

CONCLUSION

This chapter has demonstrated that pawning was one of the institutions by which women and girls were dominated by men through entrenched cultural norms in the immediate period after abolition of domestic slavery in the Gold Coast and into the twentieth century. It demonstrated that sexual abuse of women had intensified with the dependence on pawning as the main source of credit in the area with examples of cases reported to the colonial courts. It showed that boys went to school while girls helped to cater to the needs of younger ones and managed the home due to patriarchal values in the nineteenth and twentieth century. It highlighted that men in this period married to gain the labor of their wives on their farms or for sexual reasons. These desires were sometimes against the wish of the women involved since most marriages were contracted out of convenience by the families involved. Marriage was either to pay a debt or obtain a loan for the girl's family. Furthermore, customary marriage encouraged promiscuity among the people. In addition, the acts of pawning, traditional marriage, and patriarchy in nineteenth and twentieth-century Ghana were a challenge to the Basel Missionary and went contrary to the Christian doctrine. In summary, the act of pawning had become so worrisome that the colonial government sought diverse means to put an end to it in the twentieth century.

NOTES

1. Aryeetey Bortei-Doku, "The Participation of Women in the Economy," in *Economic Reforms in Ghana: The miracle and the Mirage,* ed. E. Ayeetey, Harringan and M. Nissanke (Accra, Ghana: Woeli Publishing, 2000), 331; see also, Jette Bukh, *The Village Woman in Ghana* (Copenhagen: Centre for Development Research, 1979), 52, 54.

2. Kwabena O. Akurang-Parry, "Transformations in the Ferminization of Unfree Domestic Labour: A Study of "Abaawa" or Prepubescent Female Servitude in Modern Ghana," *International Labor and Working-Class History,* no. 78 (Fall 2010): 28–30, http://www.jstor.org/stable/40931302; see also, Beverly Grier, "Pawns, Porters and Petty Traders: Women in the Transition to cash crop Agriculture in Colonial Ghana," in *Pawnship in Africa: Debt Bondage in Historical Perspective,* ed. Toyin Falola and Paul E. Lovejoy (Boulder, CO: Westview Press, 1994), 161–189.

3. For further definitions of pawnship, see for example, Justin Willis, "Debt Bondage," review of *Pawnship in Africa: Debt Bondage in Historical Perspective,* by Toyin Falola and Paul E. Lovejoy, ed., *The Journal of African History* 36, no. 2 (1995): 323–324; see also, Akosua Perbi, *A History of Indigenous Slavery in Ghana: From the 15th to the 19th Century* (Legon: Sub-Saharan Publishers, 2004), 49;

Idem, "Slavery in Africa and its Global Effects," paper presented at the International Conference of the UCIP/UCAP, Accra, June 19, 2005), 7.

4. PRAAD, Accra, SCT5/4/16, Reported case of assault to the Judicial Court, Record Book vol. 26 dated May 5, 1875–September 29, 1875, 44–48 (Hereafter SCT5/4/16, 1875). See also, PRAAD, Accra, SCT 5/4/14, and PRAAD, Accra, SCT5/4/15.

5. SCT5/4/16, 1875.

6. PRAAD, Kumasi, ARG1/2/30/1/2, Chief Commissioner of Ashanti's letter to the Colonial Secretary dated May 20, 1908 (Hereafter ARG1/2/30/1/2, 1908).

7. SCT5/4/16, 1875.

8. For studies on the early colonial labour problem in West Africa, see for example, A.G. Hopkins, *An Economic History of West Africa* (Cambridge: Cambridge University Press, 1973), 222.

9. SCT5/4/16, 1875.

10. SCT5/4/16, 1875.

11. SCT5/4/16, 1875.

12. For further information on sexual abuse of women and girls, see Kofi E. Boakye, "Culture and Nondisclosure of Child Sexual Abuse in Ghana: A Theoretical and Empirical Exploration," *Law & Social Inquiry* 34, no. 4 (Fall 2009): 951–952, https://www.jstor.org/stable/40539387; see also, Tijani I. A. Oseni, Osagie E. Lawani and AderemiI. Oyedeji, "A Case Study of Sexual Abuse of a Minor," *African Journal of Reproductive Health* 20, no. 1 (March 2016): 109.

13. SCT5/4/15.

14. SCT5/4/15.

15. SCT5/4/15.

16. PRAAD, Accra, ADM. 11/ 1/ 1094, Paul Jenkins, The report of Friedrich Ramseyer to Inspector Pratorious, no. 9 dated November 16, 1882 (Hereafter ADM. 11/ 1/ 1094). This is a voluminous file on Basel Mission correspondence in the Gold Coast which was written in German but translated to English.

17. ADM. 11/ 1/ 1094, Report on new convert's education in Fankyeneko and Anyinam dated 1881.

18. For studies on low attendance of school by girls compared to boys in Ghana, see Lebo Moletsane and Takyiwa Manuh, "Ghana: Girls don't quit school by choice," *Agenda: Empowering Women for Gender Equity*, no. 41 (1999): 86–88, https://www.jstor.org/stable/i385815.

19. ADM. 11/ 1/ 1094, Sitzler's report on the West Akyem Mission area on marriage problems, no.108 dated July 1, 1890.

20. Grier, "Pawns, Porters and Petty Traders," 166.

21. Free born people in the Akan society referred to royals or people who had neither been enslaved or in any form of bondage.

22. Grier, "Pawns, Porters and Petty Traders," 167.

23. Grier, "Pawns, Porters and Petty Traders," 167.

24. Head-money is a token of money offered by a husband to be to a woman's lineage in order to contract a marriage between his family and a woman's lineage before the woman is allowed to move in to live with the man. Marriage among the

Akan was a union between the families of the couples involved and not just the couples.

25. ARG1/2/30/1/2, 1908.

26. For studies on female pawns working on cocoa farms in Ghana after the abolition of domestic slavery up to 1950, see for example, Gareth Austin, "Human Pawning in Asante, 1800-1950: Markets and Coercion, Gender and Cocoa," in *Pawnship in Africa: Debt Bondage in Historical Perspective*, ed. Toyin Falola and Paul E. Lovejoy (Boulder, CO: Westview Press, 1994): 122–123.

27. Austin, "Human Pawning in Asante," 173.

28. Gareth Austin and Ugochukwu Uche, "Collusion and Competition in Colonial Economies: Banking in British West Africa 1916-1960," *Business History Review* 81(Spring 2007): 1–26, https://www.jstor.org/stable/25097296; see also, Marika Sherwood, "Elder Dempster and West Africa, 1891- 1940: The Genesis of Underdevelopment?," *The International Journal of African Historical Studies* 30, no. 2 (1997): 258, https://www.jstor.org/stable/221228.

29. PRAAD, Accra, ADM 11/975, Memorandum on the vestiges of slavery in the Gold Coast by J. C. de Graft Johnson in Accra dated October 1927, 19; Also available in Austin, "Human Pawning in Asante," 139.

30. For further information on polygyny in Ghana, see for example, Roger Klomegah, "Socio-Economic Characteristics of Ghanaian Women in Polygynous Marriages," *Journal of Comparative Family Studies* 28, no. 1 (Spring 1997): 73–74, https://www.jstor.org/stable/41603480; see also, Kofi Abrefa Busia, "Some Aspects of the Relation of Social Conditions of Human fertility," in *Culture and Human Fertility: A Study of the Relation of Cultural Conditions to Fertility in Non-Industrial and Transitional Societies*, ed. Frank Lorimer et al. (Paris: UNESCO, 1954), 346.

31. ADM. 11/1/1094, Akyem Abuakwa, 1888–1914.

32. ADM. 11/1/1094, Akyem Abuakwa, 1888–1915, 33.

33. ADM. 11/1/1094, Akyem Abuakwa, 1888–1915, 33.

34. ARG 1/2/30/1/2, Executive Instructions.

35. SCT5/4/16, 1875.

36. ARG 1/2/30/1/2, Executive Instructions.

37. ARG 1/2/30/1/2, Executive Instructions.

38. ARG 1/2/30/1/2, Executive Instructions.

39. Head-money was the fee paid to the family of a female who was given in marriage under customary law.

40. ARG 1/2/30/1/2, Executive Instructions.

41. ARG 1/2/30/1/2, Executive Instructions.

42. ARG 1/2/30/1/2, Minutes by His Excellency the Governor dated December 12, 1905. The governor's minutes is in accordance with proposals to end pawning before the introduction of the executive instructions with regard to pawns and slaves in Ashanti in 1907. These instructions were applicable to both the Ashanti and the whole of the Gold Coast.

43. ARG 1/2/30/1/2, Minutes.

44. ARG 1/2/30/1/2, Executive Instructions.

45. ARG 1/2/30/1/2, Executive Instructions.

46. ARG 1/2/30/1/2, Executive Instructions.
47. ARG1/2/30/1/2, Domestic Slavery.
48. CSO21/17/2.

BIBLIOGRAPHY

Akurang-Parry, Kwabena O. "Transformations in the Feminization of Unfree Domestic Labour: A Study of "Abaawa" or Prepubescent Female Servitude in Modern Ghana." *International Labor and Working-Class History*, no. 78 (Fall 2010): 28–47. http://www.jstor.org/stable/40931302.

Austin, Gareth and Ugochukwu, Uche. "Collusion and Competition in Colonial Economies: Banking in British West Africa, 1916-1960." *Business History Review* 81 (Spring 2007): 1–26. https://www.jstor.org/stable/25097296.

Boakye, Kofi E. "Culture and Nondisclosure of Child Sexual Abuse in Ghana: A Theoretical and Empirical Exploration." *Law and Social Inquiry* 34, no. 4 (Fall 2009): 951–979. https://www.jstor.org/stable/40539387.

Bortei-Doku, Aryeetey. "The Participation of Women in the Economy." In *Economic Reforms in Ghana: The Miracle and the Mirage*, edited by Ernest Aryeetey et al., 331. Accra: Woeli Publishing, 2000.

Bukh, Jette. *The Village Woman in Ghana*, 1. Copenhagen: Center for Development Research, 1979.

Busia, Kofi A. "Some Aspects of the Relation of Social Conditions of Human Fertility." In *Culture and Human Fertility: A Study of the Relation of Cultural Conditions to Fertility in Non-Industrial and Transitional Societies*, edited by Frank Lorimer et al, 341–348. Place de Fontenoy, Paris: UNESCO, 1954.

Grier, Beverley. "Pawns, Porters and Petty Traders: Women in the Transition to Crop Agriculture in Colonial Ghana." In *Pawnship in Africa: Debt Bondage in Historical Perspective*, edited by Toyin Falola and Paul E. Loveoy, 161–189. Boulder, CO: Westview Press, 1994.

Hopkins, Antony G. *An Economic History of West Africa*. Cambridge: Cambridge University, 1973.

Klomegah, Roger. "Socio- Economic Characteristics of Ghanaian Women in Polygynous Marriages." *Journal of Comparative Family Studies* 28, no. 1 (Spring 1997): 73–88. https://www.jstor.org/stable/41603480.

Moletsane, Lebo and Takyiwaa Manuh. "Ghana: Girls Don't Quit School by Choice." *Agenda: Empowering Women for Gender Equity*, no. 41 (1999): 86–91. https://www.jstor.org/stable/i385815.

Oseni, Tijani I. A., E. Osagie Lawani and Aderemi I. Oyedeji. "A Case Study of Sexual Abuse of a Minor." *African Journal of Reproductive Health* 20, no. 1 (March 2016): 109–113.

Perbi, Akosua. *A History of Indigenous Slavery in Ghana: From the 15th Century to the 19th Century*. Accra: Sub-Saharan Publishers, 2004.

———. "Slavery in Africa and its Global Effects." Paper presented at the International Conference of the UCIP/UCAP. Accra: GIMPA, June 19, 2005, 7.

Sherwood, Marika. "Elder Dempster and West Africa, 1891- 1940: The Genesis of Underdevelopment?" *The International Journal of African Historical Studies* 30, no. 2 (1997): 253–276. https://www.jstor.org/stable/221228.

Willis, Justin. "Debt Bondage." In *Review of Pawnship in Africa: Debt Bondage in Historical Perspective*, edited by Toyin Falola and Paul E. Lovejoy, 323–324. *The Journal of African History* 36, no. 1 (1995).

Chapter 8

Patriarchy, Gender Inequality, and Housework in Sefi Atta's *Everything Good Will Come*

Joyce Agofure

Throughout most of history, women have been held down by the iron fist of gender power structures and configurations which have spread gender inequality into every sphere of the society. In this regard, Lilia Monzo states that:

> Women live everyday with the mortifying knowledge that their lives are not their own, often feeling powerless to break free. This humiliating existence often feels as if women have spent an eternity held by the throat, unable to breathe. For many women this chokehold is not a mere metaphor depicting their pain and humiliation but an actual terrifying threat that defines their everyday reality.[1]

Consequently, in addition to patriarchal chauvinism and gender inequality, the fundamental question of "housework" and the concept of "unpaid work" explain and foreground the ways in which women are oppressed through systems of gender roles, capitalism, private property, and traditional gender ideals. In view of this, "countless efforts by feminists to tackle and address gender gaps, identify women's unpaid housework as "work" thereby rendering it visible"[2] has become vital.

In recent times, the issue of housework has become a valid subject to recognize gender imbalance, as noticeable in Sefi Atta's selected novel,

> to recognize women's activities at home as "work," to show that, not being present in public life and in the labor market was not women's individual choice, to show the meaning of women's reproductive labor for economy and to reveal the material basis of women's oppression.[3]

The pivotal concern of this chapter is to shed light on the construction of gender practices, subjugation in patriarchal social relations, and how women's unpaid house work shapes their self-status, self-perception, and consciousness.

The expression "patriarchy" literally means the rule of the father or the patriarch. It is used to describe a specific type of male-dominated family, of a large household which includes women, younger men, children, and domestic servants all under the rule of a dominant male. Conversely, "gender" is the personal feature and social position that members of a society attach to being male or female. It stresses culturally conceived and learned principles about appropriate appearance, conduct, mental, and emotional characteristics for male and female. Patriarchy and gender-labeling breed discrimination, domination, inequality, and their corollaries give absolute priority to men and a secondary status to women. In this regard, Sefi Atta's *Everything Good will Come* examines the struggles women face in a patriarchal conservative Nigerian society.

The novel centers around the gender stratification which burdens the protagonist Enitan, starting from her childhood into her adult life, and her experiences of growing up with her father, a lawyer and her mother, a typical homemaker, who spends most of her time in a "white garment" church after the loss of her son. It also follows the events that trails Enitan's best friend, Sheri. For the most part, the novel explicates the diverse ways the lives of married women are confined by prejudice, social oppression, and a disproportionate share of family responsibilities in terms of household work. The text demonstrates the extent to which society treats the subordination of women as a "natural" condition of existence even as women's lives are deformed by domestic violence at the hands of their husbands. The choice of Marxist feminist theory underpins how gender differences and capitalism aids the family to suppress the female in relation to unpaid housework. The value of the unpaid labor women perform within the family sustains the current work force and nurtures the next generation, yet it comes at no cost in a gender-stereotyped production space/system.

MARXIST FEMINISM: A THEORETICAL DISCOURSE

Before delineating the concept of Marxist feminism, it is crucial to explain the terms "Marxism" and "feminism." Marxism deals with

> a form of inequality that arises from the class dynamics of capitalism.[4] It understands class inequality as the primary axis of oppression in capitalist societies. Feminism deals with the inequality between the sexes and recognizes gender inequality as the primary axis of oppression in patriarchal societies.[5]

This keeps women in the domestic sphere and men in the administrative center. Thus, Marxist feminism is an intersection of Marxism and feminism. Although, Marxism and feminism differ in terms of their focal concern with different forms of oppression—gender relations and class relations in all sorts of ways—understanding and converging reciprocal effects between gender and class is at the heart of Marxist feminism. Consequently, Marxist feminists align themselves with the theories and economic philosophies of Karl Marx. Marxist feminists focus on investigating and explaining the ways in which women are oppressed through systems of capitalism and private property. It examines "forms of systematic inequalities that lead to the experiences of oppression for marginalized individuals."[6] For Nancy Holmstrom, "Marxist feminism is an emancipatory, critical framework that aims at understanding and explaining gender oppression in a systematic way. It provides an account of how social arrangements of patterned disparity can be internally rational yet unjust."[7] Thus, Erik Olin Wright expresses that Marxist feminists capture the following assumptions:

(1) Women are systematically harmed in many ways by the gender relations within which they live, and thus, those relations can be described as oppressive.
(2) They establish that these relations are not alterably given by biology but are society or culturally constructed.
(3) They analyze various social, economic, and cultural processes in contemporary societies which undermine or reproduce existing forms of gender oppression and thus create the context for transformative struggles through the agency of women.[8]

Marxist feminism maintains that economic inequality, dependence, and unhealthy social relations between men and women are the root of women's domination in the current social context. Marxist feminists point out that in capitalist economies, reproductive labor is usually considered to be exclusively women's labor. This creates a system in which women's labor is separated from men's labor and is less valuable because it does not earn monetary compensation.

Supporters of this theory believe that because women's labor are devalued, women as a group are devalued and oppressed. In view of this, Marxist feminism helps to illuminate how institutions of family are related to capitalism and how women's works are trivialized and not considered as "real work." In other words,

in a capitalist society, house work does not produce exchange-value although, it does produce pre-capitalist use-value hence, it is not viewed as 'real' work i.e.

socially necessary labor. Thus, the observation that wives and mothers usually love the people for whom they work does not mean that cooking, cleaning and childcare are not productive work.[9]

To expatiate further, Fredrick Engels in *The Origin of the Family, Private Property, and the State* writes about how matrilineal societies were violently replaced by patriarchal societies; individual wealth and private property became key. Engels avers that "in societies based chiefly on hunting and gathering, where all members of the tribes worked, and all property was owned communally, women did not have second-class status. The subordination of women arose alongside the development of distinct social classes based on private property."[10] The supposition from this is that male supremacy in varying forms have characterized all known civilizations; it is not the product of hard-wired biological distinctions between sexes but rather a historically determined phenomenon. Though, women's unique capacity for child bearing and nursing gave rise to a natural division of labor along sex lines in primitive society, this distinction did not automatically translate into lesser status. It was only with the advent of class society that women gradually became relegated to the household. The subjugation of women under the capitalist-free market is

rooted in their central role in the family as unpaid provider of the domestic services necessary for the maintenance of society. These functions include primary responsibility for food, clothing, and cleaning for the care of the very young, aged and meeting of emotional and psychological needs of all members of the household.[11]

It is palpable therefore that the female gendered role is a social creation. Accordingly, Ferguson and Hennessey argue that

gender oppression is closely related to class oppression, and the relationship between men and women in society is like the relations between the proletariat and the bourgeoisies. Thus, women's subordination is a function of class oppression, maintained like racism because it serves the interests of capital and the ruling class. It divides men against women, privileges working class men relatively within the capitalist system to secure their support and legitimate the capitalist's class refusal to pay for the domestic labor assigned, unpaid to women.[12]

They, therefore, emphasize that women be loyal to the patriarchal order. However, male dominance still prevails as a legacy of the capitalistic, gendered division of labor, traditional roles of female and masculine implications that have consistently placed women at the second-class status. On this account, women are often assigned to the domestic sphere where the labor is inexpensive, exploited, and uncompensated in supporting the workforce. Amazingly, amidst the daily onslaught of untold injustices, exploitation, free domestic labor, social restrictions that serve to control women, there remains societal expectation that women play the "happy wife."

Furthermore, in the "nuclear family—the power dynamic dictates that domestic work is exclusively to be completed by the woman of the household."[13] Little wonder, Marxist feminists maintain that the exclusion of women from productive labor leads to male control in the public and private domains. Therefore, the goal of the Marxist feminist framework is to liberate women by transforming the conditions of their oppression and exploitation.[14] By deploying Marxist feminist theory on Sefi Atta's *Everything Good will Come* sheds light on the condition of women and the question of unpaid house work in a male-centered society. Women as sources of unpaid domestic labor create avenue for capitalists and their cohorts to make more profits. In view of this, *Everything Good will Come* shows how women continually provide free labor in the home and end up being exploited by their husbands and their husbands' relations thereby making women second-class citizens.

In essence, the representations of housewives in docile roles across the home and public spheres reaffirm that patriarchy as a system of power and control is firmly connected to capitalist economic modes where women's labors are most often expropriated. The gender disclosure of patriarchy, as male supremacy, provides the sexual hierarchical ordering of society and control, while capitalism as an economic class driven by profit feeds off the patriarchal ordering of domination and suppression of women. This is because, women often get suppressed through physical, financial, psychological, and sexual abuse, not just in Nigeria but all over the globe, there by compromising women advancement and human rights.

WOMEN AND HOUSEWORK IN SEFI ATTA'S *EVERYTHING GOOD WILL COME*

The gender stereotyping of women in Sefi Atta's text brings to fore the predicament of women in a male breadwinner and female homemaker family structure. Women face discrimination in both private and public arenas. This is obvious in the home environment of the text where characters such as Enitan's mum, Sheri, and Sheri's stepmums who as stay-at-home wives were incessantly at the beck and call of their breadwinner husbands who shuttle them back and forth given that the women were economically dependent on them. These men's attitude illuminates "Marxist feminist perspectives that women's sex class as well as economic class plays a role in women's oppression."[15] For instance, Enitan's father, a lawyer, coerces and compels Enitan's mum, a full-time housewife, into having a son in a bid to have an heir apparent who turns out to have poor health. Shei experiences physical and psychological trauma till the child dies. By this, Sefi Atta addresses the concern of gender discrimination, birth control, and the view that "motherhood is an alienating experience for women especially when exclusively . . . men decide the policies and laws that regulate women's reproductive choices . . . to bear as many children as possible."[16] The novel reveals that elite men are dominant over women of lower social classes. Hence, the demands to be a perfect mother, wife, child nurturer, and caregiver without a husband's assistance drives Enitan's mum to misery as she collapses into church extremism as a means of escape from her many disillusions. Not long after, she degenerates into resentment, alienation, and death.

Sheri also recounts the sundry events and occurrences that stared her stepmothers and children in the face when her father died. She recounts the grief "when my father died who remembered me? We didn't even know where our next meal would be coming from and no one cared. Not even my uncle who took all his money."[17] The excerpt portrays how men's control of property alters the family form into a gendered and patriarchal one where the woman becomes a property of the husband, father, or uncle. Patriarchal ideology which merely views women as wives and mothers rather than as workers, disinherit women, renders them property-less and perpetrates male dominance. This upholds Marxist feminist tenet which says, "[W]omen are systematically harmed in many ways by the gender relations within which they live thus, those relations can be described as oppressive."[18] Since women are solely into housework and child rearing, they tend to depend on their husband's wealth. Along these lines, to surmount the challenge of motherhood, livelihood, inequality, and women's rights in the home/workplace, the novel explains that Bakare's wives started a business in their home to fend for themselves. The narrator puts it thus: "The Bakare's started their catering business . . . it wasn't difficult a transition for them. Their house in Victoria Island was spacious and part of their backyard was conveniently cemented."[19] However, Sheri laments the outcome of the situation:

> I'm not even sure we can continue the business. My uncle comes to the house complaining that we are misusing his property. He wants to take the house from us, I'm sure. He can't do that! Why not? She said. He took everything else under native law as my father's rightful heir. Why should the house be different?[20]

The above excerpt substantiates the extent to which Sheri's uncle marginalizes the women and would not allow them to have freehand or economic independence. Such mindset produces continuous insecurity, exploitation and keeps the women bound to the home, thereby validating feminist analysis of patriarchy intermixed with Marxist's analysis of capitalism perpetuated by male chauvinism against women self-sufficiency.

Other instances of unpaid housework alongside male supremacy and male violence in the home are brought to light in Sheri's relationship with her different husbands. In Sheri's first marriage, a vivid scene of how she over-worked and enslaved herself to the point of becoming "a kitchen martyr and . . . forgett[ing] how to flaunt her mind"[21] is portrayed. Furthermore, the narrator explains Sheri's dilemma in her second marriage:

> I saw how she limited her involvement in the family business to please her brigadier. She tidied . . . she dusted with cleaning rags, sometimes with her fingers . . . . The rest of her time she spent preparing for Brigadier Hassan: her hair, her nails dabbing perfumes and cooking meals.[22]

Throughout the novel, *Everything Good will Come*, Sefi demonstrates how Sheri's husbands at diverse instances made her stay-at-home condition horrible with series of violence and beatings even after "personally servicing" them not just with house care but with emotional comfort. Therefore, making her to be insecure, economically exploited, and socially repressed. In view of this, the novel of study sustains the Marxist feminist stance that "various social, economic, and cultural processes in contemporary societies which undermine or reproduce existing forms of gender oppression . . . create the context for transformative struggles through the agency of women."[23] Also, the novel turns attention to the habitual work which women do in the domestic sphere and which men naturally do not do. By explicating these concerns, the author suggests that women must break out from their subservient positions to be liberated.

Subsequently, Enitan recognizes that her mother was never remunerated or compensated for all her housework commitment to support her father. After pondering all that her mother perseveres while with her father, Enitan supports her mother's decision to take possession of her husband's property as she states "if my mother took a house, two houses . . . , she deserved them. The power had always been in my father's hands."[24] Afterwards, Enitan compels her father to transfer the documents of one of his houses as compensation to her mother. Nonetheless, this intent was addressed with so much negligence by Enitan's father.

To overcome the domineering patriarchal system, the writer, Sefi Atta, just like many Marxist feminists have confidence that women can gain consciousness of themselves as a class of workers by insisting that women's domestic/house work be recognized as real work. This must be remunerated or compensated for women to achieve full liberation and parity with men in their home environment. As well, the novel captures Sheri employing the services of Enitan's father, a renowned legal representative to challenge in a court of law her uncle's dispossession of the family's inheritance and business venture. It is therefore apparent that patriarchy and gender inequality in all ramifications outlines the institutionalized system of male dominance which allows inequality and reinforces the material base among men which enable them gain power and dominance to control women.

CONCLUSION

This study evaluates Sefi Atta's *Everything Good will Come* by raising deep-seated concerns regarding patriarchal and gender differences undervaluing women's housework, intimidating women into stay-at-home wives, and depriving women of monetary compensation for domestic work in the family. Sefi Atta's novel highlights the extent to which gender domination and oppression marks and mars women's lives from the cradle to the grave. These fundamental formations by male bias and prejudice stifle women's economic independence; hence, the necessity and clamor for house cleaning, meal preparation, and childcare to be adequately paid for. This would go a long way to expedite the eradication of dependency, poverty, exploitation, and male supremacy over the woman. The novel suggests and calls for the incorporation of women, on feminist terms, into all corporate structures. It demands for gender equality, access to family resources, and the dire need to liberate women from the overwhelming dependence on men in contrast to the downgrading of women under dominant power structures in postcolonial societies. Taken together, Marxist feminism is a productive tool which draws attention to the gender contradictions piloting women's suppression and second-class status in the home and other domains till date.

NOTES

1. Lilia Monzo, "Women and Revolution: Marx and the Dialectic," *Knowledge Cultures* 4, no. 6 (2016): 97.
2. Gilman Acrar-Savran, *Body Labor History: For a Dialectical Feminism* (Istanbul: Kanat Press, 2003), 34.
3. Susan Himmelveit, "The Discovery of Unpaid Work: The Social Consequences of the Expansion of Work," in *Inside the Household: From Labor to Care*, ed. Susan Himmelveit (London: Macmillan, 2000), 102.
4. Sheivari Rahi, "Marxist Feminism," in *Encyclopedia of Critical Psychology*, ed. Teo Thomas (New York, NY: Springer, 2014), 34.

5. Sheivari, "Marxist Feminism," 42.

6. Barbara Ehrenreich, "What is Socialist Feminism?" in *A Reader in Class, Difference and Women's Lives*, eds. Rosemary Hennessey and Chrys Ingraham (London: Routledge, 1976), 65.

7. Nancy Holmstrom, *The Socialist Feminist Project: A Contemporary Reader in Theory and Politics* (New York, NY: Monthly Review Press, 2002), 54.

8. Erik Olin Wright, *Interrogating Inequality: Class Analysis, Socialism and Marxism* (London: Biddles, 1994), 7.

9. Margaret Benston, "The Political Economy of Women's Liberation," *Monthly Review* 41, no. 7 (1989): 31.

10. Fredrick Engels, *The Origin of the Family, Private Property, and the State* (London: Penguin Classics, 2010), 550.

11. Ann Ferguson and Rosemary Hennessey, "Feminist Perspectives on Class and Work," in *Stanford Encyclopedia of Philosophy* (London: Routledge, 2010), 65.

12. Ferguson and Hennessey, "Feminist Perspectives," 68.

13. Carole Mccann and Kim Seung-Kyung, *Feminist Theory Reader* (London: Routledge, 2013), 34.

14. Rahi, "Marxist Feminism," 48.

15. Rosemarie Tong, *Feminist Thought: A More Comprehensive Introduction* (Charlotte, NC: Westview Press, 2014), 97–98.

16. Tong, *Feminist Thought*,110.

17. Sefi Atta, *Everything Good will Come* (Lagos: Farafina, 2005), 104.

18. Wright, Interrogating Inequality, 7.

19. Atta, *Everything Good*, 135.

20. Ibid., 138.

21. Ibid., 106–107.

22. Ibid., *Everything Good*, 157.

23. Wright, *Interrogating Inequality*, 7.

24. Atta, *Everything Good*, 153.

BIBLIOGRAPHY

Acar-Savran, Gilman. *Body Labor History: For a Dialectical Feminism*. Istanbul: Kanat Press, 2003.

Atta, Sefi. *Everything Good will Come*. Lagos: Farafina, 2005.

Benston, Margaret. "The Political Economy of Women's Liberation," *Monthly Review* 41, no. 7 (Dec. 1989): 31–45.

Ehrenreich, Barbara. "What is Socialist Feminism?" In *A Reader in Class, Difference and Women's Lives*, edited by Rosemary Hennessey and Chrys Ingraham. London: Routledge, 1976.

Engels, Fredrick. *The Origin of the Family, Private Property and the State*. London: Penguin Classics, 2010.

Ferguson, Ann and Rosemary Hennessey. "Feminist Perspectives on Class and Work." In *Stanford Encyclopedia of Philosophy*. London: Routledge, 2010.

Hennessey, Rosemary. *Materialist Feminism: A Reader in Class, Difference, and Women's Lives*. London: Routledge, 1997.

Himmelveit, Susan. "The Discovery of Unpaid Work: The Social Consequences of the Expansion of Work." In *Inside the Household: From Labor to Care,* edited by Susan Himmelveit. London: Macmillan, 2000.

Holmstrom, Nancy. *The Socialist Feminist Project: A Contemporary Reader in Theory and Politics*. New York, NY: Monthly Review Press, 2002.

Mccann, Carole and Kim Seung-Kyung. *Feminist Theory Reader*. London: Routledge, 2013.

Monzo, Lilia. "Women and Revolution: Marx and the Dialectic." *Knowledge Cultures* 4, no. 6 (2016): 97.

Sheivari, Rahi. "Marxist Feminism." In *Encyclopedia of Critical Psychology,* edited by Teo Thomas, 34–48. New York, NY: Springer, 2014.

Tong, Rosemarie. *Feminist Thought: A More Comprehensive Introduction*. Charlotte, NC: Westview Press, 2014.

Wright, Erik Olin. *Interrogating Inequality: Class Analysis, Socialism and Marxism*. London: Biddles, 1994.

Chapter 9

Women as Composers in Nollywood

Evidence of Absence or Absence of Evidence?

Emaeyak Peter Sylvanus

Nollywood is Nigeria's unique and globally recognized film industry with productions that date back to 1992. The early 1990s thus signaled the birth of a creative and cultural industry that "metamorphosed from the existing traditions of dramatic presentations in festivals and rituals, the traveling theatre, television drama, and so on."[1] In nearly three decades (1992–2020), the scholarship on Nollywood has intensified and resulted in several publications on different aspects of the industry and its cinematic productions.[2] However, the literature on women in Nollywood limits women's activities to a descriptive and/or representative form—neither nuancing their status and unique contributions beyond the cinematic gaze, nor how the society's construction of gender roles impacts such women's behavior.[3] This observation has, in addition to the sustained roles of such women film directors, producers, and writers as Emem Isong-Misodi, Uche Jombo, and Mary Njoku, motivated film scholars like Oghomwen Edward of the University of Salford to prioritize the upper end of the industry's hierarchy in her ongoing doctoral research.

The focus on gendered power and how it structures Nollywood is critical to understanding "the power dynamics that framed and continue to frame both women's impact in media and their presence in the historical record."[4] Broadly, the debate on underrepresentation of women in music is not new, and many scholars within mainstream musicology/ethnomusicology have made this argument.[5] Susan McClary's *Feminine Endings* notably inspired criticisms and polarized opinions.[6] However, the backlash from other writers have failed to prevent renewed interests in feminist issues in both popular culture and literature.[7] While such renewed interests are laudable, I argue that they have not gone far enough, especially given the apparent decline in the scholarship devoted to women's music in the creative and cultural industries. So, this text encourages queries about whether or not, for example, there should be different selection requirements and standards for women composers and their works in the creative and cultural industries. Specifically, my study is a unique departure in focus as it examines how questions of gender and gendered politics have shaped film music and its practice in Nollywood. It is the first to focus on the contributions of women in Nollywood film music. Here, I address three questions: the degree to which the Nollywood film music industry is regulated by gender; whether or not men and women occupy distinct roles and how these, if at all, have changed in nearly three decades; and the implications of this study on the broader cultural, historical, and analytical debates around gender in Nollywood Studies.

To answer these and other related questions, this text relies on a range of sources such as film credits, oral histories, practitioners' (personal and professional) notes, relevant literature, and the transcripts of interviews with such established composers as Stanley Okorie, Shadrach John, Chimere Emejuobi, and Austin Erowele. To be clear, data from a few of these sources have been difficult to assemble because, until recently, music was not the focus of the scholarship in Nollywood. The dearth of documentation is further intensified by the absence of an archiving tradition and archival sources. Another obstacle in the search for evidence of women composers is the absence of a guild of composers, which critically diminishes a Nollywood composer's influence and social identity.[8] Together, these challenges forced me to look diagonally for evidence, including interviewing and focusing on the role of Chimere Emejuobi (figure 9.1), who is fondly referred to as the "Queen of Nollywood soundtrack." Overall, the current study represents a provisional yet long overdue starting point on women as film music composers in Nigerian cinema.

As an outline, the first half of this essay presents an overview of the Nollywood film music industry—citing, among other things, its structure, the eras of the practice, the unique attributes of those eras, as well as who the composers were, their gender, agenda, and defining roles. The second half of the essay is a case study of Chimere Emejuobi who is the only surviving woman composer in Nollywood. According to Emejuobi:

> I am retiring [from the practice] in search of greener pastures. I have tried as the last woman standing. I have spent nearly twenty years since 1997 when I joined Nollywood. I have now decided to move to Washington DC, USA next year [2017]. (Emejuobi, excerpt from interview recorded on October 23, 2016)

Emejuobi's retirement is instructive because it leaves the Nollywood film music industry without an established woman composer. The gender vacuum occasioned by her exit requires that we scrutinize the value and role of women composers in Nollywood.

Figure 9.1   Chimere Emejuobi. Photo credit: Author. Used with permission.

AN OVERVIEW OF THE NOLLYWOOD
FILM MUSIC INDUSTRY

This section broadly references two of my earliest works on Nollywood film music studies in which I analyzed the industry's structure and proposed three eras of the creative and business practice. Both structurally and hierarchically, the Nollywood film music industry is rather linear, less complex, and involves very few persons. The head of this hierarchy is always the executive producer/marketer (EPM). Although there is a film director, the next important person to the EPM, in context of the soundtrack, is the film composer. In other words, the film director has no responsibility in the film music process. The redundancy of the film director is unique to mainstream Nollywood because it is not guided by the Euro–American auteur-driven model, which suggests that "the unity of a film—its totality of decisions [including music]—must be rooted in the director's agency."[9] So, whereas the EPM and composer occupy a privileged position, the sound editor, singers, and other audio studio personnel make-up the lowest tier of this hierarchy. The need to foreground structure and hierarchy subsists in what it reveals later about the gender dynamics/roles and value of women in the Nigerian film music industry.

As already suggested, three periods of the Nollywood film music indus-
try/practice emerged from an earlier study. These include the Mimetic
(1992–1996), Pragmatic-expressive (1997–2009), and Opaque (2010 to date)
eras. In the current text, these periods offer the background for delineating
and nuancing the entries and exits of composers, as well as the attributes and
classifications of their works within Nollywood. Specifically, the Nollywood
Mimetic era was characterized by an overwhelming reliance on preexisting
European and American art and popular music. The feature films of this era
emphasized much dialogue and drama, and thus frustrated the potential for
unique film music aesthetics (e.g., *Devil's Money* [1994]). Within the practice, the composers of the Mimetic era were entirely men such as Sammie
Okposo, Abbe Eso, Mike Nliam, and Stanley Okorie. Save Stanley Okorie,
every other composer before him has either retired from the industry or tran-
sitioned onto another role.[10] Broadly, these men ran the film music industry in
a manner that arguably foreclosed women composers. Enter Stanley Okorie:

> The general understanding was that acting was the main attraction for most
> women; it was their aspiration. You have to also know that you needed to be
> a gifted songwriter to be entrusted with a soundtrack job in those days. Some
> of the women like Thelma O'kahz had very good [singing] voices; but most of
> us [composers] and the marketers [EPM] in particular were not convinced that
> they [the women] could do well as soundtrack producers. So, I personally got
> her [Thelma] to take up the role of a singer in a few of the soundtracks that I
> composed.

Okorie's comment highlights the earliest subtle signs of gender prejudice
within the film music industry. I say so because the business of Nollywood
film music has been (and continues to be) conducted within a noninstitution-
alized vertical integration wherein there are no barriers to entry or exit. It
has, essentially, remained a single-artist endeavor and an all-comers affair
regardless of gender.

Moving on, the Nollywood Pragmatic-expressive era was a period of
intense critical engagements with the potentials of/for a localized film music
tradition. It ended the preceding era's limited use of music in both the opening and closing credits of a film. Through the art of prefiguring (i.e., the use
of music to predict dialogue and scenes), Nollywood soundtracks acquired a
new (cultural) meaning and value for all parties, including filmmakers, composers, and the local audience.[11] Consequently, the feature films of this era
contained more songs and demonstrated a deliberate effort to further establish
the industry's unique film music identity in comparison to, say, Hollywood
and/or Bollywood (e.g., *Karishika* [1998], *Endtime* [1999], and *The Master*
[2005]). From viewers' perspectives, there was a functional relationship

between the background music and the narrative, arguably because they could watch a Nollywood film as much with the ears as with the eyes. In other words, the soundtrack was (and still is) an artistic tool for "singing the film."[12] This second era underpinned the evolution of a creative process with a strong desire for collaboration, contracting, and general restrategizing. The forces of individualism, originality, and competition suddenly became activated, and these developments ushered in a style of sound–visual synergy that would define Nollywood soundtracks for succeeding decades.[13] As part of a process to mark the departure from the relentless and monotonous use of preexisting music in the Mimetic era, Nollywood soundtracks quickly became something of a song-text rendition of the synopsis of the screenplay. As well, these soundtracks drew extensively from the varieties of Nigerian popular music genres and, consequently, redefined the notion of genre as conceptualized in both film and music.[14]

Emerging soundtrack composers in this era were predominantly men with the capacity to adapt to and satisfy the immediate musical demands of film producers. Records from film credits and oral accounts of practitioners reveal that there were no women composers in Nollywood until 1999. This entry date represents a duration of about ten years from the establishment of Nollywood itself. Of this, Emejuobi declares:

> There were no women soundtrack producers or composers when I joined Nollywood in early 1999. I was the only woman among big names like Stanley Okorie, Sammie Okposo, Shadrach John, and Albert Kalu. But I was determined to surprise the marketers and critics who did not give me any chance to show what I can create. And you cannot blame them because until I joined that part of the industry, women were mainly interested in certain roles like make-up and acting. To be honest, I only decided to try [composing] soundtracks after failing to land [secure] acting roles. By 2002, I wrote the soundtrack for the acclaimed film, *A Cry for Help*.

Emejuobi's quote overly suggests that music as a field of production in Nollywood was deeply gendered and masculinized. My research specifically reveals that the recruitment of women in the field of soundtrack production during the Pragmatic-expressive era was largely linked with semiskilled or "dispensable" roles such as backup singers, sound-editing trainees, instrumentalists, and microphone operators. Second, Emejuobi's claim that she composed the soundtrack of *A Cry for Help* (2002) is, on the one hand, debatable, particularly because the film credits it to two men named Albert Kalu and Craig David.[15] On the other hand, the singing voice in the film's soundtrack is unequivocally Emejuobi's. This theoretically supports her claim as the composer because the Nollywood film music tradition requires that soundtracks are performed in the composer's own singing voice for different reasons, including the avoidance of any litigation following copyright infringement.[16] As such, the only logical reason for not crediting Emejuobi with this soundtrack would be the gendered politics of composing for film in Nollywood. Enter Emejuobi:

> Like I told you [before the interview], I was naïve during those initial years. The truth is that I wrote, sang, and recorded that soundtrack. But when it was time to pay me, the film producer insisted on having sex with me as part of the [contractual] conditions. I was surprised. He invited me to his studio in Lagos where he claimed that I will be paid. When I refused to sleep [have sex] with him, he called one Albert to do the job. But as you can tell from the film music, Albert did not do anything: they simply took [appropriated] my intellectual property and put their names there. They did this to punish me for refusing his terms.

This is the first verifiable instance of gender discrimination and sexual harassment in the Nollywood film music industry, which Emejuobi's own words supports (discussed later). However, between 2004 and 2009, Emejuobi's success would inspire other prospective women composers such as Darlene Asuquo and Amara Okoh. Even so, Emejuobi affirms that the careers of both newcomers ended almost at the same time as the Pragmatic-expressive era was being overshadowed by the next.

> For almost five years [between 2000 and 2005], I remained the only woman actively doing soundtrack business. But I was later joined by two other wonderful ladies like Amara Okoh who, unfortunately, did not last long as a soundtrack producer. I know this because when you stop hearing a person's voice [in Nollywood film soundtracks] for some time, it is possible that the person has not been given [a film] job or contract to execute. Another wonderful lady is Darlene Asuquo. She started strong but it has been ages (and I am talking about a time before 2010) since I last heard her voice. I do not think that she is still into it.

That said, the synthesis of approaches and soundtrack imports of both the Mimetic and Pragmatic-expressive eras as well as other forms of experimentations had, by 2010, given birth to a third era—one with a rather unclear path. I label this the Opaque era (i.e., 2010 and beyond). As a fledgling new era booming with greater exploits and sophistry, speed, aesthetic awareness, and reward and refinement, unfolding events in the Nollywood film and film music industries began to shape genuine efforts at mediating and reforming existing practices. For example, in the last quarter of 2010, private sector investors decided to partner with the existing government to build a

Hollywood-type estate called Nollywood city. This "city" would be located in Abuja and equipped with such state-of-the-art facilities as studios, post-production workstations, digital synthesizers, and accommodation, as well as security. The Nollywood city will be the crucible where, according to entrepreneur Mike Audu, "[A]ll dreams of Nollywood will come alive."[17] Although this project was never actualized, the announcement itself triggered a sudden rethink in approach, especially in terms of quality, aesthetics, and representation. In order to redefine the practice, the desire and intensity to conquer the shortcomings of the previous eras in terms of technique, piracy, infrastructure, creative collaboration, outreach, and quality, created an impasse.

An important reason for the impasse was the emergence of New Nollywood (a parallel national film industry) in 2012. New Nollywood prompted changes to technological and marketing/distribution preferences, thematic preoccupation, as well as an upward evaluation of budgets, quality, audience appeal, and new forms of shooting and releasing movies such as in cinemas and online streaming outlets like Iroko TV. As these changes occurred, more women such as Emem Isong-Misodi, Uche Jombo, Genevieve Nnaji, Mary Njoku, Mo Abudu, and Rita Dominic moved into prominent roles as film directors, producers, and screenwriters. By contrast, however, there was barely any change in gender composition within the film music industry. Essentially, the "boy's club" only expanded to include more men like Maxwell Chidebere Leonard and Michael Truth Ogunlade. So, whereas there was no noticeable increase in the number of women composers, New Nollywood itself polarized practitioners' creative views about soundtrack. This leads to the second reason for the impasse: the existence of three schools of thought regarding how film music is presently conceived in Nollywood. Briefly, these are the Nollywood Traditionalist, Temperate, and Pro-Hollywood film music schools.[18] In all, the Opaque era presents a nest of ideas and overlapping approaches from preceding eras but with no definitive cultural identity for its soundtracks. Perhaps, it is too soon to say what the era is characterized by, but it certainly cannot be exclusively called any of the previous two.

In terms of gender representation to date, the stakeholders of the Nollywood film music industry are fundamentally men. The gross underrepresentation of women as film composers in Nollywood raises queries about gender- and industry-related behaviors, as well as how intergender relations affect the practice. Arguably, this underrepresentation is fundamentally the product of patriarchy: there is an unspoken social construction that recognizes and privileges men composers over their women counterpart, in part, because the film music industry is significantly run by men. Given that Chimere Emejuobi is "the last woman standing," it is fair to conclude that men constitute a very disproportionate percent of the total number of stakeholders, including soundtrack producers, songwriters, sound engineers, sound editors, composers, sound designers, and studio owners. Even the film makers, including some women film directors seem more at ease in their relationships with men composers. As such, most Nollywood cinematic productions reflect the positions and wishes of this phallus-dominated industry.

In what follows, I share the oral account of Chimere Emejuobi whom I interviewed in autumn of 2016. In that interview, she spoke about her early days in the industry: her music, her background, issues of social identity, the sociocultural and economic opportunities, frustrations, and how being female and single is instantly an item to explore and exploit within what might be termed the zone of possible agreement. For the avoidance of doubt, I have pared the lengthy and interesting interview to focus on the most important and relevant questions and responses for this publication. Also, I have occasionally tweaked some grammar and sentences to facilitate a smooth read in written form.

CHIMERE EMEJUOBI AND THE ZONE
OF POSSIBLE AGREEMENT

Emaeyak Sylvanus (ES): Did you join Nollywood primarily as a composer?

Chimere Emejuobi (CE): No. I was drawn to acting first. Later, I thought to myself: there are other parts of the industry that I can do better in. So, because I was already experimenting with music for short plays in the past, I felt [that] I would function better in the soundtrack area of Nollywood. I tried to convince some of the movie marketers that I can do it. Yet some of them kept asking me if I can do it better than Stanley [Okorie] who was the main face of Nollywood soundtrack then.

ES: Interesting. Your soundtrack seems quite similar in style to those of a few others in the industry, particularly Stanley Okorie's. Did you understudy anyone, including Stanley?
CE: No. I did not even work under anybody. I only knew that these guys ran things in the industry. I only always saw the names of men as soundtrack writers or producers on films. I never saw a woman's name.
ES: Was it (and is it still) harder for a woman composer to get a contract for film music in Nollywood?
CE: Yes. I think it is more difficult now. Just look back in time: when I joined, I was the only woman. Most of the contracts were given to the men. I struggled

to prove that I can do even better. I even showed some of my earliest works to some of the film makers then, just as a way to back up my claim. But they generally laughed it off. The few who even gave it a thought wanted sex first. And so, I thought to myself that this is very unfair: how can I use my God-given talent to write a song and then offer my body as added bonus before qualifying for a job? Many female actors who wanted quick fame actually complied. This is my worry with that industry. There is so much sexual harassment. It is even worse now. As the only woman in soundtrack, I believed that I had a duty to myself and to other women in the film music business to keep a high moral standard. I mean, how many men am I going to have sex with before I earn the right to equal treatment and pay in the industry? And do you know what these men do? They discuss the women! The moment they have sex with one for a contract, they will tell the rest and those ones will equally insist that the sex is part of the contract. It is such a shame. If you refuse to give them sex they will try to make sure that you do not get any job [film music project] in the industry. They did it to me in the early years. There are a few civilized men but overall, sex is always on the plate when it comes to the man and woman work relationship in Nollywood. And for your information, it does not matter if you are married or single. The men will make efforts [advances] at the women. Apart from sex, some of these powerful men even demand material gifts like phones and wristwatches, which really is a bribe, for them to give you a contract. This is true. I know some female actors who have done so as a substitute for sexual intercourse.

ES: What specific experiences in relation to gender discrimination did you have as a woman composer in Nollywood?

CE: There are many but I will share one with you. Sometime between 2000 and 2002, there was an opportunity to write a soundtrack for a film called *Anointed*. The producer told me that two other men [composers] were interested but that he had decided to "give me a chance to do something." Well, I went away and put in a lot of hard work into that soundtrack. I wrote the lyric, recorded the music in a studio, and sang both the solo and backup parts. In fact, I traveled to Lagos just to produce a good job. The [film] producer said it was a good piece [of work] and used it in the film. Now, the first shock I got was that he paid me 7000 Naira [in Nigerian currency] for the work instead of the agreed 65,000 Naira. When I asked him why, he said: "Nobody knows you in the industry. I am even taking a risk with you." But you see, he would not do it to a man who is new in the industry. He just intimidated me. As if that was not enough, when the film came out, he did not even credit the soundtrack to me. He just put his name on it because nobody knows me. I was so upset. I swore never to work with that producer again. My only source of encouragement was that many viewers and friends could identify my [singing] voice in the soundtrack. That was the only way of proving that I did [compose] the soundtrack.

ES: How has this industry behavior been checked (if at all)?

CE: Checked? I said that it is even worse now. Who is checking [whom]? We do not have the laws to protect women's rights for a start. Even if I try to be patriotic and say that we have such laws in the industry or country, nobody is enforcing them. I'm sorry to say that the men do what they like. It is a part of the culture where men feel entitled to women and their bodies. This is part of why I decided to quit after putting in twenty years into the job. There was really no time in those years when I felt at ease in dealing with the men. Some will just walk up to you in the name of a business deal and smack your buttocks. Like I said, they do this because the woman cannot complain to any court of law or police officer. Even if you complain, you will be [made] a source of caricature, especially if they know that you are unmarried. If we had laws that worked, I would have used it to my advantage many times. But there are none; and I feel [that] this is why the two or three other women in soundtrack business left [prematurely]. In America, for example, you can report such a behavior and be sure that justice will take its course. But in Nigeria, you dare not even mention the name of the man. Even now, I still cannot mention their names because anything can happen to me, and nobody will ask why. These men have means and they can destroy one's career. So, I have concluded that it is better for me to leave the industry. Moreover, the economy of the country is down. There was a time when the business boomed. This was between 2002 and 2014. Now, the soundtrack business is not paying very well to support my standard of living. So, you combine sexual harassment, the discrimination, and poor [monetary] value for the soundtrack and you know why I am leaving [both] the industry and country.

DISCUSSION

What has been presented so far arguably indicts an industry and society wherein gender inequality has become enduring and firmly inscribed in the collective oblivious. This statement aligns with Pierre Bourdieu's theory of life's experiences, which he suggests are "internalized as second nature and so forgotten as history."[19] Broadly, this state of mind plays an active role in the construction of gender dispositions within the film music industry in Nollywood. Thus, the issue of gender and intergender relations in the industry are, to paraphrase Bourdieu, nearly always present in "perception, thought, and action."[20] Consequently, the Nollywood film music industry has inadvertently constructed the quality of being a woman to be as diametrically opposed to a man's, and regardless of creative ability. This kind of construction leads to what Kate Huppatz indicates as a "consistency in practice over time so that gendered dispositions often appear relatively stable."[21] Indeed, the Nollywood film music hierarchy and gender order are, to paraphrase Huppatz, "particularly entrenched because masculine domination is predominantly legitimated."[22] This order also thrives because the notion of domination is lodged in "a biological nature that is [in and of] itself a naturalized social construct."[23] One means by which this domination is sustained is via a "legitimate authority." Within the Nollywood film music industry, the bulk of those with legitimate authority are men. The implication, and following CE's statements, is that composing for film is actively constructed as men's work.

Moreover, this authority is strengthened through the use of money and a system that rewards the men more (or at least reacts favorably toward men who bargain for higher pay) for doing the same kind of work. The evidence of this is not far-fetched: men control the film projects, the funds, and such facilities as studios which they may offer at prohibitive fees to the women composers as a way to discourage rivalry. Finally, there is the matter of sexism and sexual harassment, which is both constantly and consciously activated to degrade the social identity of the woman composer. In other words, women, whether as composers or actors, are regularly subjected to the sexual needs and exploitation of the male ego. This too is misogyny, which some scholars define as "the hatred or disdain of women. It is an ideology that reduces women to objects for men's ownership, use, or abuse."[24] This practice has crystalized over the years within Nollywood and, thus, affirms the notion that "social identity is defined and asserted through difference."[25] Taken together, the evidence suggests that patriarchy influences the degree to which the Nollywood film music industry is regulated by gender. Significantly, patriarchy ensures that the men and women who practice film music in Nollywood occupy distinct roles that have remained nearly unchanged since the early 1990s.

NOTES

1. Adetayo Alabi, "Introduction: Nollywood and the Global South," *The Global South* 7, no. 1 (2013): 1–10. Also see, Emaeyak P. Sylvanus, "A Brief History of TV and TV Music Practice in Nigeria," *Muziki* 15, no. 1 (2018): 37–57.

2. For example, Moradewun Adejumobi, "Nigerian Videofilm as Minor Transnational Practice," *Postcolonial Text* 3 (2007): 1–16; Jonathan Haynes, *Nigerian video film* (Athens, OH: Ohio University Press, 2000); Matthias Krings and Onookome Okome, *Global Nollywood: The Transnational Dimensions of an African Videofilm Industry* (Bloomington, IN: Indiana University Press, 2013); Brian Larkin, "Indian Films and Nigerian Lovers: Media and the Creation of Parallel Modernities," *Africa* 67, no. 3 (1997): 406–440; Foluke Ogunleye, *African Videofilms Today* (Manzini, Swaziland: Academic Publishers, 2003); Uchenna Onuzulike, "Nollywood: The Influence of the Nigerian Movie Industry on African Culture,"

144 *Emaeyak Peter Sylvanus*

Journal of Human Communication 10, no. 3 (2007): 231–242; Jean-Christophe Servant, "Nigeria: Straight to Video," *World Press Review* 48, no. 5 (2001): 40–41.

3. See Carmela Garritano, "Women, Melodrama, Political Critique," in *Nigerian Video Film*, ed. Jonathan Haynes (Athens, OH: Ohio University Press, 2000), 165–191; Jumoke Giwa-Isekeije, "Peeking through the Opomulero Lens: Tunde Kelani's Women on Center Stage," *The Global South* 7, no. 1 (2013): 98–121; Kenneth W. Harrow, *African Cinema: Post-colonial and Feminist Readings* (Trenton, NJ: Africa World Press, 1999); Agatha Ukata, "The Image(s) of Women in Nigerian (Nollywood) Videos" (PhD diss., University of Witwatersrand, 2010).

4. Kate Lacey and Michelle Hilmes, "Women and Soundwork," *Feminist Media Histories* 1, no. 4(2015): 2.

5. For example, Ellen Koskoff, *Women and Music in Cross-cultural Perspectives* (Urbana, IL: Illinois University Press, 2005); Susan McClary, *Feminine Endings: Music, Gender, and Sexuality* (Minneapolis, MN: University of Minnesota Press, 1991); Karin Pendle, *Women and Music: A History* (Bloomington, IN: Indiana University Press, 1991); Ruth A. Solie, *Musicology and Difference: Gender and Sexuality in Music Scholarship* (Berkeley, Los Angeles, CA and London: University of California Press, 1993).

6. Including, but not limited to, Elaine Barkin, "Either/Other," *Perspectives of New Music* 30, no. 2 (1992): 206–233; Paula Higgins, "Women in Music, Feminist Criticism, and Guerrilla Musicology: Reflections on Recent Polemics," *19th Century Music* 27, no. 2 (1993): 174–192.

7. For example, Joan Cartwright, "Conscious Inclusion of Women Musicians," *Gender Studies* 11 (2012): 235–42.

8. See Emaeyak P. Sylvanus, "Scoring without Scorsese: Nollywood's Divergent, Creative Process," *Musicology Research* 2, no. 1 (2017): 117–140.

9. Jeff Menne, "The Cinema of Defection: Auteur Theory and Institutional Life," *Representations* 114, no. 2 (2011): 36–64.

10. Transitioning from one role to another is commonplace within Nollywood because competition is not suffocated, and there is very limited emphasis on formal training, professional licensing, and institutional regulation. For more, see Emaeyak P. Sylvanus and Obiocha P. Eze-Emaeyak, "The Business of Film Music in Mainstream Nollywood: Competing without Advantage," *Journal of Cultural Economy* 11, no. 2 (2018): 141–153.

11. Discussed further in Emaeyak P. Sylvanus, "Prefiguring as an Indigenous Narrative Tool in Nigerian Cinema: An Ethnomusicological Reading," *Ethnomusicology* 63, no. 2 (2019): 159–183.

12. Discussed in Emaeyak P. Sylvanus, "Performing Ethnicity in Nollywood Film Music: The Power of Texted Music," *Journal of the Musical Arts in Africa* 15, no. 1 (2018): 93–109.

13. Discussed in Emaeyak P. Sylvanus, "Locating Nollywood Film Music at the Intersection of Individualism and a Commodified Identity," *Black Camera* 11, no. 2 (2020): 85–105.

14. Also discussed in Emaeyak P. Sylvanus, "Popular Music and Genre in Mainstream Nollywood: Introduction," *Journal of Popular Music Studies* 30, no. 3 (2018): 99–114.

15. See minute 01:41 of the opening credits of the film at https://www.youtube.com/watch?v=OCkTqeo1UfQ, posted online by Africaine Films on 14 July 2016.

16. Refer to Sylvanus, "Scoring," 117–140.

17. Chief Mike Audu conveyed this idea to the Actors Guild of Nigerian [AGN] at Abuja in 2010. More details can be found at http://www.sunnewsonline.com/webpages/news/abujareports/2010 (accessed October 7, 2017).

18. For more, see Emaeyak P. Sylvanus, "Composing for Film in Nollywood: Schools of Thought," *Quarterly Review of Film and Video* (Summer 2020), https://doi.org/10.1080/10509208.2020.1778979.

19. Pierre Bourdieu, *The Logic of Practice*, trans. Richard Nice (Cambridge: Polity Press in association with Basil Blackwell, 1990), 56.

20. Pierre Bourdieu, *Masculine Domination*, trans. Richard Nice (Cambridge: Polity Press, 2001), 8.

21. Kate Huppatz, *Gender Capital at Work: Intersections of Feminity, Masculinity, Class and Occupation* (New York, NY: Palgrave Macmillan, 2012), 18.

22. Huppatz, *Gender Capital at Work*, 19.

23. Bourdieu, *Masculine Domination*, 23.

24. Teri M. Adam and Douglas B. Fuller, "The Words have Changed but the Ideology Remains the Same: Misogynistic Lyrics in Rap Music," *Journal of Black Studies* 36, no. 6 (2006): 938.

25. Pierre Bourdieu, *Distinction: A Social Critique of the Judgment of Taste*, trans. Richard Nice (London: Routledge, 1984), 172.

BIBLIOGRAPHY

Adam, M. Teri and Douglas B. Fuller. "The Words have Changed but the Ideology Remains the Same: Misogynistic Lyrics in Rap Music." *Journal of Black Studies* 36, no. 6 (2006): 938–957.

Adejumobi, Moradewun. "Nigerian Videofilm as Minor Transnational Practice." *Postcolonial Text* 3 (2007): 1–16.

Alabi, Adetayo. "Introduction: Nollywood and the Global South." *The Global South* 7, no. 1 (2013): 1–10.

Barkin, Elaine. "Either/Other." *Perspectives of New Music* 30, no. 2 (1992): 206–233.

Bourdieu, Pierre. *Distinction: A Social Critique of the Judgment of Taste*. Translated by Richard Nice. London: Routledge, 1984.

Bourdieu, Pierre. *Masculine Domination*. Translated by Richard Nice. Cambridge: Polity Press, 2001.

Bourdieu, Pierre. *The Logic of Practice*. Translated by Richard Nice. Cambridge: Polity Press in association with Basil Blackwell, 1990.

Cartwright, Joan. "Conscious Inclusion of Women Musicians." *Gender Studies* 11 (2012): 235–242.

Garritano, Carmela. "Women, Melodrama, Political Critique." In *Nigerian Video Film*, edited by Jonathan Haynes, 165–191. Athens, OH: Ohio University Press, 2000.

Giwa-Isekeije, Jumoke. "Peeking through the Opomulero Lens: Tunde Kelani's Women on Centre Stage." *The Global South* 7, no. 1 (2013): 98–121.

Harrow, W. Kenneth. *African Cinema: Post-colonial and Feminist Readings.* Trenton, NJ: Africa World Press, 1999.

Haynes, Jonathan. *Nigerian Video Film.* Athens, OH: Ohio University Press, 2000.

Higgins, Paula. "Women in Music, Feminist Criticism, and Guerrilla Musicology: Reflections on Recent Polemics." *19th Century Music* 27, no. 2 (1993): 174–192.

Huppatz, Kate. *Gender Capital at Work: Intersections of Feminity, Masculinity, Class and Occupation.* New York, NY: Palgrave Macmillan, 2012.

Koskoff, Ellen. *Women and Music in Cross-cultural Perspectives.* Urbana, IL: Illinois University Press, 2005.

Krings, Matthias, and Onookome Okome. *Global Nollywood: The Transnational Dimensions of an African Videofilm Industry.* Bloomington, IN: Indiana University Press, 2013.

Lacey, Kate, and Michelle Hilmes. "Women and Soundwork." *Feminist Media Histories* 1, no. 4 (2015): 1–4.

Larkin, Brian. "Indian Films and Nigerian Lovers: Media and the Creation of Parallel Modernities." *Africa* 67, no. 3 (1997): 406–440.

McClary, Susan. *Feminine Endings: Music, Gender, and Sexuality.* Minneapolis, MN: University of Minnesota Press, 1991.

Menne, Jeff. "The Cinema of Defection: Auteur Theory and Institutional Life." *Representations* 114, no. 2 (2011): 36–64.

Ogunleye, Foluke. *African Videofilms Today.* Manzini, Swaziland: Academic Publishers, 2003.

Onuzulike, Uchenna. "Nollywood: The Influence of the Nigerian Movie Industry on African Culture." *Journal of Human Communication* 10, no. 3 (2007): 231–242.

Pendle, Karin. *Women and Music: A History.* Bloomington, IN: Indiana University Press, 1991.

Servant, Jean-Christophe. "Nigeria: Straight to Video." *World Press Review* 48, no. 5 (2001): 40–41.

Solie, A. Ruth. *Musicology and Difference: Gender and Sexuality in Music Scholarship.* Berkeley, Los Angeles, CA and London: University of California Press, 1993.

Sylvanus, P. Emaeyak. "A Brief History of TV and TV Music Practice in Nigeria." *Muziki* 15, no. 1(2018): 37–57.

Sylvanus, P. Emaeyak. "Composing for Film in Nollywood: Schools of Thought." *Quarterly Review of Film and Video* (2020). https://doi.org/10.1080/10509208.20 20.1778979.

Sylvanus, P. Emaeyak. "Locating Nollywood Film Music at the Intersection of Individualism and a Commodified Identity." *Black Camera* 11, no. 2 (2020): 85–105.

Sylvanus, P. Emaeyak. "Prefiguring as an Indigenous Narrative Tool in Nigerian Cinema: An Ethnomusicological Reading." *Ethnomusicology* 63, no. 2 (2019): 159–183.

Sylvanus, P. Emaeyak. "Performing Ethnicity in Nollywood Film Music: The Power of Texted Music." *Journal of the Musical Arts in Africa* 15, no. 1 (2018): 93–109.

Sylvanus, P. Emaeyak. "Popular Music and Genre in Mainstream Nollywood: Introduction." *Journal of Popular Music Studies* 30, no. 3 (2018): 99–114.

Sylvanus, P. Emaeyak. "Scoring without Scorsese: Nollywood's Divergent, Creative Process." *Musicology Research* 2, no. 1 (2017): 117–140.

Sylvanus, P. Emaeyak and Obiocha P. Eze-Emaeyak. "The Business of Film Music in Mainstream Nollywood: Competing without Advantage." *Journal of Cultural Economy* 11, no. 2 (2018): 141–153.

Ukata, Agatha. "The Image(s) of Women in Nigerian (Nollywood) Videos." PhD diss., University of Witwatersrand, 2010.

Chapter 10

An Analysis of Gender Roles around Water and Sanitation in Rural Uganda

Christiana Smyrilli

This chapter presents the author's study on investigating gender roles in water and sanitation infrastructure and practices, in southern, rural Uganda.[1] As the literature acknowledges the different roles that men and women play in water, sanitation, and hygiene (WASH), this research aims to expand the knowledge base for researchers and practitioners, through an evidence-based study. It discusses the interrelationship between WASH and gender, looking at how they affect each other. It also identifies how factors such as education and governance may influence these interrelationships, in order to provide a more holistic evidence-based understanding.

LITERATURE REVIEW

Water and Gender Movements in Development

Improving water and sanitation has been part of development objectives for at least half a century, driving programmes, projects, and policies within the development sector across the globe.[2] The first international drinking water supply and sanitation decade (1981–1990) resulted in 1.2 billion people gaining access to clean water, while 770 million people gained improved sanitation.[3] Simultaneously, a paradigm shift from women in development in the 1970s, to gender and development in the 1980s and 1990s expanded the attention from women to the gender relations and power structures within a society that affect women's position relative to the men's.[4] These movements encouraged development programmes to address women's empowerment and female participation in projects,[5] with practitioners gaining understanding of factors affecting women's equal involvement in programmes.[6] Despite the concurrence of these two developments, there was still little focus on gender specifically within WASH projects due to lack of awareness of gender roles around WASH practices.

The new millennium introduced the United Nations Millennium Development Goals (UN MDGs), with Target 7C addressing access to water and sanitation: "By 2015, [we aim to] halve the proportion of people without sustainable access to safe drinking water and basic sanitation."[7] According to global average figures, the target for drinking water was met in 2010; however, the proportion of people with access to improved sanitation remained well below the targets, especially in Africa. Furthermore, the indicators used by the UN to monitor the progress of the MDGs highlighted that rural populations had significantly less access to drinking water and sanitation infrastructure in 2015. Although the MDGs also emphasized the need for gender equality through MDG3: "Promote gender equality and empower women," they did not link gender and WASH.

The second international decade for action "Water for Life" (2005–2015) gave specific focus to the gender divide within the WASH sector in the poorest regions of the planet, emphasizing women's (and girls') roles as carriers of water, managers of water resources and hygiene within the household, and the importance of good quality water for maternal care and childbirth,[8] demonstrating an increasing awareness that gender is inherently important within the WASH sector and filling in an apparent gap in the MDGs.[9] The 2000s additionally saw global partnerships forming, which recognized and promoted the need for gender considerations within the WASH sector, such as the gender water alliance[10] and the Women for Water Partnership.[11] Finally, in 2010, access to water and sanitation was officially recognized as a basic human right.[12] According to the UN:

> The right to safe drinking water and sanitation is an internationally recognized human right and integral to the realization of other human rights, most notably the right to life and dignity, to adequate food and housing, and to health and well-being, including the right to healthy occupational and environmental conditions.[13]

The Sustainable Development Goals (SDGs) followed on from the MDGs in 2015, expanding the targets, adopting seventeen "integrated and indivisible" goals, and recognizing the interrelationships between different aspects of development.[14] SDG 6 refers to the availability and sustainability of water and sanitation for all, with the targets aiming to provide safe drinking water to all by 2030, while sanitation and hygiene access calls for appropriate consideration to the needs of women and girls.[15]

Sub-Saharan Africa and Uganda

In 1990, the WHO/UNICEF Joint Monitoring Programme (JMP) for water supply and sanitation was established to report the progress made in improving WASH across the world. Since 2017, JMP introduced updated ladders[16] on water and sanitation, and a new ladder for hygiene was introduced.[17] According to the latest report, in Sub-Saharan Africa, the figures display 42 percent of the population having inadequate access to clean water.[18] There are big gaps between rural and urban coverage of improved water supply, particularly in Sub-Saharan Africa, suggesting that "water quality in small systems is of particular challenge."[19] The JMP report also states that a significant proportion of the population of sub-Saharan African countries spends more than thirty minutes on the task of water collection.[20] This burden, as well as the general participation in household activities, falls primarily on women, due to various belief systems and sociocultural norms.[21]

Sanitation situation is worse, with 2.3 billion people worldwide estimated to still lack access to basic sanitation services. In Sub-Saharan Africa, only 28 percent have access to basic sanitation as of 2017 (with insufficient data to estimate safely managed services). It is noted that in both cases, the access to "safely managed services"[22] for both water and sanitation is lower in the rural areas than in the urban areas.[23] Finally, it is estimated that only 15 percent of the population in Sub-Saharan Africa has access to facilities with soap and water for hand washing, while population growth increased in the number of people practicing open defecation (from 204 to 220 million between 2000 and 2015), emphasizing the need to address proper hygiene for the purpose of improved health and quality of life.[24] This highlights that despite the efforts of the last fifty years, more work needs to be employed in improving WASH services.

In Uganda, the rural population has been increasing since the 1960s, reaching almost 33 million by 2017,[25] with poorer families having more children to act as active labor within the household, helping with tasks like water collection, waste removal, and agriculture.[26] This makes it important to provide rural areas with adequate WASH services. Between 1990 and 2000, the rural water supply coverage increased from 40 percent to 46 percent, while the rural sanitation coverage decreased from 82 percent to 72 percent.[27] This is comparative to other countries in the East African region, with Uganda doing slightly better in terms of water supply but slightly worse in terms of sanitation coverage.[28] By 2015, 27 percent of rural Ugandan population drinks water from an unprotected source or from surface water such as rivers and lakes.[29] Sixty nine percent collect water from an improved source, but most spend more than minutes roundtrip doing so. Only 4 percent has a water supply on premises. Various studies in Uganda explore the WASH sector in the country.

A 1998 study pointed to the shortfalls of water and sanitation policy in Uganda.[30] It found that this had a negative impact on water quality, water quantity, as well as the effectiveness of water committees and communities' willingness to maintain their water infrastructure schemes. The introduction of the UN MDGs in 2000 encouraged the Ugandan government to acknowledge the need for improvement of the WASH services in the country, by prioritizing water and sanitation in its poverty eradication action plan and the national development plan.[31] In 2015, the Ugandan Ministry of Water and the Environment reviewed the progress in the country, noting that although the target for water supply was met, with 71 percent of the rural population having improved water sources, only 34 percent have improved sanitation which is slightly less than half of the targeted 70 percent.[32] However, this figure is debatable, as the JMP estimates that Uganda has an improved sanitation coverage of only 17.3 percent.[33]

A study published by Thomson *et al.*[34] revisited communities in Kenya, Uganda, and Tanzania that were initially studied by the authors of Drawers of Water,[35] examining changes in the WASH sector, particularly in domestic water use, hygiene, and heath, over thirty years. In this time period, water had changed from a public good to an economic good, where more emphasis is given to the beneficiaries being willing and able to pay for their water (infrastructure). Additionally, there seemed to be a major change in the state institutions; the select East African governments took a regulating role, accepting increased and continuing support from donors, as well as other private actors in the sector, such as NGOs and CBOs, while also giving a greater focus to develop rural areas than they did thirty years ago, leading to an increased access improved water supplies. Thompson *et al.* state that women are still remained, after three decades, the main carriers of water, although the introduction of the jerrycan has increased the number of young men collecting water for sale. The overarching conclusion is that poor people bear the "choice" between using up their limited income on water due to nonaccess in public services or piped systems, or bearing the cost of risk of ill health, inconvenience, and long distances when they collect water from alternative sources, with most of the responsibility and therefore disadvantages falling on women.

A more recent five-year study in Lwengo District[36] shows that women, as the main managers of water resources and responsible for carrying water for home use, suffer the most when there are water shortages, inadequate provision of infrastructure, or inefficient decision-making. Women's position within the communities and cultural expectations define women roles in terms of water management within the household, such as meeting men's water demands for drinking and washing. Despite increased focus by practitioners and government to raise women's participation in formal decision-making structures, for example, in village water committees, factors such as the individual's agency, or the perceived personal and social costs associated with it, such as being stigmatized by the community as "loose women" or "unfit mothers," influence women's decision in participation.[37]

METHODOLOGY

A mixed-methods approach was followed to collect ethnographic data from rural communities in Uganda, in various districts all located on the southern belt of the country. Focus group discussions were conducted separately with male or female participants to encourage them to express themselves honestly, as the aim is to capture the opinions and feelings of men and women with respect to their experience with water supply and sanitation. These discussions were complemented with interviews one-to-one or group interviews, and observations near WASH infrastructure. The participants were identified through two nonprobability sampling methods: (a) purposive sampling, where participants were selected because they collect water from the point-sources and/or own a pit latrine that represent the population and allow the researcher to meet the specific research aims[38] and (b) snowball sampling, when relevant contacts were identified or suggested by other participants.[39] This meant that participants were either "experts" and knowledgeable in the WASH sector in Uganda or represented the general population of a community studied.

The sites visited were identified by NGOs (local or international) working in Uganda, which provided access to the researcher to conduct the study in geographical areas they have worked in. The communities were chosen because they have a point-source infrastructure for water collection (a protected spring, rainwater harvesting tanks, surface water, or a borehole with hand pump) and pit latrines. Data was collected from communities in the southern part of Uganda, in the districts of Manafwa and Mbale, Busia, Kabale, Mukono, Mpigi, Wakiso, Kayunga, and Luwero, over a total period of six weeks. This chapter presents and discusses the findings from the study, using qualitative data and supported by photographs from the field.

DISCUSSION OF GENDER ROLES IN WASH: CAUSES AND IMPACTS

The research's overarching theme is that there are still distinct roles within WASH practices in rural Uganda, which affect men and women in different ways and to different extents. This section will discuss the specifics of gender roles within WASH, as experienced through fieldwork conducted, looking at both the causes of the assumed gender roles, as well as the impacts of WASH from a gender perspective.

Water Supply and Gender

Despite the last fifty years of work around improvement in water supply, and the increased focus on women and gender issues, data from the communities visited highlight that very little progress has been done with regards to gender roles around water supply, both within the household and the community structures. Women, with help from children, remain the primary carriers of water for household use, in many cases observed walking for at least one kilometer and spending a long-time queuing for water, hence classifying the source as "limited" according to the JMP. However, access is difficult beyond time and distance. A lot of the protected springs visited and observed were located in remote areas, surrounded by vegetation and only accessed through dangerous paths (that become muddy after rain) or are down steep slopes (see figure 10.1). For example, in Buikwe village in Mukono district, the protected spring used by the community is located at the bottom of a small hill, which is risky to descend due to the dusty nature of the soil, with

Figure 10.1 **"A Protected Spring in Mukono District, Surrounded by Vegetation and Accessed through a Remote Path."** Photo credit: Photo from author's personal library, 2018.

women and children carrying 20-liter jerrycans up the hill to their house on return.

When men were observed collecting water, it was under certain circumstances. Unmarried men living with their parents and single men living alone would collect water for household use; men would collect water for household use with the help of their bicycles or motorbikes as this is more culturally acceptable than men carrying jerrycans—and also enables them to carry multiple jerrycans per trip—(see figure 10.2); or they would collect water for business, such as brick laying. Men are primarily viewed as income earners and would rarely collect water for household use if the wife and children were available, as they expressed fear of social stigma if they are seen carrying water, particularly on their heads, and doing "a woman's job."

Gender roles are defined by both culture and society. A woman leader working in Buyaka—a village in Mbale district stated that "the men are spoon-fed," and "expect to have everything ready when they come home for lunch," including food, water to drink and bathe, and clean clothes. Another female interviewee in Matwa village, Mbale district, further noted that women may face, in the best case, complaints and, in the worst case, abuse or violence if they failed to provide water. This clearly demonstrates that women are expected to provide for their husbands, not only for consumption, but also for cooking, bathing, and cleaning, thereby increasing their workload especially with regards to water collection. The women would have to

Figure 10.2 "A Man Is Collecting Water from a Borehole Using His Bicycle." Photo credit: Photo from author's personal library, 2018.

go multiple times and carry each jerrycan separately (usually on their heads, sometimes at the same time with two hands carrying a child on their back, or holding one by hand, as shown in figure 10.3), thus experiencing increased physical strain and health risks. They combine their role of providing for the family while also tending to their child-caring responsibilities, indicating that women need to multitask.

Even when pregnant, women are still expected to fulfill their duties, walking long distances with heavy water loads. In support of this, a young woman interviewed stated that after birth-giving, women are expected to return promptly to their duties, so they must carry their children with them on their

Figure 10.3 **"A Woman Collecting Water from a Borehole with a Baby on Her Back."**
Photo credit: Photo from author's personal library, 2018.

backs when accessing the water points. Discussions with women in multiple communities revealed that if women are unable to complete their water collection duties, then, the responsibility falls on the husband's sisters, or the woman's sisters, but not on the husband, showing that the women even have to bear the burdens associated with their extended families. Additionally, older participants in the discussions mentioned that a grandmother takes over the caring of the children when the mother is unable to do so. Nonetheless as women are getting older, health problems make it more difficult for them to cope with tasks they "have to do," such as collecting and carrying water.

In addition to physical health problems, the insufficient provision of infrastructure for water supply creates other issues. Both male and female discussants noted that women walk to the water points before sunrise, in order to promptly return home and fulfill their household activities, as failing to do so may resort to domestic violence, as explained by multiple female interviewees. Moreover, accessing water points in darkness, or far from the village, causes stress to the women, as it makes them vulnerable to falling down unstable paths or getting injured on them, being bitten by snakes, or falling victims to physical abuse and sexual violence. The men also expressed fear for their wives undertaking such tasks while it is still dark, as "different people have different motives," recognizing the harassment risks women face.

Household and community structures determine time allocation for tasks. Women were observed to collect water at dusk, after 6 p.m., showing that their working days are long, while on the other hand, men have leisure time as they were observed drinking alcohol at the same time their women were queuing at water points. At most of the springs and boreholes visited in the morning and the evening, women spend long time in queues (see figures 10.4 and 10.5). The women claim that "peak time" queuing is mostly a problem for women who are inflexible with their working days, referring to those, for instance, who want to collect water and promptly return home to prepare lunch for example. During discussions, women explained that they can only fill up 1 to 2 jerrycans at once, even if they have more with them, as other people are waiting too. Such long queues have occasionally resulted, according to narratives, in disagreements and fights between community members, due to the stress over time.

During the interviews and discussions, the data collected on the average consumption per person per day among all communities visited revealed 25 liters, which is half of the proposed minimum amount by WHO for good health and living standards.[40] Better infrastructure provision and coverage could help provide the quantity and quality of water required by WHO standards. Thus, leadership and education were identified to be driving factors in improving the water situation in all these communities. Observations from the communities studied indicate that active leaders strive to improve their

Figure 10.4 **"A Long Queue of Jerry Cans at a Borehole."** Photo credit: Photo from author's personal library, 2017.

Figure 10.5 **"Queueing for Water at a Protected Spring."** Photo credit: Photo from author's personal library, 2017.

communities, initiating proposals to the district office for a water source, such as a protected spring or a borehole, and mobilizing the people in the community to become active agents of change, for example, collecting money for the maintenance of the infrastructure or providing the construction team of the NGOs with resources such as bricks. However, the data suggests that both men and women can assume active leadership roles. Susan, a female representative in Mbale district managed to secure the first water tank in her community through a local community-based organization (see figure 10.6), while Peter, a community chief in Manafwa district attained both a community borehole by the district council (see figure 10.7) as well as a water tank for his home through a local organization. Literacy is crucial as it enables community members to send written applications requesting improved water infrastructure. This was highlighted during a focus group discussion with women who were attending functional adult literacy (FAL) groups who claimed to feel empowered to request for a better water supply system.

It is important to note that provision of water infrastructure improves the economic capacity of households. For example, men could start a brick-laying business near springs, as a constant flow of water is necessary for making bricks. Other men could start enterprises through the sale of water transported to households for a fee. On the other hand, women who had the financial capacity and upon agreement with their husbands, could buy water from such vendors freeing up time to participate in income-earning activities. For instance, an interviewed woman in Mukono district mentioned that she

Figure 10.6 "A Rainwater Harvesting Tank Installed at a Household." Photo credit: Photo from author's personal library, 2017.

Figure 10.7 "A Non-Functional Borehole with a Chlorine-Pastilles Bucket." Photo credit: Photo from author's personal library, 2017.

would buy water for her hairdressing business, while a lady from Wakiso district stated that she would buy water to produce juice to sell for profit. This highlights the capacity of water infrastructure in challenging social norms and the traditionally formed gender roles of women working in the house, encouraging wholesome development and improving people's living conditions.

Sanitation, Hygiene, and Gender

Even though households in the communities visited have pit latrines, open defecation is still practiced, with both men and women experiencing poor sanitation. In Mbale district, for example, members of one of the villages visited explain that the sanitation practices involve the use of pit latrines and African pots at home, but it was noted that men also practiced open defecation while they work in the fields. Women would also resort to such practices if they were far from the house, despite feeling ashamed to do so. This practice was equally reflected in all the other communities visited in other districts. Community members acknowledge the problems open defecation causes, such as contamination of the water source leading to health issues and disease, but they indicate that they have no choice if they are far from the home and a pit latrine. According to the JMP ladder, the practices of these communities would be classified best as "open defecation" because, despite pit latrines being available, they are not always used.

Despite being of classified as "basic" infrastructure, pit latrines were identified to have positive impacts on people's lives, especially the women who state that they feel cleaner and more protected using them. They also feel less ashamed to host guests, as they can provide them with sanitation facilities. In Matwa district, a female interviewee noted that since the construction of pit latrines in households, they have been experiencing illnesses, such as diarrhea, less frequently. In different communities, various research participants also mentioned incidents of crime, and people, particularly women, being attacked while practicing open defecation, as they had to walk to faraway places alone. Incidences of illness and crime have decreased with each household being sensitized to the benefits of using pit latrines and having access to one.

It is important to note that in terms of hygiene, as defined by the JMP ladder, only two households visited (one in Ngando village, Buyenda district and one in Buikwe village, Buikwe district) comply with the "basic" standard, of having a place for washing hands with soap (see figure 10.8) after using the sanitation facilities. In all other households visited, "no services" were observed near the pit latrines for hand washing. More emphasis was given to this in public or community spaces, such as church, community center, schools, and medical centers, which all offered water and soap for washing hands. Observations and discussions indicate that both men and women are aware of the benefits and proper etiquette of hygiene practice; however, it remains uncertain how they would comply with this at home, out of the public eye. Data suggests that hygiene is still a big issue and highly neglected in rural Uganda.

Education Changes Behaviors

Seven out of the focus group discussions were carried out with participants in FAL programmes. These programmes were initiated in 1997 by the Ugandan government, in collaboration with NGOs and donors, to improve literacy rates among adults and "empower [them] to participate fully as equal partners in development programs."[41] Part of the curriculum discusses the importance of good sanitation and hygiene practices, as well as the impacts these have on health. The members of the seven groups (totaling 126 people) were primarily women, while only nine men participated.

All of the FAL group members noted an enhanced appreciation of the use of the pit latrines, with women particularly expressing increased feelings of dignity and pride. For instance, a male member from the FAL group in Busia district felt proud because he is "one step further in development," showing that these feelings are important to both men and women. Moreover, hygiene practices were improved as a lady specifically acknowledged learning the

Figure 10.8 "A Man Washing His Hands Outside His Pit Latrine." Photo credit: Photo from author's personal library, 2017.

importance of hand washing after using a latrine, and accepted that "throwing away waste is not good because it leads to diseases." A lady from another FAL group in the district stated that the pit latrines provide them with privacy, an important issue to them, while in general women "also feel less marginalized now." In conclusion, FAL groups result in positive changes in sanitation and hygiene practices.

Women's Role in Sanitation and Hygiene

The discussions with the FAL groups highlighted women's unofficial leadership role in promoting sanitation and hygiene both within their households and in the communities. A female participant from one FAL group in Busia district admitted that although she and her family had a household pit latrine previously, her family did not understand its value, so they were not using it. After her education, she talked to her husband and children and now everyone in her family is using it. This was a universal finding across all FAL groups visited; interviewees stated that they now appreciate the use of pit latrines, and all of them have constructed a pit latrine at their abodes. The fact that more women participate in FAL groups indicates that women act as catalysts in their households and their communities. Participating in the educational programmes encourages them to mobilize their husbands in building a pit latrine, influencing the family for improved sanitation and hygiene practices. Collectively, this improves health in the community.

Community mobilization through the female FAL group participants resulted in the provision of pit latrines to all the households within each community interviewed. The men, although not personally participating in FAL education, acknowledge and appreciate the importance of good sanitation and hygiene, and assume a more "manly" role: those who have the skills to construct the latrines built them for the households who didn't have the skills or the labor force. This improved infrastructure provision and coverage within the communities. FAL groups are thus empowering women to become the driving force for change, but narratives suggest the need for collaboration and coherency between all the members of the community.

The aforementioned findings highlight the role of women as active agents of change within their community, through education and empowerment. This agrees with Okech's studies in eight different districts in Uganda,[42] where the author argues that education improves a community's WASH practices, where all members, regardless of attendance to the FAL programme, follow better practices.

Baguma *et al.*[43] have stated that "given the low levels of education and the poor reading culture in developing countries, encouraging women to join local active water-related associations would improve the women's knowledge about water resource management." The findings from focus group discussions with FAL groups indicate that educating women, with curriculum especially targeted towards WASH, has positive impacts towards improvement in communities and development of WASH infrastructure and practices.

Menstruation: Women's Burden

Privacy is also important for women, who expressed dissatisfaction when the facilities are in public view. Additionally, women express stronger feelings of shamefulness and uncleanliness, as inadequate access to sanitation infrastructure and water for washing makes menstruation hygiene management

(MHM) difficult. This increases the risk of infections and abdominal pains, due to unhygienic menstrual management. During an interview with community leader Susan, an elected district representative and health worker, she stated that the government was trying to improve MHM through educating and sensitizing women on proper sanitation and hygiene practices. Young girls feel ashamed during menstruation, (as it is considered a taboo in the communities), and do not attend school during their menstrual period to avoid any "accidents" that will make them the topic of discussion at school for the whole year. Furthermore, they are unprepared for menstruation because their mothers do not talk to them about it, and women and girls "do not even talk to the doctors about it," as stated by a young woman during a focus group discussion in Busia district. As menstruation remains a taboo subject, women and girls face a number of problems, both in health risks due to poor sanitation and hygiene practices, and psychological trauma as they feel ashamed, unclean, embarrassed, and marginalized. Thus, it is important to acknowledge that menstruation remains a big barrier for women's development and equality in communities in rural Uganda, with proper sanitation and hygiene infrastructure being the first step forward in overcoming issues beyond the health implications of inappropriate management.

RECOMMENDATIONS FOR RESEARCHERS AND PRACTITIONERS

This chapter encourages researchers and practitioners to have a multidisciplinary approach to WASH infrastructure provision, as gender roles communities around WASH practices are very distinct in rural communities around. Gender-sensitive infrastructure has the potential to challenge cultural norms, while improving both men's and women's lives across different aspects such as health, economic situation, and role within the community.

CONCLUSION

This chapter presents the findings from research conducted in rural Uganda. The main finding suggests that despite fifty years of global efforts to address access to water and sanitation, as well as address the importance of gender in development, gender roles around WASH are still prevalent. Women, and children, remain the main collectors of water for household use, bearing the physical burden, as well as the associated health risks with walking long distances carrying heavy loads. This plight additionally makes them vulnerable to attacks from animals, sexual harassment, and violence.

With regards to sanitation and hygiene, the study indicates that both men and women are affected by the lack of adequate infrastructure, although in fundamentally different ways, as women also have to deal with biological factors such as menstruation, increased feelings of shamefulness, and higher risks of harassment or violence when there is inadequate privacy.

Through data from various communities, the researcher identified that encouraging leadership is an important factor to drive change. Active leaders attract attention to the lack of infrastructure in their communities, through engagement with the district office or local organizations, and submitting applications for funding or WASH projects. Additionally, they organize their community around creating a water user committee for managing the water infrastructure, such as collecting fees from the users for its maintenance. The cases studies portrayed both men and women in leadership roles who attained WASH infrastructure provision in their communities, although it was noted that women leaders are generally more active in the sensitization of other community members towards proper sanitation practices, such as improving menstruation management. Women leaders also seem to be generally more aware of the gender issues related to WASH, and seem to be more passionate in driving change.

Education was also identified as a driving force for improved WASH practices. The findings from discussion with seven FAL groups signify that education has a strong, positive impact on WASH and the provision of infrastructure. Higher literacy rate enables communities to send applications to local organizations or the district office requesting water infrastructure such as boreholes or protected springs. The data suggests that both male and female leaders are active with regards to this. Additionally, it was evident that women are empowered to act as catalysts for improved practices in their communities, driving change by influencing men's participation in development such as building pit latrines.

These findings suggest that education programmes and promotion of leadership initiatives challenge the stereotypes that see women as solely household managers or mothers, and can lead to improvements in the WASH sector and community development. With a general understanding of the gender–WASH interrelationship, WASH infrastructure can be a driver of social change, challenging existing gender roles.

NOTES

1. I would like to thank my mentor and supervisor, Prof. Allan McRobie, and my supervisory team from the University of Cambridge for the continual support and inspiration. Additionally, I thank Newnham College, the Engineering Department at

the University of Cambridge, and the EPSRC for funding this research. Above all, I would like to extend my sincere thanks to all the people, organizations and participants in Uganda that enabled me to undertake this piece of research.

An earlier version of this chapter was published as Smyrilli, Christiana and Allan McRobie, "The Relationship Between Gender and WASH Development Projects in Rural Uganda," *Global Journal of Women Studies* 1, no. 1 (2017): 7–17.

2. WHO and UNICEF, *Global Water Supply and Sanitation Assessment 2000 Report* (n.p.: WHO and UNICEF, 2000).

3. UN General Assembly, "Proclamation of the International Drinking Water Supply and Sanitation Decade," 1980, http://www.un.org/documents/ga/res/35/a3 5r18e.pdf; Hari Srinivas, "International Decade for Clean Drinking Water, 1981-1990," The Global Development Research Center, 2005, https://www.gdrc.org/uem/water/decade_05-15/first-decade.html.

4. Julie Fisher et al., "Mainstreaming Gender in the WASH Sector: Dilution or Distillation?," *Gender & Development* 25, no. 2 (2017): 185–204; Shahrashoub Razavi and Carol Miller, *From WID to GAD: Conceptual Shifts in the Women and Development Discourse*, Geneva: UNRISD, 1995.

5. Saskia Ivens, "Does Increased Water Access Empower Women ?," *Development* 51, no. 1 (2008): 63–67; Sally Baden, *Practical Strategies for Involving Women as Well as Men in Water and Sanitation Activities* (Sussex: BRIDGE [development-gender] 1999); Shibesh Chandra Regmi and Ben Fawcett, "Integrating Gender Needs into Drinking-Water Projects in Nepal," *Gender & Development* 7, no. 3 (1999): 62–72; Wendy Wakeman, *Gender Issues Sourcebook for Water and Sanitation Projects* (Washington, DC: The World Bank and Water and Sanitation Collaborative Council, 1995).

6. Audrey Lubisi, "Women's Participation in Water Projects," *Water and Sanitation for All - Partnerships and Innovations: Proceedings of the 23rd WEDC International Conference, Durban, South Africa, 1-5 September 1997*, ed. J. Pickford et al. (WEDC, Loughborough University 1997), 325–327; Rachel Masika and Sally Baden, *Infrastructure and Poverty: A Gender Analysis* (BRIDGE [Development-Gender] Report, no. 51 (1997): 16.

7. United Nations, *The Millennium Development Goals Report 2015*.

8. WHO and UNICEF, *Water for Life; Making It Happen* (Geneva: WHO and UNICEF 2005).

9. United Nations, "International Decade for Action 'WATER FOR LIFE' 2005-2015," accessed December 10, 2018, http://www.un.org/waterforlifedecade/background.shtml.

10. Gender and Water Alliance, "About GWA," 2003, http://genderandwater.org/en/about-the-gender-and-water-alliance.

11. Women for Water Partnership, *Women and Water: Charting Pathways to Equitable and Sustainable Development* (The Hague: Women for Water Partnership, 2015).

12. United Nations General Assembly, "The Human Right to Water and Sanitation," resolution 64/, 2010; John Scanlon, Angela Cassar, and Noemi Nemes, *Water as a Human Right?* (Gland, Switzerland and Cambridge, UK: IUCN, 2004);

United Nations, *The Human Right to Water and Sanitation Milestones* (UNW-DPAC, 2011).

13. United Nations, *The United Nations World Water Development Report 2016: Water and Jobs*, 2016.

14. United Nations General Assembly, "Transforming Our World: The 2030 Agenda for Sustainable Development," resolution 70/1, 2015.

15. Ibid.

16. The JMP service ladders are used to benchmark and compare service levels across countries.

17. WHO and UNICEF, *Safely Managed Drinking Water - Thematic Report on Drinking Water 2017* (Geneva: WHO, 2017); Joint Monitoring Programme, *Progress on Drinking Water, Sanitation and Hygiene*, launch version (Geneva: WHO, 2017).

18. Joint Monitoring Programme, "Progress on Drinking Water"; WHO and UNICEF, "Joint Monitoring Programme," *WASH Data*, accessed January 9, 2019, https://washdata.org/data/household#!/dashboard/new.

19. WHO and UNICEF, *Safely Managed Drinking Water.*"

20. Ibid.

21. Ibid.; David Baguma et al., "Safe-Water Shortages, Gender Perspectives, and Related Challenges in Developing Countries: The Case of Uganda*," Science of the Total Environment* 442 (2013): 96–102.

22. According to the JMP, safely managed sources for water are defined as access to "drinking water from an improved water source which is located on premises, available when needed and free from fecal and priority chemical contamination." On the other hand, they define sanitation as the "use of improved facilities which are not shared with other households and where excreta are safely disposed in situ or transported and treated off-site"

23. Jo-Anne Geere and Moa Cortobius, "Who Carries the Weight of Water? Fetching Water in Rural and Urban Areas and the Implications for Water Security," *Water Alternatives* 10, no. 2 (2017): 513–540; Joint Monitoring Programme, "Progress on Drinking Water."

24. WHO and UNICEF, "Joint Monitoring Programme," 5.

25. World Bank, "Uganda Rural Population," *Data*, 2017, https://data.worldbank .org/indicator/SP.RUR.TOTL?locations=UG.

26. WHO and UNICEF, *Global Water Supply and Sanitation Assessment 2000 Report*; Baguma et al., "Safe-Water Shortages."

27. WHO and UNICEF, *Global Water Supply.*

28. John Thompson et al., *Drawers of Water II: 30 Years of Change in Domestic Water Use and Environmental Health in East Africa* London: IIED, 2001.

29. WHO and UNICEF, "Drinking Water, Sanitation and Hygiene Service Levels in Uganda (2015)," *WASH Data*, 2015, https://washdata.org/data/household#!/dash-board/1875.

30. George Bagamuhunda and Gilbert Kimanzi, "In the Light of Experience - Water Policy and Usage in Uganda," *Waterlines* 16, no. 3 (1998): 19–20.

31. Ministry of Finance Planning and Economic Development, *Millennium Development Goals Report for Uganda 2010.*

32. S. Mutono et al, *Water and Sanitation for the Poor and Bottom 40% in Uganda: A Review of Strategy and Practice since 2006* (World Bank report no. ACS13381, April 24, 2015), 27.

33. WHO and UNICEF, "WHO/UNICEF Joint Monitoring Programme (JMP) for Water Supply and Sanitation," accessed December 10, 2018, https://www.wssinfo.org/.

34. Thompson et al., *Drawers of Water II.*

35. A. U. White, G. F. Bradley, D. J. White, *Drawers of Water. Domestic Water Use in East Africa* (Chicago, IL: University of Chicago Press, 1972).

36. Joyce Mpalanyi Magala, Consolata Kabonesa, and Anthony Staines, "Lived Experiences of Women as Principal Gatekeepers of Water Management in Rural Uganda," in *Water Is Life, Progress to Secure Safe Water Provision in Rural Uganda*, ed. G. Honor Fagan et al. (Rugby: Practical Action Publishing, 2015), 31–42.

37. Christina Geoffrey Mandara, Anke Niehof, and Hilje van der Horst, "Women and Rural Water Management: Token Representatives or Paving the Way to Power?," *Water Alternatives* 10, no. 1 (2017): 116–133.

38. Bruce L. Berg, "Designing Qualitative Research," in *Qualitative Research Methods*, 5th ed., ed. Jeff Lasser (Boston, MA: Pearson Education, Inc., 2004), 15–42; Colin Robson, "Surveys and Questionnaires," in *Real World Research: A Resource for Users of Social Research Methods in Applied Settings*, 3rd ed., ed. Colin Robson (Chichester: John Wiley, 2011), 235–277.

39. Robson, "Surveys."

40. Guy Howard and Jamie Bartram, *Domestic Water Quantity, Service Level and Health* (Geneva: WHO, 2003).

41. Ministry of Gender Labor and Social Development, *National Report on the Development and State of the Art of Adult Learning and Education (ALE) in Uganda* (Kampala, 2008).

42. Anthony Okech, *Evaluation Practices in Adult NFE and Literacy Programmes in Uganda: A Situational Analysis* (Hamburg: UNESCO Institute for Education, 2005); Anthony Okech, *Adult Literacy Programs in Uganda* (Washington, DC: The World Bank, 2001).

43. Baguma et al., "Safe-Water Shortages", 101.

BIBLIOGRAPHY

Baden, S. *Practical Strategies for Involving Women as Well as Men in Water and Sanitation Activities.* Sussex: BRIDGE (development-gender), 1999.

Bagamuhunda, G. and G. Kimanzi. "In the Light of Experience - Water Policy and Usage in Uganda." *Waterlines* 16, no. 3 (1998): 19–20.

Baguma, D. et al. "Safe-Water Shortages, Gender Perspectives, and Related Challenges in Developing Countries: The Case of Uganda." *Science of the Total Environment* 442 (2013): 96–102.

Berg, B. L. "Designing Qualitative Research." In Qualitative Research Methods, 5th edition, edited by Jeff Lasser, 15–42. Boston, MA: Pearson Education, Inc., 2004.

Fisher, J. et al. "Mainstreaming Gender in the WASH Sector: Dilution or Distillation?," *Gender & Development* 25, no. 2 (2017): 185–204.

Geere, J. and M. Cortobius. "Who Carries the Weight of Water? Fetching Water in Rural and Urban Areas and the Implications for Water Security." *Water Alternatives* 10, no. 2 (2017): 513–540.

Gender and Water Alliance. "About GWA," 2003. http://genderandwater.org/en/about-the-gender-and-water-alliance.

Howard, G. and J. Bartram. *Domestic Water Quantity, Service Level and Health.* Geneva: WHO, 2003.

Ivens, S. "Does Increased Water Access Empower Women?" *Development* 51, no. 1 (2008): 63–67.

Joint Monitoring Programme. *Progress on Drinking Water, Sanitation and Hygiene.* Launch Version. Geneva: WHO, 2017.

Lubisi, A., "Women's Participation in Water Projects." In *Water and Sanitation for All - Partnerships and Innovations: Proceedings of the 23rd WEDC International Conference, Durban, South Africa, 1-5 September 1997*, edited by J. Pickford et al., 325–327. WEDC, Loughborough University, 1997.

Magala, J. M., C. Kabonesa and A. Staines. "Lived Experiences of Women as Principal Gatekeepers of Water Management in Rural Uganda." In *Water Is Life, Progress to Secure Safe Water Provision in Rural Uganda*, edited by G. Honor Fagan et al., 31–42. Rugby: Practical Action Publishing, 2015.

Mandara, C. G., A. Niehof and H. van der Horst. "Women and Rural Water Management: Token Representatives or Paving the Way to Power?" *Water Alternatives* 10, no. 1 (2017): 116–133.

Masika, R. and S. Baden. *Infrastructure and Poverty: A Gender Analysis.* BRIDGE (Development-Gender) Report No. 51 (1997).

Ministry of Finance Planning and Economic Development, Uganda. *Millennium Development Goals Report for Uganda 2010.*

Ministry of Gender Labor and Social Development. *National Report on the Development and State of the Art of Adult Learning and Education (ALE) in Uganda.* Kampala, 2008.

Mutono, S. et al. *Water and Sanitation for the Poor and Bottom 40% in Uganda: A Review of Strategy and Practice since 2006.* World Bank Report no. ACS13381, April 24, 2015.

Okech, A. *Adult Literacy Programs in Uganda.* Washington, DC: The World Bank, 2001.

Okech, A. *Evaluation Practices in Adult NFE and Literacy Programmes in Uganda: A Situational Analysis.* Hamburg: UNESCO Institute for Education, 2005.

Razavi, S. and C. Miller. *From WID to GAD: Conceptual Shifts in the Women and Development Discourse.* Geneva: UNRISD, 1995.

Regmi, S. C. and B. Fawcett. "Integrating Gender Needs into Drinking-Water Projects in Nepal." *Gender & Development* 7, no. 3 (1999): 62–72.

Robson, C. "Surveys and Questionnaires." In *Real World Research: A Resource for Users of Social Research Methods in Applied Settings*, 3rd ed., edited by Colin Robson, 235–277. Chichester: John Wiley, 2011.

Scanlon, J., A. Cassar, A. and N. Nemes. *Water as a Human Right?*. Gland, Switzerland and Cambridge, UK: IUCN, 2004.

Srinivas, H. "International Decade for Clean Drinking Water, 1981-1990." *The Global Development Research Center*. https://www.gdrc.org/uem/water/decade_05-15/first-decade.html.

Thompson, J. et al. *Drawers of Water II: 30 Years of Change in Domestic Water Use and Environmental Health in East Africa*. London: IIED, 2001.

UN General Assembly. "Proclamation of the International Drinking Water Supply and Sanitation Decade." November 10, 1980. https://undocs.org/pdf?symbol=en/A/RES/35/18.

UN General Assembly. "The Human Right to Water and Sanitation." Resolution 64/292, 2010.

UN General Assembly. "Transforming Our World: The 2030 Agenda for Sustainable Development." Resolution 70/1, 2015.

United Nations. "International Decade for Action 'WATER FOR LIFE' 2005-2015." http://www.un.org/waterforlifedecade/background.shtml.

United Nations. *The Human Right to Water and Sanitation Milestones*. UNW-DPAC, 2011.

United Nations. *The Millennium Development Goals Report 2015*.

United Nations. *The United Nations World Water Development Report 2016: Water and Jobs*. 2016.

Wakeman, W. *Gender Issues Sourcebook for Water and Sanitation Projects*. Washington, DC: The World Bank and Water and Sanitation Collaborative Council, 1995.

White, A. U., G. F. Bradley and D. J. White. *Drawers of Water. Domestic Water Use in East Africa*. Chicago, IL: University of Chicago Press, 1972.

WHO and UNICEF. "Drinking Water, Sanitation and Hygiene Service Levels in Uganda (2015)." *WASH Data*. https://washdata.org/data/household#!/dashboard/1875.

WHO and UNICEF. *Global Water Supply and Sanitation Assessment 2000 Report*. Np: WHO and UNICEF, 2000.

WHO and UNICEF. "Joint Monitoring Programme," *WASH Data*. Accessed January 9, 2019, https://washdata.org/data/household#!/dashboard/new.

WHO and UNICEF. *Safely Managed Drinking Water - Thematic Report on Drinking Water 2017*. Geneva: WHO, 2017.

WHO and UNICEF. *Water for Life: Making It Happen*. Geneva: WHO and UNICEF, 2005.

WHO and UNICEF. "WHO/UNICEF Joint Monitoring Programme (JMP) for Water Supply and Sanitation." 2015. https://www.wssinfo.org/.

Women for Water Partnership. *Women and Water: Charting Pathways to Equitable and Sustainable Development*. The Hague: Women for Water Partnership, 2015.

World Bank. "Uganda Rural Population." *Data*, 2017. https://data.worldbank.org/indicator/SP.RUR.TOTL?locations=UG.

Part III

WOMEN IN POWER AND
MALE DOMINANCE

Chapter 11

Patriarchy, Gender, and Deliberative Democracy

How Does It Play Out in the Ugandan Parliament?

Hannah Muzee and Joyce Bayande M. Endeley

BACKGROUND

For centuries, patriarchy and gender relations have regimented women's lives to suit and maintain the status quo. To date, majority of women have little or nothing to say about the way they should live their lives. Their social, political life, and sexuality have been controlled and needless to say been ordered to serve the patriarchs. Thus, even when women's presence in a political institution (parliamentary structures) has increased, their increase is not necessarily proportionate to their voices. In Uganda, the increase of women in politics and other public structures has been accredited to the National Resistance Movement (NRM) under President Museveni.[1] The NRM government established a system of people participation that led to the evolution of the council system from village to national legislative levels. This system included marginalized social groups such as women, youth, and disabled citizens who through mandatory spaces can rise and participate in mainstream politics.

Consequently, this affirmative action policy ensured that each district in Uganda received a female representative. Nonetheless, scholars have questioned the motive of this affirmative action policy. They have instead dubbed it as one that has tended to create an ideologized intimate relationship between the president and women, where the women, instead of using it as a stepping stone, are pushed into a position of compromise and blind loyalty to the president whom they seem to see as their godfather.[2] Thus, unless otherwise, it is assumed if the president the patriarch is not in support of any policy or initiative by the women legislators, the chances of it being passed into law are slim.

Therefore, even when the affirmative action policy in Uganda increased women's presence in parliamentary structures, their increase in numbers did not afford them a majority status because compared to men they are still the numerical minority. These and other factors have militated against women legislators' voices during deliberations in parliament. In addition, since parliament was originally a male-dominated institution, there tends to be the presence of unspoken rules and customs that uphold male superiority and peg women as passive actors in the political process.[3] Lerner, therefore, argued that for as long as the rules were made and written by men, there was no way women would gain real equality. She, therefore, argued that the liberation of women would require a conscious evaluation of the patriarchal mindset, it is nuances and effect on women's voices during deliberations in parliament.[4]

Women's voices during deliberations are often silenced both actively and passively by powerful male voices with the capability to suppress and marginalize them during debate sessions.[5] Women's voices are not only continuously stifled by lack of numerical advantage but also by discriminatory practices, humiliating stereotypes, and cultural practices that forbid women from speaking in public ("Women are to be seen and not heard") and thus deemed unfit for leadership.[6] Thus, in an environment that is seemingly unwelcome, women legislators have to constantly find a way of ensuring that their voices are heard or else remain invisible even when physically present.

This chapter, therefore, intends to explore patriarchal manifestations in the Ugandan parliament during deliberative sessions and how women parliamentarians have navigated through its limitations to attain visibility and voice during deliberations. The chapter proceeds with a theoretical review of literature on women's political participation, methodology data analysis, and empirical evidence of how women parliamentarians in Uganda have been able to navigate and overcome patriarchal attitudes and culture to ensure visibility and voice.

A THEORETICAL REVIEW OF THE LITERATURE

The search for a critical mass of women in parliamentary structures has propelled many countries like Rwanda in Africa to parity levels of women and men in parliament, while other countries struggle to attain and maintain the 30 percent internationally set threshold. According to the critical mass theory, Kanter posited that the numerical composition of a group of individuals affected their behavior. For instance, in skewed and tilted groups with a ratio of 85:15 and 65:35, respectively, the numerically dominant type controlled and determined the culture of a group, while the minority was tokenized, treated more as symbols and less of individuals. Thus, the minority become more susceptible to stereotyping, making it harder for women to achieve their status; instead they conformed to the stereotypical biases as noted in the case of affirmative action policy and women in the Ugandan parliament.[7] Despite this disadvantage, the theory propounds that the token status of minorities increases their propensity for coalitions and collective action. Through which, they can be able to affect the culture of group.[8]

But, even with a slightly higher critical mass of women in the Ugandan parliament at 34.8 percent presently,[9] scholars have argued that their substantive impact on policy formulation is curtailed by patriarchal prejudice, inadequate government support, and constricted multiparty-political space.[10] The reason for this is that mainly men occupy top positions and in turn manage the functioning of political machinery and party initiatives while women's voices are muffled throughout the process, or used to their disadvantage. This action makes belief that the solution did not entirely lie in an increase of number but more in a critical mass of feminists, hence women's voice and the ability to voice women's concerns.[11]

All the same, scholars have argued that gender composition and critical mass are necessary ingredients for quality deliberation in parliament. Logically, the more the women in parliament, it becomes apparent to witness the feminized style of politics characterized by a kinder and gentler style of debating.[12] Similarly, a study of board representation found boards of at least three directors of each gender 79 percent to be more active compared to those that had a deficit in representation. The explanation behind the surge in performance was the fact that women directors found it easier and more comfortable to participate with a presence of more women in attendance.[13] However, there is a need to underscore the importance for a fit of rules to numbers to create a necessary atmosphere for women voices because an increase in number amidst a restrictive set of rules and norms will not create the desired effect.[14] Hence, there is a need to eliminate patriarchal attitudes toward women as a prerequisite for women to gain entrance into governance. Nevertheless, the women should be capable and knowledgeable of the function of government systems to freely express themselves on equal footing with men.[15]

Even then, when ideal deliberative democracy advocates for equality among participants, with mutual respect in situations of public argumentations, this is far from reality. For there are many factors and situations that cause inequalities among participants such as differences in education levels that limit the full and equal participation of all citizen[16]. On the disadvantaged end are women who usually have limited or no access to wealth, education, and other material resources, consequently predicting their inability to participate on equal footing with men during deliberative sessions.[17] As argued by Ahikire, women confront a glass ceiling in public deliberations due to the patriarchal nature of political systems.[18] Besides, these inequalities are evident in deliberative political settings where women more than often are themselves constantly interrupted, speak for shorter times than men or get their submissions ignored.[19] Thus, the argument stands that deliberative environments mostly favor those of better social standing, with vocal strength—and mostly men enjoy this privilege. This element, therefore, defeats the equity aim and aspiration of deliberative democracy for all participants.

According to Cohen, deliberative democracy theory posits an ideal of democratic association in which justification of terms and conditions of association proceed through public argumentation and reasoning among equal citizens.[20] Tutui further asserted that political equality is a value of deliberative democracy with effective political competition that excludes political coalition which automatically creates permanent minorities.[21] Hence, as earlier on mentioned, women unfortunately are on the disadvantaged end concerning this equality conundrum. Mushemeza noted that because of patriarchy and insufficient gender mainstreaming in the determination of policy choices and legislation on the quality of life for both women and men in areas of family, health, and education, women find it difficult to influence legislation and policy formulation.[22] As a result of these irregularities, inequalities are evident in deliberative settings especially where men have always had a privileged position in most societies.[23] These irregularities and differences are usually evident in deliberative sessions regarding class, status, race, or gender. Moreover, in reference to gender, women's limited influence in deliberative situations is also attributed to their low education achievement compared to the men who have the privilege of a better education.[24]

Besides, the fact that parliament and public deliberation were initially male-dominated institutions, this meant that they tended to favor a male style of speech characterized by assertion and confrontational speech and were less accommodative toward exploratory speech usually associated to women.[25] Consequently, because of institutional patriarchy, women more than often find themselves sidelined in the system. In addition, male domination in public and private spheres deprives women of their legal rights and opportunities to move freely, associate, and socialize. Also, in the workplace, patriarchy subordinates women through discrimination, disregard, insult, and control.[26] Unfortunately, political structures strengthened by patriarchal undertones thrive on the domination of women.[27] Thus, even when women venture into political structures, patriarchal power which is contingent on the provision of sexual and economic services by women in the domestic realm, restricts and expects them to perform similar tasks due to androcentric mentalities.[28] Patriarchy, therefore, a combination of social structures and practices that consistently dominate, oppress, and exploit women,[29] would require an assortment of strategies to eliminate its hold on women's active political participation, voices, and agency.

METHODOLOGY

By utilizing a qualitative research design, this study aimed to identify and describe the lived experiences of ten women and four male parliamentarians in Uganda. Through interviews and analysis of two debate transcripts of the domestic violence and children's [amendment] bills, the study hoped to identify patriarchal manifestations during deliberations in the Uganda parliament and how women parliamentarians went about addressing these challenges. The textual analysis of the debate transcripts hoped to provide the researcher with evidence of patriarchal manifestations during deliberations.[30] In addition, the study adopted a constructivist and interpretivism approach to qualitative research, which allowed the researcher to rely as much as possible on the views of the participants in the situation being studied.[31] The following section, therefore, presents a description of the participant's views on how they as women parliamentarians in Uganda were able to deal with patriarchal attitudes, norms, and culture to enhance their voices during deliberations in parliament.

PATRIARCHAL MANIFESTATIONS
AND PARTICIPANT'S VOICES

An analysis of the number of interventions between men and women parliamentarians who participated during the deliberations of the Domestic Violence Bill, 2009 and the Children's [Amendment] Bill, 2015, showed that in both bills, the number of deliberators equaled parity (see Table 11.1). However, despite the parity levels, the male parliamentarians seemed to intervene more than the women.

Although barely a 10 percent difference between the interventions made by the women and men in the children's [Amendment] bill, the data shows a significant disparity even when the issues under discussion were related to women. The frequency of participants' voices can measure inequality in deliberative sessions with the aim of identifying who dominates over the other during a discussion.[32] Thus, based on the findings of disparity in table 11.1, it is evident that men dominated women. Bachtiger *et al.* argued that to achieve equality in participation, the share of participation should be proportional to the formal standing of a specific group. In this case, if the women

Table 11.1   Number of interventions by deliberators in the selected bills

		Gender		
Element	*Bills*	*Male*	*Female*	*N*
Deliberators	Domestic Violence Bill	9	10	19
	The Children's [Amendment] Bill	17	18	35
Interventions	Domestic Violence Bill	64	38	102
	The Children's [Amendment] Bill	105	96	201

Source: Compiled by the Researcher from the parliament of Uganda transcripts, 2009 and 2015.
Note: Deliberators=the legislators both women and men who participated during the debate of the bills both at committee and plenary stages of parliament; Interventions=represents the number of times a particular legislator had something to say during the deliberations of the bills; Bills=include two bills, the domestic violence bill and the children's [Amendment Bill] bill all now acts of parliament; Gender=the number of male and female.

and men's numbers almost equal parity, then it is expected that their voices or participative share should equal the same. Unfortunately, this was not the case revealing the androcentric and patriarchal nature of political deliberations in parliament even when the agenda was feminist.[33]

Furthermore, during the deliberations of the Children's [Amendment] Bill 2015, a female member of parliament expressed concern and insisted that a male member of parliament be called to order for assuming that she as a laywoman who did not know the law.

> You know me like a very laywoman, but I understand that there is a law known as the Children Act and it has very explicit provisions for adoption of children. I know that possibly, it provides for those orders. However, why is it in the interest of all those law firms, including that of *Honorable. John* [not real name]) which is known to have participated in securing so many of these guardianship orders; why it is that they do not want to follow the provision of the Children Act to get these children adopted properly?

> Is it therefore in order, Madam Chairperson, for *Honorable. John* to do two things: one, to come here and not declare the interest of his law firm in this legal guardianship; and two, to tell me, a laywoman, that there is no proper statute when the Children Act is there? Is it in order?[34]

Besides, during the deliberation of the Children's Amendment Bill, a female member of parliament called for protection from the speaker of parliament while being rudely interrupted by a male colleague, to which the speaker responded "you are protected."

Woman MP: Thank you very much, *Hon. Joyce* [not real name]. Let me first agree with *Hon. Norah* [not real name] that we can draft something to take care of that local situation, as part of an additional amendment; that should be okay. However, the information I would like to—(Interjection)—Madam Chairperson, please protect me from *Honorable Festus* [Not real name].[35]

The illustrations above present some of the patriarchal manifestations that are evident in deliberative political sessions. Even when interruptions are expected as one is deliberating on the floor of parliament, the fact that the women parliamentarians were able to stand up to interruptions and demand to be listened to, showed that they had the voice and confidence to stand up to political deliberative bullying by their male counterparts. Mendelberg *et al.* posited that since women's discursive styles are different from those of men, they are less likely to be listened to and hence disadvantaged during deliberative sessions that favor more authoritative discussion.[36] Therefore, to overcome these patriarchal challenges, women to some extent need to embody specific masculine attributes such as assertiveness and boldness where need be. Confidence on women's part to call out men on their "bullshit" is necessary in especially male-dominated settings.

As per other factors that enhanced women's voices during deliberations in parliament, the participants acknowledged that a higher level of education was a sure path to women's empowerment. The participants however noted that in comparison to men, the level of education of women legislators was considerably low. The participants noted that "the education of women was for a long time neglected and that is why there are very few women with higher educational qualifications." Therefore, without equal educational qualifications to the men, women cannot confidently deliberate on equal footing with men. Mendelberg argued that the difference in the levels of education between men and women caused inequalities during deliberations. Better quality and higher education qualifications provide individuals with a higher status which in turn grants them a smooth path to participation and influence during deliberations. Unfortunately, women tend to find themselves at the disadvantaged end.[37] O'Neil and Domingo further asserted that a woman's political engagement depends on her family background, socio-economic status, and parents' attitude to education for girls in particular higher education.[38] Therefore, if society and parents are still bent on encouraging girls toward education that promotes domesticity, women will not acquire the necessary intellectual skills from subjects like law, political science that are essentials for them to effectively participate in the western politics.[39]

Besides the inequality in educational achievement, the participants also noted that the presence of a lady speaker in the parliament played a significant role in enhancing their voices during deliberations. A participant said that the speaker is very supportive of women and sometimes she protects them on the floor of parliament: "Let them speak," she says. The women participants noted that the speaker "does not want women to be interfered with when speaking and is quite exceptional while dealing with women." Also, in order to encounter the male-dominated leadership of parliament, the women through Uganda women parliamentary association advocated for a 40 percent women leadership in committees. One noted,

> We agreed that we need to have a 40 percent women leadership of committees. We said that if the chairperson is a woman the vice should be a man and vice versa and we have followed and achieved it if it not 50 per cent at least 40-38 per cent in the leadership of the committee.

Furthermore, a daycare facility with qualified staff for women members of parliament (MPs) was established. The institution of daycare facilities was done consciously to enable breastfeeding mothers the ability to "come to work and follow the debate of the day." A participant noted that women are "so stressed out, they have to run the family unit, attend to parliamentary duties." Therefore, "social responsibility from all sided spreads the women thin, and it thus becomes hard for her to execute her legislative duties effectively." Hence, the presence of a daycare facility helped mitigate the gender challenges that women face regarding the cumbersome nature of the multiple roles of both the domestic and parliamentary duties.

The women MP participants also decried the social norms and stereotypes against women in leadership. One participant argued that "society was not liberated in their perception of women in leadership." The participants noted that society hardly takes women leaders seriously and therefore called for the education of the society on the potential of women as leaders.

Therefore, the willingness of society, according to Markham, to accept new ideas about gender roles is essential for women's meaningful political participation. Markham claimed that a more inclusive and gender equal political environment helped alleviate the burden of socio-cultural constraints coupled with patriarchal structures, stereotypical gender biases, the double burden of professional and family tasks that continuously exclude women from active political life. These factors tended to reinforce the cultural norms of women as caregivers and limit the time they would have otherwise committed to their political engagements.[40]

The male participants also acknowledged that culture and patriarchal indoctrination negatively influenced women's voices during deliberations in parliament. One male participant argued that most "women still believed that a man is supposed to be a leader and thus more has to be done to convince and educate women that they can do better." Another male participant also avowed to the influence of African culture as a significant inhibitor to women's voice in parliament.

> First of all, women have a problem not of their making but a cultural problem. In that women are presumed to be under men, and that is carried from childhood even those that have gone to the university. If you do not succumb to that, you are not looked upon very kindly. So that one is a big problem, they may want, but they have to face that negative cultural attitude, and you find that women who are vocal are those who are not potential wives. This makes it very unfortunate for women who are very intelligent, but who these cultural things restrain. So, when it comes to the parliament very few can talk, and for those who talk you see come from which regions—some of these regions have very "humble women." Education helps but at the end of the day they have to go back to the people who harbor these discriminative cultural beliefs. It is indeed a pity for the women, culture is really against them, and the men are reluctant to release the supremacy, and that is the real problem.

While another male participant argued that "it was important for women to acquire higher levels of education claiming that at the lower levels of education, women have two problems, one of being a woman and the other of lower education." Hence, there is a need for women to have equal opportunities as the men to higher education. Bishaw affirmed that education did not only give women voice against social and political injustices but also freedom to express themselves.[41]

The male participants further argued that cultural stereotypes and norms further affect women's inferiority complex and thus limit their participation levels.

> Women are coming into what has been a male-dominated community, so they still have an inferiority complex with the assumption that a woman belongs to the kitchen, looking after children, and keeping the home. Much as they are still speaking on the floor, they still speak like they have not come out of the kitchen, but that perception is changing. You get some women who can articulate some issues.

Child and Lovenduski too argued that women's inferiority complex is affected by the male-dominated nature of parliament which is also insulated by formal and informal rules of exclusion which can be improved on by feminizing legislature.[42] This involves making deliberate plans such as the daycare facilities instituted by the parliament of Uganda to alleviate the gender burden that women face regardless of their level and status in society, and other gender-sensitive rules and regulations like equal committee leadership that allow for women to take center stage during deliberative sessions. Women are often silenced and sent into invisibility in the political process by the patriarchal nature of political power which constrains women from speaking in public.[43] Thus, because of some of above mentioned cultural inhibition and prohibitions, women are reluctant to run for political office, let alone speak in front of men in public.[44] Hence, the need for government programs that provide both technical and social support to women's activities and enhance their voices in politics.[45]

CONCLUSION

Therefore, even when Uganda may have made some impressive strides concerning the descriptive (numerical) representation of women parliamentarians, the parliament and political system largely remain androcentric riddled with camouflaged patriarchal attitudes toward women's political leadership and participation. The women parliamentarians have to continually figure out ways of dealing with the patriarchal nature of the parliamentary institution in order to perform as effectively as their male counterparts. This chapter described some of the patriarchal manifestations in the Ugandan parliament and how the removal of some of these barriers is central to women's voices during deliberation in parliament. Of particular importance in this study was the assertiveness and boldness of some of women parliamentarians to speak out against any patriarchal notions. Besides, the ability of the parliamentary administration to provide facilities like daycares for the women to counter impediments to their political participation set a significant revolutionary move toward enhancing women's voices in an African setting. The double burden of women's political or economic and unpaid domestic work affects women from all works of life and it is imperative that institutions take deliberate steps to alleviate this burden to enhance women's voices and agency.

NOTES

1. Josephine Ahikire, "Towards Women's Effective Participation in Electoral Processes: A Review of the Ugandan Experience," *Feminist Africa* 3 (2004): 8–19.

2. Sylvia Tamale, *When Hens Begin to Crow: Gender and Parliamentary Politics in Uganda* (Kampala: Fountain Publishers, 1999).

3. Georgina Waylen, "Gender, Institutions and the Quality of Democracy: Engendering the 'Crisis of Democracy'" (2015), https://www.semanticscholar.org/pap er/Gender%2C-Institutions-and-the-Quality-of-Democracy%3A-Waylen/56f30eaf71 534278e16124d5e514fa355dd09856.

4. Gerda Lerner, *The Creation of Patriarchy*, vol. 1, Woman and History (Oxford: Oxford University Press, 1986).

5. R Simpson and P Lewis, *Voice, Visibility and the Gendering of Organisations* (New York, NY: Palgrave Macmillan, 2007).

6. A.M Tripp, "The New Political Activism in Africa," *Journal of Democracy* 12, no. 3 (2001): 141–155, https://doi.org/10.1353/jod.2001.0060.

7. Rosabeth Moss Kanter, *Men and Women of the Corporation*, 1993 ed. (New York, NY: Basic Books, 1977).

8. Pamela Oliver and Gerald Marwell, "A Theory of the Critical Mass. I. Interdependence, Group Heterogeneity, and the Production of Collective Action," *American Journal of Sociology* 91, no. 3 (1985): 522–556.

9. "Uganda Parliament," Inter-Parliamentary Union (IPU), accessed May 6, 2017, https://www.ipu.org/parliament/UG.

10. Daisy-Cynthia Nneamaka Adi, "Critical Mass Representation in Uganda," *Independent Study Project (ISP) Collection* 674 (2009), https://digitalcollections.sit.edu/isp_collection/674.

11. Donley T Studlar and Ian McAllister, "Does a Critical Mass Exist? A Comparative Analysis of Women's Legislative Representation since 1950," *European Journal of Political Research* 41, no. 2 (2002): 233–253. https://doi.org/10.1111/1475-6765.00011.

12. Rita Grunenfelder and Andre Bachtiger, "Gendered Deliberation? How Men and Women Deliberate in Legislatures," (ECPR Joint Sessions, Helsinki, 2007): 1–27.

13. Miriam Schwartz-Ziv, "Gender and Board Activeness: The Role of a Critical Mass," *Journal of Financial and Quantitative Analysis* (2015): 1–55, http://doi.org/10.2139/ssrn.1868033; Sarah Childs and Mona Lena Krook, "Critical Mass Theory and Women's Political Representation," *Political Studies* 56 (2008): 725–736, https://doi.org/10.1111/j.1467-9248.2007.00712.x.

14. Tali Mendelberg, Christopher F Karpowitz, and J. Baxter Oliphant, "Gender Inequality in Deliberation: Unpacking the Black Box of Interaction," *Perspectives on Politics* 12, no. 1 (2014): 1–27, https://doi.org/10.1017/S1537592713003691.

15. Karen Celis, "Substantive Representation of Women (and Improving It) What It and Should It Be About?," *American Political Science Association* (2008): 1–24.

16. Joshua Cohen, "Deliberation and Democratic Legitimacy," in *The Good Polity*, ed. Alan Hamlin and Philip Petit (New York, NY: Blackwell, 1989), 17–34; Jurg Steiner et al., *Deliberative Politics in Action: Analyzing Parliamentary Discourse* (Cambridge, UK: Cambridge University Press, 2004).

17. James Bohman and William Rehg, *Deliberative Democracy: Essays on Reason and Politics* (Cambridge, MA: MIT Press, 1997).

18. Ahikire, "Towards Women's Effective Participation in Electoral Processes: A Review of the Ugandan Experience."

19. Alice Siu, "Deliberation and the Challenge of Inequality," *The American Academy of Arts and Sciences* 146, no. 3 (2017): 1–10, https://doi.org/10.1162/DAED_.

20. Cohen, "Deliberation and Democratic Legitimacy."

21. Viorel Tutui, "Theoretical Models of Deliberative Democracy: A Critical Analysis," *Argumentum. Journal of the Seminar of Discursive Logic, Argumentation Theory and Rhetoric* 13, no. 2 (2015): 179–205.

22. Elijah Dickens Mushemeza, "Contribution of Women in Influencing Legislation and Policy Formulation in Uganda (1995-2005)," *Africa Development* 34, no. 3 & 4 (2009): 167–206.

23. Siu, "Deliberation and the Challenge of Inequality."

24. Tali Mendelberg, "The Deliberative Citizen: Theory and Evidence," *Political Decision Making, Deliberation Ad Participation* 6 (2002): 151–193; Mary Wollstonecraft, *Vindication of the Rights of Women with Strictures on Political and Moral Subjects* (London: Printed for J. Johnson, 1792).

25. Sarah Childs, "A Feminized Style of Politics? Women MPS in the House of Commons," *British Journal of Politics and International Relations* 6 (2004): 3–19, http://www.web.pdx.edu/~mev/pdf/Childs.pdf; Francesca Polletta and Pang Ching Bobby Chen, "Gender and Public Talk: Accounting for Women's Variable Participation in the Public Sphere," *Sociological Theory* 31, no. 4 (2013): 291–317, https://doi.org/10.1177/0735275113515172.

26. Abeda Sultana, "Patriarchy and Women's Subordination: A Theoretical Analysis," *The Arts Faculty Journal* (2011): 1–18.

27. Linda McDowell, "Beyond Patriarchy: A Class-Based Explanation of Women's Subordination," *Antipode* 18, no. 3 (1986): 311–321.

28. Lerner, *The Creation of Patriarchy.*

29. Sylvia Walby, *Theorizing Patriarchy* (Oxford: Basil Blackwell Ltd, 1990).

30. Dey Ian, *Qualitative Data Analysis* (London: Routledge, 2005).

31. John W Creswell, *Research Design: Qualitative, Quantitative and Mixed Methods Approaches*, 4th ed. (Thousand Oaks, CA: SAGE Publications Inc., 2014).

32. Jennifer Stromer-Galley, "Measuring Deliberation's Content: A Coding Scheme," *Journal of Public Deliberation* 3, no. 1 (2007): 1–37, http://www.publicdeliberation.net/jpd/vol3/iss1/art12.

33. Andre Bachtiger et al., "Dinentangling Diversity in Deliberative Democracy: Competing Theories, Their Blind Spots and Complementarities," *Journal of Political Philosophy* 18, no. 1 (2009): 32–63.

34. Parliament of Uganda, *The Children's Amendment Bill* (2015). Both parliamentary debate transcript and interview quotes use pseudonyms.

35. Ibid., 33.

36. Mendelberg, Karpowitz, and Oliphant, "Gender Inequality in Deliberation: Unpacking the Black Box of Interaction."

37. Mendelberg, "The Deliberative Citizen."

38. Tam O'Neil and Pilar Domingo, "The Power to Decide Women, Decision-Making and Gender Equality" (Overseas Development Institute, 2015), https://www.odi.org/publications/9910-power-decide-women-decision-making-and-gender-equality.

39. Nakanyike B. Musisi, "Colonial and Missionary Education: Women and Domesticity in Uganda, 1900-1945," in *African Encounters with Domesticity* (New Brunswick, NJ: Rutgers University Press, 1992).

40. Susan Markham, *Women as Agents of Change: Having Voice in Society and Influencing Policy* (Washington, DC: World Bank Institute, 2013), https://openknowledge.worldbank.org/handle/10986/21031.

41. A. Bishwa, "The Impact of Education on Rural Women's Participation in Political and Economic Activities," *International Journal of Educational Administration and Policy Studies* 6 (2014): 23–31, https://doi.org/10.5897/IJEAPS2013.0316.

42. Sarah Childs and Joni Lovenduski, "Political Representation," in *The Oxford Handbook of Gender and Politics*, ed. Georgina Waylen, Karen Celis, Johanna Kantola and S. Laurel Weldon (Oxford: Oxford University Press, 2012), 1–26.

43. Simone De Beauvoir, *The Second Sex* (Paris: Editions Gallimard, 1949); Sarah Childs and Mona Lena Krook, "Analysing Women's Substantive Representation: From Critical Mass to Critical Actors," *Government and Opposition* 44, no. 2 (2009): 125–145, https://doi.org/doi:10.1111/j.1477-7053.2009.01279.x.

44. Tripp, "The New Political Activism in Africa."

45. Susan Markham, "Strengthening Women's Roles in Parliament," *Parliamentary Affairs* 65, no. 3 (2012): 1–11, https://doi.org/doi:10.1093/pa/gss024.

BIBLIOGRAPHY

Adi, Daisy-Cynthia Nneamaka. "Critical Mass Representation in Uganda." *Independent Study Project (ISP) Collection* 674 (2009). https://digitalcollections.sit.edu/isp_collection/674.

Ahikire, Josephine. "Towards Women's Effective Participation in Electoral Processes: A Review of the Ugandan Experience." *Feminist Africa* 3 (2004): 8–26.

Bachtiger, Andre, S. Niemeyer, Michael A. Neblo, Marco Steenbergen and Jurg Steiner. "Dinentangling Diversity in Deliberative Democracy: Competing Theories, Their Blind Spots and Complementarities." *Journal of Political Philosophy* 18, no. 1 (2009): 32–63.

Beauvoir, Simone. *The Second Sex*. Harmondsworth: Penguin Books, 1949.

Bishwa, A. "The Impact of Education on Rural Women's Participation in Political and Economic Activities." *International Journal of Educational Administration and Policy Studies* 6 (2014): 23–31. https://doi.org/10.5897/IJEAPS2013.0316.

Bohman, James and William Rehg. *Deliberative Democracy: Essays on Reason and Politics*. Cambridge, MA: MIT Press, 1997.

Celis, Karen. "Substantive Representation of Women (and Improving It) What It and Should It Be About?" *Comparative European Politics* 7 (2009): 95–113. https://doi.org/10.1057/cep.2008.35.

Childs, Sarah. "A Feminised Style of Politics? Women MPS in the House of Commons." *British Journal of Politics and International Relations* 6 (2004): 3–19. http://www.web.pdx.edu/~mev/pdf/Childs.pdf.

Childs, Sarah and Mona Lena Krook. "Analysing Women's Substantive Representation: From Critical Mass to Critical Actors." *Government and Opposition* 44, no. 2 (2009): 125–145. https://doi.org/doi:10.1111/j.1477-7053.2009.01279.x.

———. "Critical Mass Theory and Women's Political Representation." *Political Studies* 56 (2008): 725–736. https://doi.org/10.1111/j.1467-9248.2007.00712.x.

Childs, Sarah and Joni Lovenduski. "Political Representation." In *The Oxford Handbook of Gender and Politics*, edited by Georgina Waylen, Karen Celis, Johanna Kantola and S. Laurel Weldon, 1–26. Oxford: Oxford University Press, 2012.

Cohen, Joshua. "Deliberation and Democratic Legitimacy." In *The Good Polity*, edited by Alan Hamlin and Philip Petit, 17–34. New York, NY: Blackwell, 1989.

Creswell, John W. *Research Design: Qualitative, Quantitative and Mixed Methods Approaches*. 4th ed. Thousand Oaks, CA: SAGE Publications, Inc., 2014.

Dey, I. *Qualitative Data Analysis*. London: Routledge Taylor and Francis Group, 2005.

Grunenfelder, Rita and Andre Bachtiger. "Gendered Deliberation? How Men and Women Deliberate in Legislatures." Presented at the European Consortium for Political Research (ECPR) Joint Sessions, Helsinki, (2007): 1–27.

Inter-Parliamentary Union (IPU). "Uganda Parliament." Accessed May 6, 2017. https://www.ipu.org/parliament/UG.

Kanter, Rosabeth Moss. *Men and Women of the Corporation*. 1993rd ed. New York, NY: Basic Books, 1977.

Lerner, Gerda. *The Creation of Patriarchy*. Vol. 1. Woman and History. Oxford: Oxford University Press, 1986.

Markham, Susan. "Strengthening Women's Roles in Parliament." *Parliamentary Affairs* 65, no. 3 (2012): 1–11. https://doi.org/doi:10.1093/pa/gss024.

———. *Women as Agents of Change: Having Voice in Society and Influencing Policy*. Washington, DC: World Bank, 2013. https://openknowledge.worldbank.org/handle/10986/21031.

McDowell, Linda. "Beyond Patriarchy: A Class-Based Explanation of Women's Subordination." *Antipode* 18, no. 3 (1986): 311–321.

Mendelberg, Tali. "The Deliberative Citizen: Theory and Evidence." *Political Decision Making, Deliberation and Participation* 6 (2002): 151–193.

Mendelberg, Tali, Christopher F. Karpowitz and J. Baxter Oliphant. "Gender Inequality in Deliberation: Unpacking the Black Box of Interaction." *Perspectives on Politics* 12, no. 1 (2014): 1–27. https://doi.org/10.1017/S1537592713003691.

Mushemeza, Elijah Dickens. "Contribution of Women in Influencing Legislation and Policy Formulation in Uganda (1995-2005)." *Africa Development* XXXIV, no. 3 & 4 (2009): 167–206.

Musisi, Nakanyike B. "Colonial and Missionary Education: Women and Domesticity in Uganda, 1900-1945." In *African Encounters with Domesticity*, edited by Karen Tranberg Hansen, 172–194. New Brunswick, NJ: Rutgers University Press, 1992.

Oliver, Pamela and Gerald Marwell. "A Theory of the Critical Mass. I. Interdependence, Group Heterogeneity, and the Production of Collective Action." *American Journal of Sociology* 91, no. 3 (1985): 522–556.

O'Neil, Tam and Pilar Domingo. "The Power to Decide Women, Decision-Making and Gender Equality." Overseas Development Institute, 2015. https://www.odi.org/publications/9910-power-decide-women-decision-making-and-gender-equality.

Parliament of Uganda. *The Children's Amendment Bill* (2015).

Polletta, Francesca and Pang Ching Bobby Chen. "Gender and Public Talk: Accounting for Women's Variable Participation in the Public Sphere." *Sociological Theory* 31, no. 4 (2013): 291–317. https://doi.org/10.1177/0735275113515172.

Schwartz-Ziv, Miriam. "Gender and Board Activeness: The Role of a Critical Mass." *Journal of Financial and Quantitative Analysis* (2015): 1–55. http://dx.doi.org/10.2139/ssrn.1868033.

Simpson, R. and P. Lewis. *Voice, Visibility and the Gendering of Organisations*. New York, NY: Palgrave Macmillan, 2007.

Siu, Alice. "Deliberation and the Challenge of Inequality." *The American Academy of Arts and Sciences* 146, no. 3 (2017): 1–10. https://doi.org/doi:10.1162/DAED_.

Steiner, Jurg, Andre Bachtiger, Markus Sporndli and Marco Steenbergen. *Deliberative Pollitics in Action: Analysing Parliamentary Discourse*. Cambridge: Cambridge University Press, 2004.

Stromer-Galley, Jennifer. "Measuring Deliberation's Content: A Coding Scheme." *Journal of Public Deliberation* 3, no. 1 (2007): 1–37. http://www.publicdeliberation.net/jpd/vol3/iss1/art12.

Studlar, Donley T. and Ian McAllister. "Does a Critical Mass Exist? A Comparative Analysis of Women's Legislative Representation since 1950." *European Journal of Political Research* 41, no. 2 (2002): 233–253. https://doi.org/10.1111/1475-6765.00011.

Sultana, Abeda. "Patriarchy and Women's Subordination: A Theoretical Analysis." *The Arts Faculty Journal* (2011): 1–18.

Tamale, Sylvia. *When Hens Begin to Crow: Gender and Parliamentary Politics in Uganda*. Kampala: Fountain Publishers, 1999.

Tripp, A. M. "The New Political Activism in Africa." *Journal of Democracy* 12, no. 3 (2001): 141–155. https://doi.org/10.1353/jod.2001.0060.

Tutui, Viorel. "Theoretical Models of Deliberative Democracy: A Critical Analysis." *Argumentum: Journal of the Seminar of Discursive Logic, Argumentation Theory and Rhetoric* 13, no. 2 (2015): 179–205.

Uganda, Parliament. *The Children's Amendment Bill* (2015).

Walby, Sylvia. *Theorizing Patriarchy*. Oxford: Basil Blackwell Ltd, 1990.

Waylen, Georgina. "Gender, Institutions and the Quality of Democracy: Engendering the 'Crisis of Democracy,'" 2015. https://www.semanticscholar.org/paper/Gender%2C-Institutions-and-the-Quality-of-Democracy%3A-Waylen/56f30eaf71534278e16124d5e514fa355dd09856.

Wollstonecraft, Mary. *Vindication of the Rights of Women with Strictures on Political and Moral Subjects*. London: Printed for J. Johnson, 1792.

Chapter 12

New Dimensions to Discrimination against Party Women and Women in Power

Victor Chidubem Iwuoha

This study examines the nature and context of internal party politics and the level of opportunities same provide to women in political parties in Nigeria. This will establish the extent to which democratic consolidation in Nigeria has impacted on women's political inclusion. The study attempts to spur the interest of gender advocates and scholars, as it expands new vistas of inquiry in asking whether there are still some level of discrimination and marginalization against women occupying elected or appointed political positions in Nigeria. There is no law protecting women occupying elective and appointive positions in Nigeria against certain denials and discrimination from enjoying maternity leave, with necessary benefits. Similarly, grand mothers who are in power face challenges and are not protected from taking a leave of *omugwo*[1] (after birth care or postnatal care).

This study adopted the qualitative methods of data collection and content analysis to elicit and analyze data generated from major political parties that have won legislative seats in Nigeria, including the People's Democratic Party (PDP), All Progressive Congress (APC), Action Alliance, All Progressive Grand Alliance, Accord Party, and Labour Party among others. The study draws from Agina-Ude's[2] criteria for assessment of women's acceptability or marginalization in internal political party affairs. Focusing on national and subnational representation of women in elective and appointive positions in Nigeria, this study attempts to address three research questions: How has the implementation of the National Gender Policy (NGP) in the internal selection processes of political parties impacted on the representation of women in elective positions in Nigeria? To what extent are the rights of women in elective and appointive positions protected against discrimination and unfair treatment in their official capacities? How has the change of party in power—from the ruling PDP to APC—affected the level of women's participation and representation in politics in Nigeria?

The study establishes that only a few impactful gender equality bills have been passed in Nigeria. However, implementation remains very poor. The experiences of women in the past elections between 1999 and 2015 show that political parties have refused to integrate women's needs and concerns in the business of internal democracy.[3] The constitutions of most parties commit women to gender affirmative action but few have met the 35 percent target.[4] As this study will show, mere insignificant increases were recorded in the proportion of seats held by women in the national parliament.[5]

WOMEN AND INTERNAL PARTY POLITICS

Following the political party primaries for candidates in the Nigerian 2011 and 2015 elections, it became evident that the elimination of women from party positions through a well-orchestrated process of manipulating the outcome of most primaries was virtually party policy across board. Thus, most of the women who competed in the primaries were eliminated from nomination; although, the parties had previously promised that many female aspirants would be encouraged and supported in their quest for nominations. Indeed, the primaries were a charade because many popular female candidates and other unlucky male candidates were edged out by party barons and replaced by other candidates who enjoyed the support of state and party executives.

This study assessed the challenges of registered female political aspirants in the major political parties that have won legislative seats in Nigeria, in line with Agina-Ude's criteria for assessment of women's acceptability or marginalization in political parties.[6] The findings reveal the following means used to marginalize women at internal party selection processes:

Labeling as a Strategy of Exclusion:
Subverting Affirmative Action

Female candidates reveal that they have never been taken seriously by their party leadership. This is partly because female contestants have little financial muscle to compete with their male counterparts. Women who mount pressure on their parties for a waiver on nomination fees are perceived by party executives as having insufficient commitment to the party. Conversely, party executives remark that male candidates are more committed because they make their financial contributions willingly.

Labeling Women Aspirants as Cultural Deviants

The female folk in key political parties in Nigeria confess that their parties are still entangled in traditional beliefs which does not accept assertive, public, or leadership roles for women. As a result, most party executives secretly work against female contestants in their parties despite gender-sensitive claims and the rhetoric being advertized during party campaigns. Many party officials made overt or covert statements about some female aspirants being too assertive and independent and therefore not capable of being team players. This hallmarks the chauvinistic attitude of men and their manipulative tendencies against women in their parties.

The Politics of the Invective

Most of the female aspirants accused their fellow male contestants of adopting invectives—that is, abusive language—to demoralize and delegitimize their political ambition. Many of the female candidates were subjected to smear campaigns and direct insults centered on their alleged flirtatious lifestyle. In some instances, party women were linked to romantic affairs with powerful politicians by their "male" detractors who claim that only loose women get political appointments.

The Indigeneity Ploy

The provision of indigeneship in the 1999 Constitution of Nigeria has been subverted to discriminate against Nigerian citizens who are not indigenous to the places where they live and work. In this respect, women married to men who are nonindigenes of their local governments suffer worse forms of discrimination. Similarly, in their own constituencies, they are told that by marrying outside their places of birth, they have lost their indigeneity. In their husband's constituency, they are told they do not really belong because indigeneity is based on the consanguinity principle. Invariably, only very few women who are lucky enough to marry from their own local communities stand a chance to be accommodated and allowed to take active participation in internal party politics, if at all.

Other Techniques for the Elimination of Popular Women Aspirants in Internal Party Elections

Nigerian parties used a wide range of techniques to eliminate women from party primaries, including:

- A declaration by powerful "party owners," party barons, state governors, godfathers, and so on that those entitled to vote must support a particular candidate and that other aspirants must withdraw. Since these people (male candidates) are very powerful and feared in their communities, their declarations carry much authority.

- Money, a significant factor in party primaries, is used to bribe officials and to induce voters to support particular candidates. Since the godfather generally has more money than the "independent" aspirants trying to gain access to political office, many women were outcompeted because they simply cannot match their opponents' spending.
- Another disturbing technique is what Nigerians call "results by declaration," whereby an aspirant wins a nomination or election, but polling officials simply disregard the results and declare the loser as the winner.[7]

SECOND-GENERATION DISCRIMINATION AGAINST WOMEN IN POWER

This study also identified "second-generation discrimination" against women in power. Women occupying political positions are denied the opportunity to enjoy maternity leave, and/or *omugwo* with its attached benefits. There is no law protecting women occupying elective and appointive positions in Nigeria against these denials and discrimination. This challenge continues to debar and shut out prospective nursing and young mothers from engaging in politics.

From the above, it is evident there is an inherent lack of confidence in party women by their male counterparts and the party leadership. Men are often viewed as more viable and marketable candidates and are given preference to female candidates. As a result, political party leaders are under the illusion that fielding a female candidate is a "passport to failure." Even when women possess the characteristics that make for acceptable candidates, they often are not encouraged to step forward to become candidates. Selective mentoring is an effective strategy and determinable outcome which male politicians have been using to groom young men who will replace them in politics. This reality is captured thus:

> As of today, in Nigeria, there is marginal participation of women in governance and they have remained invisible in the party system, which claim to encourage their participation in elective positions through free nomination, yet are discriminated against in practice. While one cannot deny that the Nigerian government has scored well on adopting and or formulating measures to address gender injustice, they have however failed to allocate resources critical to the implementation and ensure proper functioning of these measures.[8]

More importantly, vestiges of masculine domination of political leadership have become extremely challenging and responsible for the difficulty in working out a positive framework for greater participation of women in party electoral processes. Party manifestoes and activities are yet to fully reflect women's political issues. Aluko Yetunde asserts:

> Vestiges of masculine domination of political leadership weigh on iterations of change, which also vary by context. It is therefore clear that political leadership in Nigeria is stratified on the bases of gender distinction, thereby calling to question the assertion of gender neutrality in the political arena. Political parties in Nigeria have always been and are still dominated by men, and there is an unwillingness to include women high on the electoral list during elections, make women issues high on their list of priorities or even include them in decision-making positions within the party. Party manifestoes and activities are yet to fully reflect women's issues; instead they remain confined to the women's wing of the various parties where they are treated as subordinates and mere supporters instead of equal partners.[9]

To say the least, the nature of internal party politics in Nigeria is nearly antiwomen and nongender sensitive. It is hardly a gender-balanced political milieu especially with regards to implementing gender-friendly policies and creating the enabling political platform for women to favorably contest elections and/or be elected into political offices. Women are said to be among the poorest people in the world and a poor person cannot play a significant role in politics. If political participation does not involve money, the story may have differed and there would have been, perhaps, more women in politics. In connection to this, Lisa Denny maintains that:

> The final challenge women face in getting elected in Nigeria relates to financial constraints. The costs of running an electoral campaign are high—even more so in the context of Nigeria where politics is highly monetized. Aside from paying for the campaign itself and the materials and coverage that go along with this, many candidates also dispense "patronage," in the form of cash handouts, to voters. Women are at a disadvantage in this regard as they consistently earn less than their male counterparts and are usually not in charge of household finances, limiting their ability to make independent decisions. While many candidates receive donations from patrons, there are few patrons willing to risk their money on female candidates, given the low likelihood of them being elected. As a result, women's campaigning is frequently smaller scale, with less coverage than that of men.[10]

Since Nigeria's democratic experience in 1999, successive governments have found it most difficult to deepen democratic structures and internal party democracy that would lap up gender-friendly actions and encourage women's political engagement. Salaam observes that political parties limit the opportunities of women from contesting internal party primaries by increasing the cost of indication of interest forms.[11] Hence, women who are less economically advantaged are unable to mobilize enough resources to compete with their male counterparts since politics is often heavily "monetized" due to the high cost of electioneering campaign in political parties. For example, in the 2006 primaries for the 2007 general elections, thirty-one presidential aspirants obtained nomination forms at N5 million each (totaling 155 million naira), while three female aspirants were exempted from payment as a way of encouraging the participation of women. However, female aspirants still paid the compulsory 10,000 naira for the expression of interest (totaling 310,000 naira) just like their male counterparts. The expression of interest fee was also applied to all electable positions at all levels of government. The costs of the nomination form for gubernatorial, senatorial, and house of representative aspirants were pegged at three million, one million, and 500,000 naira, respectively. On the other hand, aspirants to the State House of Assembly paid 100,000 naira each.[12]

In 2015, the ruling party APC purposely hiked the cost of these forms as a strategy to directly confront and undermine the benefits and prospects of the "Not-Too-Young to Run" Bill. Thus, the APC inflated its presidential expression of interest and nomination fees from 7 million to 45 million; its gubernatorial forms to N22.5 million; its senatorial forms to N7 million; its House of Representatives forms to 3.85 million; and its State House of Assembly forms to N850,000. This in itself is clear machination and an orchestrated plan to discourage qualified women from contesting. The noninclusivity of the political parties' program is one of the fundamental reasons for the low participation of Nigerian women in politics.

Although nomination fees are often waived for women by their political parties, this practice also works against them. For instance, party chieftains argued that women who did not purchase forms cannot take precedence over men who paid huge nomination fees.[13] Moreover, Section 93 (1-12) of the 2006 Electoral Act, which stipulates the election expenses, did not reduce it for the benefit of female contestants who are more likely to be financially vulnerable. This further limits the capacity of female contestants from electioneering activities. In particular, the election expenses are as follows: presidential candidate (N500 million), governorship candidate (N100 million), senatorial candidate (N20 million), house of representative candidate (N10 million), House of Assembly candidate (N5 million), LGA chairmanship candidate (N5 million), and LGA councillorship candidate (N500,000 thousand) (Okocha, 2009).

Furthermore, women are seldom found where the party programs and strategies are drawn and the main politics of the party take place. Alternatively, they are too busy with the women's wing. The formation of the women's wing of the political parties is as a result of women accepting their "second-fiddle" status. It shows that they unknowingly do not deem it fit to take part in the day-to-day running of the party except they are separated from the men. They have to conform to the exclusionary norms of the parties. Worse still, any woman who attempts to break this exclusion is seen as a nonconformist and treated with scorn even by fellow women. The real problem is with the hypocrisy of the patriarchal nature of the Nigerian politics in which every women seeking a role in public life is commonly seen as a "busybody."[14]

Broadly speaking, several hurdles hinder Nigerian women's successful participation in politics. Lack of internal democracy in the political parties hinders women's emergence as candidates for elective positions. Godfathers who fund the political party machineries wield excessive power and have preference for male candidates. Since men are usually in the majority in the political party setup, they tend to dominate the party hierarchy and are therefore at an advantage in influencing the party's internal politics. Women's underrepresentation in party membership arises from the social, cultural, and religious attitudes of different Nigerian societies which most often relegate women to the background. As a result, only very few men, even among the educated, allow their wives to participate in politics.[15]

REPRESENTATION OF WOMEN IN ELECTIVE POSITIONS IN NIGERIA

The introduction of the NGP in 2007 did not translate into tangible increase in women representation in politics. For instance, only about a 3 percent increase in women representation in considerable positions occurred in 1999; 4 percent in 2003 and 6 percent in 2007. Although the NGP set a target of 35 percent as a benchmark toward gender parity in Nigeria, much work is still required.

For the 2011 Presidential elections, only one woman—Chief (Mrs) Ebiti Ndok, of United Nations Development Program—emerged as a candidate. In the National Assembly elections, only 9.1 percent of the candidates were female. Only twelve women contested under various political parties for the 2011 governorship position out of 338 contestants (representing 3.5 percent) while sixty-two women out of 338 contested for the position of deputy governorship—a paltry 18 percent. Many of these female candidates contested under relatively new and unknown political parties.[16] Indeed, a close examination of the participation of women in 2011 elections shows that only a few women were given the opportunity to represent their parties in the general elections. As Irabor contends, "internal party selection processes and outcomes during the 2011 elections suggest that in all political parties few women were elected to contest seats; and that those were selected were given seats that were hard to win."[17] Table 12.1 depicts the marginal number

Table 12.1   Number of Women Contestants in Various Political Parties in Nigeria, 2011

Office Contested	Gender		
2011	*Female Candidates*	*Male Candidates*	*Total*
Presidents	1(0)	19(1)	20
Vice Presidents	3(0)	17(1)	20
Governors	13(0)	340(36)	353
Deputy Governors	58(1)	289(35)	347
Senatorial	90(7)	800(102)	890
House of Reps	220(19)	2,188(341)	2408

Note: The numbers in bracket represent elected candidates. Nigerian Bureau of Statistics, "Social Statistics in Nigeria," *Nigeria Bureau of Statistics*, http://nigerianstat.gov.ng/download/169, accessed on June 3, 2013.

of women who contested the 2011 elections in different political parties in Nigeria as well as the few winnings recorded.

Table 12.1 shows that women did not compete for the president and governorship positions in any of the political parties. Only 9 percent of the candidates for the National Assembly elections in April 2011 were women. Similarly, only 4 percent of the candidates who contested on behalf of various political parties for the office of governor were women. A mere 9.06 percent representing 909 of the 10,037 candidates for available seats were women. Following the election of only twenty-five women elected to the 360-member House of Representatives, Nigeria was ranked 118 out of 192 countries in terms of gender parity in 2012. At 9 percent, the low representation of women in Nigeria's House of Representatives is significantly below the global average (15 percent), and far behind South Africa's and Rwanda's representation (43 percent and 56 percent, respectively). Thus, Nigeria's sixty-three-registered political parties have failed to deliver gender parity in political representation at the national level.

Representation at the local government level is equally low. As at 2012, only about 4 percent of Nigeria's councilors were women, compared with South Africa's 38 percent.[18] In the twenty-nine states where governorship elections held in 2011, the representation of women seeking the office of governor and deputy governor stood at 22.9 percent—representing eighty-seven out of the 380 candidates running for the positions. That pathetic figure was made up of candidates from less known political parties, amounting to no significant increase in women's representation. In the contest for senatorial seats, 122 women out of 747 candidates, representing 16 percent, were cleared by Independent National Electoral Commission (INEC) to run. However, only eight of them eventually won elections to the upper chamber equating to101 men against eight women in the Senate. In the lower chamber, the situation was not any better as 267 women out of a total of 1,774 candidates ran for seats at the House of Representatives. This is just 15 percent of the total.

Table 12.2 shows the number and percentage distribution of women elected to public office at the national level.

Table 12.2   Percentage Distribution of Women elected to Political Offices in Nigeria, 1999–2011

Office	*1999*		*2003*		*2007*		*2011*	
	Seats available	Women	Seats available	Women	Seats available	Women	Seats available	Women
President	1	0	1	0	1	0	1	0
Senate	109	3(2.8%)	109	4(3.7%)	109	9 (8.3%)	109	7(6.4%)
House of Representatives	360	7(1.9%)	360	21(5.8%)	360	27(7.5%)	360	25(6.9%)
Governor	36	0	36	0	36	0	36	0
State House Assembly (SHA)	990	24(2.4%)	990	40(3.9%)	990	57(5.8%)	990	68(6.9%)
SHA Committee Chairpersons	829	18(2.2%)	881	32(3.6%)	887	52(5.9%)	887	-
LGA Chairpersons	710	13(1.8%)	774	15(1.9)	740	27(3.6%)	740	-
Councilors	6368	69(1.1%)	6368	267(4.2%)	6368	235(3.7%)	6368	-

Source: Nigerian National Bureau of Statistics, "Profile of Women and Men in Nigeria," www.nigerianstat.gov.ng; *National Bureau of Statistics, Profile of Women and Men in Nigeria,* (Abuja: Federal Government of Nigeria, 2009), http/www.nigerianstat.gov.ng, accessed on June 3, 2013.

The 2011 figures as presented in table 12.2 underscore a sharp and consistent retrogression from women's position in 2007. Hence, there has been an overall regression in women's representation in political decision-making positions.[19] Seven out of 109 (6.42 percent) senators elected in 2011 were women compared to nine (10 percent) in 2007, while only twelve out of 360 (3.33 percent) were members of the House of Representatives, down from twenty-six in 2007. Out of Nigeria's thirty-six states only one—Lagos State—voted in a woman deputy governor; but no woman was elected governor.[20] Based on this, Oladoye argues that setting an agreed quota system within and between the parties could be a useful starting point to entrench gender equality.[21] Evidence from countries like South Africa and Rwanda that have managed to increase women's participation in politics suggests that until women candidates are nominated at party level to contest winnable seats, any talk of equity in gender representation will be slow and may not be achievable in the short term.

WOMEN'S POLITICAL PARTICIPATION IN THE 2015 ELECTION IN NIGERIA

According to data provided on the INEC website, only one female presidential candidate contested the 2015 elections; while there were four female vice-presidential candidates, one main governorship contender, and five deputy governorship candidates; and 266 contestants for House of Representatives and 127 contestants for Senate seats in the said 2015 elections. However, only eight women eventually won seats into the Eighth Senate, out of the 109 seats available. Three of the eight female senators were of the APC. The five other women were from the PDP.[22]

In the House of Representatives, the situation was not much different, although the return rate was not as dismal as that recorded in the House of Senate. Only fourteen women out of a total of 256 female candidates cleared for the House of Representatives elections were elected on the platform of the APC and PDP, the two leading political parties. On the other hand, the gubernatorial elections produced four female deputy governors. They were Oluranti Adebule (Lagos State), Mrs. Yetunde Onanuga (Ogun State), Ipalibo Banigo (Rivers State), and Cecilia Ezeilo (Enugu State).[23]

A total number of 755 female candidates were cleared by the INEC to contest the 2015 general elections into the various Houses of Assembly across all the political parties in the entire country. On a state by state basis, Enugu State had the highest number of female candidates at sixty-seven, followed by Anambra with sixty-five candidates, while Yobe and Katsina states recorded an all-time low of one candidate each. On the basis of Nigeria's six geopolitical zones, the south west had the highest number with 252 female House of Assembly candidates, followed by the south east with 203, then, the north central with 108 and the south with 96, while the north west and north east geopolitical zones had fifty-seven and thirty-nine female candidates, respectively cleared to contest the elections.

However, when compared to the number of male candidates cleared for the same election, these numbers of female candidates pale into insignificance as a total of 4520 male candidates emerged against 755 females nationwide for the House of Assembly elections. The highest number of male candidates for that election came from Oyo state with 234, followed by Kano with 220, and Imo with 218 candidates. It is surprising that Oyo state with a high number of male candidates had only twenty-eight females contesting and thus had the highest differentials between male and female at 206. Similarly, Kano with 220 male candidates had only nineteen females with a difference of 201, followed by Imo State with at 188, Sokoto at 169, and Katsina at 162. Of all, Enugu and Osun with a fair number of both female and male candidates recorded the lowest number of thirty-one and forty-five, respectively.[24]

In the 2015 election, women performed poorly in the aspect of National Assembly positions attained. Nigeria had only three women out of 109 available seats in the House of Senate in 1999—a doleful 2.8 percent. Nonetheless, this was a slight improvement in the total number of elected women from 2003 when four women made it to the upper chamber (3.7 percent) and this number further increased to nine (8.3 percent) in 2007. Conversely, there was a slight decline in 2011 when only seven women made it to the Senate (6.4 percent) despite an increase in gender advocacy among civil society organizations. By 2015, representation was still at 7.3 percent as only eight women were elected to the Senate. Likewise, in 1999, twelve women were elected into the House of Representatives out of the 360 available seats. This is only a representation of 3.3 percent in a country where women comprise almost 50 percent of the population. Nigeria had 5.8 percent female representation in 2003 when twenty-one women were elected. In 2007, it improved with an increase to twenty-five women being elected (6.9 percent) and twenty-six women 7.2 percent in 2011. Disappointingly, the numbers dropped in 2015 as only fourteen women were elected representing just 3.8 percent of the house.[25]

In contradistinction to the National Assembly, the State House of Assembly elections have seen a steady improvement since 1999. In 1999, out of the 991 members of the State Houses of Assembly twenty-four were women; comprising only 2.4 percent of members of the State Houses of Assembly across Nigeria. In 2003, Nigeria had forty (3.9 percent) women representation in State Houses of Assembly. In 2011, women's representation in the State Houses of Assembly stood at 5.8 percent with fifty-seven women. In 2007 and 2011, there were sixty-eight women out of the 991 State Houses of Assembly legislators across Nigeria representing a meager 6.8 percent. In 2015, according to the analysis of the results published by INEC, out of the 919 seats contested, women won only forty-six seats, bringing their total representation to only 4.6 percent. Some states lacked a single female in the State Houses of Assembly. Unfortunately, most of the states where there were no female legislators are found in the north east, north west, and north central—these states include Jigawa, Kano, Kaduna, Katsina, Gombe, Kebbi, Benue, and Kogi.

Women's Performance in Major Appointive Posts

Representation has been lopsided for Nigerian women in top public offices. In the Eighth Senate, none of the principal officers was a woman, and only eight of the 109 senators were women. The House of Representatives had only one female principal officer. However, only twenty-four (7 percent) of the 362 members were women. The figures of women in Nigerian politics are in contrast with the situation in countries such as Rwanda, where women make up sixty-one of 106 parliamentarians (58 percent), and Senegal where women occupy sixty-five of the 150 parliamentary seats (43 percent). In Nigeria's thirty-six states, there is no female governor, and the country does not appear ready to have a woman as president. All of these realities exist despite the country's NGP's promise to support women to occupy 35 percent of elective positions in Nigeria.[26]

Table 12.3 summarizes the level of women's participation in major appointive positions in Nigeria between 1999 and 2011.

Table 12.3   Statistics on Women's Performance in Major Appointive Posts, 1999–2011

Office Type	No. Available	1999 Men	1999 Women	2003 Men	2003 Women	2007 Men	2007 Women	2011 Men	2011 Women
Vice President	1	1	Nil	1	Nil	1	Nil	1	Nil
Senate President	1	1	Nil	1	Nil	1	Nil	1	Nil
Speaker of the House of Representatives	1	1	Nil	1	Nil	1	1	1	Nil
Deputy Governors	36	35	1	34	2	34	2	30	6
Speaker of the State Houses of Assembly	36	35	1	34	2	35	1	34	2
Deputy Speakers of the State Houses of Assembly	36	36	Nil	35	1	35	1	35	1
Cabinet Ministers	49	45	4	43	6	39	10	39	10

Source: Nigerian Bureau of Statistics, "Social Statistics in Nigeria," *Nigeria Bureau of Statistics*, http://nigeri-anstat.gov.ng/download/169, accessed on October 28, 2015.

Table 12.3 indicates unacceptable and insignificant increases in the number of women that gained appointive positions in Nigeria since 1999. A comparative juxtaposition of the lackluster success achieved in the period 1999–2007 and after (i.e., 2007–2011) shows that no robust attempts had been made toward the enforcement of NGP to the extent of creating an obvious impact on Nigerian politics.

Ministerial Portfolios

Women have equally suffered the same fate in appointive or nonelective positions. Remarkably, President Olusegun Obasanjo's administration saw to the inclusion of a greater number of women in ministerial positions. In his first tenure out of forty-one ministerial positions, seven women were eventually appointed. Even though this administration involved women in governance, their positions were nonetheless mostly subordinate, especially as Ministers of State, in which they served as deputies under men who occupied the substantive portfolios.

Similarly, in the Yar'Adua/Goodluck Jonathan-led government, more women were appointed from 2007 yet mostly as Ministers of State. On the other hand, Jonathan's administration retained some important women who served during Yar'Adua's tenure as ministers while he made a few new female appointments. However, Jonathan appointed more women than any other president's his special advisers. Table 12.4 depicts the trend of women ministerial portfolio in Nigeria between 1999 and 2011.

Table 12.4 highlights that women have not achieved any significant increase in appointive positions in Nigeria within the said period.

Table 12.4   Trend of Women Ministerial Portfolios/Special Advisers in Nigeria, 1999 and 2011

Year	Tenure	Number of Available Portfolios	No of Seat Allotted to Women	Portfolio	Name
1999	Olusegun Obasanjo	40	8	Aviation	Mrs. Kema Chikwe
				Defense/state	Mrs. Dupe Adelaja
				Finance/state	Madam Adamu Ciroma
				Health/state	Dr. (Mrs.) Amina Ndalano
				Solid Minerals/ state	Dr. Bekky Ketebuigwe
				Science & Tech/ state	Mrs. Pauline Tallen
				Women Affairs	Mrs. Aishat Ismali
				Women Affairs/ Special Adviser	Chief (Mrs.) Titilaya Ajanaku
2006	Olusegun Obasanjo	42	7	Education	Dr. Oby ezekwesili
				Foreign Affairs	Mrs. Nenadi Usman
				Finance	Dr. Ngozi Okonjo iwuala
				Women and Youth	Mrs. Maryam Ciroma
				Health/state	Mrs. Helen Esuene
				Special Duties	Mrs. Grace Egbuche
				Water Resources/ state	Mrs. Salome Jakande
2007	Umaru Musa Yar'Adua	41	14	Education	Prof. Ruquayyatu A. Rufai
				Finance/state II	Mrs. Sulamatu Suleiman
				Commerce and Industry/state	Mrs. Josephine Tapgun
				Women Affairs	Mrs. Iyom Josephine Anenih
				Petroleum	Dr. Diezani Allison-Madueke

(Continued)

Table 12.4   Trend of Women Ministerial Portfolios/Special Advisers in Nigeria, 1999 and 2011 (Continued)

Year	Tenure	Number of Available Portfolios	No of Seat Allotted to Women	Portfolio	Name
				Aviation	Mrs. Fidelia Njama
				FCT/state	Mrs. Jumoke Akinjide
				Finance	Dr. Ngozi Okonjo Iweala
				Aviation	Mrs. Stella Odua-Ogiemwonyi
				Niger Delta Affairs/state	Hajia Zainab Ibrahim Kuchi
				Foreign Affairs/ state	Mrs. Viola Onwuliri
				Women Affairs	Hajia Zainab Maina
				Defense/state	Mrs. Erelu Olusola Obada
				Land and Housing	Mrs. Ama Pepple
2011	Goodluck Jonathan	44	10	Aviation	Mrs. Stella Odua-Ogiemwonyi
				Defense	Mrs. Erelu Olusola Obada
				Education	Prof. Ruquayyatu A. Rufai
				FCT/state	Mrs. Jumoke Akinjide
				Finance	Dr. Ngozi Okonjo Iweala
				Foreign Affairs/ state	Mrs. Viola Onwuliri
				Niger Delta Affairs/state	Hajia Zainab Ibrahim Kuchi
				Petroleum	Dr. Diezani Allison-Madueke

(Continued)

Table 12.4   Trend of Women Ministerial Portfolios/Special Advisers in Nigeria, 1999 and 2011 (Continued)

Year	Tenure	Number of Available Portfolios	No of Seat Allotted to Women	Portfolio	Name
2011	Goodluck Jonathan	**Advisers**		Science and Tech	Mrs. Ita Okon Bassey
				Women Affairs	Zainab Maina
				Ethics and Value	Mrs. Stella Jibril
				National Assembly Matters	Senator Joy Emodi
				Social Development	Mrs. Serah Akuben Pane
				Gender Issues	Mrs. Asma'u Abdulkadir

Source: Nigerian Bureau of Statistics, "Social Statistics in Nigeria," *Nigeria Bureau of Statistics*, http://nigeri-anstat.gov.ng/download/169, accessed on June 3, 2013.

CONCLUSION

This paper established that there are still obvious aspects of women discrimination in both electoral and appointive positions in Nigeria. Women's political participation in Nigeria has remained marginal and worse off than it was expected to be, although in Nigeria's 2015 general elections, women recorded far better participation than the 1999, 2003, and 2011 elections, respectively. However, the much expected balance is yet to be achieved therefore there is yet no effective women's participation in Nigerian politics. The much anticipated 35 percent affirmative action as declared in the 2007 NGP is still far away from reality. The political parties are without a quota system or reserved seats for women in their leadership structures and they tend to have very few women leaders. More especially, party leadership is skewed against women contesting internal party primaries by increasing the cost of indication of interest form. Lack of internal party democracy is also a major limitation to women's political ambitions. These fundamental impediments have critically undermined the chances of women winning party tickets in elections in Nigeria.

Political parties should therefore implement vital and balanced policy that reflects the aspirations and needs of the women contenders. Internal party processes should be demonetized so that most women with lean financial muscles will not be elbowed out of the race from the onset. A twinning system is being proposed to ensure that if, for example, the governorship

candidate is a male, the deputy will be a female. This strategy may likely improve the participation of women in Nigerian politics.

NOTES

1. This is a longstanding Igbo custom. Shortly before the due date of a pregnant woman, her mother arrives to stay with her for the birth and at least 2 months postpartum. Her mother (the grandmother) bathes the baby, does all the cooking. She also bathes her daughter, the new mother, helping her massage important areas like the abdomen with hot water. The new mother is not expected to lift a finger during *omugwo* or go outside the house. She just eats and nurses her baby and others take care of the chores.

2. Ada Agina-Ude, "Strategies for Expanding Female Participation in the 2003 Elections and Beyond," *The Nigerian Social Scientist* 6, no. 1 (2003): 3–7.

3. Amina A. Salihu, "Nigeria Women's Trust Fund: Politics Strategy and Sustainability" (Abuja: The Nigerian Women's Trust Fund, 2011).

4. San Mahdi, "Political Context for Development and Gender Equality in Nigeria," (Lagos: British Council, 2011).

5. This record is below the global average and well behind other African countries such as South Africa and Rwanda.

6. Agina-Ude, "Strategies."

7. Ibid., 12

8. Victor Iwuoha, "ICT and Elections in Nigeria: Rural Dynamics of Biometric Voting Technology Adoption," *Africa Spectrum* 53, no. 3 (2018): 89–113; Charles Umeha, "Women: The Journey to Political Relevance," *Champion Newspapers*, January 16, 2010, 14.

9. Aluko Yetunde, "The Consequences of Gender and Women's Political Leadership in Nigeria Context" (proceedings of the 16th Annual Conference on The Social Dimension of Nigerian Democratizing Process, University of Ilorin, Nigeria, August 9–11, 2011).

10. Lisa Denny, "Nigeria: Women on the Outskirts of Politics," *Open Democracy*, 2012, accessed June 3, 2013, http://www.opendemocracy.net/5050/lisa-denney/nigeria-women-on-outskirts-of-politics.

11. Titi Salaam, "A Brief Analysis on the Situation of Women in Nigeria Today," (Abuja: Democratic Socialist Movement, 2003), accessed on September 8, 2013, http://www.socialistnigeria.org/women/1-3-03.html.

12. Jonah Ojo, "The Challenge of Electoral Reform through Enhanced Political Party Management and Internal Democracy," (paper presented at the 1st National Conference and General Assembly of Society for Peace Studies and Practice, Abuja, Nigeria, June 17, 2008).

13. Sulaiman Y. Kura, "Political Parties and Democracy in Nigeria: Candidate Selection, Campaign and Party Financing in People's Democratic Party," *Journal of Sustainable Development in Africa* 13, no. 6 (2011): 268–298.

14. Oby Nwankwo, "Women & 2011 Elections in Nigeria," *Heinrich Boll Stiftung*, accessed on September 12, 2013, http://www.ng.boell.org/web/gender-231.html.

15. Bonn Nwanolue, Chike Osegbue, and Victor Iwuoha, "Between Universality and Political Reality: A Reflection on the Inclusiveness of Women in Nigerian Politics, 1960-2012," *ANSU Journal of Peace and Development Studies* 1, no. 1 (2012): 12–27.

16. Dan Oladeye,"In Retrospect: 2011 April Polls and Gender Ranking in Nigeria," accessed August 7, 2013, http://www.cp-africa.com/2011/05/17/in-retros pect-2011-april-polls-and-gender-rankingin-nigeria/#/news.

17. Favour O. Irabor, "Women's Participation and Performance in Nigerian Politics: Challenges and Solutions," (paper presented at a round table discussion on the Empowerment of Women In Politics, Abuja, Nigeria, December 13, 2012), 2.

18. British Council, "Gender in Nigeria Report 2012: Improving Lives of Girls and Women in Nigeria," 1, accessed June 3, 2013, http:/www.britishcouncil.org/Af rica-ng-gender-report-2012.

19. National Bureau of Statistics, *Profile of Women and Men in Nigeria* (Abuja: Federal Government of Nigeria, 2009), accessed June 3, 2013, http/www.nigerianstat .gov.ng.

20. National Bureau of Statistics, *Annual Abstract of Statistics* (Abuja: Federal Government of Nigeria, 2011).

21. Oladeye, "In Retrospect."

22. Anambra and Ekiti States produced two candidates each and the other candidate wasfrom Cross River State.

23. Ekwy P. Uzoanya and Tobi Awodipe, "Nigerian Women's Scorecard in 2015 Polls," *The Guardian*, April 18, 2015, https://guardian.ng/features/nigerian-womens-scorecard-in-2015-polls/.

24. Nse E. Akpan, "Men without Women: An Analysis of The 2015 General Elections In Nigeria," accessed July 25, 2017, http://www.inecnigeria.org/wp-conte nt/uploads/2015/07/Conference-Paper-by-Nse-Etim-Akpan.pdf.

25. International Republican Institute, "2015 Nigeria Election Observation Report" (Washington, DC: International Republican Institute, 2015), accessed October 5, 2017, http://www.iri.org/2015%20Nigeria%20Election%20Observation%20Report /1/assets/basic-html/page39.html.

26. International Republican Institute, "2015 Nigeria Election," Federal Ministry of Women's Affairs and Social Development, *National Gender Policy* (Abuja: Federal Ministry of Women's Affairs and Social Development, 2006).

BIBLIOGRAPHY

Agina-Ude, Ada. "Strategies for Expanding Female Participation in the 2003 Elections and Beyond." *The Nigerian Social Scientist* 6, no. 1 (2003): 3–7.

Akpan, Nse E. "Men Without Women: An Analysis of the 2015 General Elections in Nigeria," *INEC Online Publication*, 2015. Accessed July 25, 2017.http://www

.inecnigeria.org/wp-content/uploads/2015/07/Conference-Paper-by-Nse-Etim-Ak
pan.pdf.

British Council. "Gender in Nigeria Report 2012: Improving Lives of Girls and
Women in Nigeria," *British Council Report*, 2012. Accessed June 3, 2013
http:/www.britishcouncil.org/Africa-ng-gender-report-2012.

Denny, Lisa. "Nigeria: Women on the Outskirts of Politics," *Open Democracy*, 2012.
Accessed June 3, 2013. http://www.opendemocracy.net/5050/lisa-denney/nigeria
-women-on-outskirts-of-politics.

Federal Ministry of Women's Affairs and Social Development. "National Gender
Policy." Abuja: Federal Ministry of Women's Affairs and Social Development,
2006.

International Republican Institute. "2015 Nigeria Election Observation Report."
Washington DC: International Republican Institute, 2015.

Irabor, Favour O. "Women's Participation and Performance in Nigerian Politics:
Challenges and Solutions." Paper Presented at a Round Table Discussion on the
Empowerment of Women in Politics, Abuja, Nigeria, December 13, 2012.

Iwuoha, Victor C. "ICT and Elections in Nigeria: Rural Dynamics of Biometric
Voting Technology Adoption." *Africa Spectrum* 53, no. 3 (2018): 89–113.

Kura, Sulaiman Y. "Political Parties and Democracy in Nigeria: Candidate Selection,
Campaign and Party Financing in People's Democratic Party." *Journal of
Sustainable Development in Africa* 13, no. 6 (2011): 268–298.

Mahdi, San. *Political Context for Development and Gender Equality in Nigeria.*
Lagos: British Council, 2011.

National Bureau of Statistics. *Profile of Women and Men in Nigeria.* Abuja: Federal
Government of Nigeria, 2009.

National Bureau of Statistics. *Annual Abstract of Statistics.* Abuja: Federal
Government of Nigeria, 2011.

Nwankwo, Oby. "Women & 2011 Elections in Nigeria." *Heinrich Boll Stiftung*,
2011. Accessed September 12, 2013. http://www.ng.boell.org/web/gender-231.h
tml.

Nwanolue, Bonn, Chike Osegbue and Victor C. Iwuoha. "Between Universality and
Political Reality: A Reflection on the Inclusiveness of Women in Nigerian Politics,
1960-2012." *ANSU Journal of Peace and Development Studies* 1, no. 1 (2012):
12–27.

Ojo, Jonah. "The Challenge of Electoral Reform through Enhanced Political Party
Management and Internal Democracy," Paper Presented at the 1st National
Conference and General Assembly of Society for Peace Studies and Practice,
Abuja, Nigeria, June 17, 2008.

Oladeye, Da. "In Retrospect: 2011 April Polls and Gender Ranking in Nigeria." *CP
Africa*, 17 May 2011. http://www.cp-africa.com/2011/05/17/in-retrospect-2011-
april-polls-and-gender-rankingin-nigeria/#/news.

Salaam, Titi. *A Brief Analysis on the Situation of Women in Nigeria Today.* Abuja:
Democratic Socialist Movement, 2003.

Salihu, Amina A. "Nigeria Women's Trust Fund: Politics Strategy and Sustainability."
Abuja: The Nigerian Women's Trust Fund, 2011.

Umeha, Charles. "Women: The Journey to Political Relevance." *Champion Newspapers*, January 16, 2010.

Uzoanya, Ekwy P. and Tobi Awodipe. "Nigerian Women's Scorecard in 2015 Polls." *The Guardian*, April 18, 2015. https://guardian.ng/features/nigerian-womens-score card-in-2015-polls/.

Yetunde, Aluko. "The Consequences of Gender and Women's Political Leadership in Nigeria Context." Proceedings of the 16th Annual Conference on the Social Dimension of Nigerian Democratizing Process, University of Ilorin, Nigeria, August 9-11, 2011.

Chapter 13

Silence and Power in Yejide Kilanko's *Daughters Who Walk This Path*

Nneoma Onwuegbuchi

Literature is essentially, art. As art, it takes shape by itself and it is this very quality according to Sosthenes Ekeh that "undergirds its significance."[1] The implication of this self-sufficiency is what accounts for art's ability to divorce itself from external referents. In essence, the self-sustenance of art highlights the ambiguity of the literary object because art's framework—in Frye's words—involves an "inductive survey of the literary field."[2] More so, the literary text's plurivocity is such that emphasizes its ambiguity: an intelligibility that is interrogated in Yejide Kilanko's *Daughters Who Walk This Path*. To a great extent, this resonance is entrenched in a depth that is underlain by symbols both at the mythic and at the primary level. Against this backdrop, this paper unveils the matrix that underlies the myth of sexual violation that the mythological image of Philomela enshrouds. This myth is illuminated by Morayo, the text's central protagonist, who models markedly the mythological figure of Philomela.

Furthermore, this paper interrogates the various shades of silence exhibited by Morayo, especially upon her desecration by Bros T, and aims to bring to the fore how phallocratic socialization processes within the text's world foster this silence. This mythical mediation on sexual defilement is not without an anchor as this paper aims to articulate the primary symbol of power. The premise of this investigation is directed at the demonstration of the interplay of power relations and silence in the text under study. Therefore, this paper evinces how the dominant group, by enforcing silence, attains control and power over the "Other." The study also emphasizes how the compliant group regains power through the subversion of this tool of domination—a phenomenon which is regarded as "unsilence." The discussion is solely guided by the discourse of poststructuralism.

Criticism tends to bring a work of art to the forefront of discussion. In other words, no work attains the status of being literary by virtue of its publication alone. The validity of this is evinced by *Daughters Who Walk This Path*, a work which since its publication is yet to receive a remarkable amount of attention by literary critics. So far, the only evaluations of *Daughters Who Walk This Path* have been reviews sourced from online journals and blogs as well as critiques that do not project its introversion. For instance, Shamila Dodhy engages this text from a critical viewpoint; however, her reading reflects the replication of colonial violence—a testament to a decay of the Nigerian civil body politic. Thus, in her treatise, she maintains that "[t]he novel exposes the hypocrisy and corrupt activities of politicians through the character of Chief Omoniyi."[3]

It is at this point that this essay deviates from what is avowed in Dohdy's argument as it asserts that despite Dohdy's critical standpoint and other distinctive reviews, such readings are merely tantamount to, in Ekeh's terms, a "casual vulgarization of textual integrity."[4] To this end, this paper engages Kilanko's text at the level of its "textual unconscious."[5] It suffices this study to assert that although no critical engagement that depicts the introvertedness of Kilanko's text has been undergone; the absence of such recognition does not in any way denote its unliterariness as it is in Jacques Derrida's phrase "pure literature."[6] Largely, this sparseness of critical appraisal can be traced to the fact that the text divorces itself from the everyday norm. Therefore, this study maintains that the lacuna created as a result of this sparse critical attention stems from the fact that the selected text does not readily subscribe to the level of Holoquist's "social dynamics."[7]

Against this backdrop, this work identifies this dearth of poststructural criticism and sets out to fill this gap by demonstrating how mythical symbols can be utilized to articulate primary symbols. To achieve this aim, it appropriates the myth of Philomela as a veritable tool for the articulation of the primary symbol of power. Therefore, at stake in this paper is the delineation of a pervading silence which reveals the dialectics of dominance and subservience that further highlights the imbalance that characterizes power structures.

Fundamentally, any interrogation into the mythical symbol of silence and female incapacitation traces its way to Ovid's account of Philomela in Book 6 of his *Metamorphoses*. Here, the establishment of otherness is buttressed by the violent rape of Philomela by Tereus, King of Thrace. This is buttressed when the omniscient narrator asserts: /And Tereus dragged her with him/To the deep woods, to some ramshackle building/Raped her, a virgin, all alone./[8] Tereus also pitilessly cuts off her tongue: subduing her further into submission. Nevertheless, by weaving her story into a tapestry, Philomela regains her voice as she relays her ordeal to Procne, her sister.

At this juncture, it becomes important to note that although this essay utilizes Ovid's original account as a premise, it adopts a somewhat divergent view. This is evinced by the absence of an ethos of infanticide in this study. This deviation buttresses the countless interpretations which mythic thought is capable of recuperating. Even so, this paper stays true to the fact that defiance and female solidarity remain viable paths for disavowing patriarchal, linguistic incapacitations.

For various myth critics, mythic ideation presents itself as the fulcrum on which most literary narratives rest. In "The Structural Study of Myth," Claude Levi-Strauss posits that if myth is essentially language, then "in order to preserve its specifity [*sic*] we should put ourselves in a position to show that it is both the same thing as language, and also something different from it."[9] What Strauss clearly dictates in the above assertion is the manner in which the language of myth constitutes the language of literature. As such, Strauss argues for the universality and timeless nature of literature since myths date back to times unaccounted for. Close to Strauss on the matter is Bronislaw Malinowski who avows that mythic thought constitutes not only a system of language but also illuminates the "widest context of human behaviour."[10] As regards this, Malinowski justifies mythic thought as the conduit through which the collective consciousness of a people can be relayed.

Similarly, Paul Ricoeur distinguishes between two types of symbolic orders—the mythical symbol and the primary symbol: the latter because it can be articulated in a narrative. As such, he posits: "Mythical symbols are more articulated; . . . and tell the Beginning from the End of experience of which primary symbols are the avowal."[11] In other words, Ricoeur affirms that mythical symbols never exhaust primary symbols. This is against the backcloth that a primary symbol "always exceeds every representation of it."[12] In Literature, several of these primary symbols abound and they include fear, hope, evil, guilt, power, and so on. For Northrop Frye, "The narrative aspect of literature is a recurrent act of symbolic communication."[13] With regard to the above, this study affirms that while, in literature, mythical symbols enshroud mythological images; contrarily, primary symbols are unknowable, inarticulate and can only be incorporated into narratives through the appropriation of mythical symbols.

Still on the path of interrogating mythic thought, James Frazer asserts: "Recent researches into the early history of man have revealed the essential similarity with which, under many superficial differences, the human mind has elaborated its first crude philosophy of life."[14] What can be gleaned from Frazer's position is that myths proliferate and erupt a myriad of thoughts while accounting for humanity's unity. As Amechi Akwanya maintains, it is only mythic thought that is capable of apprehending occurrences within the confines of fear and hope. The relevance of this position is made distinct

when Akwanya posits: "The difference between scientific thought and mythical thinking is that the former seeks to establish a connection among disparate
phenomena, whereas mythic thought apprehends each occurrence in isolation
and often under the aspect of fear or hope."[15]

From these preceding stances, power as a primary symbol underlies the
display of violence by patriarchal ogres like Bros T and Chief Omoniyi. On
this ground, the study plumbs the milieu of silence and female incapacitation
in *Daughters Who Walk This Path* in order to demonstrate how the solidarity between Morayo and Aunty Morenike reflects the camaraderie of the
mythological figures—Philomela and Procne, and to delineate subsequently
the manner in which primary symbols can be articulated through mythical
symbols.

THE POETICS OF POSTSTRUCTURALISM

The shift from structuralism to poststructuralism involves a radical departure
from the logocentric conventions of the former. This swing in theoretical
approach informs the attempt of poststructuralists to unsettle the binary oppo-
sitions in a text's structure. Although language and antihumanism constitute
important kernels shared with structuralism, poststructuralism, however,
involves an incisive critique of the parochial Saussurean sign system of
language. It is with regard to this that the two dominant features of poststructuralism involve the decentring of the origin and an overriding emphasis
placed on signifiers. In his treatment of the poststructuralist framework, Terry
Eagleton posits that the transition following structuralism to poststructuralism involves,

> A shift from seeing the poem or novel as a closed entity, equipped with definite
> meanings which it is the critic's task to decipher, to seeing it as irreducibly
> plural, an endless play of signifiers which can never be finally nailed down to a
> single centre, essence or meaning.[16]

The critical theory of poststructuralism also projects the deconstructive
affirmations of Jacques Derrida; whose positions serve as the forerunner or
predecessor of the literary theory under focus. It is against this backdrop that
his position almost coincides with the emergence of poststructuralism. Little
wonder that he asserts that: "The centre is not the centre. The concept of the
centre . . . is contradictorily coherent."[17] Additionally for Jacques Lacan, the
French psychoanalyst whose positions involve a break from the traditional
Freudian assertions, language is appropriated as a tool for establishing individual identities. It is therefore against this backdrop that he highlights that

language inaugurates the distinction of "the principal 'I' from a host of other subjectivities."[18] Julia Kristeva, on the other hand, inaugurates the theory of intertextuality to explain the way that "the novel, seen as a text, is a semiotic practice in which the synthesized patterns of several utterances can be read."[19]

Considering the immensity of the variant critical approaches to poststructuralism, the present study becomes unable to explore, appropriately, all the strands of the aforementioned theory. It is with regard to this that attention shall be directed solely at poststructuralism from the outlook of Roland Barthes whose perspectives in *The Pleasure of the Text* constitutes the yardstick used in the analysis of the selected text.

Although earlier works of Roland Barthes develop a structuralism informed by Saussurean linguistics, in his much later treatises, he relegates the tenets of structuralism to the background. Principally, this is what informs his glide from structuralism to a poststructuralist stance. In furtherance of his idea of evacuations, he observes that, "As institution, the author is dead: his civil status, his biographical person have disappeared; dispossessed, they no longer exercise over his work the formidable paternity whose account literary history, teaching and public opinion had the responsibility of establishing and renewing."[20]

Adopting a paradigm shift from the logocentricism of structuralism, Barthes further asserts that the pleasure of the text is ensconced in the process of *ecriture*. It is with recourse to this that Barthes argues that "the text you write must prove to me that it desires me. This proof exists: it is writing."[21] In addition, Barthes also pleads in favor of the euphoric nature of the text which is also elicited by the impersonal process of reading. Arguing for the autonomy of the text's pleasure, Barthes further posits that pleasure is not "a naïve residue and is not dependent on a sensation."[22] The implication of the above articulated position is that the meaning of a text, which evokes pleasure, is not necessarily streamlined to the existence of a dominant signifier. It is with regards to this; therefore that Barthes establishes language as a temporal process of meaning making as the text involves "a transmutation of . . . a new philosophic state of the language substance."[23]

In a bid to capture the gratifying nature of the text, Barthes pleads further in favor of the "atopic" nature of language; which he considers to be "always outside of place."[24] This assertion appears to echo or reawaken one of the tenets of poststructuralism which is the subversion of a privileged centre. Subsequently, it is with regard to this—the unstable nature of language—that Barthes articulates that the text is unpredictable. Little wonder then he asserts that, "everyone can testify that the pleasure of the text is not certain: nothing says that the text will please us a second time."[25] By virtue of the similitude of sympathy, Barthes establishes how the text bears semblance to a tissue; as its meaning or truth is worked out by an interweaving of complexes. Strikingly, this position appears to be dissimilar to the tenets of structuralism where all meaning is woven around a dominant signifier. Succinctly, this tracking of resemblance is highlighted when Barthes asserts that:

> But whereas hitherto we have always taken this tissue as a product, a ready-made veil, behind which lies, more or less hidden meaning (truth), we are now emphasizing in the tissue the generative idea that the text is made, is worked out in a perpetual interweaving; lost in this tissue-this-texture-the subject unmakes himself, like a spider dissolving in the constructive secretions of its *web*. Were we fond of neologisms, we might define the theory of the text as an hyphology.[26]

In view of all this, Barthes' perception of the text as *hyphos* proves to be in unity with Eagleton's who reechoes the former's perception of the *hyphos* when he posits that: "Each sign in the chain of meaning is somehow scored over or traced through with all the others, to form a complex tissue which is never inexhaustible."[27] In all, it can be surmised that poststructuralism, as a literary theory or set of theories, strives to decenter a privileged core. This it achieves by dispersing meaning along a chain of signifiers. Primarily, this working definition plays a significant role in the analysis of *Daughters Who Walk This Path*. As regards this, this paper explores the manner in which various signifiers expound the apotheosis of male tyrants and how this contributes to female incapacitation.

This study explores three major highlights: dynamics of silence; specters of power, and conceptualizing unsilence. By the first, this paper hopes to examine the various shades of silence in the text, while projecting the dominant mode expressed in the selected text. By the second, this paper delineates a skewed power structure and how otherness is established through the perpetration of false ideals. In other words, this section delineates the manner in which women are made to participate in their own oppression. By the last, the study celebrates the comeback of Morayo: a process which this paper conceptualizes as unsilence.

Dynamics of Silence

Silence as a discourse formative in the literature generates a myriad of interpretations. Contrary to the traditional notion of silence as tranquillity, Onunkwo Chibuzor *et al.* argue for the ability of silence to attain a marvelous blend with sound. This is evinced when they assert: "That the text is full of sound ought to depict a world of lively and exuberant activities."[28] Correspondingly, this paper hinges its foci on the demonstration of the interplay of silence and sound in *Daughters Who Walk This Path*. As such, this essay adopts a paradigm shift from the traditional notion of silence, thereby emphasizing its novelty. The thrust of this essay aligns with the perception of silence as inertia; despite a flourish of "exuberant activities."[29] Hence, silence is conceptualized as inaction, dormancy, and self-immolation. This is geared toward the revelation of the docile state of Morayo, the central protagonist against which other characters' loom large.

Within the hub of the text, the initial boisterousness of Morayo is paralleled with her much later reticence. This ill-fated transition is interpreted as a consequence of her sexual violation. In *Daughters Who Walk This Path*, the initial exuberance of Morayo is buttressed by the joy with which she receives the news of her newly born albino sister and by her happy experiences in childhood against which she asserts: "Eniayo and I danced around in our compound. With pink tongues striking out to taste the rain, we laughed at the display at the heavenly fireworks that lit up the wide open skies."[30] From the above, it becomes discernible that, in this Bildungsroman text, the silence cum inertia of Morayo is elicited by the gruesome incest-rape perpetrated by Bros T, her cousin cum kinsman. Strikingly, this parallels the violation of Philomela by King Tereus.

Against this background, this paper demonstrates the manner by which female sexuality is exploited to satisfy the uncanny appetites of predatory males. Hence, the hunter-hunted dialectics becomes suggestive of the way in which power is wrested from Morayo and Aunty Morenike. Most debilitating about this incest-rape is the breach of trust which had been conferred on Bros T by Morayo. This override helps to illuminate the multifarious implications arising from female sexual violation. As the hub of the text unfolds, the initial liveliness of Morayo gives way to dormancy and this is revealed by her detachment from school activities. Little wonder that she bemoans her fate: "Some days I wanted to tell Tomi what had happened with Bros T. My mouth would open and close several times. Yet I knew that I could not tell her anything."[31]

By tracing the proliferation of signifiers, in *Daughters Who Walk This Path*, one begins to notice its revelation of varied forms of silence. The first form of silence demonstrated is tension and unease and this is captured by the electrified atmosphere in Morayo's home that is reflected by Bros T's ghost which "still walked around [their] house."[32] More so, this is demonstrated by the strained conversation between Morayo and her mother where the former laments, "There were days when it seemed as if mummy wanted to talk to me."[33] In this paper, the type of silence that is explored is not just restricted to taciturnity alone but also embraces inaction. This perception of silence deviates largely from silence as muteness and is buttressed when Morayo exclaims to her parents: "Bros T has been coming to my room at night.[34] Morayo's dormancy is reflected by her attempts at self-immolation—all of which reveal her inability to deal with Bros T's violation. This is also evidenced by is her multiple strings of amorous affairs against which she proudly asserts that: "If a boy at the library smiled at me, I smiled back and we would leave together."[35] This kind of illumination captures explicitly "the infestation of silence with sound"[36]

In *Daughters Who Walk This Path*, although Morayo remains the central character under analysis, Aunty Morenike is paralleled with the former. This is done to elucidate the text's reconciliation with the Ovidian demonstration of filial relationships. Therefore, it can be said that Aunty Morenike attains identification with Morayo: a similarity between Aunty Morenike and Morayo that is captured in Michael Focault's assertion on resemblances: "No equality or relation or order can be established between two things unless their resemblance has at least occasioned their comparison."[37]

By function of this, this paper reveals Aunty Morenike—Morayo's second cousin—as a character also plagued by the oppressive forces of patriarchy. This is demonstrated by the violation of young Morenike at fifteen by Chief Komolafe—her father's friend. As with Morayo, this accounts for her aloofness from self and from her immediate environment. This is also evinced by the fact that, "Morenike stared into space."[38]

Specters of Power

Right from the unveiling of its matrix, an atmosphere of violent power is inaugurated in *Daughters Who Walk This Path*. This is demonstrated by the binary of the oppressed versus the oppressor along which the primary symbol of power is interrogated. As with Ovid's account of sexual violation, inertia remains the premise against which power is investigated. Echoing this is Tochukwu Ngwu who asserts that: "Although the overwhelming existences do not show the potency of destruction, their silence leaves the selves in fear."[39] This skewed power relation which silence introduces is further buttressed when Ngwu posits that: "Although they show no tendency to destroy the speaker and other selves who seek acceptance and protection under their power, their profound silence to the plea of the speaker engenders anxiety and tenseness of tone."[40]

In the text under analysis, both Bros T and Chief Komolafe appropriate enforced silence as a tool for the enslavement of Morayo and Aunty Morenike. Thus, like Tereus who incapacitates Philomela by raping her and cutting off her tongue, Bros T participates in the objectification of young Morayo. In addition to the use of force, by virtue of which Bros T "immediately clamped his other hand tightly around [her] throat,"[41] silence is enforced by Bros T's hegemonic ideas: an ideological tool which he uses to "interpellate [Morayo] into her own suffering."[42] Within the heart of *Daughters Who Walk This Path*, these false notions which heighten Morayo's inertia are captured when Bros

T tells her—upon her body's favorable response to his violation—that: "It is what you want. You just don't know it yet."[43] This is made profound when he also tells her: "Listen, if you say anything to Aunty Bisoye, you will be responsible for what happens to Eniayo."[44] Thus, by threatening to perpetrate the same mode of violence against Eniayo, her younger sister, Bros T gains full control of Morayo's psyche.

Similarly, Aunty Morenike's violation by Chief Komolafe who rapes and impregnates her emphasizes the interplay of silence and power. Therefore, even without it being explicitly mentioned in the text, one can readily surmise that what is at the heart of this text is the primary symbol of power.

Conceptualizing Unsilence

The term "unsilence," the antonym of the root word silence, emphasizes the return from a state of inertia; however, in this paper, it is not indicative of noise. This term receives a figurative interpretation by Onukwo *et al.* who define it as: "To do something [the right thing of course], whether in deed or in kind, in order to salvage a situation."[45] In *Daughters Who Walk This Path*, a return from dormancy is achieved through the filial bond established between Aunty Morenike and Morayo. Similar to the camaraderie existent between Procne and Philomela, this paper establishes the subversion of the dominating tool of silence through Aunty Morenike and Morayo's solidarity.

Under the auspices of Aunty Morenike's influence, Morayo is reinvested with a power that was initially wrested from her by Bros T's. And despite Aunty Morenike's rape-induced pregnancy, her will to gain a university degree together with her activism strengthen Morayo's resolve to launch out of inertia. In the text, Morayo's reliance on Aunty Morenike is revealed when she asserts that, "Aunty Morenike is different from my other female cousins. She does not treat me as if I was an annoying child."[46] This dependence is made even more evident by their shared experience of sexual defilement. Hence, when Morayo laments to Aunty Morenike that, "Even though I didn't want him to come into my room, what he did felt good," the latter reassures her by stating: "It was not your fault."[47]

As the hub of the text unfolds, Morayo's eventual unsilence—despite her attempts at self-immolation—transforms into a passion for political activism. More so, the cordial filial relationship established between Aunty Morenike and Morayo serves as an outlet through which the latter is rid of her shame, guilt, and silence. In her article, Martha Cutter maintains that in Alice Walker's novel, Philomela is given a voice which "successfully resists the violent patriarchal inscription of male will onto the silent female body."[48] This is clearly evinced by the manner in which Morayo celebrates the fullness of her being despite Bros T's violation. Similarly, King-Kok

Chueng argues that the novel, *The Color Purple*, violates the "paternal warn-ing against speech."[49] Subsequently, both treatises emphasize resistances against the linguistic incapacitation fostered by punitive patriarchy. However, unlike Cheung's views, this paper argues against silence as hushed quietude. Contrarily, it pleads in favor of silence as inertia. In *Daughters Who Walk This Path*, Morayo's eventual resistance against oppression as well as her reawakening are buttressed by her reunion and marriage to her lost love, Kachi, against which the ghost of Bros T sublimes.

CONCLUSION

This study acknowledges that every reading of a text, according to Ekeh, "offers a different critical dimension to a work."[50] The central thrust of this paper remains the articulation of the primary symbol of power through silence. To achieve this, the study explores Morayo and Aunty Morenike as models of the mythological figures, Philomela and Procne. This is done to reveal how female solidarity can be weaponized to subvert oppressive, patriarchal domination. Nevertheless, this paper does not project a uniform account of the Ovidian myth that was used for analysis, and this is buttressed by its relegation of the ethos of infanticide. It is in relation to this deviation that the study demonstrates how mythical symbols can generate "a web of numberless re-mediations."[51]

NOTES

1. Sosthenes Ekeh, "The Density of the Literary Object: A Modernist Reading of Wilfred Owen's 'Dulce et Decorum Est,'" *The Muse* 43 (June 2015): 30.

2. Northrop Frye, *Anatomy of Criticism* (New Jersey: Princeton University Press, 1957), 21.

3. Shamalia Dohdy, "Political Sagacity in the Fictional World of Yejide Kilanko's *Daughters Who Walk This Path*," *Journal of Academia* 5, no. 1 (December 2017): 95, http://myjms.moe.gov.my/index.php/joa/article/view/8060.

4. Ekeh, "The System of Dispersion," *The Muse* 45 (June 2017): 168.

5. Fredrich Jameson, *The Political Unconscious: Narrative as a Socially Symbolic Act* (New York: Cornell University Press, 1981), n.p.

6. Jacques Derrida, *Of Grammatology*, trans. Gayatri Spivak (Baltimore, MD: John Hopkins University Press, 2001), 59.

7. Michael Holoquist, *Dialogism: Bakhtin and his World*, 2nd ed. (London: Routledge, 1990), 66.

8. Pablo Ovid, *Metamorphoses*, Book 6 (Bloomington, IN: Indiana University Press, 1955), 239.

9. Claude Levi-Strauss, "The Structural Study of Myth," *The Journal of American Folklore* 68, no. 270 (1955): 430.

10. Bronislaw Malinowski, *A Scientific Theory of Culture and Other Essays* (New York, NY: Oxford University Press, 1960), 5.

11. Paul Ricoeur, *The Conflict of Interpretations*, 4th ed. (Evanston, IL: Northwestern University Press, 1974), 298.

12. Amechi Akwanya, *Discourse Analysis and Dramatic Literature* (Enugu: New Generation Books, 2014), 236.

13. Frye, *Anatomy of Criticism*, 276.

14. James Frazer, *The Golden Bough* 1, 3rd ed. (London: Macmillan, n.d), 21.

15. Akwanya, *Verbal Structures: Studies in the Nature and Organizational Patterns of Literary Language* (Enugu: New Generation Books, 2014), 135.

16. Terry Eagleton, *Literary Theory: An Introduction*, 2nd ed. (Oxford: Blackwell, 1983), 120.

17. Jacques Derrida, "Structure, Sign and Play in the Discourse of the Human Sciences," *Modern Literary Theory,* 4th ed., ed. Patricia Waugh and Philip Rice (New York, NY: Oxford University Press, n.d), 196, http://www.scribd.com/doc ument/383877230/Philip-Rice-and-Patricia-Waugh-Modern-Literary-Theory-A-Rea der-pdf.

18. Jacques Lacan, "The Mirror Stage as Formative of the Function of the I as Revealed in Psychoanalytic Experience," *Modern Literary Theory,* 4th ed., ed. Patricia Waugh and Philip Rice (New York, NY: Oxford University Press, n.d), 190, http://www.scribd.com/document/383877230/Philip-Rice-and-Patricia-Waugh-Mod ern-Literary-Theory-A-Reader-pdf.

19. Julia Kristeva, *Desire in Language* (New York, NY: Columbia University Press, 1980), 36.

20. Roland Barthes, *The Pleasure of the Text* (Canada: Harper Collins, 1975), 27.

21. Barthes, *The Pleasure of the Text*, 6.

22. Barthes, *The Pleasure of the Text*, 23.

23. Barthes, *The Pleasure of the Text*, 3.

24. Barthes, *The Pleasure of the Text*, 34.

25. Barthes, *The Pleasure of the Text*, 52.

26. Barthes, *The Pleasure of the Text*, 64. (brackets in original; emphasis mine)

27. Eagleton, *Literary Theory*, 128.

28. Chibuzor Onunkwo et al., "Silence and Blindness in Richard Wright's *Native Son*," *International Journal of Applied Linguistics and English Literature* 6, no. 5 (September 2017): 108, https://doi.org/10.7575/aiac.ijalel.v.6n.5p.107.

29. Ibid.

30. Yejide Kilanko, *Daughters Who Walk This Path* (London: Penguin, 2014), 11.

31. Kilanko, *Daughters*, 93.

32. *Daughters*, 93.

33. *Daughters*, 180.

34. *Daughters*, 120.

35. *Daughters*, 200.

36. Onunkwo et al., "Silence and Blindness," 108.

37. Michael Focault, *The Order of Things: An Archaeology of the Human Sciences* (London: Routledge, 1989), 74.
38. Kilanko, *Daughters*, 113.
39. Tochukwu Ngwu, "The Self before Stronger Existences in Okoro's 'Potter's Wheel' and Okigbo's 'The Passage,'" *The Muse* 45 (June 2017): 138.
40. Ngwu, "The Self Before," 141.
41. Kilanko, *Daughters*, 73.
42. Onyemuche Ejesu, "Representations of Women in African Poetry" (*African Poetry*, University of Nigeria, Nsukka, April 2015).
43. Kilanko, *Daughters*, 194.
44. Kilanko, *Daughters*, 79.
45. Onunkwo et al, "Silence and Blindness," 109. (Brackets in original text)
46. Kilanko, *Daughters*, 55.
47. Kilanko, *Daughters*, 102.
48. Martha Cutter, "Philomela Speaks: Alice Walker's Revisioning of Rape Archetypes in *The Color Purple*," *MELUS* 25, no. 3/4 (Autumn-Winter 2000): 163, https://doi.org/10.2307/468241.
49. King-Kok Cheung, "Don't Tell: Imposed Silences in *The Color Purple* and *Woman Warrior*," *Modern Language Association of Nigeria* 103, no. 2 (March 1988): 162, https://doi.org/10.2307/462432.
50. Ekeh, "The Density of the Literary Object," 28.
51. Samanta Trivellini, "The Myth of Philomela from Margaret Atwood to . . . Chaucer: Contexts and Theoretical Perspectives," *Interferences Litteraires/Literaire Interferenties* (November 2015): 85, http://www.interferenceslitteraires.be/index.php/illi/article/view/129/81.

BIBLIOGRAPHY

Akwanya, Amechi. *Discourse Analysis and Dramatic Literature*. Enugu: New Generation Books, 2014.
———. "Structure, Sign and Play in the Discourse of the Human Sciences." *Modern Literary Theory*, 4th ed., edited by Patricia Waugh and Philip Rice, 194–209. New York: Oxford University Press, n.d. http://www.scribd.com/document/383877230/Philip-Rice-and-Patricia-Waugh-Modern-Literary-Theory-A-Reader-pdf.
———. "The System of Dispersion in Akwanya's *Orimili*." *The Muse* 45 (June 2017): 166–186.
———. *Verbal Structures: Studies in the Nature and Organizational Patterns of Literary Language*. Enugu: New Generation Books, 2014.
Barthes, Roland. *The Pleasure of the Text*. Canada: Harper Collins, 1975.
Cheung, King-Kok. "Don't Tell: Imposed Silences in *The Color Purple* and *Woman Warrior*." *Modern Language Association of Nigeria* 103, no. 2 (March 1988): 162–174. https://doi.org/10.2307/462432.

Cutter, Martha. "Philomela Speaks: Alice Walker's Revisioning of Rape Archetypes in *The Color Purple*." *MELUS* 25, no. 3/4 (Autumn-Winter 2000): 161–180. https://doi.org/10.2307/468241.

Derrida, Jacques. *Of Grammatology*. Translated by Gayatri Spivak. Baltimore: John Hopkins University Press, 2001.

Dohdy, Shamalia. "Political Sagacity in the Fictional World of Yejide Kilanko's *Daughters Who Walk This Path*." *Journal of Academia* 5, no. 1 (December 2017): 92–97. http://myjms.moe.gov.my/index.php/joa/article/view/8060.

Eagleton, Terry. *Literary Theory: An Introduction*. Oxford: Blackwell, 1983.

Ekeh, Sosthenes. "The Density of the Literary Object: A Modernist Reading of Wilfred Owen's 'Dulce et Decorum Est'." *The Muse* 43 (June 2015): 26–39.

Focault, Michael. *The Order of Things: An Archaeology of the Human Sciences*. London: Routledge, 1989.

Frazer, James. *The Golden Bough* 1. London: Macmillan, 2003.

Frye, Northrop. *Anatomy of Criticism*. New Jersey: Princeton University Press, 1957.

Holoquist, Michael. *Dialogism: Bakhtin and his World*. London: Routledge, 1990.

Jameson, Fredrich. *The Political Unconscious: Narrative as a Socially Symbolic Act*. New York, NY: Cornell University Press, 1981.

Kilanko, Yejide. *Daughters Who Walk This Path*. London: Penguin, 2014.

Kristeva, Julia. *Desire in Language*. New York, NY: Columbia University Press, 1980.

Lacan, Jacques. "The Mirror Stage as Formative of the Function of the I as Revealed in Psychoanalytic Experience." In *Modern Literary Theory*, 4th ed., edited by Patricia Waugh and Philip Rice, 190–195. New York, NY: Oxford University Press, n.d. http://www.scribd.com/document/383877230/Philip-Rice-and-Patricia-Waugh-Modern-Literary-Theory-A-Reader-pdf.

Levi-Strauss, Claude. "The Structural Study of Myth." *The Journal of American Folklore* 68, no. 270 (1955): 428–444.

Malinowski, Bronislaw. *A Scientific Theory of Culture and Other Essays*. New York, NY: Oxford University Press, 1960.

Ngwu, Tochukwu. "The Self Before Stronger Existences in Okoro's 'Potter's Wheel' and Okigbo's 'The Passage'." *The Muse* 45 (June 2017): 132–148.

Onunkwo, Chibuzor, Andrew Chigbu, Mary Okolie and Uzoma Ginikachi. "Silence and Blindness in Richard Wright's *Native Son*." *International Journal of Applied Linguistics and English Literature* 6, no. 5 (September 2017): 108–112. https://doi.org/10.7575/aiac.ijalel.v.6n.5p.107.

Ovid, Pablo. *Metamorphoses* Book 6. Bloomington, IN: Indiana University Press, 1955.

Ricoeur, Paul. *The Conflict of Interpretations*, 4th ed. Evanston, IL: Northwestern University Press, 1974.

Trivellini, Samanta. "The Myth of Philomela from Margaret Atwood to . . . Chaucer: Contexts and Theoretical Perspectives," *Interferences Litteraires/Literaire Interferenties* 17, (November 2015): 85–99. http://www.interferenceslitteraires.be/index.php/illi/article/view/129/81.

Chapter 14

Becoming Man, Becoming Kola Nut

Rite of Passage in Abani's GraceLand

Ali Zamanpour

Chris Abani illustrates two parallel ceremonies, in *GraceLand,* the kola nut ritual, and the ceremonial and disciplinary procedures that inculcate male role and subjectivity into the young Igbo male body. Both appear through fragments in different chapters of the novel, and are entangled by the smells and tastes of Elvis' deceased mother's recipes. The story's mise en scène fluctuates geographically and also through time, back and forward from a small fishing town, Afikpo, to Lagos, the most populous city in the western part of Nigeria, and throughout the life of its protagonist. The kola nut ceremony deeply rooted in Igbo patriarchy is presented as deeply sacred and exclusive to male members of the community and regulated by a strict hierarchical order, while the initiation ceremony, in *GraceLand,* is the first stepping stone of becoming a man. Abani creates an *agencement* (assemblage) from the disciplinary procedures that designate male role and subjectivity into the young Igbo male body: the initiation ceremony in *Graceland,* in the context of the postcolonial struggle of a ghettoized underclass living in the shadow of skyscrapers and resort beaches. Between the dialectical relation of global and local, it addresses complex problematics of the relationship between masculinity, marginality, and liminality. The loose assemblages of affects, gender performance, rituals, and events, in *GraceLand,* allow a thorough transdisciplinary investigation of masculinity and liminality.

The relatively old concept of "liminal" describes the position of the subject on the threshold. The concept has been introduced and developed again by some recent critics. Arnold van Gennep's discourse of liminality rediscovered by scholars such as Arpad Szakolczai, Bjørn Thomassen, Kath Woodward, and others is not limited to its earlier anthropological contexts. It has the potential to open up new transdisciplinary possibilities to address gender fluidity with regard to displaced and marginalized "male subjectivity."

The aim is to create "rhizomatic" (Deleuze) frameworks and horizons that theorize and make visible the paradoxical experiences of deconstruction and revitalization of old forms, as well as the emergence of new forms of masculinity in Chris Abani's *GraceLand*. This investigation follows Bhabha's principle in *The Location of Culture*: "It does not make a claim to any specific or essential way of being"; rather, it goes "beyond" and toward the "unknowable, unrepresentable, without a return to the 'present' which is the process of repetition."[1]

MASCULINITY, LIMINALITY, AND DEATH

Liminality and death seem to be very much entwined, particularly, when scholars consider liminal states as forms of structural collapse. Liminal states are naturally ambiguous, challenging cultural networks of social classification. They extend beyond van Gennep's initial investigation of "rites of passage" in historical and cultural contexts. Liminality conveys different meanings in different literary, philosophical, cultural, and historical contexts. Some scholars such as Lucy Kay, ZoëKinsley, Terry Phillips, Alan Roughley[2] prefer to use the plural form of the term, "liminalities," to highlight the heterogeneity of the concept. Turner, in turn, represents almost any "limbo of statuslessness"[3] as a liminal experience.[4] For Turner, "[t]he 'Liminal' and the 'inferior' conditions are often associated with ritual powers and with the total community seen as undifferentiated."[5] Liminality then, in this context, is a paradoxical copresence or an escape from opposites or hierarchy—high/low; good/bad; beginning/end. The liminal state, for Szakolczai and Thomassen, describes society as a whole in a time of crisis or transition, while for Turner, it symbolizes the womb and refers to an egalitarian communitas of the poor, the deformed, the marginals, and "the inferiors."[6] Such a definition also connects the discourse of liminality with the Bakhtinian grotesque and carnivalesque. For Turner, it is the revolutionary egalitarian potential of the communitas that makes "those concerned with the maintenance of 'structure' to regard it as dangerous and anarchical or polluting to persons, objects, events and relationships."[7] Nevertheless, Turner and Szakolczai both describe the moments of becoming (change of status) as liminal.[8]

Masculinity can also be explored through the ways the "male" subject appropriates death. Such appropriation must be explored by the way the death of a family member or a loved one brings the other members into "a liminal phase," melancholia, and eventually mourning. The investigation must also address the ways the subject perceive its own *negativity* and the inevitability of "not being there." The relation of death and liminality, in literature, is reciprocal and of a complex basis. The singularities of such relation, in

GraceLand, highlight a significant link with masculinity. For instance, liminality might be seen, in *GraceLand*, as overcoming the limits of life (knowable) and sovereignty over the body. The proximity with death and to some extent dead body (necropolitics) could also trigger a liminal phase and put to the test the subject's belief in his individual autonomy. Mbembé's idea of "the romance of sovereignty" is a belief based on the subject's individual autonomy that makes it "the master and the controlling author" of his or her own meaning, limits, and body.[9]

Elvis, Abani's protagonist, a teenager who is "still so stubborn, still so proud," experiences a series of events that contribute to his transformation and transgressions.[10] Abani's storytelling gradually becomes more violent toward the end of the novel and reaches the point of subliminal horror where Elvis shakes from "the cumulative effect of all the terror he had witnessed."[11] He watches how people stone an "accused thief" to death in a scene his friend calls "necklace of fire."[12] The narrator describes the scene as "comically biblical, yet purely animal" when the crowd "baptizes" the man with petrol and sets him on fire with a tire around his neck.

Abani plays with the subliminal affect of horror when he calls the fire horrifying, "yet strangely beautiful."[13] In the novel, sublime horror also can be found in the quest of the colonel, a villain, who personally supervises the tortures and takes pictures throughout. One of his men calls him an artist who is "looking to find de beauty of death."[14] In one of the last scenes, Elvis, who is hired unknowingly for a job by the colonel's people, smuggles teenagers from Nigeria to Ghana to sell them for the harvesting of their parts for organ transplant in American hospitals. Elvis and his friend, Redemption, find themselves between coolers with separated heads and "de spare parts" and living bodies of drugged kidnapped "kids."[15] Abani illustrates a form of dissociation with the body in Elvis when he understands that he is part of the trading of the spare parts: "He stared out of the window, but kept seeing the heads in the iced cooler. He felt strange, like there were two parts of him, each watching the other, each unsure. He watched from another place as his hands trembled and his left eye twitched uncontrollably."[16]

For Stenner and Moreno, the (antistructural) liminal moment of transition is only temporary and should be endured only until the subject "is able to cobble together and incorporate a new identity status,"[17] which some critics such as Peter Messent call "postliminal identity."[18] The postliminal phase can also be related in different ways to the Deleuzian notion of reterritorialization as a form of restructuring of a place or territory in an abstract sense.

In another scene, Elvis' friend, Okon offers him a drink and some food, paid by the money he earned selling his blood. Here, the structural bodily threshold shatters, in the confrontation of "bare life" (Agamben) with death. When the body returns to its naked form, the options seem to be limited to self-immolation or selling the body: "If you eat well, you can give four pints in four different hospitals, all in one day. It's illegal, of course, but it's my blood, and it's helping to save lives, including mine. Right?"[19] Back in the room, Elvis applies makeup to his face and becomes Elvis. Looking as much like the real Elvis Presley as possible, he admires himself from many angles and thinks that "it was a shame he couldn't wear makeup in public."[20]

Elvis also imagines sharing the fate of the transvestites that "haunted the car park"; like them, "he would be a target of some insult, or worst, physical beatings, many of which were meted out by the police, who then took turns with their victims in the back of their vans."[21] As the boundaries of Elvis' body fall, he becomes more perceptive of the forces of biopolitics and questions his "colonial mentality" that wishes he had been "born white," or even "just American."[22] He thinks of himself as a "hairless panda" and without knowing why, he begins crying through his cracked face powder. Later, when Redemption involves "a boy in a man's work" and teaches him to pack cocaine into small pellet-like packages for the "couriers," he understands that "the body" itself, in its "alive" and "dead" forms, becomes the last stage of resistance and/or exploitation. In Redemption's words, a courier swallows the packages and depending on the person capacity, they fit to swallow between two hundred and four hundred packages: "Dat's around two to four kilos. Dat's why we packed dem like dat. So deydon't burst in de stomach, and de last glove make it easy to swallow."[23] Abani's flirtation with death and the deadly, and the way *GraceLand* connects it with Igbo masculinity, seems to go beyond the "motto of survival."

Death as "man's negativity" is also present in Mbembé's concept of "necropolitics." Mbembé borrows this notion of death from Hegel's *The Phenomenology of Spirit* and Bataille's "Hegel, Death and Sacrifice," wherein "spirit attains its truth only by finding itself in absolute dismemberment."[24] In *GraceLand*, Igbo masculinity, therefore, often becomes death that lives a human life. For Mbembé, "[I]t is the definition of absolute knowledge and sovereignty: risking the entirety of one's life"[25] and to "walk through the valley of the shadow of death."[26] Death, in such contexts, illustrates the world of violence wherein, "the sovereign"—often embodied in a male figure—as Bataille argues, "is he who is, as if death were not"; "he has no more regard for the limits of identity than he does for limits of death, or rather these limits are the same: he is the transgression of all such limits."[27]

BECOMING MAN, BECOMING KOLA NUT

Elvis' transitions, transformations, and transgressions can also be observed anthropologically through the eyes of scholars such as Szakolczai, and Turner since Abani also begins most of his fragmented *Bildungsroman*[28] by short anthropological notes regarding kola nut ceremony. "The transition from the liquid sensitivity of moments of becomings" in traditional societies, as Szakolczai affirms, was carefully structured and always supervised by an experienced master of ceremonies, for example, shamans, elders, or medicine men. Not unlike Foucault's definition of heterotopia,[29] the location of the "event" (of becoming) must be kept in the margins of public life, on the edges of the society, and carefully guarded by taboos.[30] "The affectivity summoned during a liminal transition calls for a highly ritualized and ceremonial framing such that a hard crust of ritual might protect the liquid sensitivity of moments of becomings, the better to pattern them into a socially authorized form."[31]

The process of reterritorialization or, as defined by Szakolczai, the "genuinely formative experience of transition," should be monitored carefully as the subject might change fundamentally. The risk, here, is that the process might not go as planned and/or it cannot be reversed.[32] Here, the liminal seems to refer to an in between state that begins with the seperation/detachment from a hierarchical position and ends with the incorporation of a culturally acceptable upper position in the hierarchy.

The first moment of becoming, in *GraceLand*, is when Elvis confronts his teenage cousins and a group of teenage boys who welcome Elvis "on his first step to manhood as dictated by tradition."[33]Amanda Aycock in "Becoming Black and Elvis" claims that Abani does not celebrate such ceremonial becoming, as the ceremony has lost its function and exists solely as something "to get on with it,"[34] "for the sake of appearances than a meaningful observance of custom."[35] Aycock leaps forward and maintains the idea that the metaphorical and symbolic failure of a ceremony suggests "the fraught implications of attempting to achieve/enforce normative identity in the modern, globalized—yet intertwined—world."[36] Aycock reads *GraceLand* as a transgression from the familiar and the conventional, or traditional *Rite of Passage,* and celebrates the moments when things "fall apart" or become outmoded. Aycock explains Abani's "genetics" of writing as "Mongrelisation" ("of culture and identity"), which she calls Abani's "thematic backbone."[37] The term, "mongrelisation," explains the "biracial heritage" of the writer and his lived experience as "Nigerian-born Igbo-English novelist and poet now lives in Los Angeles."[38] By that, Aycock explains the "nomadic existence' and fluid categories of Abani's protagonists and their identity that is always in flux. One can also read Abani's characters, such as Elvis and Madam Caro, as "too big for that world"; as they are characters that "traditional society [cannot] peg into a role."[39] I believe that one should also focus on Abani's multiple levels of storytelling, and the way he negotiates the local and the global. As for him, the Igbo/Yoruba culture is not only "an ordered ideal over a chaotic and random world," it is also "a symbiotic and fluid exchange of understandings that are in constant flux and change and in constant negotiation appearing static only in the moment."[40] Abani explains this permanent

impermanence liquid force or the so-called "ike" in Igbo or "chi" in Yoruba/
Igbo as a flux that is processed and given shape always via the trope of a journey. Abani's "global Igbo," not unlike Campbell's monomyth, has only one
journey; there are many roads and many paths, but only one journey regardless of the many detours. This journey is a process of choosing an ideological
basis for the metaphor of our social contract, which in Igbo culture is the basis
for all philosophy, art, and metaphor. Abani negotiates a realistic but ideal-
ized narrative of identity in its historical fluidity. The becoming "human," in
Abani's interpretation of Igbo culture, is something we journey toward.

On the other hand, Abani views his "job as a scholar not to give any power
or centrality to any particular narrative but to trouble the narratives all the
time."[41] For Abani, creating such a narrative for a writer is a difficult task
as the writer's body is the subject of the same kind of alienation. Thus, the
difficulty lies upon being in that place (body) and, at the same time, resisting
the doctrine that subjugates it and finding innovative narratives to transcend
the body, gender, race, religion, and nation.

The initiation ceremony, in *GraceLand,* begins with Sunday, Elvis' father,
teasing him: "It is time to cut your apron strings"; "Dis is about being a
man. No women allowed." Sunday maintains that "he has to learn how to
be a man."[42] Sunday, "an out-of-work drunk," is the one who emphasizes on
exclusive gender territoriality of masculinity. For the community, Sunday is
just another "good man who has lost his way."[43] Even when the father might
seem to be incapable of fulfilling his role, it is the rituals that take responsibility to convey a designative gender role to the young boys. Not unlike the
kola nut ritual, women take no part in the ceremony and female guests are
"never presented with kola-nuts."[44] Elvis gets to know the big picture of the
ceremony: "You are going to kill your first eagle."[45] Sunday presents the act
of killing the eagle as the first step into manhood: "When you are older, de
next step is to kill a goat, and den from dere we begin your manhood rites.
But dis is de first step."[46] Joseph, Elvis' uncle, paints and prepares him for the
ceremony and sends his son out to summon the male elders. He hands Elvis
"a small homemade bow with an arrow strung in it. On the end of the arrow,
pierced through its side, was a chick. It was alive and it chirped sadly."[47] The
metaphorical substitution of an eagle with a chick, for Abani, demonstrates
the cultural flexibility of Igbo rituals. A ritual, as part of the tradition, is an
event, "like the sunset, or rain, changing with every occurrence. So too, the
kola ritual has changed. Christian prayers have been added, and Jesus has
replaced Obasi as the central deity"[48]:

"Is this an eagle chick?" Elvis asked.
Joseph laughed. "Elvis, you funny. No, it is chicken, eagle is too expensive."[49]

The Igbo's symbolic orders, in Abani's view, has the potential to transform. Therefore, the eaglet can be substituted by a chick. It even can be purchased and pierced through its side on the end of the arrow, before the symbolic act of hunting/killing:

"It is alive," Elvis said.

"Of course it is. You just shot it," Joseph replied.

"I didn't."

"You did," Sunday said.[50]

Becoming man, in *GraceLand*, at first, seems more about facing death than the act of killing. Abani traces the connections between male subjectivity and death in moments where being/becoming man is only possible in an exchange with death. For Mbembé, however, the confrontation with death is not mainly a male issue, or in his own words, "the human being truly *becomes a subject*—that is, separated from the animal—in struggle and the work through which he or she confronts death."[51] To uphold death, for Mbembé, is the Hegelian definition of "the life of the Spirit;" "The life of the Spirit, [As Hegel] says, is not that life which is frightened of death, and spares itself destruction, but that life which assumes death and lives with it."[52] Being man, in *GraceLand*, is also about assuming death and living with it. The ceremony, in the novel, ends with representing the "hunted chicken" to the elders:

"Do we have a kill?" they asked in Igbo, all speaking as one.

"Yes, we have a kill," Joseph replied.

"Was it a good kill?" the old men asked.

"Yes," Joseph said.

"Where is the kill?"

Joseph pointed, and Elvis stepped forward. The old men smiled and looked at one another.

"In our day it was a real eagle."

"Let's just get on with it," Sunday said.[53]

Sunday's "getting on with it," for Aycock, is a symbolic refusal of the rigid order and harmonious collaboration of tradition and postcolonial/neocolonial world. Aycock undermines to some extent the liquidity of becoming, the ceremonial transformation of an event (an assemblage of hunting/death) into the embodied affect of manhood. Another essential part of the ceremony is the etiquette and the patriarchal order of seniority.

The "boy" must present the kill to the elders. The same way he should present the kola nut to the eldest in the kola nut ceremony. The youngest male should also bring the wooden kola bowl and demonstrate it to the guests "in order of seniority and in order of clan."[54] On the other hand, it is the oldest man in the gathering who must offer the kola nut to the guest as a symbol of respect and hospitality;[55] the oldest guest is the one who blesses the bowl;[56]and passes it to the next guest in line by seniority.[57]Thus, the kola proceeds round the room and is observed by "the eldest of all the clans."[58] Abani explains the complexity of the ritual by the voice of an ethnograph highlighting the way age and lineage are traced among Igbo: "Certain Igbo groups trace lineage along matrilineal lines, though others are unapologetically patriarchal. The kola nut ritual provides a ritual space for the affirmation of brotherhood and mutual harmony while also functioning as a complicated mnemonic device."[59]Abani's effort is mostly focused on the cultural mapping of male subjectivity in Igbo culture.

Abani is also observant of the discriminatory position of women and demonstrates his awareness of the privileged position of the male subject and the different forms of discrimination toward "female" agency. For instance, in her last days, Elvis' mother insists to her Mama, Oye, Elvis' grandmother, that she wants to be reborn as a boy next time:

We'll call you back to be reborn into the lineage again.
As a boy next time!
Why? They are such limited creatures.[60]

She reminds her mother that "de songs dat de women would sing when a boy was born"; "ringing from hamlet to hamlet, dropped by one voice, picked up by another until it had circled de town. Andde ring of white powder we would wear around de neck to signify de boy's place as head of de family."[61] Elvis' mother compares this to the "mournful" song, "carried by solo voices" to alert the town "of de sadness of de family." She also mentions that "de only reason Sunday hasn't taken another wife" is "because [she] bore him a son."[62] For Abani, there is also a "deeper philosophy to these rituals, a connection to land and history that cannot be translated".[63] "It [the ritual] is not as easy as it seems as it also defines being"[64] and he mentions several stages in the rites of passage for the Igbo male. Abani highlights the importance of the understanding of the kola nut ritual: "At the heart of the ritual is the preservation, orally, of the history of the clan and the sociopolitical order that derives that history."[65] In the final stage of the ceremony, Elvis is lifted up onto the shoulders of Innocent, his oldest cousin: "He felt very grown-up sitting up there, seeing the world from that high."[66] They are accompanied by the group of young men, singing the praises of Elvis as a great warrior and hunter. The elders free the chick, tying it upside down to a branch next to others that are in several stages of decay and an old man plucks a tail feather from the bird and sticks it in

Elvis's hair. The elders cut the tree bark, dipping their fingers in the sap, trace patterns on his face.[67]

For Elvis' father, manhood is not about a failed or a successful hunt, since Joseph and he have prepared everything in advance for Elvis. "Being man" is about not turning away from death. Sunday picks Elvis up and holds him close to the decaying birds. Elvis turns away from the smell. Sunday reacts: "Don't turn away from death. We must face it. We are men."[68] For Innocent, his oldest cousin, it is also about having a warrior's heart with which to confront the upcoming events: "De trials of dis world things come as surprise, so you must have a warrior's heart to withstand dem. Dat's why your papa no tell you about today."[69] It is of course also about drinking with men: "Ah Elvis done taste him first blood, so as a man, he must drink with men."[70]Abani, as Aycock explains, celebrates "the perpetuality of 'becoming' as the meaningful, beautiful (if painful) aspect of life."[71]

In *Graceland*, becoming often begins with a separation. This is often an event that creates traumatic, epistemic rupture in the permanence of experience. For Mark Fisher, trauma ruptures "the very fabric of experience itself."[72] It is the traumatic break from the past that allows "the new to emerge."[73] For Abani, "there are things that cannot be contained, even in ritual. The Igbo have a saying: Oya bu uto ndu. That is the joy of life."[74] This separation, for the Igbo, is divided into different stages and the boy should kill an eaglet and later a goat and might eventually lead to the subject's metaphorical death (dying as a child). Abani once again interrupts the logic of his narrative to demonstrate the ugly side of the transgression outside the boundaries of manhood. Sunday defines parental love to Elvis and explains to Elvis why they are a lot of deformed children begging: "Because their parents know dey have no future. So at birth, before de child knows pain, dey deform it because it increases its earning power as a beggar. Do you see de love?"[75] The expressive quality of masculinity and even love, for Sunday, consists fundamentally in the exercise of sovereignty or the exercise of power outside the law (*ab legibus solutus*). In *GraceLand*, such an extreme interpretation of manhood does not limit Joseph, Elvis' uncle in anyways, when he rapes Elvis and Efua, but it makes Sunday to silence Elvis and threaten to kill him if he ever talks about it.

The ceremony determines a subject's position; a subject position in social and cultural structures provides/recognizes and negotiates identities, rights, responsibilities, and expectations. In Elvis's cross dressing, Abani's mise en scène takes a Foucauldian turn. This time, becoming man takes effect not through a ceremonial framework but through discipline and punishment. Aycock persuasively argues that Elvis' cross dressing is just a "gendered experience" in search of love and affection from an absent father. Aycock claims that the nine-year-old Elvis associates the girls' appearance, their

hairdos, their "femininity" with "the promise of love," and he believes that
his father will like him better, show him affection if he acts like a girl.[76]
Sunday's stand is clear: "No son of mine is going to grow up as a homo-
sexual!"[77] Sunday makes himself clear for Aunt Felicia who is trying to save
Elvis from the beating: "When you have your own children, you can do what
you like. But Elvis is my son. Son, not daughter."[78] In the final scene, Sunday
holds Elvis tightly between his knees to keep him from making any sudden
moves and shaves Elvis' head, to make a man out of him again.

Abani evokes the contact of the razor as "the rough lick of a cat's
tongue,"[79] putting the whole event to Elvis' seeking attention. At the end of
the chapter, Elvis' docile body calms between the pain of the beating and
the joy of fatherly care: Elvis feels "himself relaxing into his father's body."
Sunday continues that "I'm only doing dis for your own good. It's not easy
to be a man. Dese are trying times. Not easy."[80] Abani's scene reminds the
readers of Butler's argument in *The Psychic Life of Power* that the attention
and love necessary to a child's existence are exploitable.[81] Abani depicts Igbo
patriarchal rules as rigid but also forgiving, accepting that "mistakes are
expected until the boy becomes a man."[82] The journey to manhood and to life
is difficult and "Manhood is not achieved in a day."[83] Abani notes the peril in
this: "the loss of face is not only on the young neophyte, it is on his clan, as
they have not taught him well."[84]

In *GraceLand*, Igbo culture is depicted as an open-ended entanglement of
ways of being and the learning of such an assemblage happens through the
unravelling of its knots, one of which is through the open-ended entanglement
with kola nut: "The king's head is the kola nut's apex or head. The lines of
the star clearly imprinted on it that determine the number of lobes the kola nut
will have."[85] This number is the key to the Igbo mathematical system. This
number holds the truth of the clan.[86] Abani states that "omenala"[87] is only one
path and that "there is only one history which is Igbo,"[88] but he views tradition itself as a fluid force and in constant negotiation. Tradition, for Abani,
is an event, similar to a sunset, or rain, "changing with every occurrence."[89]
Tradition, for Igbo, is not "a system of code," it is an uncodable force even
when it seems that "the protocol is followed strictly."[90] In this perspective,
Abani emphasizes a longing for "a pure lyric moment."[91] Therefore, the kola
nut ceremony is a metaphorical ritual that preserves and transmits cultural
norms of masculinity from generation to generation.

Even though those norms might change through time, the transformative
ability of the Igbo culture, for Abani, is the essence of its survival. The kola
nut ceremony works as an educative medium. It is "part hospitality, part etiquette, part protocol and part history lesson."[92] Abani goes even further and
writes on kola nut's role on the Igbo belief system as sacred and a blessing.[93]
"He who brings kola, brings life."[94] *GraceLand* illustrates the "greatest"

way of worshiping is "the offering of kola in communion, the soul calling unto life."[95] Through this particularly formed perspective, kola nut has a Eucharistic quality: "[I]t is the representative of a life that invokes a supreme deity and by association, the implication that the consumption of one [is] equal to that of the other."[96] The number of lobes is also used in divination by *dibias* (healers) to discern the path of petitioners.[97] The number of lobes, determined by the line running across the kola nut's apex, determines what kind of person petitioner is.[98] Igbo assigns the kola nut a particularly important role in their culture, cosmology, and human collectivities. For Abani, it becomes a question of integrating it into the path one takes in the future. "We do not define kola, it defines us."[99] Becoming kola in that sense is integrating nature and culture that is in line with the Igbo male communion and environment. Abani's rhizomatic and "spidery" writing—not unlike Beatrice, Elvis' mother—spreads across *GraceLand* to claim "an ancient kingdom" not only through the over-coded politics of gender but also through a *Bildungsroman* made by interlacing threads of becoming: "this is the kola nut. This seed is a star. This star is life. This star is us."[100]

NOTES

1. Homi K. Bhabha, *The Location of Culture* (London: Routledge 1994), 3–4.

2. Lucy Kay and Zoe Kinsley and Terry Phillips and Alan Roughley, *Mapping Liminalities: Thresholds in Cultural and Literary Texts* (Berlin: Peter Lang 2007), 7–17.

3. Victor W. Turner, "Liminality and Communitas," in *The Ritual Process: Structure and Anti-Structure*, ed. Victor W. Turner (Chicago, IL: Aldine Publishing, 1969), 100.

4. Ibid., 97.

5. Ibid., 100.

6. Ibid., 110.

7. Ibid., 108–109.

8. Arpad Szakolczai, "Liminality and Experience: Structuring Transitory Situations and Transformative," *International Political Anthropology* 2, no. 1 (2009): 141–169.

9. Achille Mbembé and J. Libby Meintjes, "Necropolitics," trans. Libby Meintjes *Public Culture* 15, no. 1 (2003): 5.

10. Abani, *GraceLand*, 165.

11. Ibid., 228.

12. Ibid.

13. Ibid.

14. Ibid., 165.

15. Ibid., 237.

16. Ibid., 242.

17. Paul Stenner and Edwardo Moreno, "Liminality and Affectivity: The Case of Deceased Organ Donation," *Subjectivity* 6, no. 3 (2013): Sub 6.3,244.

18. Peter Messent, "Liminalities, and Trauma in Hemingway's," in *Mapping Liminalities: Thresholds in Cultural and Literary Texts*, ed. Lucy Kay (Berlin: Peter Lang 2007), 138.

19. Abani, *GraceLand*, 77.

20. Ibid.

21. Ibid.

22. Ibid.

23. Ibid., 110.

24. Mbembé and Meinrjes, "Necropolitics," 14.

25. Mbembé and Meinrjes, "Necropolitics," 15.

26. Psalm 23:4 as quoted inChris Abani, *GraceLand*, 171.

27. Quoted by Achille Mbembé and J. Libby Meintjes, "Necropolitics," 16.

28. *Merriam-Webster Dictionary. s. v.* "Bildungsroman is the combination of two German words: *Bildung,* meaning "education," and *Roman,* meaning "novel." Fittingly, a "bildungsroman" is a novel that deals with the formative years of the main character–in particular, his or her psychological development and moral educa-tion." Accessed July 30, 2019, https://www.merriam-webster.com/dictionary/bildung sroman.

29. Michel Foucault, "Of Other Spaces: Utopias and Heterotopias," *Architecture/ Mouvement/Continuité,* trans. Jay Miskowiec (1967), 4. Michel Foucault elaborated the concept of heterotopia to describe the space of 'otherness' that is simultaneously physical and mental. Foucault describes many types of heterotopia or spaces that exhibit dual meaning: a crisis heterotopia, heterotopia of deviation, time, ritual or purification and others: "[T]hese places are absolutely different from all the sites that they reflect and speak about, I shall call them by way of contrast to utopias, heterotopias."

30. Arpad Szakolczai, "Liminality and Experience: Structuring Transitory Situations and Transformative," *International Political Anthropology* 2, no. 1 (2009): 148.

31. Stenner and Moreno, "Liminality and Affectivity," 25

32. Ibid., 25.

33. Abani, *GraceLand,* 20.

34. Ibid., 20.

35. Amanda Aycock, "Becoming Black and Elvis: Transnational and Performative Identity in the Novels of Chris Abani," *Safundi: The Journal of South African and American Studies* 10, no. 1 (2009): 13.

36. Ibid., 12.

37. Ibid., 11.

38. Ibid.

39. Abani, *GraceLand*, 25.

40. Chris Abani, "Global Igbo" (lecture presented at the 26th annual Chicago Humanities Festival, citizens, October 24, 2015), accessed July 30, 2019, https://www.youtube.com/watch?v=mofJiqcrzr8.

41. Abani, "Global Igbo".
42. Abani, *GraceLand*, 19.
43. Ibid., 27.
44. Ibid., 172.
45. Ibid., 18.
46. Ibid., 19.
47. Ibid.
48. Ibid., 291.
49. Ibid., 19.
50. Ibid.
51. Achille Mbembé and Melintes, "Necropolitics," 14.
52. Ibid.
53. Abani, *GraceLand*, 20.
54. Ibid., 183.
55. Abani, *GraceLand*, 154.
56. Ibid., 223.
57. Ibid., 230.
58. Ibid., 240.
59. Ibid., 209.
60. Ibid., 37.
61. Ibid.
62. Abani, *GraceLand*, 37.
63. Ibid., 230.
64. Ibid., 252.
65. Ibid., 34.
66. Ibid., 21.
67. Ibid.
68. Ibid.
69. Ibid, 22.
70. Ibid., 22.
71. Aycock, "Becoming Black and Elvis", 12. Parentheses are in the original citation.
72. Mark Fisher, *The Weird and the Eerie* (London: Repeater, 2016), 22.
73. Ibid.
74. Abani, *GraceLand*, 299.
75. Ibid., 188.
76. Aycock, "Becoming Black and Elvis," 15.
77. Abani, *GraceLand*, 62.
78. Ibid.
79. Ibid., 63.
80. Ibid.
81. Butler, *The Psychic Life of Power,* 8.
82. Abani, *GraceLand*, 274.
83. Ibid., 284.
84. Ibid., 263.

85. Ibid., 24.
86. Ibid., 24.
87. Ibid., 291. "History is at the heart of the ritual, marked in Igbo by the word omenala, which literally means 'the way we have always done it" (224).
88. Ibid., 299.
89. Ibid., 291.
90. Ibid., 196.
91. Ibid., 291.
92. Abani, *GraceLand*, 172.
93. Ibid., 3.
94. Ibid., 3.
95. Ibid., 17.
96. Ibid.
97. Ibid., 46.
98. Ibid., 60, 70. "Just like the kola nut, people have distinct lobes of energy. These determine their life plan. Four is the highest number, the king nut. The sorcerer. Three is the seer, the singer, and the shaper. Two is, the struggle to learn love."
99. Ibid., 46.
100. Ibid., 3.

BIBLIOGRAPHY

Abani, Chris. "Chris Abani: Global Igbo." Lecture presented at the 26th annual Chicago Humanities Festival, citizens, recorded on October 24, 2015. Accessed August 20, 2020. https://www.youtube.com/watch?v=mofJiqcrzr8.

———. *GraceLand*. New York, NY: Pidacor, 2004.

Aycock, Amanda. "Becoming Black and Elvis: Transnational and Performative Identity in the Novels of Chris Abani." *Safundi: The Journal of South African and American Studies* 10, no. 1 (2009): 11–25. https://doi.org/10.1080/17533170802 650987.

Bhabha. Homi K. *The Location of Culture*. London: Routledge, 1994.

Butler, Judith. *The Psychic Life of Power: Theories in Subjection*. Stanford, CA: Stanford UP, 1997.

Deleuze, Gilles and Felix Guattari. *A Thousand Plateau: Capitalism and Schizophrenia*. Translated by Brian Massumi. London: Minnesota UP, 1987.

Fisher, Mark. *The Weird and the Eerie*. London: Repeater, 2016.

Foucault, Michel. "Of Other Spaces: Utopias and Heterotopias." Translated by Jay Miskowiec. *Architcture/Mouvement/Continuité*. (Oct. 1984).

Foucault, Michel. *Power/Knowledge*. New York, NY: Pantheon Books, 1980.

Kay, Lucy, Zoe Kinsley, Terry Phillips and Alan Roughley. *Mapping Liminalities: Thresholds in Cultural and Literary Texts*. Berlin: Peter Lang, 2007.

Mbembé, Achille and Libby Meintjes. "Necropolitics." Translated by Libby Meintjes. *Public Culture* 15, no. 1 (Winter 2003): 11–40.

Messent, Peter. "Liminality, Repetition, and Trauma in Hemmingway's 'Big Two-Heated River' and Other Adams Stories." In *Mapping Liminality*, edited by Lucy Kay, 137–166. Berlin: Peter Lang, 2007.

Stenner, Paul and Edwardo Moreno. "Liminality and Affectivity: The Case of Deceased Organ Donation." *Subjectivity* (Aug 2013), Sub 6.3: 229–253. https://doi.org/10.1057/sub.2013.9.

Szakolczai, Arpad. "Liminality and Experience: Structuring Transitory Situations and Transformative." *International Political Anthropology* 2, no. 1 (2009): 141–172. https://doi.org/10.2307/j.ctt9qcxbg.5.

Thomassen, Bjørn. *Liminality and the Modern: Living Through the In-between.* Burlington, VT: Ashgate, 2014.

Turner, Victor W. "Liminality and Communitas." In *The Ritual Process: Structure and Anti-Structure*, Victor W. Turner, 94–130. Chicago, IL: Aldine Publishing, 1969.

Part IV

POLICY IMPLEMENTATION

Chapter 15

Transitional Justice, Sexual Violence, and Women's Status in Africa

Elsabé Boshoff and Louise du Toit

We argue in this chapter that (i) transitional justice (TJ) processes on the African continent offer a unique opportunity to enduringly address women's citizenship status in postcolonial and postconflict states. For this perspective, it is necessary to recognize systemic sexual violence against women and girls as (ii) effectively undermining a series of women's core human rights, such as their rights to physical security, sexual integrity and dignity, to freedom of movement, expression, and association, among others. Moreover, we argue that (iii) the continuities of systemic sexual violence throughout preconflict, armed conflict, and postconflict periods must be acknowledged. We claim that it is a gross injustice when sexual violence against women is (iv) only acknowledged as a crime against humanity when narrowly confined within genocidal and nationalist or ethnic conflicts. Against this narrow legal recognition, we propose that systemic sexual violence, also in peace time, constitutes (v) a form of political violence, similar to that exhibited during conflict, because it sexualizes women and strips them of political agency.

TJ processes aim at truth, accountability, and redress in exceptional circumstances. They also aim to put into place institutions, changed mind-sets and practices, policies, and procedures that build social cohesion and a lasting, just peace. We argue that TJ must therefore consider (1) how to stop systemic sexual violence during conflict and extending into peace time. In order to prevent half of the population from sinking into second-class citizenship postconflict, TJ processes must (2) expose and punish incidents of sexual violence in armed conflict as gross human rights violations. Moreover, (3) sexual violence victims must receive appropriate forms of redress, and (4) institutions must promote public awareness around sexual attack as politically equivalent to torture and punishable by law.

We critically evaluate the Protocol to the African Charter on Human and Peoples' Rights on the Rights of Women in Africa (Maputo Protocol), particularly as it relates to the rights of women to dignity, security, equal protection before the law, right to peace, protection in armed conflicts, as well as the central right to remedy. The work also draws on feminist and conflict literature.

SEXUAL VIOLENCE AGAINST WOMEN IN CONFLICT

Sexual violence has accompanied warfare since the earliest recorded times. The legend of the Rape of the Sabine Women tells of the mass abduction and forced marriage of these women to citizens of newly established all-male Rome. This triggered a war, which only ended when these same women intervened between the warring groups of men. Through their peace-brokering, the Sabine women broke out of the restrictive mold in which both groups had cast them: that of passive sex objects and prized property; essentialized as the "other of war." Arguably, female sexuality is seldom this central as the cause of armed conflict. However, we claim that some aspect of the same gendered logic of nationhood, war, and political agency associated with masculinity, and passive sexualized property associated with femininity, accompanies every instance of armed conflict. Sexual violence aimed predominantly at women and girls is therefore misconstrued as collateral or incidental damage and instead lies at the very heart of armed conflict.

Until recently, war rape was often viewed as a regrettable yet to be expected side effect of war: as male sexuality run amok due to the breakdown of civil order. The range of functions rape could serve in war were thereby obscured. It was only in the 1990s, with the important *ad hoc* Tribunals of the International Criminal Court for Rwanda (ICTR) and for the former Yugoslavia, that the systemic use of war rape as "a weapon of war," came to be better understood. Both tribunals highlighted how rape and other sexual atrocities played a strategic role in the logic of genocide and ethnic cleansing, and how they were also consciously deployed as such by the military leadership.[1] These tribunals famously saw the first convictions for war rape as torture, as a war crime, and as a crime against humanity.[2]

We welcome these developments, because they dramatically expose the power-political role of sexual violence, in conflict, but as we shall argue, also in peace time and during political transition. Simultaneously, we caution that this new focus on rape as a weapon of war should not detract from punishing more opportunistic rapes and rapes committed without a clear military aim; nor should it seduce us into a hierarchical ordering of rapes; and nor should it lead to the prioritization of "political" rapes over all "other" rapes, including peace time rapes, as if the latter were devoid of political significance. An example of such opportunistic rapes may be seen in the reports about UN peacekeepers[3] who abuse their power vis-à-vis civilians.

Nevertheless, a better grasp of this strategic usage of war rape, together with evidence of diminished prevalence where rape is expressly forbidden by military command, has debunked the ancient conception of soldiers as natural sexual predators. And it alerts us to the diverse political and military aims served by widespread rape and fear of rape. Diken and Laustsen, for example, analyze how war rape is used especially in an "identity-driven" conflict, with the aim to demoralize the enemy, to inflict long-term trauma, to destroy family ties, and to break down group solidarity within the enemy group[4] through creating embodied shame and abjection.

Such destruction is explicitly pursued when war rapes are turned into community spectacles, family members are forced to watch, and even to participate in the rapes.[5] Thus, even though rape targets one person at a time, its destructive effects usually spread throughout a community, and into the future, e.g., as children are born from war rape. Further, destructive effects include the literal clearing of territory as civilian populations flee the threat of rape and torture. On the side of the perpetrators, it initiates young men into a "brotherhood of guilt"—sometimes forcibly—and strengthens soldier bonds.[6] Rape deployed as a weapon of war can have these powerful effects because of the loaded symbolic meanings attached to sexuality in human existence.

Sjoberg explains the symbolic power of rape when she considers the gendered nature, not just of warfare, but of the nation itself. She argues that "the story of state/nation/ethnicity constitutes and is constituted by gender tropes."[7] Both the modern state and the normative citizen are imagined as masculine and as standing in a position of superior opposition vis-à-vis its other—Woman.[8] The male soldier becomes the highest expression of collective identity, and political voice. Agency and leadership are conceptualized in heroic masculine terms, particularly visible in the domain of international relations. The feminine aspect is imagined as the inferior, weak, and passive interior of the nation, in need of protection. Because of their lack of agency, voice and access to violence within the nation, unarmed women and children ("civilians") all gendered as feminine, paradoxically become important to the masculine nation, construed as its most valuable possession. Thus, women and children become prime targets carrying heightened symbolic value in times of conflict. The exclusion of women from war and violence is connected with their exclusion from full citizenship in the public-political sphere: situating women outside of politics, and in need of male and state protection.

Sjoberg[9] explains the link between woman and war thus: "The very availability of war as an option for decision-makers depends upon the assumed presence of an innocent, interior, feminized other generally—the other of war [and thus its ultimate cause and justification]—and women's needs for the protection provided by states specifically." In parallel with the logic of torture, rape must therefore be seen as strategic, because of its symbolic value. Their intimate cruelty means that torture and rape bring terror "home." Rape enacts on the perceived vulnerable body the blind power of the perpetrators' regime, as well as the impotence of the victim group. Mostly, war rape consists in male bodies raping female bodies, often indiscriminately targeting anyone from very young to very old—adding to the terror and demonstrating the inescapability of the imposing regime. It demonstrates that its power reaches everywhere and can penetrate everyone's most intimate spaces and determine their destinies. It further demonstrates that the future (symbolized by the womb) belongs to the perpetrators who even in the future are inescapable. It renders the power of the regime omnipresent and omnipotent and symbolizes that the victim group has been finally and fully vanquished because they are incapable of protecting their vulnerable interior, their hope for the future, and their loftiest reason for entering the conflict. Accordingly, symbolically, the collective is "raped." It reinforces the masculine superiority of the perpetrators by feminizing the enemy by dramatizing the phallic power of the regime. Thereby, it attempts to "remake" the shared world through rendering the enemy impotent by being gendered feminine: outside of politics, powerless, and voiceless.

Clearly, then, war rape's efficacy depends upon the gendering of nations that positions women as outside of politics, and the nation as masculine. This gendering is ongoing and firstly aimed internally, by excluding women from real power. Peace time and intracommunal rape statistics bear witness to this ordinary, yet central, political ordering, which reveals the crucial link between rapes in war and in peace. They share a fundamental political function, in that they serve to demarcate the political sphere. In peace time, they gender nations and systematically strip women of political power through domestication, and in war time, they deploy the same logic to drive enemy groupings into submission. TJ processes must address this naturalized yet covert power-political function of sexual violence, established during peace and transition, and exploited during armed conflict.

War rape, like torture, should be prioritized as a war crime during transition, in order to lay the foundation for women's full citizenship in the new dispensation. But, war rape must crucially not be prioritized in a way which diminishes postconflict and peace time rapes. Quite the inverse is required: better insight into the power dynamics of militarized sexual violence should translate into a better appreciation of the power-political function of peace time rape. The logic of war rape shows how it is systematically deployed in peace time also, to suppress women's claims to citizenship, and turn women into the depoliticized, vulnerable core of the nation.

WOMEN'S CITIZENSHIP AND HUMAN RIGHTS IN CONFLICT AND PEACE

We have so far considered the political power structures that limit women's citizenship and participation in political spaces and that yield war rape as an effective tool for destruction of an enemy. This section discusses the rights of women which are protected under international human rights, criminal and humanitarian law, particularly on the African continent, and which should be incorporated into TJ processes to restore women's citizenship. Marshall defines citizenship as "a status bestowed on those who are full members of a community. All who possess the status are equal with respect to the rights and duties with which the status is endowed."[10] According to Fallon: "Marshall distinguished between civil, political, and social rights: Civil rights focus on individual freedom and justice, political rights center on participation in and exercising of political power, and social rights highlight economic welfare and security."[11]

We argue that systemic sexual violence against women and girls in peace and war undermine women's civil, political, and social rights, denying them their fundamental citizenship and human rights. Where sexual violence occurs with impunity, irrespective of the conscious perpetrator motives, its power-political effect is to sexualize women and girls, and to suppress their claims to full citizenship status. Sexual violence and its widespread toleration is therefore the quintessential political violence. It aims to destroy[12] the very subjectivity and voice of its target and thus the prepolitical basis on which all claims to political standing ultimately rest.

International humanitarian law (IHL) is the law defining the conduct of parties to a conflict in order to "limit the effects of armed conflict, [through protecting] persons who are not or are no longer participating in the hostilities and restrict[ing] the means and methods of warfare."[13] The main instruments of IHL have done little to address sexual violence understood as a "natural" consequence of war. The 1949 Geneva Conventions and their 1977 Additional Protocols also do not include sexual violence among acts considered "grave breaches," and in the Geneva Convention relative to the protection of Civilian Persons in Time of War, sexual violence was characterized as an attack on women's honor, rather than their basic human rights and dignity.[14] Similarly, Geneva Convention II provides that "women shall be treated with all consideration due to their sex."

Additionally, the United Nations declaration on the protection of women and children in emergencies and armed conflict, and the convention on the Elimination of all Forms of Discrimination against Women makes no mention at all of sexual violence.[15] These are all indications of the blind spot concerning women's exclusion from citizenship globally. Through the naturalization of sexual violence, especially against women and girls,[16] the continuing exclusion of women from the polis is also naturalized. As discussed, sexual violence was for the first time given due consideration by the ICTY and ICTR. In the Rome Statute establishing the International Criminal Court (effective 2002), various forms of sexual violence are also recognized as war crimes and crimes against humanity.[17] The Maputo Protocol (2003) explicitly provides for the right to protection in armed conflict, providing a concomitant duty on states to

> Protect asylum seeking women, refugees, returnees and internally displaced persons, against all forms of violence, rape and other forms of sexual exploitation, and to ensure that such acts are considered war crimes, genocide and/or crimes against humanity and that their perpetrators are brought to justice before a competent criminal jurisdiction.[18]

These are powerful formulations, clearly responsive to the best and strongest findings of the ICTR and ICTY, in line with the Rome Statute and the milestone developments in international criminal law of the 1990s.

The Maputo Protocol also provides extensively for the elimination of discrimination against women, the right to dignity of women, and the rights to life, integrity, and security of their person. Under each of these rights, the protocol places a related duty on the state to ensure that measures are adopted and implemented to ensure the fulfillment and protection of these rights. Under the rights to equality and dignity, there is a duty on the state to "commit themselves to modify the social and cultural patterns of conduct of women and men through public education, information, education and communication strategies" to address inequality and discrimination in all its forms,[19] and to "adopt and implement appropriate measures to prohibit any exploitation and degradation of women."[20] The right to integrity includes a commensurate duty on states to take appropriate and effective measures to:

(a) enact and enforce laws to prohibit all forms of violence against women, including unwanted or forced sex whether the violence takes place in private or public;

(c) identify the causes and consequences of violence against women and take appropriate measures to prevent and eliminate such violence;

(d) actively promote peace education through curricula and social communication in order to eliminate elements in traditional and cultural beliefs, practices, and stereotypes which legitimize and exacerbate the persistence and tolerance of violence against women;

(e) punish the perpetrators of violence against women and implement programmes for the rehabilitation of women victims;

(f) establish mechanisms and accessible services for effective information, rehabilitation, and reparation for victims of violence against women.[21]

Additionally, the protocol provides for the rights of women to participate
in the political and decision-making process, a right to peace, including the
right to participate in the promotion and maintenance of peace, as well as a
right to remedy as a separate right for violation of any of the rights under
the protocol.[22] Read together, these substantive rights and explicit duties on
states provide a powerful tool which should be integrated into TJ approaches.
In doing so, states should be cautious that violence against women is never
isolated from core political, reconciliation and nation-building priorities: by
fully integrating the Maputo Protocol into TJ processes and tools, states will
finally take responsibility to counter the depoliticization of women. In support of this view, the African Charter on Human and Peoples' Rights (the
African Charter) provides for *all persons* the integrity of their person, respect
of the dignity inherent in a human being and to the recognition of their legal
status.

Clearly, these normative instruments provide a strong and comprehensive
framework for the protection of women against sexual violence during peace
and conflict, the role of the state in holding perpetrators accountable, paying
reparations to victims, and involving women in these processes. These policy
documents move beyond the gendered view of the nation in which women are
outside of politics, a symbolic "center of gravity" for the nation,[23] and mainly
in need of protection from armed men. Women's citizenship status itself is
highlighted as being at stake in these policies. At least, this is the direction in
which we want to push the interpretation and application of these provisions.

Having thus identified the interrelated nature of rape in war and peace, as
well as the plethora of women's rights under the current normative framework, the next section considers the ways in which TJ processes could effectively mainstream a gender perspective postconflict.

THE PRINCIPLES AND PRACTICES OF TJ IN
ADDRESSING WOMEN'S CITIZENSHIP STATUS

TJ tries to explain "how countries and societies can come to terms with
a history of violence and war, oppression and human rights violations,"[24]
and includes judicial and nonjudicial mechanisms to transition away from a
violent past.[25] Additionally, it aims to "avoid 'repeating, re-enacting, or reliv-
ing past horrors'; deter future violations; and restore the dignity of citizens
victimized by atrocity."[26] It has been suggested by Anderlini *et al.* that two
values underlie TJ, namely justice and reconciliation.[27]

Justice can be retributive, where perpetrators are criminally prosecuted, or restorative, aimed at bringing together everyone affected by the violations to address the consequences collectively.[28] Reconciliation is difficult to define and can refer to "co-existence or it can mean dialogue, remorse, apology, forgiveness and healing."[29] There are many types of TJ mechanisms: processes to hold perpetrators accountable, such as truth commissions, criminal trials, and vetting processes; "victim-oriented restorative justice processes, including reparations, monuments, and public memory projects; and amnesties that seek to officially recognize but pardon past acts."[30]

Writing from the South African experience of TJ and reconciliation, commentators concluded that the enormity of these processes is routinely underestimated. This is partly because people are misled by the grand and simplistic narrative of (the devastation) before and (the perfect future) after, and by facile metaphors such as building bridges and meeting new dawns, that suggest a quick and easy process. A good example is South African sociologist Cherryl Walker's description of how the then Minister of Land Affairs, Derek Hanekom, had guessed in 1995 that the Land Claims Commission would take about three years to complete the task of land restitution in South Africa.[31] Today, twenty-four years later, the unresolved land issue threatens to undermine democracy.

An important lesson from the South African example is that TJ processes should move more slowly, take more time, and have a broader scope than traditionally understood. A key aspect of this more comprehensive and longer-term approach to TJ is sustained attention to the creation of social, material, and political conditions that facilitate full citizenship for women—a goal which in most contexts would be a completely novel one, and not a restoration or return to an imagined golden age before the conflict. The prominence of the preposition "RE-," as in restore, reconcile, remember, restitution, and so on, might thus be deeply misleading in that it implies a return to something assumed to have existed in the past. We suggest that the ideal TJ process would be much more radical and open than this and call for an altogether new social imagination. Central to such a new imagination must be the thorough disruption of the masculinity of the nation, and thus of war and politics, and of postconflict entitlements. Du Toit proposes an approach to the TJ process that is driven by a realistic assessment of the material and symbolic interdependence of all spheres and groupings of the postconflict society.[32] He realizes that such an approach implies that the imagination around reconciliation must become centrally gendered, and a core aspect of the transformation of relationships (i.e., reconciliation) must be the transformation of gender relations.[33]

Given that women are largely denied participation in the power-politics during war and peace time, it is no surprise that they are to a large extent also still absent from TJ processes.[34] To the extent to which they are, TJ processes fail half of the population and repeat the logic which has excluded women from the nation in the past. However, it is our view that it is not just a matter of women and their primary concerns during conflict and transition that are left out by current dominant approaches to TJ, and thus what is required is not "merely" one of "including" women in every (male dominated) step. As we have explained throughout this contribution, the deeper, and enduring, structural problem is that women are systematically excluded from full citizenship, and that sexual violence before, during, and after armed conflict, is the main instrument for achieving this exclusion. It is thus not a question of "add women and stir"; instead, fully accounting for sexual violence against women as a political instrument wielded throughout war and peace will imply nothing short of a social revolution.

It would thus be a grave mistake and a furtherance of injustice, if sexual violence against women in war context were to be treated as an isolated phenomenon within TJ procedures. By this, we do not mean that it should not be recognized as a standalone crime. Such recognition is indeed an important first step: sexual violence should no longer only be recognized as genocide, or torture, and thus as a war crime only by proxy, but should be understood as a separate crime of the same magnitude. However, this understanding should not be limited to war rape and withheld from other instances of rape. As Kiran Grewal describes, within the context of the Special Court for Sierra Leone, women who had already queued up to testify about their rapes in war time were turned away by the court, because they had not been raped by someone recognized as an enemy by the SCSL; theirs was thus not "war rape," but "mere rape." As in the case of Rwanda, Sierra Leonean women discovered that it was only within the narrow context of war, and only when perpetrated by a qualifying enemy, that one's rape was taken seriously, and could even be openly discussed.[35]

Thus, in addition to streamlining gender equality into criminal justice processes, providing for full participation of women and inclusion in the agenda of issues that are important to women, there is also a need for a *qualitative* change in the values and "underlying structure" of society as part of the transitional project.[36] This idea is captured in the term "transformative equality" arising out of the appreciation that in order to achieve full equality, it is necessary to recognize that "many pervasive forms of discrimination against women rest not on law as such but on legally tolerated customs and practices of national institutions."[37] This is in line with the argument of this chapter that political structures and practices maintain the gendered nature of the state and that sexual violence is systematically deployed (and tolerated) to suppress women's claims to citizenship. Transformative equality thus requires a fundamental shift in the way gender roles are viewed, and by extension the way in which the state itself is viewed.

We argue that the Maputo Protocol embodies the potential for such transformative equality, for example, in that various clauses go beyond requiring formal and substantive equality (right to participate, right to remedy, equal standing before the law), further requiring that the state brings about change in social values. This is clear, for example, from the definition of discrimination in Article 1 which states that

"Discrimination against women" means any distinction, exclusion or restriction or any differential treatment based on sex and whose objectives or effects compromise or destroy the recognition, enjoyment or the exercise by women, regardless of their marital status, of human rights and fundamental freedoms in all spheres of life.

Thus, a recognition of their full citizenship. The transformative nature of the obligations imposed by the Maputo Protocol on states is also clear: they have a duty to modify the social and cultural patterns of conduct and actively promote peace education through curricula and social communication.

While during peace time, it is generally easier for states to comply with obligations which require of them to implement legislative change, than it is to change the opinions and views of society, TJ processes provide a unique opportunity for intensive nonlegal interventions through the whole range of TJ mechanisms. In addition, TJ periods offer another advantage and that is the wide range of stakeholders who are involved in these processes—it is usually a national project, aimed at engaging all sectors of society, thereby increasing the radically transformative and disruptive role that such a new approach to TJ could have. The disturbing other side of the coin is that if TJ processes fail to reimagine women's citizenship status, as arguably happened in the South African case, they easily become complicit in widespread sexual violence that operates postconflict to ensure women's ongoing exclusion from the national project.

Some of the practical ways in which this transformative work can be done is, for example, through ensuring that there is a gender balance in the tribunals and courts which adjudicate on war crimes; ensuring the streamlining of traditionally "female" values, such as risk-aversion and sharing in resources as well as responsibility; ensuring that "[p]eacekeeping forces [are] mixed in terms of gender, ethnicity and other identities to diversify the capacities as well as sending the right message to the civilians on the ground,"[38] and by ensuring that "reintegration [mainly of male fighters] is not simply about coming home, but defining new guiding social values and establishing corresponding relationships and institutions."[39] If done properly, TJ can "address the immediate manifestations of violent conflict as well as its structural and attitudinal causes and bring about long term change."[40]

CONCLUSION

It should be clear from our exposition that we regard sexual violence during war, and how TJ processes respond to the phenomenon after conflict, as just the tip of the iceberg we call women's citizenship status. Even though it is crucial for comprehensive and lasting peace and justice in the postconflict society that its processes treat sexual violence against women and girls as a war crime and a crime against humanity, and deal with it accordingly, it is also imperative that these crimes not be isolated from the larger question of how sexual violence in every context and instance impedes women's citizenship and undermines their subject status in society. The postconflict focus on sexual violence should therefore be accompanied by a much larger strategy to disrupt traditional ways of gendering nationhood and war, and to substitute them with a pervasive vision of a nation in which women are full and equal citizens and in which women's values, voices, and embodied presence infuse decision-making, including about war and peace. In other words, although sexual violence is only the tip of the iceberg of women's citizenship, it is also importantly a key indicator of women's actual status within society. Under such conditions, the idea of sexual violence as "natural" will be discarded and it will be consistently condemned as a political crime akin to torture and as a cruel and dehumanizing means of control, oppression, and exploitation. TJ mechanisms will be geared toward creating postconflict institutions with zero tolerance for sexual violence, with the understanding that its perpetuation threatens the new society at its core. We estimate that the Maputo Protocol already provides the legal basis for the renewal of TJ processes and mechanisms on the African continent in precisely these ways.

NOTES

1. Bülent Diken and Carsten Bagge Laustsen, "Becoming Abject: Rape as a Weapon of War," *Body and Society* 11, no. 1 (2005): 116.

2. Karen Engle, "Feminism and Its (Dis)contents: Criminalizing Wartime Rape in Bosnia and Herzegovina," *The American Journal of International Law* 99, no. 4 (2005): 781; See also the decisions of the ICTY cases of *Kunarac* et al. (IT-96-23 & 23/1) and *Furundžija (IT-95-17/1).*

3. See e.g. Associated Press "UN Seeks Inquiry into New Claims of Peacekeeper Sexual Abuse" October 6, 2018. https://www.news24.com/Africa/News/un-seeks-inquiry-into-new-claims-of-peacekeeper-sexual-abuse-20181006-2.

4. Diken and Laustsen, "Becoming Abject," 111.

5. Ibid., 112.

6. Ibid.

7. Laura Sjoberg, *Gendering Global Conflict: Toward a Feminist Theory of War* (New York, NY: Columbia University Press, 2013), 171.

8. We use the capitalized form of the word to remind the reader that we refer to the figure of the feminine within the symbolic order and not in any straightforward way to actual, individual women.

9. Sjoberg, "Gendering Global Conflict," 215.

10. T. H. Marshall, *Citizenship and Social Class and Other Essays* (Cambridge: Cambridge University Press, 1950), 28–29.

11. Kathleen M. Fallon, "Transforming Women's Citizenship Rights within an Emerging Democratic State: The Case of Ghana," *Gender & Society* 17, no. 4 (2003): 526–527.

12. It is important to note that this is what sexual violation aims at, rather than what it necessarily achieves. This emphasis is crucial, because the victims of sexual violation differ widely in their personal responses to it and it would be unfair to always expect the same harmful effects for everyone.

13. ICRC "What is International Humanitarian Law?" (2004), accessed on January 9, 2019, https://www.icrc.org/en/doc/assets/files/other/what_is_ihl.pdf.

14. Miranda Alison, "Wartime Sexual Violence: Women's Human Rights and Questions of Masculinity," *Review of International Studies* (2007): 33, 82.

15. Ibid.

16. Space does not allow us to go into the sexual violation of men and boys during war, apart from mentioning that the greater recognition of this phenomenon is also assisting in shifting the public's understanding of sexual violence as a weapon of war and politics, and away from the old naturalistic models based on the idea of male lust unleashed. Lara Stemple does important work on men as victims of rape in war, but also in prisons, the army, etc. See e.g. Lara Stemple, "Male Rape and Human Rights", *Hastings Law Journal* 60 (2009): 605–647.

17. Alison, "Wartime Sexual Violence," 82.

18. Maputo Protocol, article 11(3).

19. Maputo Protocol, article 2(2).

20. Maputo Protocol, article 3(3).

21. Maputo Protocol, article 4(2).

22. Maputo Protocol, article 25.

23. Sjoberg, (*Gendering Global Conflict,* 251) uses this term from Von Clausewitz (*On War*, 485) to discuss the status of 'the feminine' in gendered war. Clausewitz transl. Michael Howard and Peter Paret (Princeton, NJ: Princeton University Press, 1984).

24. Martina Fischer, "Transitional Justice and Reconciliation: Theory and Practice," (2011), 406, https://www.berghof-foundation.org/nc/en/publications/publication/transitional-justice-and-reconciliation-theory-and-practice/.

25. Sanam Naraghi Anderlini et al., "Transitional Justice and Reconciliation," in *Transitional Justice and Reconciliation: Inclusive Security, Sustainable Peace: A Toolkit For Advocacy and Action*, 191, https://www.inclusivesecurity.org/wp-content/uploads/2013/05/101864251-Toolkit-for-Advocacy-and-Action.pdf.

26. Tricia D Olsen et al., "Transitional Justice in the World, 1970–2007: Insights from a New Dataset," *Journal of Peace Research* 47, no. 6 (2010): 803.

27. Anderlini et al., Transitional Justice," 1.
28. Ibid., 2.
29. Ibid.
30. Olsen et al., "Transitional Justice," 803.
31. Cherryl Walker, *Landmarked: Land Claims & Land Restitution in South Africa* (Athens, OH: Ohio University Press: 2008), 8.
32. Fanie du Toit, *When Political Transitions Work: Reconciliation as Interdependence* (New York, NY: Oxford University Press, 2018), 219.
33. Ibid.
34. Judith Gardam and Hilary Charlesworth, "Protection of Women in Armed Conflict," *Human Rights Quarterly* 22 (2004): 156.
35. Kiran Grewal, "Rape in Conflict, Rape in Peace: Questioning the Revolutionary Potential of International Criminal Justice for Women's Human Rights," *Australian Feminist Law Journal* 33, no. 1 (2010): 72.
36. Sandra Fredman, "Beyond the Dichotomy of Formal and Substantive Equality: Towards New Definitions of Equal Rights," in *Temporary Special Measures: Accelerating de facto Equality of Women under Article 4(1) UN Convention on the Elimination of All Forms of Discrimination Against Women,* eds. Ineke Boerefijn et al. (Leiden: Intersentia, 2003), 111.
37. Rebecca J. Cook, "State Accountability under the Convention on the Elimination of All Forms of Discrimination Against Women," in *Human Rights of Women: National and International Perspectives,* ed. R. J. Cook (Pennsylvania, PA: University of Pennsylvania Press, 1994), 239–240.
38. Dianna Francis, "Culture, Power Asymmetries and Gender in Conflict Transformation," *Berghof Research Center for Constructive Conflict Management* (2004): 12, http://www.focusintl.com/GD169-%20Culture,%20Power%20Asymmetries%20and%20Gender%20in%20Conflict%20Transformation.pdf (accessed on January 14, 2019).
39. Elaine Zuckerman and Marcia E. Greenberg, "Gender dimensions of post-conflict reconstruction with World Bank Examples" (paper presented at the Brookings Institution, Washington D.C., USA, September 29, 2004), 10.
40. Francis, "Culture, Power Asymmetries and Gender," 6.

BIBLIOGRAPHY

African Union. Protocol to the African Charter on Human and Peoples' Rights, on the Rights of Women in Africa, November 25, 2005. https://au.int/en/treaties/protocol-african-charter-human-and-peoples-rights-rights-women-africa.
Alison, Miranda. "Wartime Sexual Violence: Women's Human Rights and Questions of Masculinity." *Review of International Studies* 33, no. 1 (2007): 75–90.
Anderlini, Sanam Naraghi, Amille Pampell Conaway and Lisa Kays. "Transitional Justice and Reconciliation." In *Transitional Justice and Reconciliation: Inclusive Security, Sustainable Peace: A Toolkit for Advocacy and Action,* by International

Alert, 191–203. https://www.inclusivesecurity.org/wp-content/uploads/2013/05/101864251-Toolkit-for-Advocacy-and-Action.pdf, 2004.

Associated Press. "UN seeks inquiry into new claims of peacekeeper sexual abuse" *News24.* October 6, 2018, https://www.news24.com/Africa/News/un-seeks-inquiry-into-new-claims-of-peacekeeper-sexual-abuse-20181006-2.

Cook, Rebecca J. "State Accountability under the Convention on the Elimination of All Forms of Discrimination against Women." In *Human Rights of Women: National and International Perspectives,* edited by Rebecca J. Cook, 228–256. Pennsylvania, PA: University of Pennsylvania Press, 1994.

Diken, Bülent and Carsten Bagge Laustsen. "Becoming Abject: Rape as a Weapon of War." *Body and Society* 11, no. 1 (2005): 111–128. https://doi.org/10.1177/1357034X05049853.

Du Toit, Fanie. *When Political Transitions Work: Reconciliation as Interdependence.* New York, NY: Oxford University Press, 2018.

Engle, Karen. "Feminism and Its (Dis)contents: Criminalizing Wartime Rape in Bosnia and Herzegovina." *The American Journal of International Law* 99, no. 4 (2005): 778–816.

Fallon, Kathleen M. "Transforming Women's Citizenship Rights within an Emerging Democratic State: The Case of Ghana." *Gender & Society* 17, no. 4 (2003): 526–527.

Fischer, Martina. "Transitional Justice and Reconciliation: Theory and Practice." *Berghof Handbook for Conflict Transformation.* By Berghof Foundation (2011), 405–431, https://www.berghof-foundation.org/nc/en/publications/publication/transitional-justice-and-reconciliation-theory-and-practice/.

Francis, Dianna. "Culture, Power Asymmetries and Gender in Conflict Transformation." *Berghof Handbook for Conflict Transformation.* By Berghof Foundation (2004), 1–16, http://www.focusintl.com/GD169-%20Culture,%20Power%20Asymmetries%20and%20Gender%20in%20Conflict%20Transformation.pdf.

Fredman, Sandra. "Beyond the Dichotomy of Formal and Substantive Equality: Towards New Definitions of Equal Rights." In *Temporary Special Measures: Accelerating de facto Equality of Women under Article 4(1) UN Convention on the Elimination of All Forms of Discrimination Against Women,* edited by Ineke Boerefijn et al., 95–123. Leiden: Intersentia, 2003.

Gardam, Judith and Hilary Charlesworth. "Protection of Women in Armed Conflict." *Human Rights Quarterly* 22 (2004): 148–166.

Grewal, Kiran. "Rape in Conflict, Rape in Peace: Questioning the Revolutionary Potential of International Criminal Justice for Women's Human Rights." *Australian Feminist Law Journal* 33, no. 1 (2010): 57–79.

International Committee of the Red Cross. "What is International Humanitarian Law?" 2004, https://www.icrc.org/en/doc/assets/files/other/what_is_ihl.pdf.

Marshall, T. H. *Citizenship and Social Class and Other Essays.* Cambridge: Cambridge University Press, 1950.

Olsen, Tricia D., Leigh A. Payne and Andrew G. Reiter. "Transitional Justice in the World, 1970–2007: Insights from a New Dataset." *Journal of Peace Research* 47, no. 6 (2010): 803–809.

Sjoberg, Laura. *Gendering Global Conflict: Toward a Feminist Theory of War.* New York, NY: Columbia University Press, 2013.

Stemple, Lara. "Male Rape and Human Rights." *Hastings Law Journal* 60 (2009): 605–647.

Von Clausewitz, Carl. *On War.* Translated by Michael Howard and Peter Paret. Princeton, NJ: Princeton University Press, 1984.

Walker, Cherryl. *Landmarked: Land Claims & Land Restitution in South Africa.* Athens, OH: Ohio University Press, 2008.

Zuckerman, Elaine and Marcia E. Greenberg. "Gender dimensions of post-conflict reconstruction with World Bank Examples." Paper presented at the Brookings Institution, Washington D.C., USA, September 29, 2004.

Chapter 16

UN Women and the Pitfalls of Gender Equality and Representation in Nigeria

Raheem Oluwafunminiyi

On a visit to Germany in October, 2016, Nigerian President, Muhammadu Buhari, was quoted to have told reporters that his wife "belongs to my kitchen, and my living room, and the other room."[1] The statement was made in response to his wife's (Aisha Buhari) criticisms about his government's dismal performance a few days before the visit in a BBC interview. Mrs Buhari, in an act rarely captured in modern Nigerian political history, criticized her husband's leadership which she claimed had been "hijacked" by a cabal. She concluded her interview by suggesting that she may not support his 2019 reelection bid except the president made some changes.[2] While the president's media handlers tried to douse the tension the president's remark had generated, angry reactions swept across the country. Social media users, in particular, took to their respective handles and timelines to express their views. Michael Buraimoh, a Twitter user from the handle, @MABSnr, for example, argued that the president's comment was not only "demeaning to all women" but also "embarrassing to Nigerians of all political persuasions."[3] Lugard Tare-Out using the handle, @Lugard_Tareotu, also tweeted that "Our women are every inch equal to our men, regardless of what the President thinks."[4] In view of the criticisms that trailed the president's statement, it was thought that an unreserved apology would be tendered to Nigerians none of which was done.

A coalition of women groups under the aegis of the Nigerian Feminist Forum, adding their voice to the debate, observed that while several African States have made immense progress in the area of women representation in government, Nigeria remain reluctant.[5] Though the controversy around the president's comment has slowly subsided, it leaves nobody in doubt about the symptomatic plight of Nigerian women today and the stiff boundaries set against them by the dominant male political class.

Given the pervasive "strangulation" of women's voice for far too long, calls for equal representation and gender equality in all strata of human life by local and international civil society groups and women's movements have heightened in the last few decades. Women groups in Nigeria, too, took up this challenge by demanding recently the full implementation of the 35 percent affirmative action clause articulated in the multifarious international and regional conventions and protocols Nigeria has been a signatory to, and in line with the 2006 National Gender Policy.[6] They as well demanded, beyond voting in elections, for fifteen ministerial posts and 35 percent of other federal appointments for women across all political platforms. These demands, it would appear, showed that women were now more than ever before aware of the prominent role they could play in a male-dominated society. They also viewed their participation in politics as an opportunity to be part of the decision-making processes that would deepen and broaden Nigeria's democracy.[7]

To support this project as well as raise awareness of the challenges women face globally in their quest for inclusion, the UN established, as part of her entity, The UN Entity for Gender Equality and the Empowerment of Women also known as UN Women, with a focus on gender equality and women empowerment. The global response was positive particularly in Africa, for instance, in Rwanda, where women won 64 percent of seats in the parliamentary elections in 2013 with swift progress made afterwards,[8] and in Namibia where strong commitments to the advancement of women have encouraged the need for gender equality and equity in the country's political space.[9] In Nigeria, however, this reality has remained a pipe dream as demands for a full implementation of the affirmative action has been strongly resisted. A reason for this is often linked to the priority area of the UN Women which encourages gender equality in political life, a goal that continues to deepen fears in the country. This chapter, therefore, challenge Nigeria's support for the UN Women mandate despite her frantic backing of those structures that perpetually hinder woman from political inclusion. While the realities of accelerating the goals on women empowerment among other priority areas may find some support, I argue that the UN Women's push for gender equality in Nigeria will make little headway until the glass ceilings against women are pulled down.

A BRIEF NOTE ON THE TRADITIONAL
ROLE OF NIGERIAN WOMEN

The traditional role of women has been a contentious issue, although arguments persist that Nigerian women in the traditional society had equal standing with the men.[10] Scholars link this majorly to the political dynamics without taking cognisance of the socio-economic and religious dimensions which, in particular, formed the basis and foundation of most traditional societies, *vis-à-vis* the women. Traditionally, the Nigerian woman had well-defined roles beyond procreation and child rearing. She was not only empowered to be independent-minded but required, in practical terms, to complement the resources of the home. Being independent was hinged on her upbringing which required her to be self-supportive. Here, she was required to take up a vocation and to earn a modest income for her personal needs. As a wife, she was not required to depend fully on her husband for her immediate needs. Although financially independent, her husband may assist to complement her personal resources as and if she desired, assisted her husband as well.

Women's role was not limited alone to economic activities but they were also engaged in decision-making, leadership attainment, and administration. They were erroneously claimed to have been mere observers yet several instances suggest otherwise.[11] Among the Yoruba, women were said to have once ruled over vast kingdoms and founded several others. They held powerful positions within palace courts and could dethrone erring kings. Bolanle Awe tells of a woman within the Egba palace tasked with the responsibility of crowning the Alake without which he could not perform his traditional duties.[12] Traditions in Ondo trace the founding of the town to a woman named *Pupupu*.[13] In the northern part of the country, the legend of *Bayajidda* and Queen Daura in the founding of the seven Hausa states also comes to mind.

Discussions on the traditional role of women in each Nigerian society would be to tasking, since each varies by history, cultural practices, and regional differences although these roles are in some respect linked. Basden's view captures this clearly: ""The most striking facts…about the woman is that they are all so extraordinarily alike…intensely conservative in their habits and ideas, and to know one is to know all… In every town [women]… exercises great influence in various directions."[14]

RECOGNIZING RIGHTS OF WOMEN:
FROM CEDAW TO UN WOMEN

Nigeria joined membership of the UN after independence in 1960, and became a party to several regional, continental, and international conventions and treaties. Some were concerned with human rights and others on gender and women rights. These treaties and conventions, in essence, are often required to be conformed to in line with the rules guiding international law. They were also full consequences for breaching them. Some of the international treaties Nigeria has signed, ratified, and acceded to since 1960 include the UN Universal Declaration on Human Rights, the International Covenants

on Economic and Social Rights (1966), the African Charter on Human and
Peoples' Rights (1983), the Convention on the Elimination of Discrimination
against Women (1985), International Covenants on Civil and Political Rights
(1993), and the Protocol to the African Charter on the Rights of Women (in
Africa 2003 and 2004) among others.[15]

Nigeria expressed the desire as far back as 1984 to recognize the rights
of women by signing that year the UN Convention on the Elimination of
Discrimination against Women (CEDAW), and in the following year ratified
the convention. The CEDAW, borne out of the determination of the commission on the status of women including pressures from international women's
rights movement, was adopted through a UN General Assembly Resolution
34/180 in 1978.[16] Since then, Nigeria has further committed itself toward the
recognition of the rights of women and undertaken steps in the elimination of
all forms of discrimination against them through the signing and ratification
of the Optimal Protocol in 2000 and 2004, respectively.[17] These obvious commitments, notwithstanding, Nigeria has made little efforts at full domestication and enforceable implementation through the instrumentality of the law.[18]

The unanimous vote in July 2010 to create a single UN body tasked with
accelerating progress in achieving equality and women's empowerment
was signed, following series of agreements, conventions, declarations, and
treaties over the past years. This birthed the formation of the UN Women
and its full operation in January 2011. It merged and built upon the work
of four previously distinct parts of the UN system: the Division for the
Advancement of Women; the International Research and Training Institute
for the Advancement of Women; the Office of the Special Advisory on
Gender Issues and the Advancement of Women, and the UN Development
Fund for Women, focusing exclusively on gender equality and women's
empowerment.

Though the UN Women merges with previous UN systems, their goals
do not conflict in that, UN Women basically aims to "enhance" rather than
"replace" the efforts of the latter.[19] As a corollary to the above, the UN
Women contends that both human development and human rights issues
are in many ways linked to gender dimensions, hence, to adequately chart
a new course that are fundamental to women's equality, focus is beamed on
priority areas. This, the UN Women believes, "can unlock progress across
the board."[20] These priority areas include: ending violence against women;
peace and security; leadership and participation; economic empowerment;
humanitarian action, governance and national planning; sustainable development agenda; and HIV and AIDS.[21] Part of its mandate, since its formation is
to work in tandem with UN member states through which agreements could
be reached on global standards regarding gender equality after which members states will effect these standards.[22] The attempt, within the context of

this study, is to interrogate one of the focus areas of the UN Women which is enhancing equality in political life and to observe if Nigeria has actualized this rather ambitious mandate.

On the founding of the UN Women in 2010, skepticism trailed the body. Most important were the fears in certain quarters that the body might not find the necessary support from all UN agencies and all UN member states. Similarly, the belief existed that members might not likely commit resources to its priority areas. And true to type, many of the fears raised have proved right today. First, albeit ironical, a handful of countries where women have a strong equal standing with men appear to show little commitments and support to the UN Women. Reluctance by developed economies in contributing to the overall budget target of UN Women which stood at (US$500 million in 2011 and 700 million in 2012), calls into question the viability of the UN Women to galvanize and give efficacy to those areas fundamental to women's equality that can unlock progress in virtually all areas.[23] While France, for instance, is not part of the top fifteen government donors to the UN Women for 2017, Senegal stood at number twenty-three among the top twenty-five core donors for 2018 well above developed economies such as Spain and Austria, respectively. Charlotte Bunch expressed this fear when she observed that, "fund raising has not reached expectations" because the UN Women "still lacks a robust, strategic, and diversified approach to raising money."[24]

Second, in the area of support, several European nations who, though joined in drumming up support for the UN Women only appear to pledge to the body but do not necessarily commit their total financial support. In 2011, France and China, two large economies, pledged a paltry US$296,296 and US$60,000, compared to less financially robust Western economies like Spain and Italy which pledged US$25,412,088 and US$961,538, respectively.[25] While only sixty-five countries out of about 150 UN member countries pledged a total of US$69,843,876, only US$33,767,897, less than half of that amount, and less than a quarter of the total annual budget, was eventually received. Records from the UN Women website show the unsupportive attitude of member nations to financially commit to the UN Women, despite decades of efforts to change the state of affairs.

Pledges and contributions to the UN Women Core Resources show the funding trajectory of UN Women, for instance, totaled US$ 33,767,897 on April 30, 2011.[26] Since this period, the body has relied heavily on voluntary monetary contributions most of which come from commitments from UN member countries. Though funding has improved in recent years with the view of extending its funding requests to the "private sector" and "emerging economies," the UN Women, by its own admission, observes that improved financial capital remain erratic.[27] As it stands, close to ninety member countries have pledged to UN Women's core budget, a significant increase from previous years. However, the body requires the strong commitments of about 150 members to maintain its diverse government donor base.[28] Given the series of serious financial challenges the UN Women faces as part of effort to carry out its "focus and priority areas that are fundamental to women's equality," it however remains to be seen how effectively women's rights could be championed under this dire financial situation.

Nigerian Women in Politics since 1999: A Brief Assessment

Since the turn of democracy in 1999, the performance of women in Nigerian politics has witnessed mixed results.[29] While women have been able to attain heights in many areas of the economy, in the political sphere, the situation remains dismal despite their vast numbers. Their aspirations and concerns appear to be undeniably tossed out. To be sure, one need to see the course at which the Nigerian woman had taken since the turn of democracy and how well they have performed in their quest for gender equality and representation within the political sphere.

In 1999, the first presidential Technical Committee was set up with the task of performing a comprehensive constitutional and electoral review. Of the twenty-four Committee members, only four were women. Their abysmal number, nevertheless, the report submitted by the Committee contained some gender-friendly provisions which would later be jettisoned. This did not, however, deter the government from taking a clear departure from the past. Four women out of the twenty-nine senior ministers and three out of eighteen junior ministers, representing 13.7 percent and 16.6 percent, respectively, were appointed. Also appointed were two senior special assistants, two women advisors, six special assistants, eight permanent secretaries, and one special assistant to the vice president.[30] There were also women appointments into executive councils and as commissioners across the states of the federation. Between 1999 and 2011, women participation in politics witnessed a modest growth, yet these positions, to quote Ngara and Ayabam, "were mostly appointive rather than elective."[31] In the case of elective positions, out of a total 469 seats in 1999 in both the Senate and House of Representatives, only fifteen women won seats, representing 3.9 percent. The figure rose to twenty-five in 2003, representing 5.33 percent and surged to thirty-four in 2007, representing 7.24 percent with a slim decline in 2011 to thirty-three, representing 7.03 percent.[32] While appointments of women into political office rose, albeit slowly, participation in key-decision-making processes remained very poor.

In 2005, 400 delegates participated at the National Political Reforms Conference (NPRC). Out of this number; only thirty women delegates were selected. For a conference aimed at reconstructing the future of the country, having a skewed representation was bound to have adverse effects on the future standing of women.[33] And as many feared, attempts by the NPRC to mainstream gender issues in its outcome failed woefully. Also, in 2007, the Electoral Reform Committee (ERC) inaugurated to review and ensure equality and standard general elections made some gender sensitive recommendations. Having submitted its (ERC) report for consideration, the National Assembly warmly adopted the only probable gender-friendly proposal which was the new clause permitting independent candidacy. Unfortunately, this clause would sooner be thrown out by the State Houses of Assembly.

The palpable situation, nevertheless, twenty-seven women won elections into parliament in the 2003 and 2007 elections, a significant improvement in women political participation and representation.[34] The experiences of women during the last two elections (2011 and 2015) show that the political parties have refused to integrate women's needs and concerns in the business of democracy. A critical look at the National Executive Councils and Board of Trustees of all political parties in Nigeria suggest a deeply gendered composition and discrimination against women. In actual fact, a good number of women who manage to get to high positions in these councils and boards are appointed heads of welfare, social organizer or ex-officio, most of which often appear politically redundant.

While several factors, beyond the obvious patriarchal machinations above, have been deduced for the abysmal failure of women's inclusion in the political process, the factor of what could be attributed to "self-infliction" cannot be totally wished away. This was not only a common feature in the 2011 elections but appear to be a new trend in subsequent elections in the country. From the foregoing, the study contends that women's performance in politics is characterized by the failure to achieve a common front against their perceived marginalization. As Olumide argues, in spite of the strong-willed campaigns held in support of women, the odds continue to show "that success of female candidates is not rising."[35]

POLITICAL REPRESENTATION IN THE MIDST OF GLASS CEILINGS

Nigeria's support for gender rights could be traced to its signing and ratification of multifarious gender-based treaties such as the CEDAW and Beijing Declaration and Platform for Action.[36] Over the years, the country has also backed several other gender-based bodies, the UN Women being one. This support was based on Nigeria's recognition of the challenges faced by women globally especially in the area of access to human rights despite years of efforts.[37] Nigeria, hence, acknowledged the efforts of the UN Women "in addressing the issues affecting not only the empowerment of women but also the advancement of women and their effective participation in their systems."[38]

To effectively address these issues, Nigeria joined a growing list of countries pledging significant financial contributions to the UN Women. In 2011, for instance, the Nigerian government approved the sum of US$500,000 as part of its donation for the UN Women core funding.[39] According to Nigeria's representative to the UN, Ambassador U. Joy Ogwu, the contribution was part of Nigeria's resolve to give strong backing to the UN Women with the conviction that the body "could do a lot for the Nigerian–and Africa–woman and girl."[40] Like Nigeria, several other countries such as India, Canada, Australia, Denmark, Holland, and Republic of Korea also donated in their own capacity.

While there is nothing wrong or defective in partnering or giving strong backing to gender-based bodies like the UN Women or in signing treaties that commits nations to gender rights, it is difficult to understand the underlying motive behind Nigeria's financial contributions to such bodies since it has done very little to break the gender barriers that often debases the rights of women across the country. Women are hardly recognized as partners and beneficiaries of development, human rights, humanitarian action, and peace and security even when they appear to be more qualified in these areas. Sadly, the hope of achieving equality in political life as one of the priority areas of the UN Women looks gloomy. A reason for this somewhat dashed hope is linked to the colonial and postcolonial perception of women as assuming purely sex roles. It is why in a deeply patriarchal society as Nigeria, a woman's fate continues to hang in the balance, especially in the political sphere.

The election of Honourable Aminu Tambuwal in 2011, as Speaker of Nigeria's Sixth Assembly, proved the above assertion true within the context of the cultural barriers set against women in politics. This is despite the anointing of Mrs Akande-Adeola, a female representative from the South-West geopolitical region, by the presidency. A commentator, while painting a grim picture of the situation observed that Akande-Adeola's gender was responsible for her loss at the speakership election "where not even fellow female Reps-elect could be swayed to back her cause."[41]

The build up to the presidential primaries of the 2011 general elections provide a further dismal performance. The case of Mrs Sarah Jibrin readily comes to mind. Since 1992, she had put herself up for presidential nomination with the 2011 election being the fifth time she would request party delegates to consider her as a candidate for the presidency.[42] At the conclusion of the party primaries, two male candidates, Mr Goodluck Jonathan and Alhaji Atiku Abubakar, garnered 2,736 and 805 votes, respectively.[43] Though nomination forms were free for women and despite the month-long campaign held nationwide by one of the candidate's (Goodluck Jonathan) wives to encourage women participation in politics, Mrs Jibrin could only muster even one vote. Women delegates at the primaries could not be swayed to vote for their own, raising concerns on equal representation for women and their viability in Nigerian politics.

With specific reference to the 2015 gubernatorial election in Taraba State, where for the first time in the nation's history, a political party fielded a woman candidate. Miss Aisha Jumai Al-Hassan tipped to make political history and finally break the jinx that had asphyxiated the Nigerian woman for years from winning at the gubernatorial polls was edged out through what a commentator called the "election malpractice antics" of the ruling party at the time.[44] Though a writer linked this to "the near success syndrome that has been the lot of many Nigerian women in politics,"[45] it is not unlikely that Miss Al-Hassan's gender was responsible for the twists and turns that would eventually deny her the mandate during and in the aftermath of the election.

In the last few years since the UN Women founding, it has made giant strides toward accelerating women's participation in politics. In view of this, and as part of its solution to halt restrictions of women in leadership and political participation, the body has initiated a series of training programs for women political candidates, civic education, advocacy, and sensitization campaigns on gender equality.[46] The Women in Politics Map 2014 which highlights the latest data on women in both executive and parliament also show the progress made across continents.[47] Though the map indicates that in general more women are now into politics and deeply involved in decision-making processes at higher levels, they do not appear to have reached "the very highest level" such as the leadership of the executive, legislative, or judicial arm of government. Nevertheless, evidence suggests that women in parts of Africa such as Ameenah Gurib-Fakim (Mauritius) and Sahle-Work Zewde (Ethiopia) were elected president, unlike what was obtained in the past, though significant gaps remain.[48] In Nigeria, glass ceilings, however, remain emboldened.

There is both constitutional and official discrimination against women which continues to debar their progress within their society. For instance, the 1999 constitution is commonly regarded as lacking gender neutrality which is seen in its use of the pronoun, "He" as much as 235 times, with very little reference to "She." The same document under Section 182 of the Penal Code declares a married man not guilty of marital or spousal rape, while Section 55 (1) of the Labour Act prohibits women from working or being employed anywhere in the country at night.[49] This is in spite of the fact the same constitution prohibits discrimination on the basis of gender. Officially, there are cultural norms or religious laws that continue to restrict women's right. An example is the insistence on female genital mutilation which often exposes the girl child to various health dangers. In the area of education, particularly in parts of northern Nigeria, as much as 80 percent of women cannot read when compared with 54 percent for the men folk.[50] Religious beliefs have also tended to reduce women to the home front and in the case of child birth, are subjected to home delivery which often leads to maternal and infant mortality. A bill which would have helped to empower women in political and economic areas and also provide them with equal opportunities in different human engagements with men was rejected by the Nigerian Senate in 2016.[51] It is through the above and many others that have set the path, sadly, for little progress and until the country commits itself to a stringent revision of virtually all discriminatory laws and practices which debars women at all levels from inclusion and participation in democratic governance, the country will, no doubt, continue to walk in cycles.

CONCLUSION

There is no doubt that no country can make meaningful progress until the right of representation and inclusion are guaranteed to the woman. To achieve societal development, therefore, adequate representation of women in decision-making positions is cardinal. By giving prime positions in all strata of the economy and especially in both appointive and elective positions, Nigeria would have guaranteed women social justice and a voice of their own.

Though a common argument observes that the very few women who eventually assume powerful political positions "are not necessarily driven by development agenda but selfish interests," and accordingly, "use the gender envelope to advance personal goals which may be visibility . . . or access to donor funding,"[52] this may not be true in certain cases. The inestimable role played by a former head of Nigeria's food and drug regulatory agency continues to reverberate across the country. Her determination to rid the country of fake drugs remains unmatched till date.

The study has been able to interrogate quite a number of issues bordering especially on the festering gender inequality and exclusion of women from the political process at all levels. The changing roles of women from colonial times, as we argued, would appear responsible for the second-fiddle role they would eventually come to play at independence. It further argues that rather than commit such huge financial resources to the UN Women, Nigeria should adopt a law to allow all obligations as CEDAW requires and commit its resources through its Women Affairs Ministry and women advocacy groups for proper mobilization and orientation. Once this internal challenge is addressed, the UN Women may likely have little work to do in terms of raising the bar on women's rights in the country.

While using the gender platform to accelerate their way to power, women must not have intentions different from the ones expected of them from the society by the time they assume higher political positions. Having ulterior motives readily places them as agents of male domination rather than flag captains of women empowerment and gender rights. This, the study believes, may help to eliminate the boundary lines and persistent structural barriers drawn against women.

NOTES

1. Sede Alonge, "My Wife Belongs in the Kitchen, President Buhari isn't Helping Nigeria," *The Guardian*, October 17, 2016.

2. For the BBC interview, see "Nigeria's President Warned by First Lady Aisha Buhari," *BBC Africa*, October 14, 2016.

3. All tweets are cited from Nosmot Gbadamosi "Nigerians React to President saying First Lady "Belongs in the Other Room," *CNN*, October 18, 2016.

4. Gbadamosi, "Nigerians React to President."

5. Sylvester Ugwuanyi, "Women Groups Slam Buhari, Describe Kitchen Comment as Demeaning," *Daily Post*, October 18, 2016.

6. Musa Njadvara, "Women insist on 35% Affirmative Action from Buhari's Administration," *The Guardian*, April 27, 2015.

7. Mojubaola Olufunke Okome, ""Unknown Soldier": Women's Radicalism, Activism, and State Violence in Twentieth-Century Nigeria," in *Gender and Power Relations in Nigeria*, ed. Ronke I. Ako-Nai (Plymouth: Lexington Books, 2013), 262–263.

8. "Revisiting Rwanda Five Years after Record-Breaking Parliamentary Elections," *UN Women*, accessed June 22, 2019, http://www.unwomen.org/en/news/stories/2018/8/feature-rwanda-women-in-parliament.

9. See Statement by H.E. Mr. Neville Gertze, Ambassador and Permanent Representative before the Third Committee of the 73th Session of the United Nations General Assembly on Agenda ITEM 29: Advancement of Women, New York, October 8, 2018.

10. Ojuolape W. "The Role of Women as a Wife, a Mother and a Career Woman" (paper presented at the Citizenship and Leadership Training Centre, Sea School, Apapa, Lagos, March 22, 2000); Fatima Sadiqi, "Changing Gender Dynamics in Africa," *CODESRIA Bulletin*, nos. 3 and 4 (2002); George U.G. "Theoretical Positions of Gender Roles in Society," in *Women and Social Change in Nigeria*, ed. 'Lai Olurode (Lagos: Unity Publishing and Research Ltd., 1990), 23-32; and Kunle Ajayi, "Gender Self-endangering: The Sexist Issue in Nigerian Politics," *Journal of Social Science* 14, no. 2 (2007): 137–147.

11. Cited in Abidemi R. Asiyanbola, "Patriarchy, Male dominance, the Role and Women Empowerment in Nigeria" (paper submitted for presentation as poster at the International Union for the Scientific Study of Population [IUSSP/UIESP] XXV International Population Conference, Tours, France, July 18–23, 2005).

12. Bolanle Awe, "Yoruba Women in History" (lecture given at the DAWN Commission's Monthly Yoruba Historical Conversation, Cocoa House, Ibadan, June 24, 2016).

13. See Olufunke Iluyemi, "Ondo Tradition and Culture: The Female Angle," in *The Evolution of Ondo Kingdom over 500 Years (1510 – 2010+)*, ed. Ibidayo Ajayi (Ibadan: Spectrum Books Limited, 2014), 50–54.

14. George T. Basden, *Among the Ibo of Nigeria* (London: Seeley, Service & Co., 1921), 94–95.

15. Sope William, "Nigeria, its Women and International Law: Beyond Rhetoric," *Human Rights Review* 4, no. 2 (2004): 229–230.

16. "Introduction to the Content and Significance of the Convention (CEDAW)," *United Nations*, accessed October 17, 2018, http://www.un.org/womenwatch/daw/ce daw/text/econvention.htm.

17. Mercy Oke-Chinda, "Beyond Rhetoric: Towards the Implementation of the Convention on the Elimination of Discrimination against Women in Nigeria," *The Journal of Law and Criminology* 7, no. 1 (2017): 3–5.

18. See, for instance, Banke Olagbegi, "Women's Right to Land Ownership in Nigeria: A Critical Examination," *ABUAD Journal of Public and International Law* 1, no. 1 (2015): 1–13.

19. "Frequently Asked Questions: UN Women—Asia and the Pacific," *Asia Pacific*, accessed October 17, 2018, http://www.asiapacific.unwomen.org/en/countries/fiji/faq.

20. "What we do," *UN Women*, accessed October 17, 2018, http://www.unwomen .org/en/what-we-do.

21. "Focus Area," *UN Women*, accessed October 17, 2018, http://www.unwomen .org/focus-areas/.

22. "UN Women Begins its Work," *UN Women*, accessed October 17, 2018, http: //unwomen.org/2011/01/un-women-begins-its-work/.

23. See "Focus Area."

24. Interview by Masum Momaya with Charlotte Bunch, Founding Member of the Gender Equality Architecture Reform (GEAR) Campaign on Friday Files as Part of the Theme for AWID 2102 Forum, February 16, 2012.

25. "Partnerships," *UN Women*, accessed October 17, 2018, http://www.unwomen .org/partnerships/?show=Donors.

26. "Pledges and contributions to UN Women Core Resources," *UN Women*, accessed February 4, 2021, http://www.unwomen.org/partnerships/?show=Donors.

27. "Government Contributors," *UN Women*, accessed October 17, 2018, http:// www.unwomen.org/en/partnerships/donor-countries.

28. "Government Contributors."

29. The year 1999 was chosen since it represents an important historic period in Nigeria's quest for uninterrupted democracy.

30. Luka R.C., "Women and Political Participation in Nigeria: the Imperatives of Empowerment," *Journal of Social Sciences and Public Policy* 3 (2011): 29–30.

31. Christopher Ochanja Ngara and Alexius Terwase Ayabam, "Women in Politics and Decision-making in Nigeria: Challenges and Prospects," *European Journal of Business and Social Sciences* 2, no. 8 (2013): 48–50.

32. Ngara and Ayabam, "Women in Politics."

33. Fatile Olufemi Jacob et al., "Feminism and Political Participation in Nigeria: An Empirical Analysis," *International Journal of Asian Social Science* 2, no. 7 (2012): 1078–1079.

34. Olumide Seye, "Women Lament Losses in April Polls as the Worst Ever," *Guardian*, June 10, 2011.

35. Olumide, "Women Lament Losses."

36. Though Nigeria ratified the CEDAW in 1985, it has failed to adopt a law to allow all obligations CEDAW requires. See "The Nigeria NGO Coalition Shadow Report to the CEDAW Committee," *International Federation for Human Rights*, accessed October 17, 2018, https://www.fidh.org/en/region/Africa/nigeria/The-Niger ia-NGO-coalition-shadow.

37. "Opening remarks by Ambassador U. Joy Ogwu, former Permanent Representative of Nigeria to the UN and President Executive Board of UN Women," *Nigeria UN Mission,* accessed October 17, 2018, http://www.nigeriaunmission.or g/index.php?option=com_content&view=article&id=177:opening-remarks-u-joy-og wu-executive-board-of-un-women&catid=49:events&Itemid=70.

38. "Opening Remarks."

39. See Growing Core Contributions to UN Women, *UN Women*, accessed October 17, 2018, http://unwomen.org/en/news/stories/2011/5/growing-core-contr ibutions-to-un-women.

40. Quoted in "Growing Core Contributions."

41. "Women in Politics: The Burden of Affirmative Action," *Saturday Tribune*, June 18, 2011.

42. Reuben Abati, "Sarah Jubrin and other Women in Politics," *Nigeria Village Square*, accessed October 17, 2018, http://www.nigeriavillagesquare.com/articles/ reuben-abati/sarah-jubril-and-Other-women-in-Politics-reuben-abati.html.

43. Abati, "Sarah Jubrin and other Women."

44. Hadiza Ibrahim, "Mama Taraba: The Curious Case of Nigerian Women Ceiling Breaker," *Daily Trust*, November 25, 2015.

45. Titilope Olalere Olusegun, "Women and Nigerian Politics: An Appraisal of 2015 General Elections" (paper presented at a Two-Day National Conference tagged: The 2015 General Elections in Nigeria: The Real Issues, at The Electoral Institute, Abuja on June 17–18, 2015).

46. See "Thematic Brief on UN Women's Work on Leadership and Political Participation," *UN Women*, accessed October 17, 2018, http://www.unwomen.org/en /what-we-do/leadership-and-political-participation.

47. For more insights, see The Women in Politics Map: 2014, launched by the Inter-Parliamentary Union and UN Women, April 13, 2012.

48. The Global Gender Gap Report, 2013, World Economic Forum Publication, 2013.

49. See Labour Act, Chapter 198 Laws of the Federation of Nigeria 1990.

50. Chinwe Julie Abara, "Tradition and Religion as Negative Factors for Gender Inequality in Nigeria" (paper presented at the Federation of International Human Rights Museums tagged: Museums and Human Rights, International Slavery Museum, Liverpool, United Kingdom, October 9–10, 2012).

51. Timothy Oshi, "Nigerian Senate Rejects Bill Seeking Gender Equality in Marriage," *Premium Times*, 15 March, 2016.

52. Abati, "Sarah Jubrin and other Women in Politics."

BIBLIOGRAPHY

Abara, Chinwe Julie. "Tradition and Religion as Negative Factors for Gender Inequality in Nigeria." Paper presented at the Federation of International Human Rights Museums tagged: Museums and Human Rights, International Slavery Museum, Liverpool, United Kingdom, October 9–10, 2012.

Abati, Reuben. "Sarah Jubrin and Other Women in Politics." *Nigeria Village Square*. http://www.nigeriavillagesquare.com/articles/reuben-abati/sarah-jubril-and-Other -women-in-Politics-reuben-abati.html.

Ajayi, Kunle. "Gender Self-endangering: The Sexist Issue in Nigerian Politics." *Journal of Social Science* 14, no. 2 (2007): 137–147.

Alonge, Sede. "My Wife Belongs in the Kitchen, President Buhari isn't Helping Nigeria." *The Guardian*, October 17, 2016.

Asia Pacific. "Frequently Asked Questions: UN Women – Asia and the Pacific." Accessed October 17, 2018. http://www.asiapacific.unwomen.org/en/countries/fi ji/faq.

Asiyanbola, Abidemi R. "Patriarchy, Male dominance, the Role and Women Empowerment in Nigeria." Poster presentation at the International Union for the Scientific Study of Population [IUSSP/UIESP] XXV International Population Conference, Tours, France, July 18–23, 2005.

Awe, Bolanle. "Yoruba Women in History." Lecture given at the DAWN Commission's Monthly Yoruba Historical Conversation, Cocoa House, Ibadan, June 24, 2016.

Basden, George T. *Among the Ibos of Nigeria*, 94–95. London: Seeley, Service & Co., 1921.

Gbadamosi, Nosmot. "Nigerians React to President saying First Lady "Belongs in the Other Room." *CNN*, October 18, 2016.

George, U. G. "Theoretical Position of Gender Roles in Society." In *Women and Social Change in Nigeria*, edited by 'Lai Olurode, 23–32. Lagos: Unity Publishing and Research Ltd., 1990.

Ibrahim, Hadiza. "Mama Taraba: The Curious Case of Nigerian Women Ceiling Breaker." *Daily Trust*, November 25, 2015.

Iluyemi, Olufunke. "Ondo Tradition and Culture: The Female Angle." In *The Evolution of Ondo Kingdom over 500 Years (1510 – 2010+)*, edited by Ibidayo Ajayi, 50–54. Ibadan: Spectrum Books Limited, 2014.

International Federation for Human Rights. "The Nigeria NGO Coalition Shadow Report to the CEDAW Committee. Accessed October 17, 2018. https://www.fidh .org/en/region/Africa/nigeria/The-Nigeria-NGO-coalition-shadow.

Interview by Masum Momaya with Charlotte Bunch, Founding Member of the Gender Equality Architecture Reform (GEAR) Campaign on Friday Files as Part of the Theme for AWID 2012 Forum, February 16, 2012.

Jacob, Fatile Olufemi, Akhakpe Ighodalo, Igbokwe Ibeto, Chinyeaka Justine and Chukwuemeka Okpo Oteh. "Feminism and Political Participation in Nigeria: An Empirical Analysis." *International Journal of Asian Social Science* 2, no. 7 (2012): 1078–1079.

Labour Act, Chapter 198 Laws of the Federation of Nigeria 1990.

Luka, R. C. "Women and Political Participation in Nigeria: The Imperatives of Empowerment." *Journal of Social Sciences and Public Policy* 3 (2011): 29–30.

Ngara, Christopher Ochanja and Alexius Terwase Ayabam. "Women in Politics and Decision-making in Nigeria: Challenges and Prospects." *European Journal of Business and Social Sciences* 2, no. 8 (2013): 48–50.

"Nigeria's President Warned by First Lady Aisha Buhari." *BBC Africa*, October 14, 2016.

Nigeria UN Mission. "Opening remarks by Ambassador U. Joy Ogwu, former Permanent Representative of Nigeria to the UN and President Executive Board of UN Women." Accessed October 17, 2018. http://www.nigeriaunmission.org/ind ex.php?option=com_content&view=article&id=177:opening-remarks-u-joy-ogwu -executive-board-of-un-women&catid=49:events&Itemid=70.

Njadvara, Musa. "Women insist on 35% Affirmative Action from Buhari's Administration." *The Guardian*, April 27, 2015.

Ojuolape, W. "The Role of Women as a Wife, a Mother and a Career Woman." Paper presented at the Citizenship and Leadership Training Centre, Sea School, Apapa, Lagos, March 22, 2000.

Oke-Chinda, Mercy. "Beyond Rhetoric: Towards the Implementation of the Convention on the Elimination of Discrimination against Women in Nigeria." *The Journal of Law and Criminology* 7, no. 1 (2017): 3–5.

Okome, Mojubaola Olufunke. ""Unknown Soldier": Women's Radicalism, Activism, and State Violence in Twentieth-Century Nigeria." In *Gender and Power Relations in Nigeria*, edited by Ronke I. Ako-Nai, 262–263. Plymouth: Lexington Books, 2013.

Olagbegi, Banke. "Women's Right to Land Ownership in Nigeria: A Critical Examination." *ABUAD Journal of Public and International Law* 1, no. 1 (2015): 1–13.

Olusegun, Titilope Olalere. "Women and Nigerian Politics: An Appraisal of 2015 General Elections." Paper presented at a Two-Day National Conference tagged: The 2015 General Elections in Nigeria: The Real Issues, at The Electoral Institute, Abuja on June 17–18, 2015.

Oshi, Timothy. "Nigerian Senate Rejects Bill Seeking Gender Equality in Marriage." *Premium Times*, March 15, 2016.

Sadiqi, Fatima. "Changing Gender Dynamics in Africa." *CODESRIA Bulletin*, nos. 3 and 4 (2002).

Seye, Olumide. "Women Lament Losses in April Polls as the Worst Ever." *Guardian*, June 10, 2011.

Statement by H.E. Mr. Neville Gertze, Ambassador and Permanent Representative before the Third Committee of the 73th Session of the United Nations General Assembly on Agenda ITEM 29: Advancement of Women, New York, October 8, 2018.

The Global Gender Gap Report, 2013, World Economic Forum Publication, 2013.

The Women in Politics Map: 2014, launched by the Inter-Parliamentary Union and UN Women, April 13, 2012.

Ugwuanyi, Sylvester. "Women Groups Slam Buhari, Describe Kitchen Comment as Demeaning." *Daily Post*, October 18, 2016.

UN Women. "Focus Area." Accessed October 17, 2018. http://www.unwomen.org/focus-areas/.

UN Women. "Government Contributors." Accessed October 17, 2018. http://www.unwomen.org/en/partnerships/donor-countries.

UN Women. "Growing Core Contributions to UN Women." Accessed October 17, 2018. http://unwomen.org/en/news/stories/2011/5/growing-core-contributions-to-un-women.

UN Women. "Introduction to the Content and Significance of the Convention (CEDAW)." Accessed October 17, 2018. http://www.un.org/womenwatch/daw/cedaw/text/econvention.htm.

UN Women. "Partnerships." Accessed October 17, 2018. http://www.unwomen.org/partnerships/?show=Donors.

UN Women. "Pledges and contributions to UN Women Core Resources." Accessed February 4, 2021. http://www.unwomen.org/partnerships/?show=Donors.

UN Women. "Revisiting Rwanda Five Years after Record-Breaking Parliamentary Elections." Accessed June 22, 2019. http://www.unwomen.org/en/news/stories/2018/8/feature-rwanda-women-in-parliament.

UN Women. "Thematic Brief on UN Women's Work on Leadership and Political Participation." Accessed October 17, 2018. http://www.unwomen.org/en/what-we-do/leadership-and-political-participation.

UN Women. "UN Women Begins its Work." Accessed October 17, 2018. http://unwomen.org/2011/01/un-women-begins-its-work/.

UN Women. "What we do." Accessed October 17, 2018. http://www.unwomen.org/en/what-we-do.

William, Sope. "Nigeria, its Women and International Law: Beyond Rhetoric." *Human Rights Review* 4, no. 2 (2004): 229–230.

"Women in Politics: The Burden of Affirmative Action." *Saturday Tribune*, June 18, 2011.

Chapter 17

Rendered as Political Pawns

Chibok Girls, Ebola, and the Exercise of Political Will

April Petillo and Jane Eggers

"What are we to believe?" asked an exasperated Nigerian father almost a year after Boko Haram abducted 270 Chibok schoolgirls.[1] Many inside and outside of Nigeria expressed this same sentiment years later. Families, community members, and even the international community were frustrated. The Nigerian national government kept "telling us [that] our girls would soon be rescued and handed over to us. Where are our girls? Are they still alive or not?" We now know the fate of those schoolgirls and many others Boko Haram abducted. Still, the question of why the government couldn't "just bring back our girls" resonates.

Months after the mass abduction, Nigeria faced Ebola, a virus that could have ravaged the country. With this crisis, Nigeria promptly identified the problem and garnered nationwide cooperation and global resources. The US Centers for Disease Control and Prevention's (CDC) case count indicates eight lives lost, a low rate likely due to the Nigerian government's quick exercise of political will to contain the potential public health crisis.

"What we are to believe" about state responses to the Chibok schoolgirl crisis specifically, and violence against women and girls generally, is important. The answer provides insight into state-recognized citizenship and state responsibilities to its citizens. This chapter contrasts Nigeria's response to these 2014 events to reflect on the interconnections between patriarchy, gender inequality, and violent extremism and how that may influence legal and social reform. We analyze the extent to which women's and girls' lives and rights are valued and realized through these events. This analysis suggests that incompetence is an inadequate explanation for the ineffective response to the Chibok girls' abduction. We argue that community involvement is essential to realizing rights and complements development goals applicable across the gender spectrum.

AGGRESSIVE WITH DISEASE, MEEK WITH ABDUCTORS

On July 20, 2014, Liberian–American Patrick Sawyer landed in Lagos and collapsed, becoming Nigeria's index Ebola patient approximately three months after the Chibok abduction and over a year before the government began to respond effectively. Mr Sawyer was treated and quarantined in Lagos by Dr Ameyo Adadevoh, Nigerian nationalist Herbert Macaulay's great-granddaughter. Although Dr Adadevoh died from Ebola exposure weeks later,[2] her decisiveness, followed by government coordination, proved pivotal to preventing widespread exposure.

Nigerian officials similarly recognized the danger, addressing the Ebola threat with international, national, regional, and local actors. The government requested health organization assistance, including the World Health Organization (WHO), the CDC, and *Médecins Sans Frontières*.[3] The Ministry of Health developed an informed, collaborative national response including an emergency operations center and management system.[4] Beyond quarantining, Nigeria's effort was multiscalar; they promptly screened, identified, and treated infected persons.[5] Mere weeks after identifying the index patient, nineteen additional people across two Nigerian states were diagnosed.[6] Only one patient evaded contact, for four days, before being located and treated.[7] These actions brought President Jonathan's administration accolades. WHO declared Nigeria Ebola-free three months after Mr Sawyer's arrival, hailing Nigeria's preventative containment a "spectacular success story."[8]

This efficient exercise of political will contrasts the seeming lack of administrative response to the gender-specific precarity of Boko Haram's mass Chibok schoolgirl abduction. The Nigerian government effectively contained Ebola, but not gendered violence and trafficking.[9] Government tracking was ineffective, leaving most Chibok girls who escaped captivity to do so on their own initiative. Navigating poor mental/physical healthcare and social stigma alone, some returned to Boko Haram.[10]

State inaction intensified the girls' vulnerability, and Boko Haram further threatened communities by coercing abducted girls to become suicide bombers.[11] Mass female abduction and abuse garnered little response from a government capable of decisive action against a viral threat shortly afterward. For this reason, the lament "what are we to believe?" resonates as a question about the state's valuation of women's and girls' rights.

CONTEXT: AN AGGRESSIVE VIRUS
AND GENDER-BASED VIOLENCE

Diseases like Ebola can have profound public health and economic consequences, as can gendered violence exacerbated by state failure to address it.[12] Nigeria's less aggressive response to the Chibok abduction illuminates how gender-based violence works in tandem with state inaction.[13]

Many national and international laws prohibit violence against women, suggesting that preventing such violence and prosecuting perpetrators should be more feasible than containing an unexpected virus. This seems especially possible in Nigeria, which has consistently low healthcare rankings[14] but has ratified numerous treaties and protocols protecting women's and girls' civil, political, economic, social, and cultural rights.[15] Nigeria has also made these international and regional instruments domestic law.[16] The Nigerian constitution protects citizens' human dignity, personal liberty, and freedom of religion, thought, and conscience (chapter IV, §34, 35, 38). However, Nigeria's inaction to violence against women can diminish these laws' effects and contribute to the problem. Nonstate actor terrorism complicates states' ability to address crimes, but so too do state actors who directly violate these rights or encourage state agents' inaction.[17] Some Nigerian police officers, whom locals could rightfully identify as state actors, epitomized this by using rape or the threat of rape to extort women's money and exert power.[18]

Nigeria's legal geography may also inform rights realization. Between 1999 and 2002, twelve primarily northern Nigerian states adopted the Shari'a Penal Code Law.[19] Some assert that this law violates rights, especially "equality before the law, equal protection of the law, torture, or degrading and inhuman punishment" and increased fundamentalist influences.[20] Federal laws requiring state action may also be affected. Nigeria's Child Rights Act (2003) protects children in conflict and prohibits child sexual abuse, labor, marriage, and exploitation. However, it is only applicable to states if passed by the thirty six state parliaments.[21] As of May 2019, eleven northern states, including Borno, which contains Chibok, had not done so.[22] Thus, areas where Boko Haram profoundly affects children's rights lack the legal protections present in less-affected regions.

Politics necessarily influenced Nigeria's responses to the Ebola and Chibok crises, though viruses like Ebola do not discriminate between sexes. Nigeria's effective Ebola response's was influenced by their comparably better health system as well as the government's swift exercise of political will and cooperation with multiple organizations.[23] Conversely, the same government refused to use political will concerning the abduction, which suggests that its infrastructures to combat gendered violence are underdeveloped or underutilized.

Discrimination undergirds acts of and responses to gender-specific violence, including systemic normalization of violence. The Nigerian government normalized the schoolgirls' harm through political passivity and false
information. Evidence found after the abductions suggested that security
forces ignored warnings that Boko Haram planned a Chibok school raid.[24]
The government then took almost a month to accept assistance despite state
claims of action.[25] In May, the government claimed to know the girls' location, and July brought rescue promises. By mid-October, President Johnson's
principal secretary publicized a deal; a notion ridiculed by Boko Haram.[26]

Nigerian governmental inaction may have also motivated further violence,
like Boko Haram's 2015 election-time attacks on northern villages and voters. [27] President Buhari was more proactive than his predecessor, influencing the October 2016 release of twenty-one abducted girls.[28] However, the
preceding seventeen months suggested that such violence is simply a part of
womanhood. This sentiment, passed from government to community, exacerbates the schoolgirls' and their community's trauma.

An unwillingness to use political will normalizes violence and portraying
violence as rare maintains it. Nigerians, particularly women, popularized
#BringBackOurGirls to protest violent insurgency and government inaction.
The campaign garnered international support, rarifying prevalent violence and
anchoring it in Nigeria. Women and girls are abducted, trafficked, assaulted,
raped, and/or murdered worldwide. Global reaction to this abduction and the
state inaction arguably frames the schoolgirls as the "Third World Female"
archetype, "thoroughly disempowered, brutalized, and victimized."[29] Yet this
view is in opposition to the reality, as the schoolgirls, who were a threat not
merely because they were receiving a "Western" education but also because
they were gaining knowledge and power. Women's and girls' education is
political and has positive effects, yet it renders them a structural threat.[30]

The girls' absence and long-term separation from their community disem-
power both.[31] Further, failure to address the harm erodes trust in government.
At a 2014 Abuja gathering calling for their rescue, an uncle of two missing
girls spoke for himself, the girls, and the community, "As far as our girls are
concerned, they have been abandoned."[32]

Local histories also influence the Chibok and Ebola crises. The Ebola crisis
may have ended differently if the index patient landed in less-resourced and
populated Northern Nigeria, rather than Lagos. Further, though Chibok is a
primarily Christian village in majority-Muslim Borno, it would be a mistake
to disregard Northern Nigeria's precolonial history of women's rights and
Islamic intellectualism.[33]

Northwestern Nigeria's Sokoto Caliphate Empire was ingrained in Islamic
values and practices and "promoted a culture of 'knowledge and intellectualism' [wherein] 'education became the yardstick for all opportunities in the

state and knowledge a ladder for climbing heights of respect and dignity'."[34] Free women, like Nana Asma'u, scholar, educator, early mother of modern African feminism, and daughter of Sokoto Caliphate founder, Usman dan Fodio, were educated.[35] Despite nearly sixty years of British colonization, Sokoto Caliphate remains a source of national and local pride.[36] Thus, Boko Haram's acts against girls' education contradict the region's sociohistorical legacy of valuing education but are consistent with resisting "Western"/historically colonizing schools.

Alongside these differences is the convergence between the Ebola and Chibok crises. Impoverishment and infrastructure problems impact virus management as well as insurgent violence. John Campbell considers Boko Haram insurgency the result of poor Nigerian governance, northeastern Nigeria's political marginalization, and the region's accelerating "impoverishment."[37] Thus, he argues that coordinated government response to Nigerian Muslim alienation would better address this insurgency. We add that this is not only the purview of federal governments; individuals and communities are essential bulwarks against this violence as well.

ADDRESSING GENDERED VIOLENCE REQUIRES EMPOWERING WOMEN AND COMMUNITIES

Gender-specific violence exists during peace and warfare, impacting communities and individuals.[38] Violence against women weakens a community's sense of safety and trust, loyalty, economy, and, by extension, the state.[39] The language of "gender-specific violence" belies the consequences for entire communities. This violence harms more than female-identified survivors; it demoralizes men stuck in patriarchal "protector" tropes. Impacted communities may live in constant fear, unable to recover a sense of wellbeing for years.[40] Gender-specific violence can also keep the threat imminent, conjuring terror of new violations like ghosts in the shared imaginary whenever community members are missing.[41] These challenges may have informed some community members' rejection of Boko Haram survivors who returned with children born from rape and forced marriage.[42]

Though nonconsensual invasion of another's body has globally signified colonized "ownership," this conquest strategy of systematically weaponizing sexual violence is only part of the story. Control of and power over another underlie gendered violence just as control of and power over peoples, land, and resources underlie colonization. Like colonizers' dehumanizing portrayal of subjugated peoples, trafficking and other forms of gendered violence socially mark certain people consumable (through excruciating work and dehumanizing treatment) and expendable (through reduced rights and minimal safety). Visibly dehumanizing some also negatively imprints the social psyche.[43] Thus, legacies remain after war and crises, informing ideas about who is violable and how to violate "effectively." These ideas, imposed on local gender definitions, can shape "particular" gender embodiment. In any state where violence against women is unaddressed, or perceived as acceptable, local conflict resolution concerning women may be skewed or obliterated. Consequently, losing locally defined resolution processes encourages dependence on external authorities, thus degrading community agency.[44] This violence and trauma can shape womanhood—bound to particular geography and religious/ethnic/communal affiliation. That locally defined "woman" is a political category signifying the friction between local independence or agency and state or powerful nonstate actor authority.

The existence of educated girls may threaten Boko Haram and others as symbols of the future and past. The lack of responsiveness suggests that the Nigerian government viewed these girls as politically insignificant. The government's refusal to act signals female bodies' expendability and the malleability of female citizenship. This inaction defines national character and identity while rendering some communities, women, and girls, outsiders.[45]

Nation-state geopolitical treatment of women and girls is not only a Nigerian issue, and precedent is not simply a legal doctrine. We cannot divorce current political understandings from histories of discriminatory cultural patterns. Critical race theorists suggest that changing centuries-old beliefs about race, gender, and sexuality requires that sovereign structural interests converge with the desired change.[46] Such convergence is rare, especially concerning marginalized intersectional identities.[47] Political action and inaction are inherently tied to social hierarchies and ensure divisions. Political inaction can write racialized, gendered displacement and colonization on certain bodies, rendering them consumable. When this occurs, the prevalence of trafficking may increase alongside decreased survivor access to justice and safety.[48] Thus, certain people live precarious, expendable lives, as objects for state or powerful nonstate entities to control, profit from, and/ or extinguish.[49] Citizenship and human rights should be less easily rendered precarious and expendable.

Violence includes physical harm and inaction, and the girls' trafficking illustrates how existing laws barely address related complexities. Although trafficking discourses focus on individual and social vulnerabilities,[50] the Chibok crisis shows that trafficking can involve using bodies for political messaging. Conversely, inaction also conveys political messages, such as support for or indifference to trafficking and, by extension, certain women's and girls' lives and rights.

Preying on individual and/or community vulnerabilities through trafficking violates international human rights law and, arguably, customary international law.[51] Nigeria ratified The Protocol to Prevent, Suppress, and Punish Trafficking in Persons, Especially Women and Children (2000). Article 3a of this protocol defines trafficking as

> the recruitment, transportation, transfer, harboring, or receipt of persons, by means of the threat or use of force or other forms of coercion, of abduction, of fraud, of deception, of the abuse of power or of a position of vulnerability or of the giving or receiving of payments or benefits to achieve the consent of a person having control over another person, for the purpose of exploitation.

This definition does not capture the range of harm, leaving Nigeria's existing legal protections insufficient to cover gaps concerning trafficking. Trafficking used to convey political messages are distinct. With trafficking in war, humanitarian and criminal laws protect civilians during armed conflict.[52] Still, there is a need for clear protection against nonstate actors' gender-specific, political violence in internal conflicts unacknowledged as noninternational armed conflict remains.

Captured girls' suicide bombing is an example of this violent messaging that can be understood as "political trafficking."[53] Coercing schoolgirls into terrorist acts reinforces Boko Haram's political message that women, particularly educated women, are unsafe. Boko Haram also used the schoolgirls to build insurgent fighter loyalty, providing the girls as personal caretakers and "morale-boosting" objects for ownership and abuse by insurgent fighters. Using the schoolgirls' bodies to encourage their own or others' harm conveys Boko Haram's power to control women and their communities. The Nigerian government's failure to act sends another political message, conveying the schoolgirls and their communities as irrelevant and exploitable. In contrast, Nigeria prioritized its Ebola response, which was decisive and collaborative, reads as not attending to gendered violence.

While the Nigerian government's response to the Chibok crisis illustrates how inaction can promote additional violence, isolated government action is not the solution. A primary task for a sovereign is protecting its citizenry and ensuring safety—all broad privileges of citizenship. The relationship between states, communities, and individuals is critical to realizing rights. Additionally, local community participation in responses to violence is imperative to these goals. Local participation, including "frontline workers," culled from community members, was critical to effectively addressing Ebola and could have also positively changed the Chibok situation.

With the mass abduction, the government relied neither on community knowledge nor support. Instead, the government offered what Chibok Council Caretaker Chairman, Mallam Ba'ana Lawan, characterized as empty promises.[54] This inaction, or refusal to exercise political will, was a lost opportunity and contributed to this governmental failure. As with the Ebola scare, large organizations are instrumental in harnessing resources to address large-scale problems. However, local organizations/actors possess community knowledge, making them critical to efficient, effective responses to fast-developing dangers like Ebola and mass abduction. Additionally, cultural negotiation is essential when regional divides influence politics.

Politics surrounding gendered violence and armed conflicts excuse neither inaction nor incompetence. This analysis suggests state inaction to the treatment or, with this example, ill-treatment of women and girls encourages more violence. Quick state response involving women and their communities can support women's and girls' rights, signaling state commitment to safety across genders.

Empowering and strengthening community response is essential because no government can always be everywhere simultaneously or nimble enough to address political insurgency seamlessly. As representatives of civil society, individuals and communities are integral to meeting local needs and ensuring states' accountability to satisfy the will of those governed. Contemporary social justice movements, such as Black Lives Matter, Standing Rock, and Say Her Name, call for fulfilling local obligations while including local perspectives in decision-making. State refusal to involve local communities and individuals ignores the will of the people who agreed to be governed, disregarding a fundamental understanding of the social contract.

LOCAL ACTION IS INTEGRAL TO REALIZING INTERNATIONAL RIGHTS AND GOALS

This analysis's broader implications involve recognizing that effective federal and national provisions, such as the Sustainable Development Goals (SDGs),[55] must relate locally to be realized locally.[56] For illustration, all goals discussed in this section are SDGs markers.

Unquestionably, violent conflicts affect community development.[57] Considering Goal 16 ("Promote peaceful and inclusive societies for sustainable development, provide access to justice for all and build effective, accountable, and inclusive institutions at all levels"), Nigeria's challenge to "significantly reduce all forms of violence and related death..." (Target 16.1) includes conflict-related women's deaths (Indicator 16.1.2) and the number of community members experiencing physical, psychological, or sexual violence (Indicator 16.1.3).

The attacks on northern Nigerian students and teachers in 2014 left "more than 300 schools damaged or destroyed and at least 196 teachers and 314 schoolchildren killed."[58] Consequently, survivors lived in fear of other insurgent attacks and without an intact educational infrastructure. Evidence of this is evidenced by the fact that the mass abduction and earlier Boko Haram incidents influenced the flight of over 800,000 children from their homes.[59] While regional geopolitics negatively impact girls' education, employing one approach throughout remains impractical if Nigeria will meet Goal 4 ("Ensure inclusive and equitable quality education and promote life-long learning opportunities for all") by 2030. This is especially true of targets 4.3 (ensuring access to affordable, quality education through university) and 4.5 (eliminating gender disparities in education and vocational training for those in vulnerable positions).

Violence against women, girls, and their communities also challenged Nigeria's progress toward Goal 5 ("Achieve gender equality and empower all women and girls"). Violence targeting schoolgirls extends to adults, from educated women to educators of any gender. Further, the direct harm created can stifle women's employment (Target 8.5 "achieve full and productive employment and decent work for all women and men . . . and equal pay for work of equal value") and create educational roadblocks (all Goal 4 targets).

An approach to the SDGs that prioritizes local involvement is consistent with meeting these national and international obligations. This shift is par-ticularly relevant for indigenous communities, whose rights and communal duties around crimes like trafficking are consistent with their sovereign obli-gations to create safety and protection for their members.[60] In nonindigenous communities, like the Chibok, local knowledge may also be practical and critical to political solution-making. Hence, engaging community assistance early in the Chibok crisis would have honored community members and international obligations.

Decisive responses to gender-specific violence, understood as a public health crisis on par with Ebola, could ensure Nigerian women's safety and protection while helping Nigeria meet long-term development goals. Further, investment in women's and girls' safety is a direct investment in women's social capital.[61]

LOCAL COMMUNITIES PLAY AN IMPORTANT ROLE IN BUILDING POLITICAL WILL

Paulo Friere, who believed that education liberates, observed that "the great humanistic and historical task of the oppressed [is] to liberate themselves and their oppressors as well. Only the power that springs from the weakness of the oppressed will be sufficiently strong [enough] to free both."[62] We agree with Friere. Governments can learn a lot from individuals and communities, especially concerning the realization and protection of their collective rights.

This analysis suggests that "what to believe" about the interconnections between patriarchy, gender inequality, and violent extremism is crucial to policy, legal, and social justice efforts. The realization of rights and good government cannot effectively exist without consent and belief in legal and government constructs. The contrast between the Nigerian government's actions during the 2014 Ebola crisis and the Chibok mass abduction[63] illustrates that government will as well as reliance on local communities and individuals can affect peoples' rights and lives. Without this web empowering individuals and communities, insurgents and authoritarians will always continue to rise.

NOTES

1. We are indebted to Dr. Leslye Obiora for her mentorship, encouragement, and insight.

2. Johnathan Cohn, "The Heroic, Tragic Story of the Doctor Who Saved Nigeria from Ebola," *New Republic*, October 25, 2014.

3. Katherine Courage, "How Did Nigeria Quash its Ebola Outbreak So Quickly?," *Scientific American,* October 18, 2014.

4. Ibid.

5. Ibid.

6. Ibid.

7. Maram Mazen, "How Nigeria is Keeping Ebola at Bay," *Time*, August 28, 2014.

8. WHO, "Nigeria is Now Free of Ebola Virus Transmission," October 20, 2014, http://www.who.int/mediacentre/news/ebola/20-october-2014/en/.

9. Although males experience all trafficking forms, international sex trafficking discourse concerns women. Inter-American Convention on the Prevention, Punishment and Eradication of Violence Against Women.

10. "'Those Terrible Weeks in Their Camp', Boko Haram Violence Against Women and Girls in Northeast Nigeria" (Report, *Human Rights Watch*, 2014).

11. Dionne Searcey, "Boko Haram Turns Female Captives into Terrorists," *New York Times*, April 7, 2016.

12. Violence against women is a global public health problem, not just a rights violation. Cheluchi Onyemelukwe, "Intersections of Violence Against Women and Health: Implications for Health Law and Policy in Nigeria," *William and Mary Journal of Women and the Law* 22, no. 3 (2016): 609–653.

13. Political responsibility concerning violence against women, "UNiTE to end violence against women." (Announcement, New York, United Nations, n.d.).

14. United Nations Development Program, "Midpoint Assessment of the Millennium Development Goals in Nigeria, 2000-2007," November 2008, 78 and Gabriel Enogolase, "Nigeria's Health System Ranks 197 of WHO's 200 Nations – NHIS," *Vanguard*. October 28, 2010.

15. Ratified treaties include Convention on the Elimination of all Forms of Discrimination Against Women (1985), Optional Protocol to the Convention (2004), Conviction on the Rights of the Child (1991), and Protocol to Prevent, Suppress and Punish Trafficking in Persons, Especially Women and Children (2001). Nigeria also signed the African Charter on Human and Peoples Rights and the Protocol to the African Charter on Human and Peoples' Rights on the Rights of Women in Africa.

16. Cheluchi Onyemelukwe, "Legislating on Violence against Women: A Critical Analysis of Nigeria's Recent Violence against Persons (Prohibition) Act, 2015," *DePaul Journal of Women, Gender and the Law* 5, no. 2 (2016).

17. State actors' and distinct/ blurred state boundaries discussion. Julie Brown, "Less is More: Decluttering the State Action Doctrine," *Missouri Law Review* 73, no. 2 (2008), https://scholarship.law.missouri.edu/mlr/vol73/iss2/8.

18. "Everyone's in on the Game": Corruption and Human Rights Abuses by the Nigerian Police Force (Report, Washington, DC: Human Rights Watch, 2010), 44–47.

19. Hauma Ibrahim and Princeton Lyman, *Reflections on the New Shari'a Law in Nigeria, Council on Foreign Relations* (June 2004): 3 and "Political Shari'a?" Human Rights and Islamic Law in Northern Nigeria. (Report, New York, Human Rights Watch, 2004).

20. Courage, "Quash Ebola."

21. Stephen Nmeregini Achilihu, *Do African Children Have Rights?: A Comparative and Legal Analysis of the United Nations Convention on the Rights of the Child* (Boca Raton, FL: Universal Publishers, 2010), 109–110.

22. Nike Adebowale, "11 States in Northern Nigeria Yet to Pass the Child Rights Law – UNICEF Official," *Premium Times*, May 12, 2019.

23. Courage, "Quash Ebola."

24. "Nigerian Authorities Failed to Act on Warning About Boko Haram Raid on School," *Amnesty International*, March 9, 2014.

25. Associated Press, "Nigeria: State of Emergency," *New York Times*, May 14, 2013.

26. Charlotte Alfred, "Remember #BringBackOurGirls? This Is What Has Happened in the 5 Months Since," *Huffington Post*, September 14, 2014, http://www.huffingtonpost.com/2014/09/14/nigeria-girls-kidnapped-5-months_n_5791622.html; "Chibok Abductions: Will Nigerian Schoolgirls Ever Be Freed?" *BBC News,* October 14, 2014, http://www.bbc.com/news/world-africa-29612345; and Ashionye Ogene, "Abandonment of 'Bring Back Our Girls,'" *Aljazeera*, October 14, 2014.

27. Aminu Abubakar and Faith Karimi, "2,000 Feared Killed in 'Deadliest' Boko Haram Attack in Nigeria," *CNN*, January 12, 2015 and Yasmin Kaye, "Nigeria: Several Feared Dead in Suspected Boko Haram Attacks: At Least 3 Dead as Militants Attack Polling Stations in Northeast Nigeria," *International Business Times,* March 28, 2015.

28. "Nigeria: Boko Haram 'releases 21 Chibok girls'," *Al Jazeera News*, October 13, 2016.

29. Ratna Kapur, "The Tragedy of Victimization Rhetoric: Resurrecting the 'Native' Subject in International/Post-Colonial Feminist Legal Politics," *Harvard*

Human Rights 1, no. 18 (2002): 18. The campaign framed the abducted as "our girls," and perpetually reinforced their "otherness," sometimes downplaying gendered violence's global pervasiveness.

30. Isaac Abrak, "Insight: Nigeria Islamists hit schools to destroy Western ideas," July 14, 2013, http://www.reuters.com/article/2013/07/14/us-nigeria-schoolkillings -idUSBRE96D01X20130714.

31. Anne Perkins, "200 Girls Are Missing in Nigeria – So Why Doesn't Anybody Care?," *The Guardian*, April 23, 2014.

32. Associated Press, "Nigeria."

33. Olufemi Vaughan and Suraiya Banu, "Muslim Women's Rights in Northern Nigeria," no. 2 (Washington, DC: The Wilson Center, April 2014), 2–3.

34. "Northern Nigeria: Background to Conflict," (Report 168, Brussels, International Crisis Group, 2010).

35. Balbasatu Ibrahim, "Contributions of Women to the Development of Hausa Literature as an Effective Means of Public Enlightenment: The Case of a 19th Century Female Scholar, Maryam Bint Uthman Ibn Foduye," *International Journal of Culture and History* 2, no. 1 (2016): 50–53.

36. Beverly B. Mack and Jean Boyd, *One Woman's Jihad: Nana Asma'u, Scholar and Scribe* (Bloomington, IN: Indiana University Press, 2000).

37. John Campbell, "U.S. Policy to Counter Nigeria's Boko Haram," (Policy Report, Washington, DC, *Council on Foreign Relations Press*, November 2014).

38. Slyvanna Falcón, "Rape as a Weapon of War: Advancing Human Rights for Women at the U.S.-Mexico Border," *Social Justice* 2, no 84 (2001): 31–50. Claudia Garcia-Morenoa and Charlotte Watts, "Violence Against Women A Priority Health Issue," *WHO Bulletin* 89, no. 1 (January 2011): 2.

39. April Petillo, "By Force or By Choice: Exploring Contemporary Targeted Sex Trafficking of Native Peoples" (Dissertation, Arizona State University, 2015).

40. Falcón, "Rape."

41. Ibid.

42. Dionne Searcey, "Nigerian Women Freed from Boko Haram Face Rejection at Home," *New York Times*, February 16, 2016.

43. Falcón, "Rape."

44. Ibid.

45. Ibid.

46. Black "racial equality will be accommodated only when it converges with the interests of whites." Derrick Bell, "Brown v. Board of Education and Interest-Convergence Dilemma," *Harvard Law Review* 518, no. 523 (1980): 523.

47. Kimberlé Crenshaw, "Demarginalizing the Intersection of Race and Sex: A Black Feminist Critique of Antidiscrimination Doctrine, Feminist Theory and Antiracist Politics," *Feminist Legal Studies* 3 (1989): 105–135.

48. Falcón, "Rape."

49. Precarious life is without security; affecting material/psychological welfare. Marxist contexts add intermittent or underemployment and predetermined social order. "Precarity" invokes Puar, Butler and Berlant. Jasbir Puar, "Precarity Talk: A Virtual Roundtable with Lauren Berlant, Judith Butler, Borjana Cvejić, Isabell Lorey,

Jasbir Puar, and Ana Vujanović," *The Drama Review – A Journal of Performance Studies* 56, no. 4 (2012): 163–177 and Judith Butler, "Performativity, Precarity and Sexual Politics," *AIBR Revista de Antropologia Iberoamericana* 4, no. 3 (2009): 321–336.

50. United Nations Office on Drugs and Crime, "An Introduction to Human Trafficking: Vulnerability, Impact, and Action, 2008." (Background Paper) http://www.unodc.org/documents/human-trafficking/An_Introduction_to_Human_Trafficking_-_Background_Paper.pdf.

51. Slavery prohibitions are *jus cogens* (Restatement of the Law, Third, Foreign Relations Law of the United States § 102 [1987]). Though contested, trafficking is regarded as slavery, arguably violating customary international law. (Office of the United Nations High Commissioner for Human Rights [OHCHR 1991]). Crimes experienced while trafficked, including rape and sexual torture, violate customary international law. Consequently, sexual violence is increasingly recognized as *jus cogens*. Kelly Askin, "Prosecuting Wartime Rape and Other Gender-Related Crimes Under International Law: Extraordinary Advances, Enduring Obstacles," *Berkeley Journal of International Law* 21, no. 2 (2003): 288–349 and Jonathan Charney, "Universal International Law," *American Journal of International Law* 87, no. 4 (1993): 529, 541.

52. Third Geneva Convention and Fourth Geneva Convention; Article 4 of Additional Protocol II; Article 27 of 4th Geneva Convention and Article 76 of Additional Protocol; Rome Statute.

53. Men/ boys experience war-related sexual exploitation/humiliation, including by Boko Haram. The schoolgirl abductions/trafficking exemplify political statements made through gendered targets.

54. Duku Joel ,eria," no. 2 (April 2014): 2–3, and Grace Obike, "Chibok Community to Fed Govt: We Want Our Girls Back Not School Building," *The Nation,* March 9, 2015.

55. These goals, adopted September 2015, were to improve Millennium Development Goals (MDGs) ending that year. "Report of the UN System Task Team on the Post-2015 UN Development Agenda," (report, New York, United Nations, 2013), 1.

56. United Nations International Children's Emergency Fund, "800,000 Children Forced to Flee Violence in Nigeria and Region," (press release, April 13, 2015).

57. Ibid.

58. Ibid.

59. Ibid.

60. Indigenous human rights jurisdictional trafficking approaches specifically and human rights generally, Jason Juran, Joseph Scovel and Hayley Weedn, "Human Trafficking & Native Peoples in Oregon: A Human Rights Report," *American Indian Law Journal* 3, no. 1 (2014): 40–158; Clare Boronow, "Note, Closing the Accountability Gap for Indian Tribes: Balancing the Right to Self Determination with the Right to a Remedy," *Virginia Law Review* 98, no. 6 (2012): 1373–1425; James Anaya, "The Human Rights of Indigenous Peoples: United Nations Developments (International Law and the Development of the Rights of

Indigenous Peoples)," *The University of Hawaii Law Review* 35, no. 2 (2013): 983–1012.

61. Obiageli Ezekwesili, "Women are Key to Achieving MDGs," *MDG Achievement Fund*, n.d., http://www.mdgfund.org/node/1528.

62. Paolo Freire, *Pedagogy of the Oppressed* (New York, NY: Herder and Herder, 1972), 44.

63. 2013 *New York Times* articles detail the Nigerian government's decisive responses after Borno state of emergency declaration.

BIBLIOGRAPHY

Abrak, Isaac. "Insight: Nigeria Islamists Hit Schools to Destroy Western Ideas." July 14, 2013, http://www.reuters.com/article/2013/07/14/us-nigeria-schoolkillings-id USBRE96D01X20130714.

Abubakar, Aminu and Faith Karimi. "2,000 Feared Killed in 'Deadliest' Boko Haram Attack in Nigeria." *CNN*, January 12, 2015.

Achilihu, Stephen Nmeregini. *Do African Children Have Rights?: A Comparative and Legal Analysis of the United Nations Convention on the Rights of the Child.* Boca Raton, FL: Universal Publishers, 2010.

Adebowale, Nike. "11 States in Northern Nigeria Yet to Pass the Child Rights Law – UNICEF Official." *Premium Times*, May 12, 2019.

Alfred, Charlotte. "Remember #BringBackOurGirls? This Is What Has Happened in the 5 Months Since." *Huffington Post*, Sept. 14, 2014. http://www.huffingtonpost.com/2014/09/14/nigeria-girls-kidnapped-5-months_n_5791622.html.

Anaya, James "The Human Rights of Indigenous Peoples: United Nations Developments (International Law and the Development of the Rights of Indigenous Peoples)." *The University of Hawaii Law Review* 35, no. 2 (2013): 983–1012.

Askin, Kelly. "Prosecuting Wartime Rape and Other Gender-Related Crimes Under International Law: Extraordinary Advances, Enduring Obstacles." *Berkeley Journal of International Law* 21, no. 2 (2003): 288–349.

Bell, Derrick. "Brown v. Board of Education and Interest-Convergence Dilemma." *Harvard Law Review* 518, no. 523 (1980): 518–533.

Boronow, Clare. "Note, Closing the Accountability Gap for Indian Tribes: Balancing the Right to Self Determination with the Right to a Remedy." *Virginia Law Review* 98, no. 6 (2012): 1373–1425.

Bourke, Joanna. "Rape as a Weapon of War." *The Lancet* 383, no. 9934 (2014): e19–e20.

Brown, Julie. "Less is More: Decluttering the State Action Doctrine" *Missouri Law Review* 73, no. 2 (2008). https://scholarship.law.missouri.edu/mlr/vol73/iss2/8.

Butler, Judith. "Performativity, Precarity and Sexual Politics." *AIBR Revista de Antropologia Iberoamericana* 4, no. 3 (2009): 321–336.

Campbell, John. "U.S. Policy to Counter Nigeria's Boko Haram." Policy Report. Washington, DC. *Council on Foreign Relations Press*, November 2014.

Charney, Jonathan. "Universal International Law." *American Journal of International Law* 87, no. 4 (1993): 529–551.

"Chibok Abductions: Will Nigerian Schoolgirls Ever Be Freed?" *BBC News,* October 14, 2014. http://www.bbc.com/news/world-africa-29612345.

Cohn, Johnathan. "The Heroic, Tragic Story of the Doctor Who Saved Nigeria from Ebola." *New Republic*, October 25, 2014.

Courage, Katherine. "How Did Nigeria Quash its Ebola Outbreak So Quickly?" *Scientific American,* October 18, 2014.

Crenshaw, Kimberlé. "Demarginalizing the Intersection of Race and Sex: A Black Feminist Critique of Antidiscrimination Doctrine, Feminist Theory and Antiracist Politics." *Feminist Legal Studies* 3 (1989): 105–135.

Enogolase, Gabriel. "Nigeria's Health System Ranks 197 of WHO's 200 Nations – NHIS." *Vanguard.* October 28, 2010.

'Everyone's in on the Game': Corruption and Human Rights Abuses by the Nigerian Police Force. Report. Washington, DC: Human Rights Watch, 2010.

Ezekwesili, Obiageli. "World Bank: Women are Key to Achieving MDGs in Africa." *MDG Achievement Fund,* n.d., http://www.mdgfund.org/node/1528.

Falcón, Slyvanna. "Rape as a Weapon of War: Advancing Human Rights for Women at the U.S.-Mexico Border." *Social Justice* 2, no. 84 (2001): 31–50.

Freire, Paolo. *Pedagogy of the Oppressed.* New York, NY: Herder and Herder, 1972.

Garcia-Morenoa, Claudia and Charlotte Watts. "Violence Against Women A Priority Health Issue." *WHO Bulletin* 89, no. 1 (January 2011).

Ibrahim, Balbasatu. "Contributions of Women to the Development of Hausa Literature as an Effective Means of Public Enlightenment: The Case of a 19th Century Female Scholar, Maryam Bint Uthman Ibn Foduye." *International Journal of Culture and History* 2, no. 1 (2016): 50–53.

Ibrahim, Hauma and Princeton Lyman. *Reflections on the New Shari'a Law in Nigeria, Council on Foreign Relations* (June 2004).

Inter-American Convention on the Prevention, Punishment and Eradication of Violence Against Women (Convention of Belem do Para), Chapter II, Article 3; Women (1993) A/Res/48/104, Article 2 (b).

Joel, Duku and Grace Obike. "Chibok Community to Fed Govt: We Want Our Girls Back Not School Building." *The Nation,* March 9, 2015.

Juran, Jason, Joseph Scovel and Hayley Weedn. "Human Trafficking & Native Peoples in Oregon: A Human Rights Report." *American Indian Law Journal* 3, no. 1 (2014): 40–158.

Kapur, Ratna. "The Tragedy of Victimization Rhetoric: Resurrecting the 'Native' Subject in International/Post-Colonial Feminist Legal Politics." *Harvard Human Rights* 1, no. 18 (2002): 1–37.

Kaye, Yasmin. "Nigeria: Several Feared Dead in Suspected Boko Haram Attacks: At Least 3 Dead as Militants Attack Polling Stations in Northeast Nigeria." *International Business Times,* March 28, 2015.

Mack, Beverly B. and Jean Boyd, *One Woman's Jihad: Nana Asma'u, Scholar and Scribe.* Bloomington, IN: Indiana University Press, 2000.

Mazen, Maram. "How Nigeria is Keeping Ebola at Bay." *Time*, August 28, 2014.

"Northern Nigeria: Background to Conflict." Report 168, Brussels, International Crisis Group, 2010.

"Nigeria: Boko Haram 'releases 21 Chibok girls.'" *Al Jazeera*, October 13, 2016.

"Nigerian Authorities Failed to Act on Warning About Boko Haram Raid on School." *Amnesty International*, March 9, 2014.

Ogene, Ashionye. "'Abandonment of 'Bring Back Our Girls.'" *Aljazeera*, October 14, 2014.

Olufemi Vaughan, Olufemi and Bantu, Suraiya. "Muslim Women's Rights in Northern Nigeria," no. 2 (Washington, DC: The Wilson Center, April 2014).

Onyemelukwe, Cheluchi. "Intersections of Violence Against Women and Health: Implications for Health Law and Policy in Nigeria," *William and Mary Journal of Women and the Law* 22, no. 3 (2016): 609–653.

———. "Legislating on Violence against Women: A Critical Analysis of Nigeria's Recent Violence against Persons (Prohibition) Act, 2015." *DePaul Journal of Women, Gender and the Law* 5, no. 2 (2016).

Perkins, Anne. "200 Girls Are Missing in Nigeria – So Why Doesn't Anybody Care?" *The Guardian*, April 23, 2014.

Petillo, April. "By Force or By Choice: Exploring Contemporary Targeted Sex Trafficking of Native Peoples." Dissertation, Arizona State University, 2015.

"Political Shari'a?" Human Rights and Islamic Law in Northern Nigeria. Report, New York, Human Rights Watch, 2004.

Puar, Jasbir. "Precarity Talk: A Virtual Roundtable with Lauren Berlant, Judith Butler, Borjana Cvejić, Isabell Lorey, Jasbir Puar, and Ana Vujanović." *The Drama Review – A Journal of Performance Studies* 56, no. 4 (2012): 163–177.

Searcey, Dionne. "Boko Haram Turns Female Captives Into Terrorists." *New York Times*, April 7, 2016.

———. "Nigerian Women Freed from Boko Haram Face Rejection at Home." *New York Times*, February 16, 2016.

"'Those Terrible Weeks in Their Camp,' Boko Haram Violence against Women and Girls in Northeast Nigeria." Report, *Human Rights Watch*, 2014.

United Nations Development Program, "Midpoint Assessment of the Millennium Development Goals in Nigeria, 2000-2007," November 2008.

United Nations International Children's Emergency Fund, "800,000 Children Forced to Flee Violence in Nigeria and Region." Press release. April 13, 2015.

United Nations Office on Drugs and Crime. "An Introduction to Human Trafficking: Vulnerability, Impact, and Action, 2008." Background Paper. http://www.unodc.org/documents/human-trafficking/An_Introduction_to_Human_Trafficking_-_Background_Paper.pdf.

"Report of the UN System Task Team on the Post-2015 UN Development Agenda." Report. New York, United Nations, 2013.

"United Nations Secretary-General's campaign UNiTE to end violence against women." Announcement. New York, NY: UNiTE, n.d.

WHO. "Nigeria is Now Free of Ebola Virus Transmission." October 20, 2014. http://www.who.int/mediacentre/news/ebola/20-october-2014/en/.

Chapter 18

"To be Introduced by My Daughter Is a Blessing"

Building Rapport between Dads and Daughters to Reduce Early Marriage in Migori County, Kenya

Paula Tavrow, Sixtus Kennedy Otieno, and Elias Muindi

Each year about twelve million girls, many of whom are African, are married before the age of 18.[1] There is growing recognition in the world community that early marriage is a human rights violation, because it stunts childhood and deprives young people of opportunities for self-realization. Marrying young entails serious social risks for girls, as it often signals the end of their education, which can limit their livelihoods, thereby exacerbating poverty, disempowerment, and social isolation.[2] Early marriage is also associated with numerous health risks for girls, including early childbearing, delivery complications, high fertility, sexually transmitted infections, HIV/AIDS, intimate partner violence, and depression.[3]

At its core, early marriage in Africa is a product of patriarchy and gender inequality. It persists mainly in traditional patrilineal societies, where fathers maintain that it is their unassailable right to negotiate with suitors and collect bride price for their sole use, without needing to consult their daughters. In Kenya, societies where early marriage is common often still perform traditional female circumcision during rite of passage ceremonies. Once a girl has undergone female circumcision in early adolescence, many believe that she is ready for marriage.[4] These communities do not prioritize girls' education because they consider women's main roles to be wives and mothers.

To most fathers in these societies, a girl's highest value is her bride price.[5] Fathers know that when a daughter marries, she will relocate to her husband's home area and is not obligated to contribute financially to her natal family, although she often does provide help to younger siblings. Communication between fathers and daughters generally is limited and cursory. Without getting to know their daughters, fathers may tend to commodify them, rather than view them as having independent interests and aspirations.[6] If a daughter is doing poorly in school or has dropped out, fathers are particularly eager to marry them off soon. Girls who get pregnant before marriage bring familial dishonor and a concomitant reduced bride price.[7] Male suitors will pay more for attractive, young, malleable brides who are uninfected with HIV.

EFFORTS TO END EARLY MARRIAGE

To date, efforts to end early marriage have been limited and mostly small-scale. While there have been some reductions in prevalence of child marriage, only a few countries have seen a major decrease of more than 10 percent.[8] The problem first received widespread attention during the International Conference on Population and Development in 1994, and later was incorporated into the millennium development goals and the sustainable development goals. In the past few decades, more programs have been introduced to try to reduce early marriage, but they remain sparse and have not had uniform success.

A major review of the evidence from 1973 to 2009 found only twenty three programs evaluated with sufficient rigor to determine their effectiveness in influencing attitudes or behaviors related to early marriage.[9] The authors categorized the programs they reviewed as having one or more of the following components: girls' empowerment, community awareness, improvements in schooling, economic incentives, and legal/policy frameworks. Those programs that were more comprehensive or "horizontal" seemed to perform better than the narrow "vertical" or policy-level activities. The typical program began with a girls' empowerment or gender equity component, and included some additional activities at the school or community level. Although about half of the programs achieved significant changes in attitudes toward early marriage, only nine achieved any positive behavior change. The authors noted that while complex horizontal programs seemed most effective, they are very challenging to manage and sustain because of their cost and multiple elements.[10]

A more recent review of interventions to prevent child marriage found eleven "high-quality" programs and evaluations in low- and middle-income countries.[11] Of these eleven programs, just six showed positive results—either in decreasing the proportion of girls married or in increasing the age of marriage. All of these positive programs focused on keeping girls in school, via tuition coverage, cash transfers, or provision of school uniforms and supplies. Some also provided sexual and reproductive health services or life skills training, to prevent unintended pregnancies among school girls, which can lead to dropouts and early marriage. Only one of the successful programs, in India, had a parental education component.

What is curious about these moderately successful programs is that they mainly addressed just one of the root causes of early marriage: poverty. Possibly the focus on poverty stemmed from the fact that it is relatively uncontroversial for donors and governments, and can yield some success. In most low-income countries, when poor parents struggle with school fees, girls are more likely to be pulled from school and married off. Providing financial incentives and resources can enable these girls to stay in school.[12] So long as a girl remains a student, she has a legitimate role in society and is shielded to some extent from pressures for her to assume the new role of wife. A school girl is also more inclined to aspire to have a livelihood, which may make her less willing to get married early if given a choice. Because early pregnancy can derail a girl's educational and career goals, two of the successful programs also included a sexual and reproductive health element.

However, while addressing poverty has shown some promise in reducing early marriage, some doubt that it is the most important driver. For instance, in Malaysia, an upper middle-income country, several prominent organizations have argued that the conservative religious culture makes the avoidance of sexual impropriety the paramount goal of fathers.[13] As a result, any school girl who shows an interest in the opposite sex will be married off quickly, even if she is underage and still a student. Regardless of a household's financial status, to the fathers, the preservation of family honor and prevention of premarital sex takes precedence over other concerns. In this context, programs based on economic incentives and school quality would be unlikely to make major inroads into early marriage.

In sum, child marriage prevention programs' impact to date may have been suboptimal because they have given insufficient attention to the *fundamental* cause of early marriage—namely, patriarchal power, which includes the undervaluing and commodification of girls and women. In other words, these programs may have sidestepped the main societal issue in order to achieve some quick but unsustainable effects. Few if any programs have directly tackled the patriarchal premise that fathers should be determining when and to whom their daughters marry. And, further, no programs in African countries seem to have questioned why fathers should be rewarded with bride price for exerting this power over their daughters. Unless these critical omissions are acknowledged and addressed forthrightly in programmatic interventions, early marriage is likely to endure for many years to come.

SITUATION IN KENYA

Globally, Kenya has the twentieth highest absolute number of child brides.[14] In the country overall, about 23 percent of girls marry before their eighteenth birthday.[15] In some counties, such as Migori and Tana River, the prevalence rate is more than double: for example, a recent study found that among adult women in Migori County, half had first married by age seventeen (compared with age twenty nationally). Men in Migori County also married younger than the national average (age twenty-two compared to age twenty-five nationally).[16] Early marriage was found only to be a problem for women, mainly because young Kuria men need to acquire sufficient bride price before they can marry, which delays their marriage age.[17]

Kenya has taken several steps to demonstrate its commitment to reducing early marriage. In 2000, Kenya ratified the African Charter on the Rights and Welfare of the Child, which includes a prohibition on child marriage. Subsequently, in 2010, it ratified the African Charter on Human and People's Rights on the Rights of Women in Africa, which sets the minimum age of marriage as eighteen. Kenya is also one of twenty countries in Africa that has committed to ending child marriage by the close of 2020. Most notably, Kenya passed a law in 2014 declaring that the minimum legal age of marriage was eighteen with no exceptions. However, an independent watchdog organization determined that Kenya is not enforcing this law and public awareness is low.[18]

In view of the need for innovative approaches to reduce early marriage in localities like Migori County, the Margaret Wanzuu Foundation—with assistance from the Kenya MenEngage Alliance, Mundo Cooperante, and the Bixby Program at the University of California at Los Angeles—decided to launch in 2017 a low-cost project to engage directly with rural fathers. While it was considered too difficult to dismantle the patriarchal premise that fathers should receive bride price from their daughters' suitors, the project team instead decided to adopt an intermediate approach. Given that men are the main decision-makers about their daughters' marriages, the team chose to aim to reduce fathers' commodification of their daughters.

Our theory of change was that if a program could build relationships between fathers and their daughters so that they came to understand and appreciate their daughters as individuals, fathers might be more inclined to support their daughters' aspirations and allow them to make critical life decisions, such as about marriage. Similarly, if daughters had better communication with their fathers, they might be able to assert themselves in choosing when and whom to marry. In addition, for both fathers and daughters, it was considered important to build community awareness about the Kenyan law prohibiting early marriage and the serious social and health risks to girls who marry young.

During the planning in June 2018 for what would become the Dads and Daughters project, the team met with key stakeholders such as local chiefs, politicians, bureaucrats, and religious leaders to get their input. All expressed enthusiasm for an activity that would encourage fathers to get to know their daughters better, and to raise awareness about Kenya's law and the negative consequences of marrying young. Some who had young daughters gave reasons for opposing early marriage, such as:

- "My daughter has the same potential as a boy, so I want her to have equal opportunities. If she marries young, she won't be able to explore her potential and make her own choices regarding her life."
- "I don't want my daughter to suffer, and I see suffering in early marriages."
- "I want her to be able to pursue her education so that she can contribute positively to society, and be a role model to others."
- "I want my daughter to have a family when she is mature and ready—to give it a best shot."
- "I want her to have a healthy life in all ways—physically, sexually, mentally, and emotionally."

SURVEY OF THREE VILLAGES

As part of the preparation for project activities, the team decided to conduct a baseline survey of rural fathers' knowledge, attitudes, and practices related to early marriage. The survey also included some demographic and household wealth indicators, as well as a census of all children from each father, their current ages, their educational level, and their age of marriage. After receiving approval from the Deputy County Commissioner in Migori County, who had been briefed by the Chief of Kehancha Township, the team selected three villages in Kuria West subcounty to conduct the survey. All interviewers were Kenyan men who conducted the survey in person in Kiswahili. Their goal was to interview fathers only, but occasionally they interviewed mothers if fathers were deceased or unavailable. At each household, an interviewer explained the purpose of the survey and asked if the head of household would like to participate. The interviews all took place in July 2018. Each interview lasted 30–45 minutes. In households where fathers had married at least one daughter early, the interviewer asked the father why the daughter had been married at that time.

Altogether, the interviewers visited 151 households, of which two had no children and three refused to participate. The final sample consisted of 146 households. In twenty households (nearly 14 percent), the father was either deceased (eight households) or not available (twelve households). Polygamy was not common: in only four households, the father reported that he had more than one wife. On average, fathers reported that they had four children (range was one to ten). The educational level of both fathers and mothers was very low: three-fifths of fathers (and nearly three-quarters of mothers) had none or only a primary education. Most fathers were subsistence farmers, with only 30 percent having formal employment. The household assets were very limited, which reflected the high amount of poverty in the area. Just two in ten households had electricity, with one in ten having a television. About one-quarter owned cows. Only one household reported having a vehicle.

Regarding the prevalence of early marriage, of those households where the father had at least one daughter aged fourteen or older, already 37 percent had married early at least one daughter. No sons had been married before the age of 18. For daughters, there was a strong association between early marriage and education: no daughter who married young had completed secondary school. When fathers were asked if Kenya has a law requiring that girls be married at the age of 18 or later, only four in ten knew the law existed.

An interesting pattern emerged of a reverse correlation between birth order and age of marriage for both daughters and sons (see table 18.1). Not only did the age of marriage decline for subsequent children, but the range of marriage age also narrowed for both genders as the family size increased. It is not known why children married earlier if they came later in birth order, but a possible reason for girls is that newly married daughters reportedly sometimes identify spouses for their siblings from among their in-laws. Also, fathers may assist

Table 18.1 **Relationship between age of marriage and birth order, by gender (N=146 households)**

Birth order:	Daughter 1 (eldest)	Daughter 2	Daughter 3	Daughter 4	Son 1 (eldest)	Son 2	Son 3	Son 4
No. in sample who were married	44	21	11	4	17	21	13	4
Age of marriage, in years (average)	17.3	17.0	16.7	16.5	21.5	20.9	19.9	19.3
Age of marriage, in years (range)	13-23	14-21	14-21	15-18	18-25	18-25	18-23	19-20
Percent married before age 18	64%	71%	73%	75%	None	None	None	None

younger sons with paying for bride price using money or cows received from the marriage of older daughters, which could facilitate earlier marriage ages.

Fathers gave a number of reasons for marrying their daughters young. The most common reason related either to the bride price or to obtaining some direct benefit from early marriage. About one-third said that the bride price helped them with their financial troubles and brought economic stability to the household. Others mentioned that their married daughters supported their younger brothers and sisters, particularly with school fees. One stated that by marrying his daughter to a chief's son, he was able to get a leadership position in the village. Some discussed their concern that if they did not marry their daughter young, she might get pregnant and would become "secondhand" or "damaged goods," thereby reducing her bride price.

However, some fathers were concerned primarily with maintaining their status and patriarchal power through early marriage of their daughters. According to one father, "If you don't marry her early, people will laugh at you. They will think that outside forces are controlling you." Fathers also generally believed that early marriage was "normal." They were skeptical of educating daughters beyond the primary level, since they felt that daughters' natural roles were to be wives, mothers, and small farmers. As one father explained, "School is not really benefiting the girl, so why keep her? She should be setting up a new household." Others maintained that from fourteen or fifteen years of age, a girl was "grown up." These fathers did not see the value of a daughter remaining unmarried until she was older.

A final purpose of the survey was to assess the extent to which the fathers knew their daughters as individuals, which was a proxy for how well they communicated with them. We chose three topics that fathers who had a good relationship with their daughters presumably would know: their daughter's career aspirations, her favorite school subjects, and her best friends. In eight of ten households surveyed ($N = 117$), there was an unmarried girl between the ages of nine and seventeen. Fathers in these households were asked to name their oldest daughter in this age range and to report whether they could answer those key questions about their daughter's life. They also were asked what they considered to be her ideal age of marriage and who should choose her husband.

As seen in table 18.2, less than one-third of fathers reported that they had knowledge about their daughter's career aspirations, favorite subjects, or closest friends—which suggests that communication between fathers and daughters in these villages is weak. Likewise, only 40 percent thought that she should be married at the legal age of marriage or above. And nearly four in ten believed that they alone should choose the daughter's husband. Just one in three felt that the daughter should have the right to choose her own spouse. The remaining fathers believed it should be a joint decision, but this

Table 18.2 Demographics of oldest unmarried daughter per household, father's knowl-edge about her life, and father's beliefs about her marriage age and choice (N=117)

For oldest unmarried daughter aged 9-17 years	Percent or mean (range)
Daughter's age, in years	15.1 (9-17)
Her birth order (whether firstborn, etc.)	2.6 (1-7)
Her marriage will occur soon (within 1-2 months)	3%
Father said he knows her career aspirations	29%
Father said he knows her favorite school subjects	27%
Father said he knows her best friends	32%
Total topics about daughter known, on average (3 maximum)	0.9 (0-3)
Father believed her ideal marriage age is 18 years or more	39%
Father believed he alone should choose her husband	40%

could mean merely that they would allow the daughter to meet ahead of time with the prospective suitor and perhaps have veto power. Overall, the results suggest that most fathers had very little involvement in their daughters' lives.

We had hypothesized that when fathers take an interest in their daughter's life and learn what is important to her, they are less likely to commodify her and more inclined to relinquish patriarchal control about her nuptials. Using multiple logistic regression modeling, we found that this was indeed the case. After controlling for various factors (father's education, household assets, daughter's birth order, daughter's age, and if the father had already married off any daughters early), we found that fathers who were more knowledge-able about their daughter's lives were 50 percent more likely to support later marriage for her, and nearly 90 percent more likely to think that she should be involved in choosing her husband.

Of the other indicators we studied, the only one that also predicted pro-gressive attitudes regarding marriage was whether the father was formally employed. This suggests that formal employment may lessen the father's need for the higher bride price associated with younger brides. In addition, it may expose fathers to nontraditional views about women's roles, thereby reducing his proclivity to cling to patriarchal dominance.

Dads and Daughters Project

The survey results helped to convince us that an intervention to increase dad–daughter communication and rapport might be effective in reducing the incidence of early marriage. In particular, we believed it was important that the intervention raise awareness about the risks of early marriage, educate fathers and daughters about Kenya's marriage law, encourage activities for fathers and daughters to engage in jointly, and create a new norm that good fathers support their daughters in their aspirations. Because early marriage is a longstanding tradition, we also recognized that it was best to work at the community level and seek to effect change by village, not by individual.

The core component of the Dads and Daughters project is multiple all-day workshops facilitated by a trained gender activist from the Kenya MenEngage Alliance. The main purpose of the workshops is to assist fathers and unmarried daughters (in the vulnerable ages of nine to seventeen years old) to learn deeply about each other and to build their relationship. One noteworthy activity in every workshop was the icebreaker. This consisted of father–daughter introductions, in which fathers and daughters interview each other on several issues and then report out to the main group. Other rapport-building activities included breaking into small groups and having the groups come up with all the ways that a father–daughter dyad resembles each other.

The workshops also included brief lectures on the Kenyan marriage law, the myriad risks of early marriage, and the benefits of girls' education. In addition, fathers and daughters learned a catchy song on the negative consequences of marrying young, which we had commissioned for the project. After the workshops, "homework" for the dyads included teaching the song to other household members and planning some joint activities. Fathers and daughters also received lunch, small stipends, and brightly colored matching t-shirts emblazoned with the project motto—*Baba Bora uBoresha Binti* (Better Dads Promote Their Daughters). Another slogan on the t-shirt was, "The Right to Be a Girl." The theme was that girls, like boys, deserve to have a childhood and be empowered to make life choices.

The workshops proved to be extremely popular with fathers in the three villages, as well as with local religious leaders, teachers, and dignitaries. Ten Dads and Daughters workshops were held from January to March 2019, usually during the weekends. Altogether, 188 dads and 232 daughters participated. The workshops took place in local community centers or schools, all within easy walking distance of the participating villages. When fathers and daughters first would arrive at the workshop, fathers would sit together at one side and daughters on the other side. The opening icebreaker would generally be awkward, with daughters sometimes covering their faces in embarrassment when they learned that they would be expected to interview their fathers. But in the ensuing games and activities, fathers and daughters started to talk more freely with each other. The workshops usually ran for about six hours. By the end, fathers and daughters were singing the song together and talking about what they had learned.

At the close of the workshops, fathers were asked to give their feedback about the experience. Some of their comments were as follows:

- "It was my first time to sit close to my daughter and listen to her. It felt good. I am very happy today."
- "I am very much excited today to learn that my daughter would like to be a doctor. This initiative should continue for us to learn more issues on parenting."
- "It was a blessing to be introduced to everyone by my daughter."

Once the COVID-19 pandemic recedes, for the next phase of the Dads and Daughters project, the team will be visiting the three villages to conduct community-wide meetings to reinforce messages from the Dads and Daughters workshops. The team will also identify six to eight progressive fathers from each village to form Fathers Leadership Groups. The main purposes of a Fathers Leadership Group are twofold: to plan events and to intervene with recalcitrant fathers regarding child marriage. The Kenya MenEngage Alliance will train members of these Fathers Leadership Groups in leadership skills, dispute resolution, and event planning. Then, they will plan activities for fathers and daughters to do together, such as games and skits to celebrate Girl Child Day (in October) and Father's Day (in June). Also, the Fathers Leadership Groups will be expected to handle complaints about fathers' treatment of their wives and children, particularly fathers who do not abide by Kenyan laws on marriage, female circumcision, and domestic violence. Through community peer pressure and role modeling, it is expected that these Fathers Leadership Groups will continue the forward momentum begun with the Dads and Daughters workshops.

The other main activity in the next phase will be to develop a facilitator's manual for the Dads and Daughters workshops, so that two to three progressive local fathers (particularly teachers) could be trained to lead future workshops in additional villages in Migori County, starting with Kuria East subcounty. The goal is to introduce workshops to at least three additional villages in Kuria East, with three to four workshops convened per village.

Finally, the project intends to hold a major annual event each year on Father's Day to bring together all former workshop participants for a Dads and Daughters Open Day to commemorate new norms, hear from supportive local leaders, and encourage more bonding between fathers and their daughters. These kinds of events help to reinforce that the Dads and Daughters project is supporting a norm-changing transformation that involves numerous communities. Afterwards, the team will conduct follow-on surveys to gauge if progress in reducing early marriage is occurring.

CONCLUSION

The determination of when and to whom a daughter marries, and the collection of bride price, is a longstanding patriarchal enterprise in many African countries. It endures mainly in traditional patrilineal societies where fathers and daughters rarely communicate, thus creating a distance between them which can cause fathers to assess their daughters' value largely on the bride price they will attract. Fathers often commodify daughters, as evidenced by referring to them as "damaged goods" if they get pregnant prior to marriage, which will reduce their bride price. Programs focused mainly on providing financial incentives and support to keeping girls in school may have some success in reducing early marriage, but they are unlikely to end the practice without challenging some features of the patriarchal order.

The Dads and Daughters project in Migori County, Kenya, has been breaking down barriers between fathers and daughters. Through all-day village-level workshops, fathers and daughters learn about each other, play games, sing songs, and are exposed to information about the health and social consequences of early marriage. This enables them to start to forge a supportive relationship between individuals, rather than as a father with his product. Fathers and daughters also engage in homework activities to help them continue to build their relationship. Planned activities will extend the Dads and Daughters workshops to new communities, reinforce progressive norms through the introduction of Fathers Leadership Groups, and encourage multiple village sharing and involvement. Preliminary data suggests that this approach may be altering patriarchal attitudes by instilling a new norm for positive fatherhood—one that entails supporting and promoting daughters to achieve their aspirations, by staying in school and delaying marriage.

NOTES

1. United Nations Children's Fund, *Ending Child Marriage: Progress and Prospects* (New York, NY: UNICEF, 2014).

2. Judith-Ann Walker, "Early Marriage in Africa – Trends, Harmful Effects and Interventions," *African Journal of Reproductive Health* (Special Edition) 16, no. 2 (2012): 231–240. See also Naana Otoo-Oyortey and Sonita Pobi, "Early Marriage and Poverty: Exploring Links and Key Policy Issues," *Gender & Development* 11, no. 2 (2003): 42–51, https://doi.org/10.1080/741954315.

3. Nawal Nour, "Health Consequences of Child Marriage in Africa," *Emerging Infectious Diseases* 12, no. 11 (2006): 1644–1649, https://doi.org/10.3201/eid1211.060510.

4. Nandera Ernest Mhando, "The Continuing Paradox of Traditional Female and Male Circumcision among Kuria in Northeastern Tanzania," *Anthropologica* 60, no. 1 (2018): 300–313, https://doi.org/10.3138/anth.60.1.a03.

5. Jane E. M. Callaghan, Yaganama Gambo, and Lisa C. Fellin, "Hearing the Silences: Adult Nigerian Women's Accounts of 'Early Marriages,'" *Feminism & Psychology* 25, no. 4 (2015): 506–527, https://doi.org/10.1177/0959353515590691.

6. Mara Steinhaus, Amy Gregowski, Natacha Stevanovic Fenn, and Suzanne Petroni, "She cannot just sit around waiting to turn twenty": Understanding why child marriage persists in Kenya and Zambia (Washington: International Center for Research on Women, 2016). Available at: https://www.icrw.org/publications/she-cannot-just-sit-around-waiting-to-turn-twenty/.

7. Siwan Anderson, "The Economics of Dowry and Brideprice," *Journal of Economic Perspectives* 21, no. 4 (2007): 151–174. doi:10.1257/jep.21.4.151.

8. UNICEF, *Ending Child Marriage.*

9. Susan Lee-Rife et al., "What Works to Prevent Child Marriage: A Review of the Evidence," *Studies in Family Planning* 43, no. 4 (2012): 287–303, https://doi.org/10.1111/j.1728-4465.2012.00327.x.

10. Ibid.

11. Amanda M. Kalamar, Susan Lee-Rife, and Michelle J. Hindin, "Interventions to Prevent Child Marriage Among Young People in Low- and Middle-Income Countries: A Systematic Review of the Published and Gray Literature," *Journal of Adolescent Health* 59, no. 3 (2016): S16–S21, https://doi.org/10.1016/j.jadohealth.2016.06.015.

12. Sudhanshu Handa et al., "Impact of the Kenya Cash Transfer for Orphans and Vulnerable Children on Early Pregnancy and Marriage of Adolescent Girls," *Social Science & Medicine* 141 (2015): 36–45, https://doi.org/10.1016/j.socscimed.2015.07.024.

13. Valentina Lai et al., *Child Marriage: Its Relationship with Religion, Culture and Patriarchy*, 2018 (Sisters in Islam and Asian-Pacific Resource and Research Centre for Women). Available at: https://arrow.org.my/wp-content/uploads/2018/03/National-Report-Child-Marriage-Single-Page.pdf.

14. Girls Not Brides (website), accessed 26 July 2019, https://www.girlsnotbrides.org/child-marriage/kenya/.

15. Suzanne Petroni et al., "New Findings on Child Marriage in Sub-Saharan Africa," *Annals of Global Health* 83, no. 5–6 (2017): 781, https://doi.org/10.1016/j.aogh.2017.09.001.

16. Government of Kenya, Demographic and Health Survey, 2014.

17. Michael L. Fleisher and Garth J. Holloway, "The Problem with Boys: Bridewealth Accumulation, Sibling Gender, and the Propensity to Participate in Cattle Raiding among the Kuria of Tanzania," *Current Anthropology* 45, no. 2 (2004): 284–288, https://doi.org/10.1086/382257.

18. UN Committee on the Elimination of Discrimination Against Women (CEDAW), 13 March 2017, List of issues and questions in relation to the eighth periodic report of Kenya. Available at: https://www.refworld.org/docid/596f24614.html.

BIBLIOGRAPHY

Anderson, Siwan. "The Economics of Dowry and Brideprice." *Journal of Economic Perspectives* 21, no. 4 (2007): 151–174. https://doi.org/10.1257/jep.21.4.151.

Callaghan, Jane E. M., Yaganama Gambo and Lisa C. Fellin. "Hearing the Silences: Adult Nigerian Women's Accounts of 'Early Marriages.'" *Feminism & Psychology* 25, no. 4 (2015): 506–527. https://doi.org/10.1177/0959353515590691.

Fleisher, Michael L. and Garth J. Holloway. "The Problem with Boys: Bridewealth Accumulation, Sibling Gender, and the Propensity to Participate in Cattle Raiding among the Kuria of Tanzania." *Current Anthropology* 45, no. 2 (2004): 284–288. https://doi.org/10.1086/382257.

Girls Not Brides (website), accessed 26 July 2019, https://www.girlsnotbrides.org/child-marriage/kenya/.

Government of Kenya, Demographic and Health Survey, 2014.

Handa, Sudhanshu, Amber Peterman, Carolyn Huang, Carolyn Halpern, Audrey Pettifor and Harsha Thirumurthy. "Impact of the Kenya Cash Transfer for Orphans and Vulnerable Children on Early Pregnancy and Marriage of Adolescent Girls." *Social Science & Medicine* 141 (2015): 36–45. https://doi.org/10.1016/j.socscimed.2015.07.024.

Kalamar, Amanda M., Susan Lee-Rife and Michelle J. Hindin. "Interventions to Prevent Child Marriage among Young People in Low- and Middle-Income Countries: A Systematic Review of the Published and Gray Literature." *Journal of Adolescent Health* 59, no. 3 Suppl (2016): S16–S21. https://doi.org/10.1016/j.jadohealth.2016.06.015.

Lai, Valentina, Shareena Mohd Sheriff, Syarifatul Adibah Mohammad Jodi and Andi Suraidah Bandy. *Child Marriage: Its Relationship with Religion, Culture and Patriarchy.* Kuala Lumpur, Malaysia: Sisters in Islam and Asian-Pacific Resource and Research Centre for Women, 2018. https://arrow.org.my/wp-content/uploads/2018/03/National-Report-Child-Marriage-Single-Page.pdf.

Lee-Rife, Susan, Anju Malhotra, Ann Warner and Allison McGonagle Glinski. "What Works to Prevent Child Marriage: A Review of the Evidence." *Studies in Family Planning* 43, no. 4 (2012): 287–303. https://doi.org/10.1111/j.1728-4465.2012.00327.x.

Mhando, Nandera Ernest. "The Continuing Paradox of Traditional Female and Male Circumcision among Kuria in Northeastern Tanzania." *Anthropologica* 60, no. 1 (2018): 300–313. https://doi.org/10.3138/anth.60.1.a03.

Nour, Nawal. "Health Consequences of Child Marriage in Africa." *Emerging Infectious Diseases* 12, no. 11 (2006): 1644–1649. https://doi.org/10.3201/eid1211.060510.

Otoo-Oyortey, Naana and Sonita Pobi. "Early Marriage and Poverty: Exploring Links and Key Policy Issues." *Gender & Development* 11, no. 2 (2003): 42–51. https://doi.org/10.1080/741954315.

Petroni, Suzanne, Mara Steinhaus, Natacha Stevanovic Fenn, Kirsten Stoebenau and Amy Gregowski. "New Findings on Child Marriage in Sub-Saharan Africa."

Annals of Global Health 83, no. 5–6 (2017): 781–790. https://doi.org/10.1016/j
.aogh.2017.09.001.

Steinhaus, Mara, Amy Gregowski, Natacha Stevanovic Fenn and Suzanne Petroni.
*"She cannot just sit around waiting to turn twenty": Understanding why child
marriage persists in Kenya and Zambia.* Washington: International Center for
Research on Women, 2016. Available at: https://www.icrw.org/publications/she-ca
nnot-just-sit-around-waiting-to-turn-twenty/.

UN Committee on the Elimination of Discrimination Against Women (CEDAW).
List of issues and questions in relation to the eighth periodic report of Kenya, 13
March 2017. Available at: https://www.refworld.org/docid/596f24614.html.

United Nations Children's Fund. *Ending Child Marriage: Progress and Prospects.*
New York, NY: UNICEF, 2014.

Walker, Judith-Ann. "Early Marriage in Africa – Trends, Harmful Effects and
Interventions." *African Journal of Reproductive Health* (Special Edition) 16, no.
2 (2012): 231–240.

Chapter 19

Gender Imbalance and Girl Child Education in Niger State, North Central Nigeria

Olawale Isaac Yemisi

Girl child education has been a burning and controversial issue in non-Western countries, including Nigeria. The widespread view is that if we educate a man, we educate one person; if we educate a woman, we educate a family and a whole nation.[1] From the above adage, the girl child is responsible for and plays a very significant role in the human socialization and development of very active citizens. It is thus imperative for policy makers, human rights organizations, and nations to promote the interest of girls in all spheres of life.

The question of the status of women in human society remains a very contentious one. This is because culture has significantly altered women roles and traditions placing "patriarchy," "masculinity," and a "male-dominated world" as the basis of societal development. Siyan Oyeweso rightly observed,

> Whether girl child and women relegation is considered in a historical or contemporaneous sense, academic and non-academic discourses on gender issues, particularly as they are related to women ... are as interesting as well as controversial.[2] He further notes that the current advocacy for feminism which encapsulates the totality of the philosophy, vision and mission of women emancipation, equity and equality in modern societies, has put the question of women's position on the front burner of politics and economies of all modern states in contemporary times.[3]

According to Namadu, increasing girl's participation in education has been identified as one of the most significant challenges facing many societies in Africa.[4] In African countries, it is estimated that if around 101 million children are not in school—more than half of them are girls.[5] These statistics summarize the nature of imbalance, inequality, and disparity in the education of the girl child. We must not also lose sight of the fact that whether the girl or boy, it is inapt for any nation to deny the education of any child, who will be future leaders of tomorrow for education is the bedrock of societal and national development.

Oduyoye gave an example from a West African analysis, stating that "the numerical insignificance of African women in most professions reflects the global situation of women's lack of equal access to education.[6] Mpayana complements Oduyoye's perspective when examining the root, the prevalent situation of education from an African family's scale of preference. He asserts that when African families face severe economic problems, they prefer to invest their limited resources in the education of boys rather than offer girls what they judge as an important and prestigious education, as in any case, girls will ultimately marry and abandon their future careers.[7]

Girls' access to education in Nigeria is still low, especially in Northern Nigeria where gender imbalance in education is crystal clear due to factors such as early marriage, ignorance, poverty, premarital pregnancy and religious belief, and so on. Osinulu[8] lamented that the girl child is discriminated against in terms of education and given out to marriage early and thereby denies her the required competences for community development. The resultant effect of such discrimination is poverty and the only key to ending poverty among womenfolk as a whole is the education of the girl child.[9] Girl child education is the process through which the girl child is made a functional member of her society[10]. She acquires knowledge, realizes her potentialities, and uses them for self-actualization through this process. It is a means of preserving, transmitting, and improving the culture of the society. In every society, education connotes the acquisition of something good, something worthwhile.[11]

In Niger State, there is still gender inequality in terms of accessibility (enrollment), low completion, and dropout to education. The issue of girl child in Niger state is more prevalent in rural societies, where the education of women has not received significant attention. The girl child in these areas still faces significant obstacles in accessing proper education because of inherent traditional societal values placed on the boy child over the girl child.[12] Due to these observed disparities, the study seeks to find out the major barrier affecting girl child enrollment, completion, and dropout at all levels of education in Niger State. The chapter will continue with a discussion on the concepts of gender, education, and the girl child.

GENDER

The concept of gender has assumed a formidable position in contemporary discourse especially in matters relating to women and inequality. The word "gender" is used to refer to the sex of a person or organism or a category of people or organisms. Gender is a term that is continually socially reconstrued in light of normative conceptions of both men and women. Gender refers to society's division of humanity, based on sex, into two distinctive categories. Gender guides how females and males think about themselves, how they interact with others, and what position they occupy in society as a whole. Based on their gender, over the years, women have been portrayed as weak, whose superficial interests lie mainly in beauty, fashion, and bearing and parenting children; thus, they cannot proffer solutions to either family or societal problems. Gender is rooted in Nigeria's cultural identity and most pronounced in northern Nigeria.

In another perspective, gender refers to social roles allocated respectively to men and women in particular societies and at particular times. Such roles and the differences between them are conditioned by a variety of political, economic, ideological, and cultural factors, and are characterized in most societies by unequal power relations. Gender imbalance can be viewed as a situation whereby females and males do not have equal conditions for realizing their full human rights and potentials; are not able to contribute equally to national, political, economic, social, and cultural development; and do not benefit equally from the results.

EDUCATION

The concept of education remains ambiguous due to the different definitions given to it by scholars, educational planners, and policy makers. However, according to A. Ray, education is any experience or practice that has a decisive effect on the mind, temperament, or physical capacity of a human being. He further contends that in a pragmatic sense, education is the procedure by which society intentionally transmits its accumulated knowledge, skills, and values from generation to generation. It is also called a method of learning and teaching in schools.[13] The acquisition of educational knowledge should not be gender isolated. It is worthy to note that education is central to development and the improvement of the lives of both genders globally, and as such, it has been identified as a priority area in internationally agreed on development goals, including the Sustainable Development Goals (SDGs).

Education is important in eradicating poverty, hunger, and in promoting sustained, inclusive, and equitable economic growth and sustainable development. There has been an increased effort towards education accessibility, quality, and affordability in every region of the world. In summary, education corresponds to a systematic, organized process, structured and administered according to a given set of laws and norms, through a curriculum, which identifies the objectives, content, and methodology through which teaching, and learning will be done.

GIRL CHILD

In this work, the girl child is defined as a biological female offspring ranging from birth to eighteen years of age, which is the period before young adulthood. This period covers the early childhood years (0–5 years), primary school years (6–12 years), and secondary school years (12–18 years).[14] Accordingly, the Convention on the Right of a Child and Section 277 of Nigeria's Child Rights Act, 2003, identifies a child as any person below the age of 18.

OVERVIEW OF GIRL CHILD EDUCATION IN NIGERIA

Academics and policy makers have made significant efforts in researching the issue of the girl child and gender disparities in education especially in Nigeria where it has become a dominant social issue. Various findings and propositions have been made. Some of these studies have focused on the problem of enrollment and dropouts among girls while others analyzed the socioeconomic, religious, and cultural barriers militating against girl child education. Some studies have also focused on comparative analysis of girl child experience in developing countries, while others analyzed the benefit of girl child education. All these studies indicated that in most developing countries, despite of the efforts put in place, gender imbalance persists and this situation permeates the educational sector.

The importance of education cannot be overemphasized. Risikat noted that "improving and widening access to education, especially basic education, is an objective in itself, as well as the channel to accelerated social and economic development in Nigeria."[15] Education is necessary for the total emancipation, improvement, and promotion of girl's status. It is key to all human development and fundamental tenets in development strategy in both developed and developing nations of the world. Education plays a crucial role in the social power structure in Nigerian societies and often disparities between girl and boy education puts girls and their future as sex objects and relegated to the background in societal participation.

A 2014 UNESCO report shows that in Nigeria, over 5.5 million girls are out-of-school.[16] The British Council Reports on girl child education in Nigeria also shows that out of the staggering 10.5 million out-of-school children in Nigeria today, the majority are girls. Niger State was among the states UNICEF identified, alongside Bauchi, Katsina, Kano, Sokoto, Zamfara, Kebbi, Gomber, Adamawa, and Taraba, with a total of 8 million out-of-school children.[17] The Universal Basic Education Commission argued that girl children constituted over 60 percent of children out-of-school. In February 2019, the Minister of Education, Alhaji Adamu Adamu in Nigeria, stated that the number of out-of-school children had risen to 16 million out of which 69 percent reside in the northern part. The Niger State Chairman for Universal Basic Education Board, Alhaji Alhassan Muhammad Bawa, in a news report dated September 12, 2020, reveals that 513,680 children are currently out-of-school in Niger State.[18] The above statistics are evidence that in spite of federal, state, and local government efforts to address this situation, girl child education is facing significant barriers.

Okernmor *et al.*[19] notes that girl child education encompasses a complex set of issues and debates surrounding (primary education, secondary, and tertiary and health education in particular) for girls and women. Omede and Agahiu also contend that in the context of Nigeria, girl child education also includes areas of gender equality, access to education and its connection to the alleviation of poverty, good governance, which are major ingredients in averting crime against women.[20] Girl child education is the process through which the girl child is made functional members of her society. It is a process through which the girl child acquires knowledge and realizes her potentialities and uses them for self-actualization and the development of her society.

In response to the aforementioned connection between girl child education and nation-building, Nigeria governments at all levels have made concerted efforts towards addressing these gender disparities at all levels of education. Mamman (2014) noted that as a result of these observed disparities, programs aimed at availing the girl child and her male counterpart of the opportunities for self-actualization and becoming useful members of the society through education were initiated by various governments of the federation since 1985. Unfortunately, the decline in the quality and support for education at various periods has left the issue intractable. What has been the nature of barrier affecting girl child education in Niger State?

BARRIERS TO GIRL CHILD EDUCATION IN NIGER STATE

Niger State is located in north central Nigeria, created on February 3, 1976, from the defunct North-Western State. It has a total landmass of 76,363.903 square kilometers making it the state with the largest landmass in Nigeria. The 2006 population census put the state population at 4,082,558. The state capital is Minna and other major cities include Bida, Suleja, and Kontogora.

The state's major indigenous ethnic groups are the Nupe, Gbayi, Kumuku, Kambari, Dkawa, Hausa, and Bakundu among others.[21] According to the Niger State Bureau of Statistics Data, 2011, Niger State had 2,922 primary schools, 443 post-primary schools, and 15 higher/tertiary institutions across her twenty-five local government.[22]

Niger State, like other states in northern Nigeria, has experienced a low enrollment of girls. Religious practices and the cultural norms of peoples of northern region of Nigeria have contributed in no small measure to the challenges faced by girls in terms of access to education. Other barriers such as poverty, early marriage, have prevented girls from attending primary, secondary, or further their education through the tertiary level. As a result, a girl's ability to meet up with socioeconomic realities of the twenty-first century is affected.

In an interview discussion, an informant attested that the enrollment and education of girl child in Niger State are considerably low and can be attributed to the geographical landmass of the state; including its largely rural environment, which makes it difficult for the state and local government to effectively curb this trend.[23] Parents in rural areas in Niger State still see no reason to send their girl child to school but rather introduce them to trade, farming, and petty businesses.[24] In another interview, an informant explained that school principals in these rural areas have resorted to begging parents to allow their wards to attend school.[25] Prolonged absence from school has stopped girls from mentally growing and consequently developing a better life in terms of economic wealth, and social mobility, that comes through education.

The gender statistics of primary school education enrollment data produced by the Niger State Bureau of Statistics in 2011 which complied data across twenty-five local government areas put the total number of female enrollment at 290,486 and male enrollment at 701,882.[26] Also, the statistics of female enrollment for secondary school was 163,738 out of 436,667 enrolled in 2011 leaving male enrollment at 272,929.[27] The next section will now treat the barriers to girl child education in detail under macro, sociocultural, and governmental.

Poverty Level as a Macrobarrier

Poverty can simply be understood as the inability of a person to meet the necessary and basic conditions of life such as food, shelter, clothing and education, health, security, and societal participation. According to several African sociologists, African women were poor, African women are poor, and African woman will keep on being poor if they aren't preparing themselves to be educated by making and changing the poor image of African women.[28] This implies that today's girl child is the woman of tomorrow and if they fail to be educated, the cycle of poverty will continue to grow and become more complicated. Observations in Niger state reveal that the prevalent level of poverty affects girl child education. This poverty can be measured in household incapacity.

Girl child education in Niger State has been hampered due to many families' inability to fund all their children's education. Hence, they adopt a gender disparity strategy by sending the boy child to school while leaving the girl child at home. Field research reveals that in Niger State's remote villages and local government areas, the issue of poverty affecting girl child education is prevalent.[29] Girls in these rural communities may have access to primary and secondary school education at most, however, they are not very devoted to school attendance. They also participate in petty commerce in front of their houses, trade in the markets, and hawk goods. An interview with a market woman[30] reveals that poverty indeed propels many parents in the rural areas to make the difficult choice of sacrificing the schooling of some of their children, especially girls. She also contends that parents in rural areas desire their children to study in major cities in Niger State, such as Minna, Suleja, and Bida; therefore, they fund the education of their sons while involving the daughters in petty trade instead. Utulu summarizes the position of parents in Niger State when she avers: "For families with limited means, undertaking additional expenses like books, uniforms and transportation and sometimes school fees, can create a financial strain that families may be less likely to endure for girls than boys."[31]

Early Marriage as a Sociocultural Barrier

The term "early marriage" is used to refer to both formal marriages and informal unions in which a girl lives with a partner as if married before the age of maturity or eighteen years.[32] In Niger State, early marriage is caused by family pressures, sociocultural values, the control of a girl child's sexual behavior, economic survival, and the need for parents to protect their young girls. It is visible that early marriage is a threat to some of the objectives of the SDGs such as no poverty, good health and wellbeing, quality education, gender equality, reduced inequalities, decent work, and economic growth.

Therefore, early marriage is clearly a barrier to girl child education in Niger State. It has a negative impact on student performance, retention ability, and academic concentration. Parents in Niger State still dwell on the outdated belief that educating their girl child will only benefit their husband's households and not them. They also argued that the girl child does not need education to effectively perform her role as a wife and mother.[33] The consequences of early marriage on the girl child's societal status are numerous as well as worrisome.

Early marriage has a highly negative consequence on their psychological, health, and education status. For one, these girls are mostly under pressure to prove their fertility in the early years of their marriage. Also, since they lack basic health-related education, they do not know how to protect themselves from diseases such as HIV and other sexually transmitted diseases. Another perceived consequence arises from male or spousal patriarchy on the family in terms of decision making, domestic violence, and sexual abuse.

For instance, one informant laments that when many girls want to continue their education after childbirth or want to begin their education after marriage; they must first seek the consent of their husband or otherwise be persecuted. If the husband refuses, whether or not she is intelligent or has great academic potentials, the matter remains so. She argues that most husbands in Niger State refuse categorically for these girl children who are victims of early marriage to start or continue with their studies.[34] Another interview informant also reveals that the girl child who received education while in her father's house was denied the opportunity to use her acquired education to promote her personal or societal development. Instead, she is married off to become a full-time housewife.[35]

Other consequences of early marriage include domestic violence and sexual abuse which are rampant with the attendant high levels of divorce cases. The girl child is at the risk of abuse because her husband is older than her and the age difference tends to introduce domination in which a rejection of such control leads to domestic violence such as beating. Furthermore, divorce, abandonment, and early widowhood are other consequences. The latter occurs when the girl child's husband dies while she is still young. This often leads to hardship and poverty which is perpetuated in her offspring. Thus, the effect of early marriage for children of an uneducated or less educated girl child is worrisome. The parental immaturity and lack of education of an underage mother undermine her capacity to nurture and bring up her child(ren). This incapacity produces the same process and continues the trend of early child marriages.

Government-Related Barriers

Nigeria's underdeveloped education sector remains a peculiar barrier to girl child education. The lack of governmental support for education has become one of the most pressing issues confronting the achievement of girl child education. With the high level of poverty and desire for quality education, parents are often pushed to gender disparity methods as private education is exorbitant and unaffordable especially with the prevalent level of poverty. The federal, state, and local governments must recognize the significance of educating a girl child and its potential thereof.

Nigeria has put in place strategies and policies to tackle the issues of girl child education. For instance, Niger State received immense support under Gender Education Programme in 2008 to develop comprehensive gender-sensitive state education sector plans.[36] However, Niger State still has a considerable number of challenges in obtaining equitable access to education such as religious/cultural internal dynamics, economic and geographical inequalities, poverty, and crisis in the implementation of national and state policies on education. These overarching policies and strategies are also been faced with the challenges emanating from the institutions in charge, lack of federal, state, and local government support after commencement, and lack of budgetary allocation to sustain such programmes.

These programmes and policies have also suffered from the lack of continuity by succeeding government administrations in Nigeria while those of international donors are also affected by short time spans of these programmes and policies. This has proved to be a limiting factor to success and in the end, the sustainability of these programmes is not guaranteed. In sum, the inability of the three Nigerian government tiers to devise a well robust and organized strategy, planned course of action, and sustainable implementation policies have affected the actualization of these policies and programme.

It is pertinent to state at this juncture that the Niger State government needs to coordinate enlightenment programs for parents emphasizing that education does not destroy culture but rather helps to portray it positively. Under the universal basic education instituted under the administration of Chief Olusegun Obasanjo and the Niger State policy of paying West African Examination Council and National Examination Council fees, primary and secondary school enrollment in the state increased. However, the federal and state governments should collaborate because free and compulsory education will not be sufficient to challenge the gender imbalance that has existed over time.

The Niger State government should incorporate and support social protection policies that support girl child education such as the conditional cash transfer (CCT) and CCT in care of the people that provide financial inducement to support families as they pay to send their girls to secondary and tertiary schools. These policies are frustrated by the lack of budgetary allocation and the lack of sustainable state institutional mechanisms that oversees the implementation process. The Niger State government has to play an interventionist role in financing institutions, building educational infrastructure in rural areas, and promoting favorable economic policies that would increase the per capita income of parents/guardians so too they can afford the education of all their wards and eliminate gender imbalance. The study argues that if these barriers are effectively and efficiently tackled, well-coordinated and the state government committed to programs aimed at availing the girl child of the opportunities for self-actualization and becoming useful members of society through education. Niger State can achieve a gender balanced state in terms of education enrolment, completion level, and decreased dropout at all levels of educational institutions.

GIRL CHILD EDUCATION AS A PANACEA FOR HUMAN AND SOCIETAL DEVELOPMENT

Over the years, the education of the girl child in northern Nigeria has been grossly neglected[37] in spite of her being a panacea to poverty, family economic shock, underdevelopment, and societal backwardness. If this imbalance continues in Niger State, the developmental growth of rural areas will be hampered as girl child education remains a long-term solution to the menace of poverty, human and societal development. Okorie states that the benefits of education extend beyond the girl by affecting her family and society as a whole.[38] The benefits to society include enhanced economic development, improved labor force, education for the next generation, healthier young girls and families, and fewer maternal deaths.

When we educate a girl child, we are investing in a strong life project, economic growth for the family and society. In the long run, we are also providing a consistent and suitable solution to problems such as family and reproductive health challenges, explosive population through family planning, infant and child mortality, and unemployment. The World Bank assertion on girl child education, as cited in Utulu, states that the cost-benefit analysis of the investment in education of females had the highest rate of return of any possible type of investment in developing nations,[39] Such benefits include reduced infant mortality and fertility rates, greater and higher economic productivity, improved family and child nutrition, better resources utilization, and longer life expectancy.

Educating a girl child is to equip her with the necessary tools to become a great potential to her society as she contributes immensely to political, economic, social, and national development. Not surprisingly, Enemuo[40] pointed out that education helps in the fulfillment of women's obligation to the society. The benefit of education for a girl and society can be explained by the effect that education has on empowering girls to acquire and use new personal, social, and economic behavior that in turn, affect societal change.[41] According to Ottaway,[42] the girl child's education has an effect on the economic wellbeing of a country. A girl child with basic education can gain employment in the formal labor force and therefore contribute not only to her family income but also to the national gross domestic profit. When girl child and women are employed, they provide financial support to their families, hence, an educated woman with good earning power can help reduce the financial constraints of the family and thus avert frustration and other related problems.

A cursory examination of girl child education and its potential benefit to the intellectual empowerment of the girl is immeasurable. Although intelligence is not truly a product of education, education however illuminates and refines intelligence. It transforms itself into useful forms and makes intelligence a resource of desirable value. Education informs, when a woman is informed, she informs her world. Education is not only the master key to a brighter future; it is also a key to survival.[43]

CONCLUSION

The chapter examined the nature of gender imbalance and girl child education in Niger State, north central Nigeria. It provided an overview of barriers affecting girl child education in Niger State. The work also explored girl child education as an impetus for societal and national development. Education is the right of every girl everywhere and key to transforming her life and the life of her community. Without education, girls are denied the opportunity to develop their full potential and to play a productive and equal role in their families, their societies, their country, and their world.

NOTES

1. Toyin Falola, "Education for Self-Employment," in *Perspectives in African Historical Studies*, ed. Ojong E. Tangban and Chukwuma C.C. Osakwe (Kaduna: Nigerian Defence Academy Press, 2013), 702.

2. Siyan Oyeweso, "Breaking the Yoke of Patriarchy: Nigerian Women in the various Professions, Politics and Governance, 1914-2014" (lecture, presented at National Conference of Association." of Women Judges of Nigeria [NAWJN], Abuja, 2014).

3. Siyan Oyeweso, "Breaking the Yoke of Patriarchy."

4. K. Namudu, "Gender perspective in Africa High Education" (paper presented at the Senior Policy Seminar on African Higher Education, University of Zimbabwe, 1992).

5. Nwanchuku Daisy, "Cultural and Psycho-Social Rots of Violence Against Women and Children in Selected African Milieux," in *Pastoral Theology's and Pastoral Psychology's Contributions to Helping Heal a Violent World,* ed. Michael G. Coedner, Surakarta (Indonesia: International Pastoral Care Network for Social Responsibility, 1996), 222–235.

6. Mercy Oduyoye, *Daughters of Anowa: African Women and Patriarchy* (Maryknoll, NY: Orbis Books, 1995), 93.

7. Mpayana N. Fulgence, *African Women's Theology, Gender Relations, and Family Systems Theory: Pastoral Theological Considerations and Guidelines for Care and Counselling* (New York, NY: Peter Lang Publishing, 2004), 51.

8. C. Osinulu, "Women's Education," in *Nigeria and Education: The Challenges Ahead.* Proceedings and Policy Recommendations of the 2nd Obafemi Awolowo Foundation Dialogue. (Ibadan: Spectrum Books, 1994).

9. D. Kasomo, "The Factors Militating Against the Education of Girls: A Case Study in Kenya," *International Journal of Sociology and Anthropology* 1, no. 7 (2009): 116–123.

10. Okorie Mercy, "An Assessment of Factors Militating against Girl Child Education in Nigeria," *International Journal of Advanced and Multidisciplinary Social Science* 3, no. 2 (2017): 49–54.

11. L. O. Ocho, *Issues and Concerns in Education and Life* (Enugu: Institute of Development Studies, University of Nigeria, 2005).

12. Connected Development (CODE), An Examination of Girls' Education Policies in Nigeria with focus on the Northeast (CODE, 2017), 6.

13. Rey A. Rey and J. Debove, *Le Petit Robert* (Paris: Le Robert, 1991), 606.

14. Chibiko G. Offorma, "Girl-Child Education in Africa" (keynote address, Conference of the Federation of the University Women of Africa, Lagos, Nigeria, July 16–19, 2009).

15. Risikat O. Dauda, "Female Education and Nigeria's Development Strategies: Lots of Talk, Little Action?," *Indian Journal of Gender Studies* 14, no. 3 (2007): 461.

16. United Nations Education, Scientific and Cultural Organisation (UNESCO), Education for All Global Monitoring Report: Teaching and Learning for All (UNESCO: Paris, 2014).

17. Azeezat Adedigba, "Eight Million out of school children in 10 Nigerian States and Abuja – UNICEF", Premium times, June 16, 2019, https://www.premiumtimes/eightmillionoutofschool.html.

18. Oyetunde Oluwatobi, How Niger State Lawmakers are under developing Education Despite Multi-million Naira Intervention Project, Sahara Reporters, September 13, 2020, https://:saharareporters.com/2020/09/13/how-niger-state-lawmakers-are-under-developing-education-despite-multimillion-naira#.

19. G.A. Okenmor, J.N. Ndit and M.A. Filshok, "The Role of Women Education in Conflict Resolution and Peace Building in the Present Political Dispensation in Nigeria," *Journal of Women in Colleges of Education* 16, no. 2 (2012): 71–77.

20. Omede Andrew and Agahiu Grace Etumabo, "The Implications of Girl-Child Education to Nation Building in the 21st Century in Nigeria," *Global Journal of Human-Social Science* 16, no. 3 (2016): 1.

21. Niger State Bureau of Statistics, Facts and Figures About Niger State, *Nigeria Statistical Development Project (NSDP)*, 2012, viii.

22. Niger State Bureau of Statistics, Education statistics, Nigeria Statistical Development Project (NSDP), 2012, 77–81.

23. Anonymous, lecturer, Niger State College of Education, Minna, interviewed by author in Minna, November 22, 2018. The interviews cited in this study have been anonymised.

24. Anonymous, student at College of Education, Minna, interviewed by author in Minna, November 23, 2018.

25. Anonymous, student, from Batati, a village in Niger, interviewed by author in Minna on November 24, 2018.

26. Niger State Bureau of Statistics, Education Statistics, Nigeria Statistical Development Project (NSDP), 2012, 77–81.

27. Niger State Bureau of Statistics, Education Statistics, Nigeria Statistical Development Project (NSDP), 2012, 77–81.

28. Mbuya Ngozie Elizabeth, United Methodist Church/North Katanga conference women coordinator, interviewed in Harare, Zambia, November 25, 2011 (As Cited in Women and Education in Africa, Moakley), 118.

29. Anonymous, student from Kutigi Village, Niger State, interviewed by author in Minna, October 25, 2018.

30. Anonymous, market woman, interviewed by author in Katunaguwari Market, Minna, on November, 2, 2018.

31. R.E. Utulu, *The Psycho-Social Burden of the Girl Child in Nigeria: Traditional Practices* (Ibadan: Nigeria Stirling-Horden Publishers, 2001), 37.

32. United Nations Children Emergency Fund, Early Marriage: A Harmful Traditional Practice: A Statistical Exploration (New York, NY: UNICEF, April 2005), https://data.unicef.org/resources/early-marriage-a-traditional-harmful-practice-a-statistical-exploration/.

33. Anonymous, business woman, information gathered in an informal group discussion, Minna, October 2, 2018.

34. Anonymous, business woman, informal group discussion, Minna October, 7, 2018.

35. Anonymous, lecturer (Female), personal discussion, Minna, October, 4, 2018.

36. Fatuma Chege, Jamiu O. Zakariya, Christiana Okojie, Omo Aregbeyen, *Girls Education Project Evaluation Report* (UNICEF &DFID Nigeria, 2008), viii.

37. O. E. Oleriebe, "Article on Neglect of Girl Child Education Bridging the Gap, A Case Study of Nigerian Agrarian Northern Community," *International NGO Journal* 2, no. 2 (2007): 30–35.

38. Okorie Mercy, "An Assessment of Factors Militating against Girl Child Education in Nigeria," *International Journal of Advanced and Multidisciplinary Social Science* 3, no. 2 (2017): 49–54.

39. R.E. Utulu, *The Psycho-Social Burden of the Girl Child in Nigeria: Traditional Practices* (Ibadan: Nigeria Stirling-Horden Publishers (Nig) Ltd, 2001).

40. F. C. Enemuo, "Gender and Women Empowerment," in *Elements of Politics*, ed. Remi Anifowose and F.C. Enemuo (Lagos: Match House Press Ltd, 1999).

41. J. Moulton, Formal and Non- Formal Education and Empowered Behaviours, "A Review of the Research Literature," Washington DC USAID/AFR/SD, (1997), https://www.eldis.org/document/A27480.

42. P. Ottaway, *Educational Challenges for the Girl-Child: The Philosophy of Education for Nigeria* (Enugu: Harris Printing and Publishing, 2000).

43. Joy Kwesiga's, *Women's Access to Higher Education in Africa: Uganda's Experience* (Kampala: Fountain Publisher, 2002).

BIBLIOGRAPHY

Azeezat, Adedigba. "Eight Million out of school children in 10 Nigerian States and Abuja – UNICEF", Premium times, June 16, 2019. https://:www.premiumtimes/eightmillionoutofschool.html.

Chibiko, Offorma. "Girl-Child Education in Africa". Keynote address, conference of the Federation of the University Women of Africa, Lagos, Nigeria, July 16–19, 2009.

Connected Development (CODE). An Examination of Girls' Education Policies in Nigeria with focus on the Northeast, CODE, 2017.

Enemuo, F. C. "Gender and Women Empowerment," In *Elements of Politics*, edited by Remi Anifowose and F. C. Enemuo. Lagos: Match House Press Ltd, 1999.

Fatuma, Chege, Jamiu O. Zakariya, Christiana Okojie, Omo Aregbeyen, *Girls Education Project Evaluation Report*. UNICEF & DFID Nigeria, 2008.

Joy, Kwesiga. *Women's Access to Higher Education in Africa: Uganda's Experience*. Kampala: Fountain Publisher, 2002.

Kasomo, D. "The Factors Militating Against the Education of Girls: A Case Study in Kenya," *International Journal of Sociology and Anthropology* 1, no. 7 (2009): 116–123.

Mbuya, Ngozie Elizabeth. United Methodist Church/North Katanga conference women coordinator, interviewed in Harare, Zambia, November 25, 2011 (As Cited in Women and Education in Africa, Moakley), 118.

Mercy, Oduyoye. *Daughters of Anowa: African Women and Patriarchy*. Maryknoll, NY: Orbis Books, 1995.

Moulton, J. Formal and Non-Formal Education and Empowered Behaviours, "A Review of the Research Literature", Washington DC USAID/AFR/SD, (1997). https://www.eldis.org/document/A27480.

Mpayana, N. Fulgence. *African Women's Theology, Gender Relations, and Family Systems Theory: Pastoral Theological Considerations and Guidelines for Care and Counselling*. New York, NY: Peter Lang Publishing, 2004.

Namudu, K. "Gender perspective in Africa High Education" (paper presented at the Senior Policy Seminar on African Higher Education, University of Zimbabwe, 1992).

Niger State Bureau of Statistics, Education statistics, Nigeria Statistical Development Project (NSDP). 2012.

Niger State Bureau of Statistics, Facts and Figures About Niger State, *Nigeria Statistical Development Project (NSDP)* 2012.

Nwanchuku, Daisy. "Cultural and Psycho-Social Rots of Violence Against Women and Children in Selected African Milieux." In *Pastoral Theology's and Pastoral Psychology's Contributions to Helping Heal a Violent World,* edited by Michael G. Coedner, Surakarta. Indonesia: International Pastoral Care Network for Social Responsibility, 1996.

Ocho, L. O. *Issues and Concerns in Education and Life*. Enugu: Institute of Development Studies, University of Nigeria, 2005.

Okenmor, G. A., Filshok M. A. and Ndit J. N. "The Role of Women Education in Conflict Resolution and Peace Building in the Present Political Dispensation in Nigeria." *Journal of Women in Colleges of Education* 16, no. 2 (2012): 71–77.

Okorie, Mercy. "An Assessment of Factors Militating against Girl Child Education in Nigeria." *International Journal of Advanced and Multidisciplinary Social Science* 3, no. 2 (2017): 49–54.

Oleriebe, O. E. "Article on Neglect of Girl Child Education Bridging the Gap, A Case Study of Nigerian Agrarian Northern Community." *International NGO Journal* 2, no. 2 (2007): 30–35.

Omede, Andrew. and Agahiu, Etumabo. "The Implications of Girl-Child Education to Nation Building in the 21st Century in Nigeria." *Global Journal of Human-Social Science* 16, no. 3 (2016): 1–5.

Osinulu, C. "Women's Education." In *Nigeria and Education: The Challenges Ahead.* Proceedings and Policy Recommendations of the 2nd Obafemi Awolowo Foundation Dialogue. Ibadan: Spectrum Books, 1994.

Ottaway, P. *Educational Challenges for the Girl-Child: The Philosophy of Education for Nigeria.* Enugu: Harris Printing and Publishing, 2000.

Oyetunde, Oluwatobi. How Niger State Lawmakers are under developing Education Despite Multi-million Naira Intervention Project, Sahara Reporters, September 13, 2020, https://:saharareporters.com/2020/09/13/how-niger-state-lawmakers-are-under-developing-education-despite-multimillion-naira#.

Rey, A. and J. Debove. *Le Petit Robert.* Paris: Le Robert, 1991.

Risikat, O. Dauda. "Female Education and Nigeria's Development Strategies: Lots of Talk, Little Action?" *Indian Journal of Gender Studies* 14, no. 3 (2007): 461–479.

Siyan, Oyeweso. "Breaking the Yoke of Patriarchy: Nigerian Women in the various Professions, Politics and Governance, 1914-2014" (lecture, presented at National Conference of Association." of Women Judges of Nigeria [NAWJN], Abuja, 2014).

Toyin, Falola. "Education for Self-Employment." In *Perspectives in African Historical Studies*, edited by Ojong, E. Tangban. and Chukwuma, C.C. Osakwe. Kaduna: Nigerian Defence Academy Press, 2013.

United Nations Children Emergency Fund, Early Marriage: A Harmful Traditional Practice: A Statistical Exploration. New York, NY: UNICEF, April 2005. https://data.unicef.org/resources/early-marriage-a-traditional-harmful-practice-a-statistical-exploration/.

United Nations Education, Scientific and Cultural Organisation (UNESCO), Education for All Global Monitoring Report: Teaching and Learning for All. UNESCO: Paris, 2014.

Utulu, R. E. *The Psycho-Social Burden of the Girl Child in Nigeria: Traditional Practices.* Ibadan: Nigeria Stirling-Horden Publishers, 2001.

Index

Page references for figures are italicized

About the Contributors

Valerie Delali Adjoh-Davoh is a doctoral "ABD" of University of Cape Coast. She obtained her bachelor's degree in History and Political Science and master's degree in African Studies from the University of Ghana in 2007 and 2010 respectively. In 2017, she received a WARA Residency Fellowship to Harvard University.

Joyce Agofure is a postdoctoral fellow, an early career scholar, and lecturer from the Department of English and Literary Studies, Ahmadu Bello University, Zaria, Nigeria where she teaches African literature. She is a recipient of many awards and fellowships such as the 2016/2017 Fulbright Foreign Student Researcher Fellowship from the University of Idaho, USA, and a 2018/2019 American Council of Learned Society of the African Humanities Program Postdoctoral Fellow (ACLS/AHP) with residency at the Rhodes University, South Africa. She is a member of the African Literature Association (ALA) and other associations. Her research interests include Comparative literature, Environmental Literary Studies, Diaspora Literature, Gender Studies, and Postcolonial Literatures. Joyce has written and published many journal articles and book chapters towards sociopolitical, environmental, and gender discourses.

Claudia Berger holds an M.A. in History and English Language and Literature. She defended her PhD thesis "Die 'Zwischenzeit' der Kapkolonie 1902–1910. Taktisches Handeln und politische Imaginationen im Transformationszeitraum" (The time "in-between": Tactical Action and Political Imagination in the Cape Colony, 1902–1910) in November 2020 at the University of Duisburg-Essen. Since May 2019, Claudia Berger is a member of the editorial staff of the German journal *WerkstattGeschichte*.

She is currently employed at the Forschungskolleg Transkulturelle Studien/ Sammlung Perthes at Erfurt University, where she is associated with the project "Kartographien Afrikas und Asiens (1800–1945). Ein Digitalisierungsprojekt zur Sammlung Perthes Gotha" (Cartographies of Africa and Asia, 1800– 1945. A Project for the Digitization of Maps of the Perthes Collection Gotha).

Elsabé Boshoff has been working as a legal assistant and thereafter a technical assistant at the African Commission on Human and Peoples' Rights since February 2017. In particular, she supports the Working Group on Extractive Industries, Environment and Human Rights as well as the focal point for the Commission's Studies on Transitional Justice and Human and Peoples' Rights and Conflict and Human Rights. She is the co-editor of a forthcoming book, *Governance, Human Rights and Political Transformation in Africa* (Palgrave Macmillan). She has, among others, also published in the *African Human Rights Yearbook* and the *Australian Journal of Human Rights*. She holds an LLM in human rights and democratization in Africa from the Centre for Human Rights, University of Pretoria.

Ngozi Edeagu holds an M.Sc. in African studies from the University of Oxford and a B.A. (first class Hons.) in History from the University of Nigeria, Nsukka. She is currently a 2019 DAAD-funded PhD researcher in African History at the Bayreuth International School of Graduate Studies (BIGSAS), Universität Bayreuth, Germany. Ngozi's publications include "Critiquing Witness Testimonies in African Colonial History: A Study of the Women's War of 1929" (2017). Her research interests cover print media, literacy, (higher) education, African history and global history. Ngozi is a lecturer in history at the Alex Ekwueme Federal University Ndufu-Alike, Nigeria.

Jane Eggers is a lawyer who represents individuals in habeas cases. She has also worked for international and state policy organizations in the US and abroad.

Joyce Bayande M. Endeley is a professor of agricultural extension education and gender studies in the Department of Women and Gender Studies, University of Buea. Her duties include teaching, research, and community outreach works. Her research interests include gender and agricultural development, and engendering development policy, program, and project in diverse fields as well as building capacity of development practitioners in the field of gender-responsive development. Administratively, she has served in top management positions in the University of Buea as the deputy-vice chancellor, director of academic affairs, vice-dean, and head of department. She does consultancy assignments for GOs and NGOs at state and international levels, supervises doctorate and master's theses and dissertations, and is an author and a co-author of several publications including books, for example: *The Social Impact of the Chad-Cameroon Oil Pipeline: How Industrial development Affects Gender Relations, Land Tenure, and Local Culture* (2007).

Ezinne M. Ezepue is a lecturer of film at the Department of Theatre & Film Studies, University of Nigeria. She has a B.A. in Theatre & Film Studies (Nigeria), an M.A. in Film and TV (Birmingham) and a PhD in Media and Cultural Studies (Birmingham). Her PhD study interrogated Nollywood's transformations as gentrification. Her current research spans through film, media, communication, and cultural studies with special focus on how emerging cultural industries develop, formalize, and gentrify. Her other research interests are in reality television and documentary film production. She is interested in film content analysis and the representations of the Nigerian woman in film/television. She organizes seminars for students and critical round table discussions with lecturers on how film studies can be effectively decolonized. She has published in both local and international journals and has book chapters to her credit too.

Catherine Cymone Fourshey is an associate professor of History and International Relations at Bucknell University. Her published research focuses on agriculture, hospitality, gender, migration, and the intersections of environment, economy, and politics in Tanzania in precolonial and colonial spaces. Additionally, Fourshey has conducted archival and field research in Tanzania, Zambia, The Gambia, and England. She has published on issues pertinent to precolonial economic and social history, gender history, and the history of Bantu speaking immigrant and refugee communities. Her published articles have appeared in the *African Historical Review, International Journal of African Historical Studies, JENdA*, and *Ufahamu*. Fourshey is a co-author of *Bantu Africa*. Currently, she is working on a co-authored project on precolonial history of eastern and central Africa through the lens of family linkages and networks. She has been a recipient of research grants and fellowships from the American Association of University Women, Fulbright, The National Endowment for the Humanities, and Notre Dame University.

Victor Chidubem Iwuoha is a senior lecturer in the Department of Political Science at the University of Nigeria, Nsukka. He also teaches peace and conflict studies in the School of General Studies at the same University. His research interests include foreign relations, diplomacy, development studies, environmental politics, diplomacy, peace and conflict studies, international political economy, strategic studies, and nuclear politics. He has published widely in reputable international journals and bagged some awards of honor in acknowledgement of his intellectual contributions.

Marla L. Jaksch is a professor in the Women's, Gender, and Sexuality Studies Department with affiliate appointments in the African American Studies Department and the International Studies Program's Africa concentration at The College of New Jersey. Jaksch, a 2010 Fulbright Scholar to Tanzania, holds a dual-title PhD in women's gender and sexuality studies and art education from the Pennsylvania State University. She has research expertise on gender and development, gender inequality in a transnational context, and fifteen years of field and archive research experience in East Africa—Kenya, Tanzania, and Ethiopia. She also provides expert testimony to gender-based violence and LGBT asylum cases to the US from East Africa.

Nyasha Mlambo holds a B.A. (Hons.) in development studies from Great Zimbabwe University. Her research interests are in the areas of urban, environmental, and gender studies.

Tasara Muguti is a senior lecturer in the History, Archaeology and Development Studies Department at Great Zimbabwe University. He holds a B.A. (Hons.) in economic history, a master of arts in African economic history and a Graduate Certificate in education, all obtained from the University of Zimbabwe. He is currently a registered PhD student with UNISA. He has several published book chapters and journal articles to his credit. His research interests are in indigenous knowledge systems, with special emphasis on African traditional medicine, land reform, human rights, democracy, and many other topical issues on contemporary Southern African history.

Elias Muindi is an activist advancing gender equality and women's health and empowerment for over ten years. He is a program officer for Kenya's MenEngage Alliance. He is a social worker by training, with a bachelor's degree in theology and a Diploma in project management. Mr Muindi is deeply committed to making sure that women and children are free from discrimination, poverty, violence, and ill health, living their lives to their full potential. He is a member of the MenEngage Africa Steering Committee and a founder and patron of the Rhodelias Foundation which works to defeat poverty and achieve social justice. His interests are in meeting people, exchanging ideas, and learning best practices.

Hannah Muzee holds a PhD in governance and regional integration from the Pan African University, Institute of Governance, Humanities and Social Sciences and the University of Yaoundé II Soa Cameroon. Her PhD dissertation project focused on deliberative politics, education and women's voices in the Ugandan Parliament. She is a lecturer in Kyambogo University. Hannah also holds a master's degree in human resource management from Makerere University, Kampala, Uganda, and a bachelor's degree in administrative science from Kyambogo University, Kampala, Uganda. She has received certificates from short courses such as UNCTAD online course on trade and gender, and is an author of a number of refereed journal articles and book chapters. Her research interests lie in gender, deliberation, feminism, human resource management, social media, governance, and politics.

G. Nokukhanya Ndhlovu recently completed her PhD in social work where she explored the research question: Youth and Gang Violence in South Africa: An intended or unintended outcome of institutional systems? She is very passionate about social justice issues and her research interests include exclusionary development, structural violence, institutional systems, gender- and people-centered development.

Samuel O. Okafor is currently a PhD student in the Department of Sociology/Anthropology, University of Nigeria, Nsukka. He is a promising scholar with multimethodological research skills in the areas of social sciences and humanities. His research interests include political sociology, policy studies, colonial and postcolonial studies, demography, medical sociology, and environmental studies. He has published a number of articles, books, and book chapters, and has presented research papers in a number of international conferences and workshops.

Raheem Oluwafunminiyi is currently affiliated to the Centre for Black Culture & International Understanding, Osun State, Nigeria. His research is located at the intersection of Yoruba cultural history and Nigerian social and political history. Raheem's interests focus on sacred water bodies (holy wells), Yoruba deities, democratization and popular culture in Nigeria. He has published in these areas in journals and in book chapters

Nneoma Onwuegbuchi received her B.A. (Hons.) from the Department of English and Literary Studies at the University of Nigeria, Nsukka (UNN). There, she served as the assistant editor of *The Muse*: the oldest and most notable student literary journal in West Africa with Chinua Achebe as its pioneer. She also served as the coordinator of Poetry Friday, UNN: a monthly celebration of page and stage poetry. Nneoma is currently a PhD student of African cultural studies at the University of Wisconsin-Madison.

Sixtus Kennedy Otieno is the program manager of the Margaret Wanzuu Foundation, and a founder member of the Kenya MenEngage Alliance

(KEMEA). He currently serves on KEMEA's steering committee. He is an experienced gender justice specialist and development practitioner. He has worked on numerous projects at local and national levels, including livelihoods, gender-based violence especially in the context of female genital mutilation and early marriages, economic empowerment, reproductive rights, and institutional development. Mr Otieno holds a bachelor's degree in development studies.

April Petillo is an assistant professor of Public Sociology, at Northern Arizona University. Her transdisciplinary work centers race and ethnicity, where law, policy, and politics meet gender, sex, and sexuality. April interrogates targeted exploitation originating in conquest logics and the resulting precarities. Her primary projects highlight legally encoded racial politics through sociolegal critical trafficking analysis and multifaceted coalition-building. Recent articles include "A Sketch of Arrivantcy: Towards Decolonized Solidarity across Indigenous and Black Divides (Frontiers 2020), "Unsettling Ourselves: Notes on Self-Reflective Listening Beyond Discomfort" (Feminist Anthropology 2020), and "Marking Embodied Borders: Compulsory Settler Sexuality, Indigeneity, and U.S. Law" (Women's Studies in Communication, 2019). April is finishing a co-edited collection on embodied methodological practice in sociological/anthropological gender-based violence research (New York University Press). Her next project defines "slaving culture," a byproduct of statecraft stemming from state-produced racial violence related to the refusal to exercise political will.

Christiana Smyrilli studied engineering at the University of Cambridge, specializing in civil, structural, and environmental engineering. She then moved on to complete her doctoral research in the Center for Doctoral Training in Future Infrastructure and the Built Environment, in the Engineering Department of University of Cambridge. Her research investigates the relationship between water and sanitation (WASH) infrastructure in rural developing areas, and how gender relates to activities performed by men and women and the use of infrastructure within WASH. Additionally, she looks at WASH–gender relationships in a disaster context, and compares the development and disaster context. Her work draws on experience from Uganda and Puerto, but Christiana has undertaken work in Mexico, India, and Peru as well.

Emaeyak Peter Sylvanus is a senior lecturer at the Department of Music, University of Nigeria, Nsukka. He holds a PhD in music from City University of London. His research focuses primarily on music in Nigerian cinema. As the pioneering scholar on Nollywood film music, Dr Sylvanus has contributed articles to high-impact journals in the arts, humanities, and social sciences. He is presently completing a chapter on music in Nollywood comedy films for publication in a book project with Palgrave Macmillan. Other projects include an extensive study of the interplay of popular music and personality cult, payday, and the liturgy in Nigeria.

Emaeyak Peter Sylvanus: https://orcid.org/0000-0002-7502-5523

Pius T. Tanga is a professor of social work and the deputy dean for research and internationalization in the Faculty of Social sciences at the University of Fort Hare in South Africa. He is also a National Research Foundation rated researcher, has published more than a hundred publications and successfully supervised more than fifteen PhDs and thirty six masters.

Paula Tavrow is an adjunct professor in Community Health Sciences at the University of California at Los Angeles (UCLA). She is also the director of the Bixby Program in Population and Reproductive Health at UCLA. Dr Tavrow was the founding co-director of the Center of Expertise in Women's Health and Empowerment at the University of California's Global Health Institute. Her main research interests are in the areas of adolescent sexual and reproductive health, early marriage, intimate partner violence, and community-based health services, primarily in sub-Saharan Africa. Prior to joining UCLA, Dr Tavrow served as the deputy research director for the USAID-funded Quality Assurance Project managed by URC, where she led operations research activities to improve health services in eight countries in East and Southern Africa. Dr Tavrow received her doctorate from the School of Public Health at the University of Michigan in Ann Arbor.

Louise du Toit is an associate professor in the Department of Philosophy at Stellenbosch University in South Africa. She was previously at the University of Johannesburg. In 2009, she published *A Philosophical Investigation of Rape: The Making and Unmaking of the Feminine self* (Routledge). She has been a visiting fellow at Stellenbosch Institute for Advanced Study (2017), at the Princeton Center of Theological Inquiry (2018), and at Bristol University Law School (Benjamin Meeker Visiting Professorship 2019). She has also been a member of the sexual violence in armed conflict international research group based at the Institute for Social Research, Hamburg, Germany. She has published widely on sexual violence in war and peace, as well as on epistemic justice and the right to interpret, African feminisms, decolonization, feminist legal philosophy, and on philosophies of sexual difference and embodiment.

Egodi Uchendu is a professor of history at the University of Nigeria. In addition to her teaching job, she has worked as a researcher in several locations in and outside Africa and received several awards and fellowships. Her studies revolve around women in conflict situations, men and masculinities, African historiography, and emerging Muslim communities in Eastern Nigeria. She currently leads the African Humanities Research and Development Circle (AHRDC) and the Centre for Policy Studies and Research at her university. For more information, visit www.egodiuchendu.com.

Olawale Isaac Yemisi is currently a postgraduate student, Department of History and International Studies, University of Ilorin, Ilorin, Nigeria. Olawale holds B.A. in history and international studies from Osun State University, Oshogbo. He served as a graduate assistant in the Department of History, Niger State College of Education, Minna (2018–2019). His experience as a research assistant has progressively shaped his academic and research pursuits. He has attended learned conferences and workshops.

Ali Zamanpour has recently completed his PhD in English studies at Université de Montréal. His research interests include postcolonial studies, gender studies, masculinities, and affect theory. His dissertation investigates the marginalized and displaced literary voices as mobile enunciative positions with the potential to address relative discourses such as liminality, in-betweenness, and becoming in migrant cultural and literary contexts.

www.ingramcontent.com/pod-product-compliance
Lightning Source LLC
Chambersburg PA
CBHW050627280326
41932CB00015B/2547